THE
TRUTH
ABOUT
MONEY

*"Because Money Doesn't
Come With Instructions"*

Ric Edelman, CFS, RFC, CMFC

GEORGETOWN UNIVERSITY PRESS

Georgetown University Press, Washington, D.C. 20007
Copyright © 1996 by Ric Edelman, Edelman Communications, Inc.
Cover Design © 1996 by Edelman Communications, Inc.
Cover Photo by Philip Kent

PRINTED IN THE UNITED STATES OF AMERICA

15   14   13   12   11   10

THIS VOLUME IS PRINTED ON ACID-FREE OFFSET BOOK PAPER

Library of Congress Cataloging-in-Publication Data

Edelman, Ric.
The Truth About Money / Ric Edelman.
    p. cm.
1. Finance, Personal.   I. Title.
HG179.E347   1996   96-11853
332.024—dc20

ISBN: 0-87840-615-8 (cloth)
ISBN: 0-87840-616-6 (pbk.)

For Jean
whose love, boundless support, endless patience, intuitive understanding,
deep personal sacrifice, endless patience, total dedication, ceaseless work, endless patience, unwavering commitment, and endless patience serve as my inspiration.
I am both grateful and humbled by her presence in my life, and
whatever success I attain is my tribute to her.

To My Dad
who taught me everything I know about business

and To My Mom
who let him

Here is Just Some of the Unique, Award-Winning Advice You'll Discover in This Book

15,273 Reasons
You Need This Book

How to Use This Book

Table of Contents

Quick Reference Guides

Foreword by Cal Thomas

The Rules of Money Have Changed by Ric Edelman

Part I — Introduction to Financial Planning

Part II — Understanding The Capital Markets

Part III — Fixed Income Investments

Part IV — Equities

Part V — Packaged Products

Part VI — The Best Investment Strategies

NON SEQUITUR WILEY

©1994 Washington Post Writers Group. Reprinted with permission.

Part VII — The Best Financial Strategies

Part VIII —The Best Strategies for Buying, Selling and Owning Homes

Part IX — Retirement Planning

BROOM HILDA   RUSSELL MYERS

Reprinted by permission: Tribune Media Services.

Acknowledgments

The TRUTH About Money began as a course I created in 1992 and which I now teach at Georgetown University. Many excellent ideas and crucial help for the original program came from Ed Moore, CFP, president of Edelman Financial Services Inc. Statistical research was provided by Graham Casserly, CFP, and the original charts were created (during many late nights) by Lisa Anderson, president of Edelman Communications Inc. Considerable effort also has been provided over the years by ECI's Kathy Renzetti.

A book version of the course came about from my frustration at being unable to "say it all" within the confines of a nine-hour program. In fact, I'd long since stopped trying. Instead, we created a series of seminars, now numbering more than 40, on such topics as debt management, homeownership, taxation, estate planning, and auto leasing — topics that simply couldn't receive their due in the core program. But this book, unfettered by limitations of time, is able to present all the information you need in just one volume.

It's one thing to decide to produce this work; accomplishing it is quite another. I need to say it all, and it all needs to be said accurately, completely — and intelligibly. To make sure I was making sense, I asked a few (well, okay, 23) of the folks on my staff to review the manuscript. To my masochistic delight, every copy came back with red ink on virtually every page. Brilliant comments all, I found that everyone found at least one problem that no one else found, yet no one found them all. (If there are any problems that remain undiscovered, everyone's fired!) I incorporated virtually all their suggestions, added more of my own, and the result follows on these pages.

Special recognition goes to Ed (again), Jack Bubon, CFP, and Andrew Massaro, CFP, CFS, each of whom who read the manuscript twice (clearly, they need a hobby), as well as to Peggy Butler, Brenda Carter, Marty Corso, CLU, ChFC, CFP, Mary Davis, CFP, Pat Day, CFP, Joe Gilmore, RFC, Jan Kowal, CPA, CFP, the late George Wood, and Rosa Zediker. Sincere thanks also to Catherine Smith and Carol Roberts (for their insurance expertise), Jim Baker, CPA (tax), Jeff Douglas (mortgage), and Susie Kieffer (title settlement), and ECI's Adrian Reilly for his wonderful illustrations (although I wish he knew how to play chess). I also am indebted to attorneys Mary Hayes Lawrence and Carolyn Newman for their review. A special thank you to my wife Jean, not only for her role as Office Mom in making sure we always had the tools necessary to pull this off, but for tolerating my constant late-night hours devoted to completing the project. And, most important of all, heartfelt thanks to Will Casserly, SOG, for his graphic design and wizardry — and especially for devoting countless hours to the layout and typesetting of the pages within, as well as the cover design. His assistance was invaluable, and I am grateful. Thanks also to the team at Georgetown University Press, for their guidance, tolerance (!) and flexibility.

To everyone involved in this effort, I thank you very much.

Foreword

Few subjects are as intimidating as money. Like the weather, almost everyone has an opinion about money, but how many know with any confidence or degree of certainty what to do about it?

Most individuals and families don't have a real financial plan, and those who do claim to have one really have based it on myth, hearsay, what their parents did, or advice given by friends, neighbors or co-workers. A lot of this advice is dangerous because it doesn't work and is not based on truth. Even the most intelligent among us who (we believe) always think and behave rationally and reasonably, display irrational and unreasonable behavior when it comes to money.

When my wife and I started making a little more money than we were paying out in bills (a mistake, I know — we should have started much earlier), we decided it was time to consult a financial advisor. We had an individual retirement account through a bank where our interest was falling and we had a little money in a savings and loan account where interest was under four percent.

Because we were fans of Ric Edelman's radio program on WMAL in Washington, D.C., we decided to call him first. We never made a second call.

Ric impressed us not only with his knowledge of money, but with his desire to work out a financial plan built upon our needs. There was no pressure. There was no attempt to sell us a particular line of stocks and bonds because he might receive a higher commission (and I'm getting nothing in return for writing this foreword except the satisfaction of sharing someone I believe in with others in need of similar help).

Actually, we weren't entirely sure what our needs were until Ric began asking questions about our circumstances, goals, and spending habits. Our visit with him was one of the most pleasurable professional experiences we have ever had. The man knows his subject and conveys a sincerity about helping his clients that is not always found in business today.

It is one thing to be knowledgeable. It is another to be able to communicate. Ric communicates with everyone, from expert to novice, without a sense of superiority, as you will discover in this book. Using humor as well as illustrations, Ric drives his points home in a way that is not intimidating (even for people like me who can't balance their checkbook and long ago gave up doing their own taxes). He makes learning about money fun and interesting and he does it without an ax to grind.

Were Ric Edelman secretary of the treasury, he would get us out of debt if his "clients" in Congress and the president would do what he says.

You could not read a better book about your money than "The Truth About Money" because Ric Edelman tells the truth — and that is one of the few things worth more than money.

So sure am I that not only are you going to like this book, but that you will benefit by following its advice, that were it my book I would offer you a money back guarantee if you don't like it. Yes, if you don't like this book, I guarantee you that you won't get your money back!

But you will like it, and while nothing is certain in life, I can safely predict that this book will make a significant contribution to your financial planning needs and when you are finished you will feel a lot more intelligent than before you started. That alone is worth the price of the book.

Cal Thomas
Syndicated Columnist

The Rules of Money Have Changed

If you're like most Americans, you are probably handling your money the same way your parents handled theirs. They, in turn, followed the footsteps of their parents. Indeed, through our own planning practice at The EDELMAN Financial Center, we have discovered that when clients come to us already owning stocks, it is usually because their parents owned stocks; when all their money is in Certificates of Deposit, it is because their parents owned CDs, too.

Although previous generations were able to succeed financially by practicing the same time-honored traditions as those who preceded them, we no longer can do so. While our parents and grandparents paid little or nothing in taxes, we lose more than a third of our incomes to the tax collector. While prices for goods and services remained stable for the first sixty years of this century, we must buy today to avoid tomorrow's price increase. Consequently, we now earn more but save less than at any time in history. We also live longer — so much longer, in fact, that most Americans face the very real risk of outliving their incomes. Even home ownership has changed: While our predecessors celebrated mortgage-burning parties as part of the American dream, today's homeowners are foolish to own their home outright.

Indeed, today's world is very different when compared with that of a few decades ago. And although the United States has been the world's preeminent economic power through-out most of the 20th century, today the U. S. controls less than half of the world's wealth. Without question, the world has changed, and **The Rules of Money Have Changed** along with it.

To succeed in this new economic environment, it is vital that you understand the new rules and learn how the truths of prior generations have been forever altered. For if we continue to operate under the old rules, we surely will fail where our parents succeeded.

I welcome you to discover these new rules, to learn for yourself how to take advantage of the realities and opportunities available to you, for both the protection and the prosperity of you and your family. Above all, I invite you to learn **The TRUTH About Money**.

Ric Edelman
October, 1996

Part I
Introduction to Financial Planning

Part I — Introduction to Financial Planning

Overview - The 11 Reasons You Need to Plan

Twenty-five years ago, financial planning did not even exist, yet today, some 200,000 people claim to be financial planners (and some of them actually are!). What is financial planning, anyway, and is it really necessary?

After all, your parents didn't plan for their future — so why should you? The reason your parents didn't plan is the same reason you haven't packed for Europe: You're not going! Likewise, our parents and grandparents never planned for their future for the simple reason that *they weren't going to have one*. Why worry about developing cancer at age 88 if you are going to be dead of tuberculosis at 45? Since people weren't expecting to live past 50 for most of this century, there simply was no need for planning.

Today, of course, things are different. And among these differences is the need for financial planning. Here are 11 reasons why you need to plan.

Reason #1: To Protect Yourself and Your Family Against Financial Risks

Notice the word *financial*. As a financial planner, I cannot protect you from the risks you face in life — no planner can — but I can protect you from suffering the financial loss that may result when any of those risks become reality. What are those risks? The four major ones are injury, illness, death, and lawsuits, and you'll learn how to manage and reduce those risks in Part X.

> **Lawsuits? You bet!** For perspective, the odds that your house will burn down are 1 in 1,200 — yet according to *Forbes* magazine, the odds are just 1 in 200 that you will be sued at some point in your lifetime. (To learn how to protect yourself from the financial threat of a lawsuit, see Chapter 69.)

3

Reason #2: To Eliminate Personal Debt

For some people, a proper goal is to become worthless. If you're in over your head with credit cards, auto loans, and student loans, becoming worthless would be a real improvement. You must move from *owing* money to *owning* money.

Indeed, total consumer debt in this country is $1 trillion. Americans hold an average of 2.3 credit cards each, with an average balance of $1,700 per card. And 15% of Americans bounced at least one check last year.

You've heard the joke about "running out of money before you run out of month," but it's not so funny to run out of money before the end of your *life!* You must make sure you don't outlive your income, and that means you've got to accumulate assets so you can support yourself for a lifetime. That's impossible to do if you have debts, so you must eliminate them. Chapter 51 will show you how.

FIGURE 1-1

Reason #3: Because You're Going to Live a Long, Long Time

At the time of the American Revolution, life expectancy at birth was 23 years. By 1900 it had climbed to only 47 years. If you were alive, you worked. There was no such thing as retirement.

Today, though, life expectancy at birth is 76; today's 76-year-olds have a life expectancy of 86. According to some estimates, by the year 2000, half of all deaths in the U.S. will occur after age 80. These life expectancies are a big part of why we need to plan.

How Old Will You Be in 2100?

Of course, these tables assume life expectancies will remain at current levels. But that might not be the case. Indeed, research suggests that people will continue to live longer and longer. In fact, even those as old as 35 today might be alive in the 22nd century.

Life expectancy tables from such diverse groups as the IRS, life insurers, the National Institutes of Health and the Center for Disease Control and Prevention all say roughly the same thing: A child born in 1995 has a life expectancy of 76 years (up from 47 in 1900); a 76-year-old today is expected to live to 86; to 92 for an 86-year-old; and there are not supposed to be 93-year-olds.

YOUR LIFE EXPECTANCY	
People who are this age today	Are expected to live to this age
0	75
15	76
25	77
35	78
45	79
55	80
65	82
75	86
85	91

FIGURE 1-2

Why are these figures important? Well, if you're wondering how much money you'll need in retirement to avoid running out of money during your lifetime, you need to project how long that lifetime will be. Based on the actuarial data provided by various government agencies, most financial planners assume their clients will live to age 85, and conservative planners (my firm included) use age 90, just to be safe (the longer you live, the more money you'll need).

> *"If you can see yourself in possession of your goal, it's half yours."*
> —Tom Hopkins

However, even "conservative" figures like age 90 could be way off the mark. Based on the relatively new fields of gerontology, microbiology, and biotechnology, some believe that people in the year 2050 could be expected to live to age 140. No typo there: That's one hundred and forty years of age.

This is not science fiction. In 2050, your kids could still be having kids. For example, in 2050, I'll be 92. Will I make it? Well, that's still six years younger than my Grandmom Fannie is at this writing. Let's face it: For many of us, 2050 is a done deal.

And now it's being suggested that lots of us who are here today could see the year 2100. The implications for society boggle the mind. Let's look closer at what such long life spans could mean.

You'll Have Multiple Marriages

First, you would be likely to have four or five spouses during your lifetime. Like all the other futurisms to follow, this one is not as far-fetched as it may first appear. After all, half of all Americans who marry eventually divorce; more than half later remarry. Thus, we're already a multiple-marriage society. It'll just become more so: More people will do it and more people will do it more often. (After all, can you imagine marrying someone at age 20 and living with that same person for the next 120 years!? Honey, I love you, but...)

Even for those who don't divorce, longer life spans often will result in one spouse outliving another by decades, which in turn will lead to more remarriages.

You'll Have Multiple Careers

Second, you will have five or six careers. You'll go to school, get a degree, develop expertise in a given field, devote yourself to it for 20 or 30 years, then quit and start again, doing something entirely different. Think that's crazy? Millions of military retirees, police officers, firefighters, and schoolteachers already do this. They "retire" at 40 or 50 with 20 or 30 years of service and, with their monthly pension checks in the mail, they head off to new challenges. This strategy will become more common in the new millennium and the phrase "double-dipper" will give way to "quintuple-dipper" as people have five or six 20-year careers in their lifetime. The notion of "retirement" as we know it today could fade away.

> *"I'd like to be rich enough so I could throw soap away after the letters are worn off."*
> —Andy Rooney

6

You'll Extend Your Rites of Passage

As our lifetimes become extended, so too will our rites of passage. As recently as 1960, it was common to marry in your late teens; the phrase "old maid" still applied to women who failed to marry by age 20. You were expected to have children (plural) before you were 25. Jerry Rubin told us not to trust anyone over 30, middle age and mid-life crises hit at 45, and the "elderly" were 65.

As I bet yours does, my own life provides examples of this brave new world: My former college roommate (now 38) is no closer to marriage now than when we were in school; my 46-year-old brother is a proud new papa (he'll be 72 when his baby girl graduates from medical school); a niece of mine has three daddies (one biological, one marital, and one legal); my 69-year-old father has announced his retirement (for the fourth time); and my 98-year-old grandmother continues to defy the actuaries.

If today's trends continue unabated, the year 2050 will find people marrying (for the first time) at age 50, having kids in their 60s (in France, they already are), facing middle age in their 80s, retiring in their 120s, and dying in their 140s.

These prognostications remind us that financial planning is a process, not a product. A financial plan must be periodically reviewed, with its assumptions challenged and altered based on changes in the economy and in your circumstances. One key circumstance is the fact that you may live much longer than you once envisioned. If you plan to retire at 65 and are assuming a life expectancy of age 90, you're assuming a 25-year retirement. But what if you live to 140? Will you have enough income for a 75-year retirement?

Finally, who's going to pay for it all?

I don't have that answer, but the question suggests that the most politically explosive social issue in America today — the right to life — will evolve into a new debate. In the 21st century, with people living for so many years beyond their resources, with society forced to pick up the tab, it is very conceivable that many will argue that those who cannot take care of themselves in old age, those who are living in pain or discomfort, those who do not have a family or support group on whom to rely, and those who cannot afford to pay for their own care should have the right to choose death. To some, Dr. Kevorkian is evil, to others he is a godsend, and to the remainder, he is a mere curiosity. Whatever you think of him, one thing is certain: Dr. Kevorkian is a prelude to the future. In the year 2050, his cause will be center stage as the nation deals with the next great social debate: euthanasia.

Welcome to the 22nd century. I hope you'll be ready.

Reason #4: To Pay for the Costs of Raising Children

You're earning — and you'll continue to earn — a huge income. Take a 35-year-old making $3,000 a month. Even if you ignore salary increases, that's more than $1 million in career earnings!

While that might sound like good news, it actually works against us. When making a lot of money, people often develop an attitude that says, "Gee, with this good income, life will take care of itself. It did for my parents. It did for my grandparents. It certainly will for me."

The issue, however, is not how much money you *earn*, but how much you *keep*. Look at the money your parents and grandparents earned over their careers. How much do they have left?

YOU ARE EARNING A HUGE AMOUNT OF MONEY		
If you are age...	...and each month you earn...	...by age 65 you will earn a total of...
35	$3,000	$1,080,000
45	$5,000	$1,200,000
55	$7,500	$ 900,000

...Even If You Never Get a Raise!

FIGURE 1-3

You easily could have little left from a lifetime of work, because you don't get to keep all the money you earn. You have expenses — lots of expenses. Can you name your biggest expense?

Children!

According to the USDA, a baby born in 1995 will cost high-income families (defined as those earning more than $56,700 per year) nearly $350,000. As shown in Figure 1-4, families earning less than $37,700 will still spend more than $176,000, while those in between will rack up expenses of nearly $239,000. That's per child — and only for the first 17 years! To learn how to examine the financial issues of raising young children, see Chapter 54.

THE COST OF KIDS

Year	Age	Household Income Below $33,700	Household Income Between $33,700 - $56,700	Household Income Above $56,700
1995	<1	$5,490	$7,610	$11,320
1996	1	5,790	8,020	11,930
1997	2	6,100	8,450	12,580
1998	3	6,570	9,140	13,510
1999	4	6,920	9,640	14,240
2000	5	7,300	10,160	15,010
2001	6	7,870	10,790	15,770
2002	7	8,290	11,370	16,620
2003	8	8,740	11,990	17,520
2004	9	9,260	12,620	18,350
2005	10	9,760	13,300	19,340
2006	11	10,290	14,020	20,380
2007	12	12,330	16,130	23,060
2008	13	13,000	17,000	24,310
2009	14	13,700	17,920	25,620
2010	15	14,220	19,170	27,620
2011	16	14,990	20,210	29,110
2012	17	15,800	21,300	30,690
Total		**$176,420**	**$238,840**	**$346,980**

FIGURE 1-4

Reason #5: To Pay for College

Guess what happens when the kids turn 18? They go to college!

It's estimated that, for a baby born in 1994, the cost of college will be $180,000 for an in-state school and $300,000 for the Ivy League. To learn the proper way to approach the cost of college, turn to Chapter 53.

THE COST OF COLLEGE

Penn State	$126,592
Maryland	145,693
Berkeley	179,971
Notre Dame	260,355
Harvard	336,492
Georgetown	336,941
Princeton	339,763
Yale	346,114

Assumes 6% annual increase in the cost of tuition, room and board — based on 1996 prices

THE COST OF A WEDDING

Flowers	$800
Invitations	350
Photography	1,500
Music	1,000
Clergy/Church	166
Limousine	201
Attendants' Gifts	200
Wedding Rings	1,004
Engagement Ring	2,285
Rehearsal Dinner	501
Wedding Dress	800
Headpiece/Veil	169
Groom's Tux	82
Reception	8,000
Total	**$17,058**

Reason #6: To Pay for a Daughter's Wedding

And if you made the foolish decision to have daughters instead of sons, get ready for another major expense: the wedding! According to *Bride's Magazine*, the average cost is $17,000; *Washingtonian* magazine puts it at $28,000.

Reason #7: To Buy a Car

With the average price of a car approaching $20,000, this is one of your biggest — and most confusing — financial decisions. Should you pay cash, accept dealer financing, or use home equity? Is leasing right for you? To learn the answer, go to Chapter 52.

Reason #8: To Buy a Home

"It's a question of priorities, Martha. Do you want lots of kids or <u>one</u> with a college education?"

Americans devote the largest portion of their income to housing. Consequently, how you handle the purchase of your home will have far-reaching implications on virtually every other facet of your financial life, including your ability to save, pay for college and plan for your retirement. For this reason, we devote five chapters (55-59) exclusively to this subject, and it's referenced in many other chapters as well, including those dealing with debt elimination (Chapter 51), paying for college (Chapter 53), and the costs of raising children (Chapter 54).

Reason #9: To be able to Retire When — and in the Style — You Want

Consider food. Assuming you and your spouse retire at 65 and live to your normal life expectancy of 85, you're going to eat 43,800 meals in retirement! (That's three meals a day, 365 days a year over 20 years for two people.) If each of those meals costs five dollars, you'll spend $219,000 on food. Where is that money going to come from?

Most people are ignorant of this message. Of today's retirees, 51% have incomes below $10,000 a year. I'm not saying these people never earned more than $10,000 a year while they were working. Rather, their income dropped below $10,000 when they retired. Also, the Social Security Administration defines financial independence as an annual income of $24,000 a year. Would you consider yourself financially independent if you earned just $2,000 a month?

> "Drive-in banks were established so most of the cars today could see their real owners."
> —E. Joseph Cossman

Another 30% of retired Americans earn $10,000 to $20,000 a year. That means only 19% of retirees earn more than $20,000 a year. The rest — 81% of all retired Americans — are financial failures.

But these masses didn't plan to fail. They simply failed to plan, because under the old rules, planning wasn't necessary. It used to be that a worker and his family could be comfortable if he retired at 62 on a pension and Social Security.

That doesn't happen anymore. Today, you don't retire as young as 62 — unless you've been downsized out of work. And you're going to live much longer than your parents and grandparents did, aren't you? Therefore, your money must last much longer. And that is the dilemma: If you fail to plan, you face the possibility of a retirement filled with poverty, welfare, and charity.

A Gallup survey showed that 75% of workers want to retire before age 60, yet only 25% think they will. That suggests people don't know how they are going to achieve their goals. One thing is sure, it's not going to happen by itself. It's going to require effort and attention. Part IX will help.

WILL YOU RETIRE WHEN YOU WANT?

Almost 75% of workers want to retire before they are 60...

AGE YOU WANT TO RETIRE

...but only 25% think they will.

AGE YOU THINK YOU'LL RETIRE

FIGURE 1-7

"If you don't know where you're going, you'll probably end up somewhere else."
—David Campbell

Reason #10: To Pay for the Costs of Long-Term Care

Prior generations did not have to deal with the costs of long-term care, but we must: Of those who reach age 65, it's estimated that one in two will require long-term care at some point. The average annual cost of a nursing home exceeds $40,000; neither your health insurance nor Medicare will pay for it. The result: 12.5 million senior citizens today are supported by others, because they don't have the money to care for themselves. For more, see Chapter 67 and Part XI.

Reason #11: To Pass Wealth to the Next Generation

This is more difficult than ever before, because living longer means it is increasingly likely that you will spend your money before you have the chance to bequeath it.

Economists call this *transference of wealth*. Historically, money was passed from father to son. It started with our immigrant ancestors, who built homes and had children. When the children married, they moved into the house with Mom and Dad. Then the kids had kids, making it three generations in one house. As the family grew larger, each generation built new rooms, increasing the size — and the value — of the family's wealth.

When the first generation died, the second generation inherited the house, later passing it to the next generation, with each growing more affluent than the previous one.

That doesn't happen today. We don't have three generations living in one house as often as we once did. Today, when our grandparents die, we're more likely to sell their house because we have our own home and we don't need theirs.

Furthermore, we find that our grandparents live so much longer than before — longer than they expected — that they often run out of assets and have nothing to leave to their children. Therefore, instead of passing wealth down to the children, the kids send money up to the parents. Thus, for the first time in our nation's history, the transfer of wealth is going backwards, and economists worry that most Americans are not prepared for this new reality. Learn how to avoid that problem by reading Part XI.

It is for all these reasons — to protect against risk; to eliminate debt; because you're going to live a long time; to handle such major expenses as children, college costs and weddings; to buy cars and homes; to afford a comfortable retirement; to protect against long-term care costs; and to pass wealth to your heirs — that **you need to create a financial plan.**

> *"Americans tend to plan for everything — except success."*
>
> —Ric Edelman

Chapter 1 - The Four Obstacles to Building Wealth

As you begin trying to accumulate wealth, you'll encounter four major obstacles. The first is the most deadly, but if you think it's the economy or taxes, you're wrong. Your biggest enemy, as I can attest from having worked with thousands of people just like you, is *yourself*. Without question, *procrastination* is the most common cause of financial failure.

You know the story of Jack and Jill. But did you know Jack was pushed down that hill? (Never mind.) As a result of his head injuries, Jack decided not to go to college. Instead, at age 18, he got a job, enabling him to contribute $2,000 to his IRA each year. After eight years, he stopped, having invested a total of $16,000.

Meanwhile, his sister Jill, inspired (guilt-ridden?) by Jack's accident, went to medical school. At age 26, she began her practice and started contributing $2,000 to her IRA. And she did so for 40 years, from age 26 to 65. She invested a total of $80,000 and she put her money into the same investment as her brother Jack. Thus, Jill started investing the same year Jack stopped, and she saved for 40 years compared to just eight years for her brother.

By age 65, whose IRA account do you think was worth more money?

CLOSE TO HOME JOHN MCPHERSON

"I've been going over our finances. According to my calculations, our monthly retirement income will be either $2,124 or $42,798, depending on whether or not we win the Publishers Clearing House sweepstakes."

"Knowledge is power."
—Francis Bacon

Assuming Jack and Jill each earned a 10% return, Jill accumulated $885,185, but Jack collected $1,035,160 — $149,975 more than his sister!

While Jack had invested only $16,000 to Jill's $80,000, his money earned interest for eight years longer than his sister. It wasn't the money that made him successful — it was the *time value of money*: Jack didn't procrastinate: By investing sooner than Jill, his account grew larger.

I have heard the complaint that procrastination does not belong at the top of my "Enemies of Money" list. There must be other, more serious causes for financial failure, right?

Wrong!

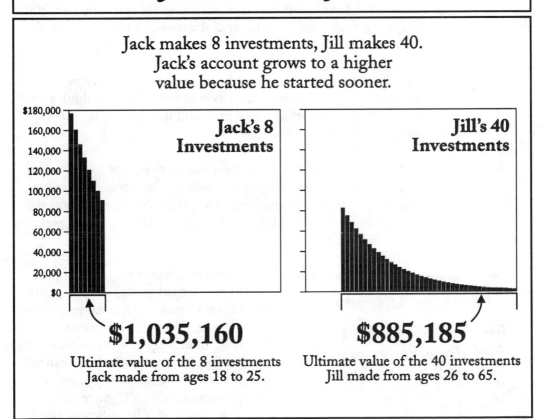

JACK AND JILL

Jack makes 8 investments, Jill makes 40.
Jack's account grows to a higher
value because he started sooner.

Jack's 8 Investments

Jill's 40 Investments

$1,035,160

Ultimate value of the 8 investments
Jack made from ages 18 to 25.

$885,185

Ultimate value of the 40 investments
Jill made from ages 26 to 65.

FIGURE 1-8

Obstacle #1: Procrastination

I cannot stress enough the need for you to get started right now. Procrastination says you'll do it tomorrow. It's easy to see why you put planning off until later: After all, who has time? You've got lots of deadlines and you don't need another one. You've got to get to work on time, get your kid to soccer practice and prepare for visiting out-of-towners this weekend. With today's deadlines, you don't have time to work on something whose effects will not be felt for 20 years. But that's okay because you're young yet and you'll still have plenty of time later! Right?

Wrong!

Maybe this is why so few of my firm's clients are under 30. It just seems that young people don't want to talk about something 40 years away: They're more concerned about this weekend's party!

In fact, I've heard all the excuses people use: If you're in your 20s, you figure you've got 40 years to deal with it, so you'll put it off until you are in your 30s...

...but by then, you've got a new house, new spouse and new kids — and you're spending money like never before. Who can think about saving at a time like this? You'll deal with it later on after things settle down in your 40s...

...when indeed you're making more money than ever, but now you find that your children are entering college. On top of that, your income growth isn't as rapid as it used to be. No problem, you say, because by the time you hit your 50s, you think your major expenses will be behind you...

> *"There are so many things that we wish we had done yesterday, so few that we feel like doing today."*
> —Mignon McLaughlin

...only to discover that your kids start to get married (with you footing the bill) and maybe they need help buying a house, too. And your parents probably need some help as well, because they're getting up in years. And you can't remember the last time you got a promotion; after all, you're now a vice president; The only way you'll get promoted is for somebody to retire or die. You're also finding that the cost of living has never been higher, so planning for retirement will just have to wait a bit longer...

...and when you hit 65, you lament your anemic savings and wish you had started 40 years ago.

I see this all the time.

If there is only one thing in this entire book that you need to take on faith, it's this: *There is never an ideal time for planning*, and while you can always find a reason to put it off, *don't*. Do it now. Procrastination will cause you financial ruin more effectively, more completely, than the worst advice a crooked broker could ever give you.

The Cost of Procrastination

There is, in fact, a specific cost to procrastination. If you are 20 years old and you want to raise $100,000 by age 65, you need to invest only $1,132 today (ignoring taxes for the moment and assuming a 10% annual return).

But a 50-year-old would need to invest nearly $22,500 to obtain that same $100,000. This is the cost of procrastination. As you can see, it's not money that makes people financially successful, it's time.

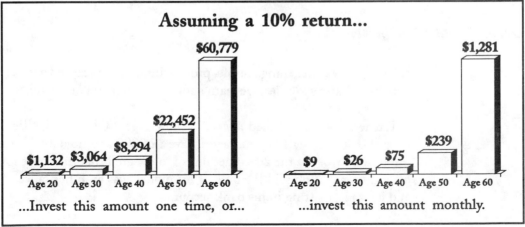

TO RAISE $100,000 BY AGE 65

Assuming a 10% return...

...Invest this amount one time, or... ...invest this amount monthly.

FIGURE 1-9

> While presenting this in a seminar, an elderly gentleman rose to object to my comments. "Excuse me," he said, "but I can't to do that."
>
> "Why not?" I asked. "Don't you have a hundred bucks?"
>
> "I have the hundred dollars," he replied. "But I don't have the 30 years!"

The cost of procrastination can be shown just as easily for those who save monthly: Our 20-year-old would need to save less than $10 a month, but the 50-year-old would need to save $239 a month. You tell me: Who has an easier task?

Why $1,200 = $37,125

A lot of folks reading this will concede the fact that starting young has its advantages. But I'm plenty young, you might be thinking, so I'll just start *next* year. After all, next year, I'll still be young enough, but I'll be making more money, and it'll be easier for me to start. After all, what difference can one year make?

A big difference.

If a 30-year-old saves $100 a month until age 65, earning 10% per year, the resulting account would be worth **$379,664**.

But if this person waited just one year, beginning her savings at 31 instead of 30, her account at age 65 would be worth only **$342,539**.

Thus, the cost of not saving $100 a month for just one year is **$37,125**. Can you really afford to blow thirty-seven grand?

Don't procrastinate. Start now.

Out the Door by Twenty-Four

Like so many other things in life, procrastination is a learned art. As with most basic attitudes, we learn about this one from our parents.

A listener, Bob, once called my radio show. Age 23, he asked, "Ric, what should I do with my money? I have $24,000 and no debt." I was impressed. Most of the 20-somethings I know are broke and have lots of credit cards. Bob said the bulk of his money was an inheritance and it was just sitting in his bank account.

I asked him about his monthly expenses, expecting Bob's reply to be in the range of $1,000 to $3,000; such an amount would be typical for folks in their 20s. To my surprise, he said, "Oh, I spend about two hundred dollars a month." Then the truth came out. Bob, 23 and a college graduate, lives at home.

Upon graduation, he became an official member of "The Boomerang Generation." Mom and Dad shipped him off to college at age 18, paid the bill, and prepared to celebrate the fact that their child-rearing and child-supporting days were over.

> *"Human beings are the only creatures on earth that allow their children to come back home."*
> —Bill Cosby

But when Bob graduated, he didn't move on with his life. Instead, he moved back home. Bob once again lives with his parents, at their expense, and his total monthly spending of $200 goes to whatever he wants — parties, hanging out with friends, going to the movies, eating out with the guys, weight-lifting at the club, and other activities of the financially secure.

Bob is able to participate in these avocations, of course, because "someone else" does his laundry, cooks his meals, and pays for the home he lives in.

Occupationally speaking, Bob is in a rut. Upon graduation, he missed the career track: Unable to get the job of his choice, he chose not to work at all. I asked, "When are you going to move out?" He said, "I'm in no hurry."

CALVIN AND HOBBES   BILL WATTERSON

> *"Life is like riding a bicycle; you don't fall off unless you stop pedaling."*
> —Claude Pepper

I can see his point. Why should he move to a 700-square-foot, three-room apartment that costs $800 per month (plus utilities and telephone)? He'd have to buy furniture and a TV, drag his laundry to the Laundromat, shop for his own groceries, and cook his own meals.

Why should Bob do that, when he can live in a 3,000-square-foot, multi-level single family home on a quarter-acre lot in the suburbs, where somebody else takes care of his laundry, does the food shopping, and prepares dinner nightly?

Let's face it, Bob's got a great thing going here, and the operative initials are M-O-M.

Bob can come and go as he pleases, has no bills to pay, and if something goes wrong, the landlord takes care of it, spelled D-A-D.

This is an issue of "tough love." Without exception, all my clients who have kids love them dearly, and they'd do anything for them — but enough is enough. Parents must recognize that at 23, these "kids" are adults who need to act like adults. Parents are not doing their children any favors by coddling and protecting them against the cold, cruel realities of life.

In Bob's case, Mom and Dad need to charge him rent, just like any other landlord. They need to collect an amount equal to (a) what Bob would pay elsewhere, or (b) what Mom and Dad would charge if Bob were a stranger.

If they were to charge $800 a month, two things would happen: Bob would get a job to pay for it, and he'd move out. Both are exactly what Bob needs to do if he's to develop and thrive in our society.

> *"If you can count your money, you don't have a billion dollars."*
> —J. Paul Getty

And to all you Moms and Dads who hate the thought of collecting rent from your own children, here's a neat trick: Collect the rent and invest it for your son or daughter without telling them. When they finally move out (we hope, one day, they will), you can give them the money as a moving-out gift, allowing them to use the money you've saved for them to help them get settled in a new home.

Don't get me wrong. I don't have a problem with kids living at home; it can be a smart financial move — for kids trying to save money. Rather, my problem is with kids who live at home as freeloaders — and there is a big difference between the two.

Take the example of Mike, one of my clients. He is 26 and like Bob lives at his parents' home. He didn't go to college, but he's been working since he was 16. Mom and Dad have always covered his expenses because Mike always has had a job and he contributes to running the household (doing chores, cooking, cleaning and shopping). He's diligent, conscientious, and — most important — Mike is good at saving money.

> *"Do not handicap your children by making their lives easy."*
>
> **—Lazarus Long**

In fact, he is *really* good at saving money: Mike has $60,000, which he saved on his own — no gifts or inheritances. He's accumulated his money throughout the 10 years he's worked.

And that's why Mom and Dad have no problem with him living at home for free: They know that rather than forcing Mike to pay rent to them or some other landlord, he's paying himself. So when he does decide to move out, he can afford to buy a place, not just rent it. Besides, like most suburbanites, Mom and Dad can afford to have Mike live in the house and they love to have him around, so it's a great deal for everybody.

The Bobs of our nation won't be 20-something forever and if they don't learn to pay their way now, if they don't start preparing to do so, they never will. Are you prepared to support your kids for your entire life?

Give your kids a push. Don't let them procrastinate. It could be the best thing you ever do for them.

CALVIN AND HOBBES   BILL WATTERSON

Obstacle #2: Spending Habits

Again, the problem is you, not the economy or world politics!

To see what I mean, look at the Newmans, married with a combined annual income of $60,000. They felt they didn't spend extravagantly, but they were nonetheless concerned that they couldn't seem to save any money. "We don't drive fancy cars or take big vacations and our kids don't have the latest Reeboks," they told me. "But we can't seem to get ahead."

Needless to say, the Newmans didn't know where their money was going, so my firm helped them figure it out. The Newmans commuted to work separately and here's what we found:

When they each got to the office, each would buy a newspaper ($.25), coffee ($.75), and a doughnut ($1.00). In a mid-afternoon break, they'd buy a candy bar ($.75). Without knowing the other was also doing this, each was spending $2.75 a day, for a daily total of $5.50.

With 20 working days per month, they were spending $110.00 per month, or $1,300 a year.

And guess what happens to the money you earn before you receive it? *It gets taxed.* In other words, the Newmans had to earn more than $2,000 in order to net the $1,300 that they frittered away on candy and soda. Then they came to us saying, "We can't seem to save any money."

CATHY CATHY GUISEWITE

I CHANGED MY MIND ON THIS.

YOU BOUGHT THIS LAST DECEMBER.

YES. WELL, I'VE HAD A RUDE FINANCIAL AWAKENING, AND NO LONGER FEEL IT'S CRITICAL TO MY LIFE.

YOU'VE OWNED IT FOR FOUR MONTHS!

I NEVER USED IT! I NEVER TOUCHED IT! I DON'T WANT IT! PLEASE TAKE IT BACK! YOU MUST TAKE IT BACK!

24 HOURS AFTER TAX DAY, AND THE 1996 RETURNS START POURING IN.

Where Does My Money Go?

Have you ever withdrawn $50 from an automatic teller machine, yet find your wallet or purse empty just a few days later?

Have you ever asked yourself, "Where does all my money go?" Like the Newmans, you probably are piddling it away. You have absolutely no idea you're doing it, because if you did know, you would stop instantly, for there isn't a rational human being in the world who would tolerate such nonsense.

> *"A study of economics usually reveals that the best time to buy anything is last year."*
> —Marty Allen

But we all piddle money away because we don't pay attention. The Newmans were spending 3% of their annual income on... *nothing!* To avoid this problem, you've got to look at your spending habits, for that's where you'll find the key to your financial future. If your spending habits are causing you trouble, you can learn how to fix them in Chapter 51.

Obstacle #3: Inflation

The most onerous of money's enemies, inflation is perhaps the best illustration of how **The Rules of Money Have Changed.**

Over the past 23 years, inflation averaged 5.8% per year. At that rate, a 50-year-old earning $50,000 a year, who plans to retire at 65 on that same income, will need a net worth of $2.2 million — and his income in his first year of retirement will be $119,000.

> *"Inflation is when the buck doesn't stop anywhere."*
> —Anonymous

INFLATION

1973	8.8%	1984	4.0
1974	12.2	1985	3.8
1975	6.7	1986	1.1
1976	4.8	1987	4.4
1977	6.8	1988	4.4
1978	9.0	1989	4.7
1979	13.3	1990	6.1
1980	12.4	1991	3.1
1981	8.9	1992	3.0
1982	3.9	1993	2.8
1983	3.8	1994	2.7
		1995	2.7

23-Year Average: 5.8%

FIGURE 1-10

$1,000 TODAY

In this many years...	$1,000 will be worth...	...and it will take this much money to buy what $1,000 buys today:
5	$742	$1,349
10	550	1,819
15	408	2,454
20	302	3,310
25	224	4,465
30	166	6,023
35	123	8,123
40	91	10,957

assuming 6% annual inflation

FIGURE 1-11

CONSUMER PRICES

	20 Years Ago	Today	20 Years from Now*
Automobile	$4,098	$18,500	$72,671
Postage Stamp	.06	.32	1.03
Gallon of Milk	1.23	2.64	8.47
Movie Ticket	1.50	7.50	24.05
Physician's Office Visit	6.75	55.00	176.39
Electric Shaver	15.00	60.00	192.43
Running Shoes	20.00	80.00	256.57
Gallon of Gasoline	.32	1.27	4.07

***based on 6% annual inflation**

FIGURE 1-12

Indeed, to look into the future, you need not 20/20 vision but an inflation-adjusted 50/50 vision!

In fact, 6% annual inflation means $1,000 will be worth barely half that much in 10 years. Put another way, you'll need $1,800 in 10 years to buy what $1,000 buys today. Do you remember when President Nixon announced a 90-day wage and price freeze? Inflation was rampant and nobody could stop it — not Congress, the Federal Reserve Board, the President's Council of Economic Advisors, the banks, or Wall Street.

Nixon and the nation panicked. Convinced that inflation was going to cause an economic calamity worse than the Great Depression, the President stopped inflation artificially. For 90 days, nobody was permitted to raise salaries or prices. And the strategy worked — until the 91st day, anyway.

When President Nixon established his freeze in 1971, the inflation rate was just four percent. If that were the case 10 years later, Jimmy Carter would have been re-elected! By the time Jimmy left office in 1980, inflation was 13% and banks were offering 15% CDs.

> *"If you had your life to live over again, you'd need more money."*
> —Anonymous

But you didn't buy them, because you were convinced that next month, CDs were going to 16% and you didn't want to be stuck with "only" 15%! So you kept your money in daily accounts. You rode the interest wave up and right back down again!

While 4% inflation once panicked our nation, that same figure today doesn't even rate a mention on the evening news. How can that be? After all, there's no difference between the 4% rate of 25 years ago and the 4% rate of today. The difference, then, is the frog.

Yes, the frog.

The Boiling Frog Syndrome

If you throw a frog into a pot of boiling water, he'll jump out. But if you place a frog into a pot of lukewarm water and slowly turn up the heat, it will boil to death.

And so it is with inflation. We've grown accustomed to inflation over the past 25 years, but that doesn't mean we don't continue to be hurt by its effect.

Obstacle #4: Taxes

It's the one we all love to hate: *taxes.*

According to the Tax Foundation, Tax Freedom Day is May 5, meaning that every dollar you earn from the first day of the year until then goes to taxes. Put another way, you work nearly three hours of each workday just to pay taxes. No wonder we find it difficult to save money!

FIGURE 1-13

"Noah must have taken into the Ark two taxes, one male and one female. And did they multiply bountifully! Next to guinea pigs, taxes must have been the most prolific animals."

—Will Rogers

"Our Founding Fathers objected to taxation without representation. They should see it today with representation."

—Anonymous

In addition to federal income taxes, you also must contend with state income taxes, as shown in Figure 1-14, plus personal property taxes, sales taxes, user taxes, intangibles taxes, excise taxes, capital gains taxes, and estate taxes.

The amazing thing is that everybody thinks taxes are a natural part of life. Have we all forgotten why we revolted against England?

Our federal income tax wasn't even created until 1913 — and it took a constitutional amendment to do it. And when the tax was established, it was quite low: There was no tax on the first $20,000 of income and only a 1% tax on income between $20,000 and $50,000 — and $20,000 was a lot of income in 1913!

You can guess what the politicians said back then, too. "Don't worry," I'll bet they claimed, "tax rates will never rise!"

It's the Boiling Frog Syndrome all over again.

CATHY CATHY GUISEWITE

STATE INCOME TAXES

State	Top Rate	State	Top Rate
Alabama	5.0%	Nebraska	6.99%
Alaska	None	Nevada	None
Arizona	7.0%	New Hampshire	5.0%
Arkansas	7.0%	New Jersey	6.65%
California	11.0%	New Mexico	8.5%
Colorado	5.0%	New York	7.5%
Connecticut	4.5%	North Carolina	7.75%
Delaware	7.7%	North Dakota	12.0%
Florida	None	Ohio	7.5%
Georgia	6.0%	Oklahoma	7.0%
Hawaii	10.0%	Oregon	9.0%
Idaho	8.2%	Pennsylvania	2.8%
Illinois	3.0%	Rhode Island	11%
Indiana	3.4%	South Carolina	7.0%
Iowa	9.98%	South Dakota	None
Kansas	6.45%	Tennessee	6.0%
Kentucky	6.0%	Texas	None
Louisiana	6.0%	Utah	7.2%
Maine	8.5%	Vermont	9.0%
Maryland	8.0%	Virginia	5.75%
Massachusetts	5.95%	Washington	None
Michigan	4.4%	Washington, D.C.	9.5%
Minnesota	8.5%	West Virginia	6.5%
Mississippi	5.0%	Wisconsin	6.93%
Missouri	6.0%	Wyoming	None
Montana	11.0%		

Average State Income Tax Rate: 6.3%

FIGURE 1-14

Chapter 2 - The Story of Taxes and Inflation

Together, taxes and inflation create a web of incredible treachery, serving as another example of how **The Rules of Money Have Changed.**

At the turn of the century, taxes and inflation were not a concern. Homes cost $5,000 (Sears used to sell them from their catalog) and if you wanted to borrow money to buy your house, the bank charged you from 4% to 6%. If you deposited money into the bank, the bank paid you 2%, keeping the difference between what it charged and what it paid as its profit.

Why were our parents and grandparents willing to accept a 2% return on their savings? Because it was profitable for them to do so: With no inflation, the 2% they earned was a real 2% and, with no taxes to pay, they got to keep it all. Thus, our parents and grandparents were able to prosper from a 2% return on their money and banks were able to prosper by charging only 4% or 6% for their loans.

Banks were willing to offer 30-year mortgages at these low rates because it had always been profitable to do so. Indeed, from 1879 to 1965, mortgage rates in the U.S. (Figure 1-15) were very stable, consistently at 5.3%, give or take half a point.

> *"Man is not like other animals in the ways that are really significant: Animals have instincts, we have taxes."*
>
> —Eric Goffman

> *"In 1790, the nation which had fought a revolution against taxation without representation discovered that some of its citizens weren't much happier about taxation with representation."*
>
> —Lyndon Johnson

MORTGAGE RATES 1879-1965

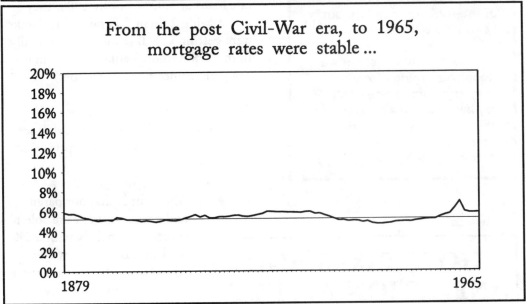

From the post Civil-War era, to 1965,
mortgage rates were stable ...

FIGURE 1-15

1966-1995

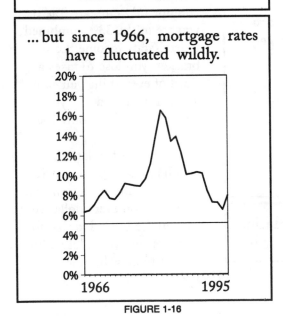

... but since 1966, mortgage rates
have fluctuated wildly.

FIGURE 1-16

> *"The farther backward you
> can look, the further forward
> you are likely to see."*
> —Winston Churchill

But something happened in 1966.
Rates began to rise and they've been
fluctuating ever since.

Amazing! Interest rates that had
remained constant since the end
of the Civil War suddenly began to
fluctuate, rocketing from 5.7% to
16.5% and crashing back down again.

What happened? Well, I'll tell you:

29

Too often, people get hung up *explaining* things rather than *accepting* them. For example, I can't explain the principles of internal combustion, but I can safely drive a car.

Handle money the same way: Recognize things for what they are, even if you can't explain them. As a judge once said, "I can't explain what pornography is, but I know it when I see it."

I don't know.

But look what happened to banks as a result: In 1965, they made 30-year, fixed rate loans at 5.83%, but by 1980, they were paying 21% in CD rates. The banks were getting killed! (I mean that literally. In the 1980s, more banks failed than in any period since the Depression.)

Bankers — some of the smartest economic minds in the nation — didn't see inflation coming, so it's no surprise that you didn't, either.

My point is that our parents and grandparents were able to succeed financially with a 2% bank account, yet if we do what they did — if we handle our money the way they handled theirs — we will fail where they succeeded.

Here's why:

Assume CD rates are 3%. If you are in the 33% combined federal/state income tax bracket, you lose to taxes a third of everything you earn. Thus, if you earn 3%, you lose 1%, and keep only 2%.

But because of inflation, which at this writing is 3%, you're actually losing, in real terms, 1% on every dollar you have in the bank. Do that for 20 years, and you'll lose 20% of your money. In other

HOW TAXES AND INFLATION AFFECT YOUR INVESTMENT EARNINGS

If You Earn	8%
You Pay Taxes of (33% Combined Fed/State Brackets)	- 2.6%
What's Left is	5.4%
Minus Inflation (23-year average CPI)	- 5.8%
Net Earnings	-0.4%

To beat the effects of taxes and inflation, you *must* earn more than 8% per year!

FIGURE 1-17

words, if you were to start with $10,000 today, you'd watch it "grow" over 20 years to $8,000. (That's why "CD" really stands for "Certificate of *Depreciation!*")

This is why many people fail financially. They focus on how much they *earn* instead of how much they *keep*. What counts is your *after-tax, after-inflation rate of return.*

As I say often on my radio and TV shows, you've got to earn more than 8% on your money in order to beat the historical level of inflation and taxes, because if you earn 8%, you lose one-third, leaving you with 5.4%. But with inflation's 23-year average of 5.8%, you actually *lose .4% per year! Thus, you must get ahead of the tax and inflation curve in order for your money to grow in real terms.*

To determine the minimum rate of return that you need to earn to beat taxes and inflation, look at Figure 1-18.

WHAT YOU MUST EARN TO MAINTAIN YOUR MONEY'S PURCHASING POWER

Inflation Rate

Tax Rate	2%	3%	4%	5%	6%	7%	8%	9%	10%	11%	12%
0%	2.0	3.0	4.0	5.0	6.0	7.0	8.0	9.0	10.0	11.0	12.0
10%	2.2	3.3	4.4	5.6	6.7	7.8	8.9	10.0	11.1	12.2	13.3
15%	2.4	3.5	4.7	5.9	7.1	8.2	9.4	10.6	11.8	12.9	14.1
20%	2.5	3.8	5.0	6.3	7.5	8.8	10.0	11.3	12.5	13.8	15.0
25%	2.7	4.0	5.3	6.7	8.0	9.3	10.7	12.0	13.3	14.7	16.0
30%	2.9	4.3	5.7	7.1	8.6	10.0	11.4	12.9	14.3	15.7	17.1
35%	3.1	4.6	6.2	7.7	9.2	10.8	12.3	13.8	15.4	16.9	18.5
40%	3.3	5.0	6.7	8.3	10.0	11.7	13.3	15.0	16.7	18.3	20.0
45%	3.6	5.5	7.3	9.1	10.9	12.7	14.5	16.4	18.2	20.0	21.8

Example: If inflation is 6% and you pay 35% in taxes, your investments must earn 9.2% to break even.

FIGURE 1-18

Everybody is lamenting today's low interest rates, compared to those of the '70s and early '80s, and my firm gets lots of calls from people complaining that interest rates have dropped. "My 8% and 10% CDs have all matured," they say. "Banks are not paying good rates any more."

> ## *"Why does a small tax increase cost you two hundred dollars and a substantial tax cut save you thirty cents?"*
> —Peg Bracken

My colleagues and I find this quite funny, because banks never paid "good rates." You're only noticing it for the first time! You see, CD rates — like all interest rates — simply track inflation. When inflation rates are high, interest rates are high, and when inflation drops, interest rates drop. In 1980, for example, when interest rates were 15%, inflation was 13%.

Do the math: If you earned 15% on a CD, you netted 10% after taxes. But with 13% inflation, you were still losing 3% per year in real terms. In other words, you were just as broke earning 15% in 1980 as you are earning 3% today. You simply never paid attention.

Now that you are thoroughly demoralized, let me assure you that there is a way out of this tax-and-inflation trap. And that leads us to the next chapter.

FRANK & ERNEST   BOB THAVES

©1996 United Features Syndicate, Inc. Reprinted by permission.

Chapter 3 - The Greatest Discovery of the 20th Century

Albert Einstein was once asked to name the greatest discovery of the 20th century. Most expected him to refer to his theory of relativity, nuclear energy, or some other important development. His answer, though: Compound interest. Was he joking? Look at these figures, then decide.

If you were to invest $10,000 at 5% interest for 20 years, your profit from the investment would be $17,126 (ignoring taxes). But if you doubled the rate of interest to 10%, how much money would you earn?

Although it would seem that doubling the rate would double the return, Einstein demonstrated that this is not the case: Increasing the rate by 100% increases the *return* by 350%. In other words, instead of earning $17,126 in interest, you would earn $63,281.

That's the power of compound interest: Money doesn't grow linearly — it grows exponentially! Take it a step further: If you earn 15% instead of 5%, your profit would be $187,155. Thus, three times the rate produces 11 times the return. And at 20% — a four-fold increase in rate — your profit would be $518,275, or a return 37 times higher than that provided by 5%.

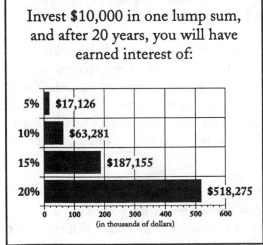

THE MAGIC OF COMPOUND INTEREST

Invest $10,000 in one lump sum, and after 20 years, you will have earned interest of:

5%	$17,126
10%	$63,281
15%	$187,155
20%	$518,275

0   100   200   300   400   500   600
(in thousands of dollars)

Invest $100 per month for 20 years (a total investment of $24,000), and you will have earned interest of:

5%	$17,103
10%	$51,937
15%	$125,724
20%	$286,965

0   50   100   150   200   250   300
(in thousands of dollars)

FIGURE 1-19

Investing monthly works just as well as when investing a lump-sum: If you invest $100 a month over 20 years, you'll have invested a total of $24,000. At 5%, your money would earn $17,103 in interest, but doubling the rate to 10% would once again increase your profit by 350%, just as before.

At 15%, you would have earned $125,724, or the same 11-fold increase as when we invested $10,000, and at 20%, you'd have earned $286,965, or a repeat of the 3,700% return.

I teach a class on this subject at Georgetown University, and it's usually about this time that my students raise a question: Where can you earn 20%?

The Secret to Earning 20% with No Risk

Wouldn't you like me to tell you how to earn 20% per year with no risk? Well, I'll tell you:

I don't know how.

And if I *did* know how, why would I tell you?

Ask yourself that question the next time someone cold-calls you with the hottest deal around. After all, if they have such a great investment, why would they tell you about it? Look, I'm a nice guy, but let's face it: If I had a "sure thing," I'd be so busy investing my own money that I certainly wouldn't have the time to tell you about it. And assuming I did have time to make a few phone calls, why would I call you — a total stranger — instead of telling my family and friends?

Actually, Wall Street has pondered the question of "why tell me?" for some time, and identified two theories: The first says that the only *sure* way to make money from investments is to earn commissions by selling them, and brokers can do that only by convincing someone that he or she will get rich in the process. Thus, this theory says a broker tells a client to buy or sell because it's good for the broker, not necessarily good for the investor.

The second theory says that Wall Street sharks who are on TV, the radio, or in some magazine or newspaper telling you to buy a certain stock often already own it, and they want to unload it. But they can't

> *"Make use of time, let not advantage slip."*
> —William Shakespeare

sell until the price goes up, or up again, and what better way to get the price of a stock to go up than by telling a few million people to buy it? So, they tout the stock on CNBC or *Wall Street Week* or *Money* magazine, and the masses oblige.

> *"The rich are taking their advice from professional financial advisors. The poor are getting their advice from Money magazine."*
> —Robert Veres

The stock briefly goes up — long enough for the guy who pitched it to get out — and he goes *back* on these programs to say, "See? I was right!"

Wall Street is full of these self-fulfilled prophecies.

You think I'm kidding? Studies have shown that in the 48 hours after a stock is touted on a popular TV show or news column, the stock rises significantly as tens of thousands of people call their brokers with buy orders. These stocks quickly return to their original levels, though, after the attention dies down, leaving investors with stocks bought at very high prices. However, these run-ups last long enough for the sharks who fed the information to the media to cash out at big profits.

Consider the example of Kidder Peabody broker A. Karl Kiplee. According to *Financial Planning on Wall Street*, Kiplee admitted that he planted inaccurate stories in the media about Epitope, Inc., a small biotech company. Allegedly, he gave CNBC and then-*Money* magazine reporter Dan Dorfman (perhaps the best-known financial journalist in the nation), false information, causing Dorfman to report in March 1994 that Epitope's AIDS test stood only a 1% chance of receiving FDA approval. This allegedly caused the stock to drop in value, yet in December of that year, the test was indeed approved.

DILBERT SCOTT ADAMS

©1996 United Features Syndicate, Inc. Reprinted by permission.

Epitope, alleging false and misleading statements, settled a suit with Kiplee, and as of this writing was even considering a suit against Dorfman, merely because Dorfman quoted Kiplee. As Dorfman later told *Business Week*, one "just can't be sure that everyone [you] speak to is 100% ethical."

But that wasn't Dorfman's only brush with controversy. *Business Week* reported in late 1995 that Dorfman was under investigation by federal authorities regarding his relationship with a Wall Street publicist. According to *Business Week*, the allegations are that corporate clients paid fees to the publicist, who is a good friend of Dorfman's, in exchange for having Dorfman say positive things about the company. At this writing, there is no indication that any money was exchanged between the publicist and Dorfman. However, Dorfman was fired by *Money* magazine; CNBC at this writing continues to allow Dorfman on the air.

Think about it. Stock prices are based on the laws of supply and demand. Supply (the number of shares of a stock that exist) is fixed; thus the price goes up and down based on demand. If lots of people want to buy, the price goes up, and if few want to buy, or if many want to sell, the price goes down.

Match these fundamentals with how one succeeds in the stock market. You make money by buying low and selling high. First, you buy a stock that has a low price. Then you go on television or radio, or get quoted in the newspaper, telling everyone that the price is really low, and that you think the price of the stock is going to go up. Better yet, get Dorfman or someone like him to do it for you.

DILBERT SCOTT ADAMS

©1996 United Features Syndicate, Inc. Reprinted by permission.

By distributing your message to millions of people, several hundred thousand will oblige, and this new demand will cause the price to rise within a day or two. You know when the show is going to air, or when the story is going to be printed (since you planted it), so you buy a few days in advance, and after the news breaks, you quickly sell while the stock is high, making a bundle. The masses, of course, get ripped-off: They bought the stock after the news report, as the stock was on its way up (they BUY HIGH) and as soon as the media attention ends (which it does quickly) demand softens and the stock falls back to its original level, causing them to SELL LOW. Thus, the not-knowing-better consumers lose money while the promoters make money.

This becomes a vicious trap for the unwary, because the promoters return to the media, saying, "The stock went up, so I was right. Therefore, you should listen to me next time and do what I tell you to do." Thus, they get invited back onto these shows, and they can be quoted again and again, and people continue to follow their "advice" and unwittingly help them make millions time after time. This is one of the reasons why there is often a big difference between *investment returns* and *investor returns* (see Chapter 37).

So whenever you see a "hot tip" touted in a financial newsletter, magazine, or newspaper, or you hear some pundit claiming on radio or TV that you need to buy or sell a certain stock, you've got to ask yourself, "What is the motivation of the person who's saying this?" After all, how relevant to your particular circumstances can the advice be when it is simultaneously being provided to millions of people?

Keep that in mind the next time you hear some financial wizard say, "The market's going to have a 20% correction." He might really mean, "The stock market's too high right now for me to buy more, so I want

DILBERT SCOTT ADAMS

©1996 United Features Syndicate, Inc. Reprinted by permission.

Even when motivation is not suspect, there's another potential problem: Lots can happen between the time an article is written and the time you read it. In its April 1995 issue, *Smart Money* magazine named Sports & Recreation as one of its "favorite midcap stocks," encouraging its readers to buy the company's shares. In the following issue, *Smart Money* apologized, saying, "Now we hate [the stock]." The magazine explained that "just as readers were starting to get their [April] issues in the mail," the stock dropped 42% in two days. Although the magazine's editors put a sell signal on the stock, readers saw the magazine's buy recommendation.

That must have been embarrassing for *Smart Money's* editors. Imagine, then, how they felt when it happened *again* in the very next issue! Yup, whereas the May issue apologized for April, the June issue found itself apologizing for May, whose cover story, "Where to Invest Now," said to buy the stock of United Wisconsin Services. Yet as *Smart Money* reported in June, "Just after we sent our [May] cover story to the printers, [there was] some disturbing news... [W]ith the May issue already in some subscribers' hands, UWS dropped a bombshell... its shares sank as low as $19, less than half their 1995 high."

To *Smart Money's* credit, they admitted their mistake. Still, you need to think again before you act on information contained in a personal finance magazine.

everyone to sell your holdings, which will force the stock market down by 20% so I can get in at the lower prices."

This is why I never tout stocks, mutual funds, or other investments by name in this book, in my newsletter, on my radio and TV shows, or in my seminars. Be wary of those who do. Like all investment advisors, I have my favorites, but I share them only with my firm's clients. My role here is to provide you with a fundamental financial education, not to get you to buy or sell something. I focus on education because once you understand how the financial world works, you'll be able to make the decisions that are best for you. And that, in turn, will enable you to ignore all the pundits and allow you to take control of your financial future.

How Did the Millionaires Get That Way?

Our inability to predict the source of 20% annual returns aside, I bet you can name the one asset that has produced more millionaires than any other. Right: It's real estate. Throughout U.S. history, real estate has been a very successful place to invest. So, let's take a little quiz:

1. Which of the following is the most valuable real estate?

    (a)   Maui

    (b)   Hong Kong

    (c)   Manhattan

    (d)   Monaco

    (e)   Tokyo

The answer is (c). Manhattan Island's real estate is the most expensive in the world.

2. From whom did we buy the island and how much did we pay?

These are easy questions. After all, you learned this in third grade! We bought Manhattan Island from American Indians, for blankets and beads worth $24.

3. What was the year?

This is a bit tougher. The year was 1626.

The Rule of 72

Before I ask you the final question, let me teach you about the Rule of 72. Great fun at cocktail parties,[1] the Rule of 72 allows you to determine how long it will take for money to double at various interest rates.

It works like this: Say you want your money to double in 10 years. To determine how much interest you need to earn, just divide 10 into 72. Therefore, in order for your money to double in 10 years, you must earn 7.2% annually. If you earn 15% and want to know how long it will take to double your money, just divide 72 by 15. The answer: 4.8 years.

So, simply divide whatever number you have — either the interest rate or the time — into the number 72, and the answer will be the number you need. If you divide the interest rate into 72, you'll get the *time*. If you divide the time into 72, you'll get the *interest rate*. What fun![2]

Now, on to our quiz's final question:

4. If the Indians had invested their $24 at 7.2% interest, so their money would double every 10 years (as the Rule of 72 shows you), how much money would they have by 1996?

By 1996, the Indians would have $3.3 trillion — on a $24 investment! The power of compounding is astounding! The key is interest earning interest on top of interest.

---

[1]Maybe not.
[2]Maybe not.

Yet many people spend the interest they earn. Do you? All too often, people deposit into their checking accounts the interest and dividends they get from CDs, stocks, and bonds and away the money goes, never to be seen again. If the Indians had done that — if they had deposited their $24 into a bank and spent the $1.73 that they earned each year (at 7.2%) instead of letting it compound — they would have earned (and spent) $640.10 in interest over the entire 370 years and the original $24 today still would be just $24.

The message is this: *Invest your money, leave it alone and don't touch it!* Allowing the interest to earn interest is the difference between six hundred dollars and $3.3 trillion.

THE POWER OF COMPOUNDING

$24 Invested at 7.2% in 1626...

```
        $24.00
         48.00
         96.00
        192.00
        384.00
        768.00
      1,536.00
      3,072.00
      6,144.00
     12,288.00
     24,576.00
     49,152.00
     98,304.00
    196,608.00
    393,216.00
    786,432.00
  1,572,864.00
  3,145,728.00
  6,291,456.00
 12,582,912.00
 25,165,824.00
 50,331,648.00
100,663,296.00
201,326,592.00
402,653,184.00
805,306,368.00
  1,610,612,736.00
  3,221,225,472.00
  6,442,450,944.00
 12,884,901,888.00
 25,769,803,776.00
 51,539,607,552.00
103,079,215,104.00
206,158,430,208.00
412,316,860,416.00
824,633,720,832.00
1,649,267,441,664.00
$3,298,534,883,328.00
```

...grows to $3.3 Trillion, by 1996!

"Money doesn't buy happiness. The fellow with $50 million is no happier than the fellow with $40 million."
—Anonymous

FIGURE 1-20

How Big is a Trillion?

Most people's eyes glaze over at talk of really big numbers. Do you really appreciate the size of a *trillion?* Let's put it this way: If you were to count from one to a trillion, counting one number each second, it would take you more than 11 days to reach one million. To reach one billion, you'd have to count for 31.7 years, while one trillion would take you *31,688 years.*

If you like to go shopping, consider this: If you were to spend $1,000 a day, here's how long it would take you to spend:

$1 million	—	3 years
$1 billion	—	3 thousand years
$1 trillion	—	3 million years

That's a lot of shopping!

Do You Want to Work Hard or Work Smart?

If you could save twice what you're saving now, you'd be twice as well off, right?

While it's true that you'd double your return if you doubled your savings, few people can afford to increase their savings by such a large amount.

But you can succeed financially *without* doubling your savings. Or rather, without doubling *the amount of money you save.* Here's what I mean:

Say you save $150 per month at a 5% annual return. In 40 years, you'd have $228,903. If you doubled your savings to $300 per month, you'd double your return, to $457,806. But clearly, in order to double the amount you save, you'd have to work harder — and most of us work hard enough as it is.

So let's try working *smarter* instead. If you continue to save the same $150 per month, but now earn 10% instead of 5%, your account in 40 years will be worth $948,612 — or *four times more* than if you had earned 5%. Indeed *working smart* is twice as profitable as *working hard.*

And if you're *really* smart, you'll do both: By boosting your monthly savings to $300 *and* earning 10%, you'll have $1,897,224.

"I am a great believer in luck, and I find the harder I work, the more I have of it."
—Stephen Leacock

Chapter 4 - The Good News and the Bad News About Planning for Your Future

Recall my comments in Chapter 1 about you needing 50/50 vision in order to succeed. I said that a 50-year-old earning $50,000 would need $2.2 million in order to retire comfortably. Did that number scare you?

All too often, the media use statistics like this one to intimidate consumers, and financial advisors often recite similar numbers to bully their clients into action. The most common use is in the area of college planning. Sadistic planners enjoy telling people that college will cost their infant children and grandchildren hundreds of thousands of dollars — effectively scaring the beejeebers out of their clients.[3]

Unfortunately, I have discovered that such numbers lead to a different reaction: Upon seeing such huge figures — numbers that certainly seem impossible to attain — clients respond by *doing nothing*. After all, clients typically say, there's no way I can save that much money, so why bother doing anything?

They have a point. Planners often discuss the future in black and white, rather than in shades of gray. They lead people to believe — or they allow people to conclude on their own — that if they fail to accumulate *every penny* that they need, none of the pennies they have collected will be of any help. Of course, that's nonsense, for while you might not be able to save a million dollars, having half a million ain't too shabby, either.

But even taking this failing on the part of planners into consideration, consumers still are getting it wrong — because they look only at the bad news, and not at the good news.

The bad news, in case you haven't already figured it out for yourself, is that *you will be unable to save all the money you need by the time you need it*. To see my point, just look at the numbers behind my 50/50: That 50-year-old earning $50,000 has 15 years until he retires. Even if he saves 100% of his gross income — with nothing siphoned off for

---

[3]Of course, I would never stoop to such a tactic in this book.

"If only God would give me some clear sign! Like making a deposit in my name in a Swiss bank account."

—Woody Allen

taxes or current needs — he'll amass only $750,000, or roughly a third of his $2.2 million goal. Thus, it seems that he won't be able to retire comfortably, for it is clearly *impossible* for him to save enough money.

That's the bad news — and it's so bad, in fact, that many people give up any efforts to plan before they even start. But that's *only* the bad news. While it is true that you will be unable to save enough money to meet all your financial goals, the good news is that *you don't have to.*

You need to go beyond my 50/50 story to our Indian story in Chapter 3: By making a one-time deposit of $24, the Indians were able to earn interest totaling $640.10 over a period of 370 years. But that $640.10, in turn, produced another $3 trillion in interest. Thus, you needn't worry about saving huge amounts of money. All you need to do is start the process: Invest the first dollar, and that dollar will do the rest. All it needs is an effective rate of return, and time.

So, when planning for your future, getting started now and saving whatever you can is half your answer. The other half is to listen to Einstein (Chapter 3) and boost the rate your savings earn — and you can learn how in Part VI.

"'A penny saved is a penny earned'? What are you, some kind of nut?"

Part II
Understanding the Capital Markets

Part II — Understanding The Capital Markets

Overview - Of all the isms, Ours is Capitalism

A society can take many forms. There's socialism, communism, fascism, and lots of other "isms" I don't pretend to understand. In America, we operate under capitalism and, whether you like it or not, whether you agree with it or not, you must take advantage of its rules if you are to succeed in our society.

Under capitalism, government and business need capital (money) to achieve their goals. Obtaining capital is their first task, for it allows them to further their objectives — whether social, political or financial.

Businesses and governments raise capital by printing and selling certificates, which they claim have value and are worth buying. Like innocent children, we believe them. This faith is vital, for without it our economic system would collapse.

All certificates, whether produced by business or government, are said to contain value because they (allegedly) will do one of two things:

- generate income   or   • grow in value.

That's it. The entire world of capitalism, our financial markets, and Wall Street can be reduced to these two premises. It's as simple as that.

To see how this concept works in the real world, let's go to the marketplace. It begins with the manufacturing process. Let's say a company manufactures a product. It then sells that product to a distributor, who distributes (sells) it to a retailer, who resells it to you — the consumer. Eventually, you do one of four things with that product:

- you consume it   • you donate it

- you throw it away   • you have a yard sale.

One of those four things happens to every product you buy.

Chapter 5 - The Manufacturing Process

You can see how this process is applied in almost any industry. In real estate, for example, a developer buys land, obtains zoning, builds roads and sewers, then sells parcels to builders.

The builders erect homes and then hire real estate agents to sell the homes to consumers (this is called the new home market). And the consumer later resells the house through the existing home market.

General Motors does the same thing: GM manufactures a car and sells it to a Buick dealer, which is a distributor; the dealer hires a salesperson to sell the car to a consumer, who later sells it to someone else through the used car market.

Corporate America does this, too, when it needs to raise cash. Say a big company needs $100 million to build a new factory. To raise the money (i.e., capital), the company manufactures (prints) certificates and proclaims they are worth $100 million. These certificates might be bond certificates, or they might be stock certificates (more on that later).

Next, the company sells the certificates to a securities broker/dealer.

By agreeing to buy the certificates from the company, the b/d now must sell them. To do so, it hires stockbrokers to peddle the certificates to investors (consumers). This process, called an Initial Public Offering, is handled in what's known as the *primary* (or first) *market*, as this is the first time these certificates are being offered to consumers.

The brokers continue to sell the certificates until they are sold out. If you buy one and later want to sell it, or if you did not buy one at first but later want to, you would do so in the secondary market, called a stock exchange. It's a place where people trade (or exchange) certificates with each other.

The New York Stock Exchange is the world's largest stock market. It's just like a grocery market, but instead of buying food, you buy certificates, and you can sell them as well. There are several secondary markets (exchanges) in the U.S.: The American Exchange, the Philadelphia Exchange, the Denver Exchange, and more. Most countries also have exchanges, although usually only one. (It's a testament to the U.S.'s size and power that it has so many exchanges. Other big ones are found in London, Frankfurt and Tokyo.) There even is a tertiary (or third) marketplace, where certificates trade electronically. There are other markets for trading commodities, such as oil, pork bellies, soybeans, and orange juice. The Mercantile Exchange and the Chicago Board Options Exchange are the biggest of these.

People often say stockbrokers and financial advisors are in the service business, but that's wrong. Wall Streeters sell products, each with its own unique features, benefits, costs, and risks — just like televisions and other products.

Since stockbrokers sell products, they are thus salespeople who work on commission, just like people who sell cars. If you go to a Ford dealer, guess what kind of car he's going to sell you? It's the same

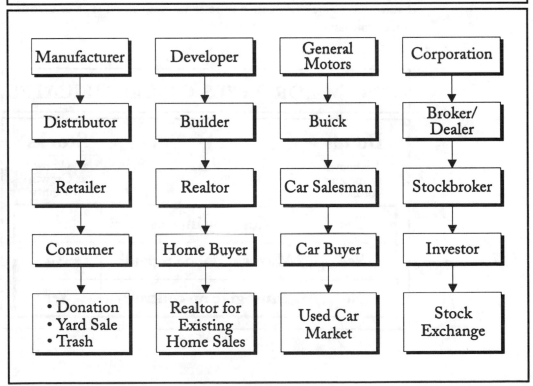

THE MANUFACTURING PROCESS

Manufacturer	Developer	General Motors	Corporation
Distributor	Builder	Buick	Broker/Dealer
Retailer	Realtor	Car Salesman	Stockbroker
Consumer	Home Buyer	Car Buyer	Investor
• Donation • Yard Sale • Trash	Realtor for Existing Home Sales	Used Car Market	Stock Exchange

FIGURE 2-1

with brokerage firms: Brokers sell whatever they have in inventory. Let's face it: If a car dealer has 27 station wagons on the lot, they're going to be selling station wagons that day. Likewise, stockbrokers have quotas and are under pressure from management to sell certain products each day, each week, and each month.

The Two Types of Certificates

There are two kinds of certificates: Bonds, also known as income or debt, and stocks, also known as growth or equity.

If Acme Widgets Inc. issues a bond certificate, it must pay you interest and eventually return your money to you, but it does not give you control of or ownership interest in the company.

If Acme issues a stock certificate, it does not have to pay dividends or ever give your money back to you, but it must give control of the company to you and others who buy the stock.

If you were Acme and needed to raise money, which type of certificate would you issue?

TWO MAJOR TYPES OF CERTIFICATES		
Bonds also known as Income or Debt	**VS.**	**Stocks** also known as Growth or Equity
Yes	Must pay interest?	No
Yes	Must capital be repaid?	No
No	Must give up control?	Yes

FIGURE 2-2

Like so many aspects in the world of money, the answer is: *It depends*, in this case, on what Acme is trying to accomplish. That's why some companies issue stock while others issue bonds — and why lots of companies do both. Let's take a closer look at these two types of certificates.

> *"The trouble with experience is that by the time you have it you are too old to take advantage of it."*
> —Jimmy Connors

If you are a bond holder, you are a *lender*. You are lending money to Acme. You do not care whether Acme makes or loses money. As long as Acme stays in business, you will receive a specific rate of interest and you will get your money back at a predefined date (called the *maturity* date). If Acme goes broke, you rank very high on the list of creditors in bankruptcy court. In fact, next to the IRS and Acme employees, bondholders typically are the highest-ranking creditors.

By contrast, a stockholder is an *owner* of the company. You have no idea how much money you're going to earn and there is no specific date on which your money will be returned. If Acme does not make any money, neither do you, and if Acme goes broke, so do you. If Acme goes bankrupt, you rank last in bankruptcy court.

All investments are either equity (meaning ownership, like stocks) or debt (meaning loanership, like bonds), although some-times they don't look like it. Wall Street pays lots of money to lots of people for creative packaging of these products. Today, you can find dozens of different types of investments, as Figure 2-3 shows. But in the final analysis, each fundamentally remains either debt or equity — just as a station wagon is still a car.

> **All the details about a particular bond are included on the bond's certificate (which is just a printed piece of paper). It states:**
>
> - **the value of the bond (known as the face value since it is printed directly on the certificate);**
> - **the interest rate;**
> - **how often the interest is paid;**
> - **who issued the bond; and**
> - **the maturity date.**

Remember that when choosing between stocks and bonds, "the greater the risk, the greater the reward." It is *impossible* to earn more money without taking a higher degree of risk, so if someone is offering you an investment that promises a better return than normal, you can be

FINANCING INSTRUMENTS

Bonds

Bankers Acceptance
Bridge Loan
Bunny Bond
Certificate of Deposit
Commercial Paper
Covered Option Security
Convertible Debt
Convertible With Premium Put
Debt With Deferred Rate Setting
Debt With Equity Warrants
Debt With a Forward Commitment
Dutch Auction Note
Dual-Currency Bond
Eurocommercial Paper
European Currency Unit Bond

Exchangeable Debt
Event-Risk Protected Debt
Flip-Flop Note
Increasing Rate Debt
Indexed Debt
Junk Bond
Floating-Rate Note
Medium-Term Note
Nondollar Debt
Option-Related Debt
Pay-in-Kind Debenture
Poison Put
Variable-Coupon Renewable Note
Zero-Coupon Bond

Stocks

Adjustable-Rate Preferred
Convertible to Preferred
Increasing Rate Preferred
Money Market Preferred
Pay-in-Kind Preferred
Poison Preferred
Remarketed Preferred

Derivatives

Debt-for-Equity Swap
Securities With a Put Option
Options
Futures
Interest Rate Swaps
Currency Forward
Options on Futures

FIGURE 2-3

sure there also is a higher degree of risk than normal. As we learn more about investments in this book, we'll look more closely at these risks.

Is a CD: (a) a stock, (b) a bond, or (c) neither?

Think about it: You have a stated rate of interest; you have a stated maturity date; and your earnings are not dependent on the profits of the bank. CDs, therefore, are bonds.

Chapter 6 - Building Cash Reserves

15,000 Reasons Why You Need Reserves

What if your car breaks down or the roof leaks? You might need cash fast. Therefore, you need cash reserves to provide you with ready cash in the event of an unforeseen crisis. The reason you need reserves, quite simply, is because every single day in America, 15,000 washing machines break down (according to Sears, which sells more washing machines than anyone).

People lose jobs, kids need braces, daughters get married, employees get laid off, businesses go broke. Like the saying, "Life is what happens while you're making other plans," something expensive is sure to happen when you least expect it. For all of life's unexpected events — both good and bad — you need cash reserves to get you through them.

Two Factors Determine How Much You Should Keep in Reserves

The amount you should keep in reserves depends on two factors: your monthly expenses and the stability of your income.

First, focus on how much you spend each month. If you don't know the amount, refer to Chapter 51. Your reserves should be a multiple of your monthly spending — say, 2x, 5x, or even 12x; the proper multiple depends on the second factor: the stability of your income. The more stable your income, the lower your multiple need be.

For example, if you and your spouse each have highly secure jobs, two months' worth of spending is probably sufficient. However, if you are single with an uncertain income, you might need to keep 12 months' worth of spending in cash reserves. The point is that you should maintain in cash reserves enough to get you through rough times. And while that's important, it's equally important that you maintain only enough, because the interest rate your reserves will earn is terribly low — lower, in fact, than what you'll earn on virtually any other investment.

And leave your reserves *alone*.

If you determine, say, that $10,000 is the right amount of reserves for you, put that $10,000 away and never touch it unless you have a crisis — just as you'd never touch your umbrella unless it started raining.

If you know you're going to incur a large expense within the next two years, such as home improvements, the purchase of a car, wedding or college costs, or other big-ticket expense, stash those amounts away *in addition to your reserves*. The same is true for occasional expenses, such as Christmas shopping. If you know you're going to spend $1,000 over the holidays, boost your reserves by that amount during the year.

The goal is to maintain your reserves at their fully-funded level at all times. If a crisis forces you to spend some or all of your reserves, your first task is to build your reserves back up again.

Once you determine how much you need for reserves, you must keep your reserves *safe* (meaning you cannot lose this money) and *liquid* (meaning you can get the money at any time without penalty).

Six Places to Store Your Reserves

Six places qualify:

- your mattress
- savings accounts
- checking accounts
- money market funds
- U.S. Treasury Bills, and
- short-term bank CDs and commercial paper

Nothing else qualifies, including everything listed next. Although the following list consists of investments that are *cash equivalents* (meaning they are the same as cash), and although many people often use these investments to store their reserves, they are nonetheless unsuitable.

U.S. Treasury Notes. Unlike *T-Bills*, which mature in as little as 30 days, *Notes* mature in two to ten years. That's too long to have to wait to get your money back so you can fix your car.

U.S. Treasury Bonds. These mature in 30 years. If the 2-year note is too long, 30-year bonds are waaaay too long.

U.S. EE Savings Bonds. These don't qualify as reserves until six months after you buy them, because you cannot cash them in for that long. That's too long to wait if you need cash in a hurry.

Bank CDs and Commercial Paper. Unless, of course, they mature within one year. Commercial paper is a CD-like investment that is offered by large corporations instead of banks.

Life Insurance Cash Value. Yes, this is a cash equivalent. (Why do you think they call it "*cash* value"?) But no, it is not suitable for use as reserves, because of potentially large surrender penalties, tax risks, and other restrictions.

Fixed Annuities. The insurance industry's version of bank CDs, typically offering a slightly higher rate, these investments offer a tax advantage discussed in Chapter 28. Annuities are not acceptable as reserves because of tax penalties and surrender charges.

SHOE JEFF MacNELLY

TYPES OF CASH EQUIVALENTS

Type of Asset	Offered By	Source of Protection	Taxable?	Suitable as Cash Reserves?
Checking Account	Banks, S&Ls, Credit Unions	Federal Deposit Insurance	Federal and State	Yes
Savings Account	Banks, S&Ls, Credit Unions	Federal Deposit Insurance	Federal and State	Yes
Certificate of Deposit	Banks, S&Ls, Credit Unions	Federal Deposit Insurance	Federal and State	If maturity is less than 1 year
Money Market Fund	Investment Companies	Based on underlying security	Federal and State, unless Tax-exempt	Yes
Treasury Bill, Note, Bond	United States Government	Federal Guarantee	Federal Only	Yes
U.S. Savings Bond	United States Government	Federal Guarantee	Federal Only	see footnote*
Life Insurance Cash Value	Insurance Companies	Guaranteed by Insurance Company	Only if withdrawn via policy surrender	No
Fixed Annuity	Insurance Companies	Guaranteed by Insurance Company	Only upon withdrawal 10% penalty if under age 59½	No
Commercial Paper	Corporations	Guaranteed by Issuer	Federal and State	If maturity is less than 1 year

FIGURE 2-4

* Because EE bonds cannot be cashed in for six months after purchase, EE bonds you currently own (and which are more than six months old) are suitable as cash reserves. New ones you buy would not be suitable for six months.

The interest rates offered by all these choices are both very similar and very low. Furthermore, the rate changes constantly, rising and falling with inflation. This becomes quite apparent in Figure 2-5, which compares the 30-day T-Bill with inflation rates. Notice that as inflation has risen or fallen, so have interest rates. That's why you were just as broke in 1980 with a 15% CD as you are today with a 3% CD.

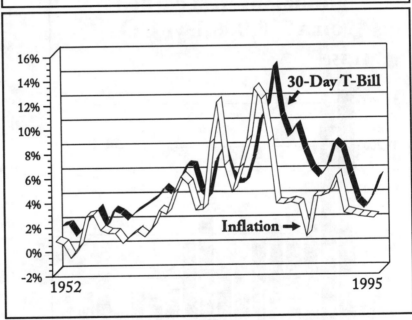

FIGURE 2-5

Although I've stated that you should place into cash equivalents only the amount needed for reserves, many Americans place 100% of their money into accounts like these. Why?

"I can't afford to gamble with my money," is the common answer. "I need to know my money is safe."

Sound familiar? The irony here is that CDs are among the most volatile of all investments. But consumers don't realize this because they don't look at CDs the correct way.

If you had invested $10,000 in a 1-year CD in 1981, your rate would have been 15.5%, meaning you would have earned $1,550 in interest that year. And who was the most likely buyer of that CD? Conservative retirees who needed income and who wanted safety for their money.

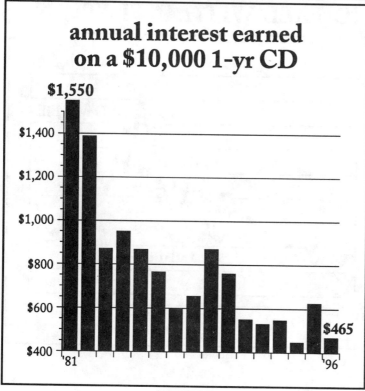

"GUARANTEED" CDs ARE ACTUALLY VERY VOLATILE

annual interest earned on a $10,000 1-yr CD

FIGURE 2-6

But that rate only lasted one year. By 1986, the rate was only 7.02%. Thus, the income on that CD dropped by more than half, to just $702. By 1996 the CD was earning only $465. Not only did retirees watch their income plummet, the cost of living jumped during that time — meaning that retirees needed $2,713 in 1996 to buy what $1,550 bought in 1981. Yet their income from CDs in 1996 was just $465!

Many retirees are going broke and they don't know why. After all, they had invested safely; they hadn't done anything wrong... had they?

This horror story is replayed over and over for people who have all their money in CDs. This is a very volatile investment, one whose income stream is both unpredictable and, ironically, far more uncertain than that the "risky" stock market.

Do you want your money to be safe? Well, you're going broke... safely!

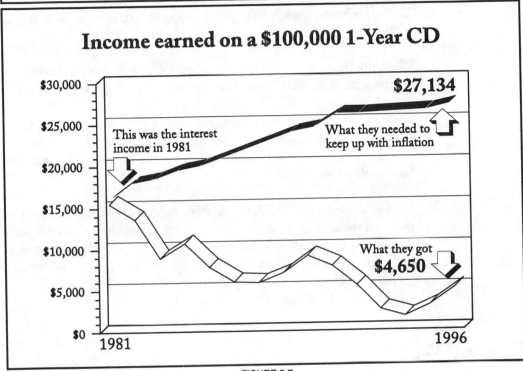

RETIREES AND THEIR CDs

Income earned on a $100,000 1-Year CD

$27,134

This was the interest income in 1981

What they needed to keep up with inflation

What they got **$4,650**

$30,000
$25,000
$20,000
$15,000
$10,000
$5,000
$0

1981

1996

FIGURE 2-7

The True Job of Banks

This is not intended to be an indictment against banks. You don't make any money in bank accounts (in real economic terms) simply because you're not supposed to. The bank is not tricking you; rather, making money for you is simply not the bank's job!

Actually, you should use a bank for only three reasons: to store your reserves, to get a loan, and to execute financial transactions. Think about it: What do you do with your paycheck? You put it in your checking account so you can write checks to pay your bills. The bank simply processes the transaction for you.

Thus, banks serve as short-term depositories of cash, as you move money from one place to another. For example, have you ever sold a house to buy another? Typically, you sell one house a few weeks or months before you settle on the other. In the meantime, what do you do with the cash you got from selling the first house? You've got to put it somewhere; you certainly don't want to gamble with it, since you need it as a down payment on the new house. So what do you do? You put it in the bank, where you receive enough interest to keep pace with inflation.

The bank thus keeps your money current with inflation, and banks do this extremely well while maintaining a very high degree of safety.

Similarly, those who have a brokerage account know that when they sell a stock, their broker automatically "sweeps" the proceeds of the sale into a money market fund, so the cash can earn interest until they buy another investment.

So if you've ever noticed that you seem to be working harder than ever and making more money than ever, yet you don't feel like you're getting ahead, now you know why: You've been keeping your money in banks, S&Ls, and credit unions, and your money — in real terms — hasn't been growing. Like pedestrians on a treadmill, money in a bank works hard but doesn't get anywhere.

The Myth of FDIC

It's ironic that those who choose banks are primarily concerned with safety, because banks are *not* the ultimate safe haven. In fact, for the savviest safety-conscious investors, banks are far too risky. Banks, after all, are nothing more than private businesses, and like any private business, a bank can go broke at any time, taking customers' money with it.

But what about FDIC? Doesn't that guarantee your money is safe?

Not at all! FDIC is widely misunderstood, so here's the truth about it:

The Great Depression saw more than 50% of the nation's banks go out of business, leaving their depositors penniless. This destroyed consumer confidence in banks. To restore that confidence, the federal government in 1933 created the Federal Deposit Insurance Corporation. Although chartered by Congress, FDIC is a private insurance company and receives no federal funding.

If you think government-sponsored deposit insurance makes your money safe, talk to a depositor at Old Court Savings & Loan. When this Maryland S&L failed, thousands of depositors thought their money was safe. Unfortunately, Old Court, like many thrifts across the country, was a member of the state deposit fund, not the federal program. When several S&Ls went broke in the early '80s, the state fund ran out of money.

In 1986, the state treasurer offered a plan to return all the money to Old Court's depositors. The plan would have required Maryland to issue new bonds. When Wall Street threatened to lower Maryland's AAA bond rating — which would have increased the state's borrowing costs — the governor rejected the plan, deciding that the state's bond rating was more important than the money its citizens had lost.

Rather, its money comes from banks, which pay insurance premiums to FDIC, much as you pay premiums to your auto insurer. Thus, when a bank fails, it files a claim with FDIC requesting that it pay off the bank's depositors, just as you would ask your auto insurer to pay your repair bill when you have an accident. Thus, FDIC was designed to reassure consumers that their money would be safe even if their bank was to fail. Similar systems were created for S&Ls (The Federal Savings and Loan Insurance Corporation), credit unions (The National Credit Union Share Insurance Fund) and pension funds (The Pension Benefit Guaranty Corporation).

These agencies, all of which have demonstrated their ability to handle occasional failures, never were designed to cope with a system-wide collapse. And indeed, the 1980s proved too much for some of them. When the S&L crisis loomed, FSLIC found itself technically bankrupt in 1986, with only 12 cents on deposit for each $100 it was insuring. FDIC was little better, with only 23 cents on hand for each hundred dollars it was protecting. Even today, FDIC, although improved, still has only $1.22 per $100.

By the late 1980s, Congress was forced to create the Resolution Trust Corporation to manage what was left of FDIC and the defunct FSLIC. Today, cleanup of the mess left by failed S&Ls and banks continues, and the FDIC, although stronger now that the wave of failures has ebbed, still has little in reserves to handle further failures.

Insurance, after all, is only as good as the company providing it, and this is too uncertain for the most risk-averse of investors. That's why, for these investors, there is only one choice for their money: U.S. Government Securities. We'll learn more about them in the next chapter.

Chapter 7 - The Most Fundamental of All Investment Risks — And How to Avoid It

Many people place their life savings in banks because they think doing so keeps their money safe. Safe? Safe from what?

As we saw in Chapter 2, money that you keep in banks is not safe from inflation, nor is it safe from taxes. So what is it that people are thinking of when they talk about bank accounts being "safe"?

The risk that banks help you avoid — even though you may not realize it — is *default risk*. Because of FDIC protection, people feel that they do not need to fear the bank going broke, taking their money with it. Like Will Rogers once said, "I am more interested in the return *of* my principal than the return *on* my principal!"

Although banks are perceived to be free of default risk, there's another — even better — way to avoid default risk: by investing in securities issued by the Federal Government of the United States, issuer of the world's safest investments.

Why are these investments so safe? Because the U.S. Government *guarantees* (not merely *insures*) them. This guarantee, printed on each bond the government issues, is a "full faith and credit obligation" of the Government of the United States of America "for the timely payment of principal and interest."

This guarantee is the investment standard of the world, because it is the only investment that absolutely frees you from default risk. This is deemed so because the United States has never defaulted on an interest or principal payment in the entire history of our nation. No other country can make this claim.

Therefore, when it comes to default risk, all investments are implicitly compared to U.S. Government Securities. Measuring default risk on a scale from low to high, U.S. Government Securities score a "none" — and it is the only asset class so ranked. Bank accounts, with their federal insurance protection, are a distant second.

The federal government issues many types of bonds, and we've already covered some of them in our discussion of cash reserves. In total, the federal government has issued securities worth $4.9 trillion, making the U.S. Government the largest issuer of bonds in the market (and the world's biggest debtor). In fact, more than $5 billion worth of U.S. Government Securities trade on Wall Street *every day*.

Did you ever wonder why U.S. Government Securities are so safe? It's because the federal government has an unlimited source of capital: If it ever runs out of money, the government just prints more to pay its bills.

I wish I could do that.

Because of Uncle Sam's unconditional guarantee, it is impossible for U.S. Government Securities to default — unless there's a collapse of the entire federal system! And if you think that's going to happen, Chapter 50 will show you how to protect yourself.

THE WIZARD OF ID PARKER & HART

By permission of Johnny Hart and Creators Syndicate, Inc.

Part III
Fixed Income Investments

Part III — Fixed Income Investments

Overview - Income Before Growth

As explained in Chapter 5, all investments are designed to produce income or grow in value (sometimes both). Of the two, income is much more reliable than growth. After all, a company's management cannot make its stock price rise, but it can pay interest to its bondholders and declare stock dividends for shareholders. Therefore, income-producing investments are considered safer (in this case, safety is defined as *reliability*) than growth-oriented investments because investors can expect to receive their income more reliably than they can expect an investment to grow in value. Therefore, we'll look first at income-producing investments.

Of course, we're talking about bonds, and there are many issuers of bonds. We'll start with the safest issuer, which is the United States Government.

Chapter 8 - U.S. Government Securities

All federal securities can be placed into two categories:

Direct obligations of the United States:

- **Treasury bills, notes, and bonds.** *Treasuries* provide money for the general use of the government.

- **Government National Mortgage Association Pass-Through Certificates.** *Ginnie Maes* provide mortgages for home buyers.

Bonds backed by an agency of the United States, including:

- **Federal National Mortgage Association.** *Fannie Mae* provides mortgages.

- **Student Loan Marketing Association.** *Sallie Mae* provides student loans.

- **Federal Home Loan Corporation.** *Freddie Mac* also provides mortgages.

Understand Ginnie Maes Before You Invest

The Rules of Money Have Changed, and nowhere is this more true than with Ginnie Maes. Tens of thousands of investors across America buy these U.S.-backed certificates, and it's a safe bet that most have no idea how Ginnie Maes work. As a result, many are in for a shock when they look to get their money back, only to find out their investment is gone, even though it was government guaranteed.

Ginnie Maes are issued by the Government National Mortgage Association, a federal agency created by Congress in the 1960s in response to concerns that banks didn't have enough cash to provide loans to tens of thousands of would-be home buyers.

Here's how GNMA works: Wally borrows $100,000 from his bank to buy a house, at 10% interest for 30 years. His bank sells the mortgage to GNMA, freeing up its capital to provide more loans.

GNMA assembles mortgages from banks throughout the nation into groups, or "pools," of $4,000,000. Each pool contains identical mortgages — the same face amount, interest rate, and maturity date. GNMA then divides each pool into $25,000 units and sells them to investors, taking half of one percent in fees.

So Wally's mortgage is now part of an investment paying 9.5% for 30 years. This is why Ginnie Maes are called "mortgage pass-through certificates."

Wally makes his monthly payment to the bank, which sends it to GNMA, which gives it to the investors who bought the pool in which Wally's mortgage is a part. GNMA payments to investors are issued monthly just like Social Security checks.

To protect investors against the possibility that Wally might default on his loan, GNMA promises to meet the obligation if Wally does not. Ginnie Maes, therefore, are direct "full faith and credit" obligations of the United States Government. The U.S. Treasury must satisfy the debt if Wally doesn't.

> *"There is nothing wrong with earning 5% or 6% on bonds; it just shouldn't take a year to do it."*
> —Anonymous

As every homeowner knows, Wally's monthly payment is part interest and part principal. Therefore, so is the monthly check that investors receive from GNMA. No other investment does this — not CDs, bonds, stocks, or mutual funds — and this unique feature is key to the confusion. While the interest portion will be relatively constant, the principal portion can fluctuate — sometimes dramatically. For instance, a Ginnie Mae investor who normally receives $140 a month ($110 in interest and $30 in principal) could suddenly get a check for, say, $3,400 — several thousand dollars more than usual.

This can occur whenever the mortgagees within the pool (e.g., Wally) increase their payments, since excesses are always applied to principal. This could happen if Wally sells his home or refinances, thus paying off his mortgage; if Wally dies, and his insurance company pays off the mortgage; or if he defaults, and GNMA pays off as required.

Because of the prepayments, the typical life of a Ginnie Mae is 12-15 years. Nowhere else can you obtain a 30-year bond that will return your money, plus interest, in a shorter period of time on a guaranteed basis. That's the good news. The bad news is that many investors don't realize their monthly check is a partial return of their own principal, so, believing it's all interest, they spend it. Ten years later they learn that because all the mortgages in their pool have been paid off, they will not get any more interest checks and, because their principal was being returned to them each month along with the interest, they are not about to receive a check for their principal, either. Realizing their principal is gone because they'd been spending it each month can be quite a shock.

But for investors who understand how Ginnie Maes work, getting principal back monthly can be a big advantage. By reinvesting this monthly return of capital — not spending it — the compounding effect can boost the total return above that provided by the Ginnie Mae itself. Some advisors, in fact, can arrange for their clients to receive only the interest each month, keeping the principal portion in an interest-bearing account on behalf of the investor. Not all financial planners or brokers perform this service; you'll have to ask.

But if you're buying Ginnie Maes, that's the smart way to treat them.

Chapter 9 - Municipal Bonds

If bonds issued by the United States Government are the safest investment, then it follows that bonds issued by state governments are the second-safest. Known as *municipal bonds* (muni's) because they are issued by state and local municipalities, they have been a primary source of capital for state and local governments since colonial days.

There are two types: *General Obligation* and *Revenue.*

G.O. bonds are guaranteed by the government issuing the bond; revenue bonds are not guaranteed.

Typically, G.O. bonds raise money for schools, highways, and other public works which do not generate revenue, while revenue bonds normally are used for projects which do, such as toll roads, airports and hospitals. Revenue bonds rely on the notion that revenue from the project repays the bond's interest and principal. But if the project fails to raise enough revenue, you will not be paid. Thus, revenue bonds are subject to default risk, while G.O. bonds are not. If you're primarily concerned with safety, you should choose a G.O. bond over a revenue bond.

G.O. bonds never default? Well, that's not entirely true: Some G.O.s actually have gone broke. Can you name the states whose G.O. bonds have defaulted?

My students at Georgetown University always guess Massachusetts, California, New York, and New Jersey. Yet none of these has ever defaulted.

If you haven't yet figured out which have, here's a hint: They lost the war. Yes, the states of the Confederacy defaulted on their G.O. bonds when they lost the Civil War. Remember: The only way a government-guaranteed bond can go broke is for that government to fail.

War aside, municipalities can't go broke because they have a never-ending revenue source. It's called (surprise!) taxes.

Municipal bonds are extremely popular. The reason is because all the interest you earn is free of federal income taxes. Of the four enemies of money, muni's beat one of them: You don't have to pay taxes to the federal government and, in 26 states, if you buy a bond from the state in which you live, you don't have to pay state income taxes, either.

Why is the interest earned on a municipal bond free from federal income tax? Why is Uncle Sam willing to give up the tax revenue?

The answer is provided by the courts. In the 1800s, Maryland sued the federal government, arguing that the feds were taxing the states on revenue the states were earning — in essence, an income tax on the states. The Supreme Court ruled (with one of my favorite quotes) that "the ability to tax is the ability to destroy." (Really? Gosh!)

The high court recognized that if the federal government taxed the states on their income, the states would retaliate by assessing property taxes against the fed for post offices and military bases. In other words, the two governments simply would tax each other endlessly.

To preserve our federal system, the Supreme Court ordered the two to stop. The federal government, said the court, may not tax state obligations and the states may not tax federal obligations. Since municipal bond interest is an obligation of the state (hence the name "General Obligation"), Uncle Sam cannot tax that revenue. Thus, there is a legitimate reason why muni interest is tax-free.

"The avoidance of taxes is the only intellectual pursuit that carries any reward."
—John Maynard Keynes

Now that you understand why muni interest is free from federal taxes, why do many states exempt muni interest from their own income taxes?

The answer is this: With 50 states plus a few U.S. territories all issuing bonds, there's a lot of competition. Thus, for Virginia to convince its residents to buy a Virginia bond instead of one from Maryland, Virginia residents demand an incentive. And what better incentive could there be than for Virginia to tell its residents that interest they earn from Virginia bonds will be free of Virginia income taxes, while interest from all other states will not be exempt? It's an effective sales tool used in 26 states. The others either do not have a state income tax, or most of their residents do not border other states. (Virginia residents, like most on the East Coast, are near four other states, and crossing state lines for goods and services is common. Other states, such as those in the midwest, find that most residents never leave, so the "sales pitch" of local tax exemption is not deemed to be a necessary inducement.)

This also explains why the U.S. government taxes you on interest you earn on its bonds. The U.S. government, after all, doesn't have any competition, so if you want the supreme safety of Uncle Sam's Treasuries, you're going to have to pay federal taxes on the interest you earn.

One Important Tax Tip!

Focus for a moment on this last point: It provides an important tip you might have missed. Just as the courts require that muni interest is free of federal taxes, the courts also require that interest on a federal bond be free of state taxes. Therefore, if you live in a state which has an income tax, you make more money on a 5% U.S. Treasury than you do on a 5% CD, because the interest you earn from the Treasury is free of state taxes while interest from a CD is not. Thus, the Treasury not only is safer, it's more profitable, too!

It drives me nuts when I hear that someone has been paying state income taxes on the interest they've earned from federal bonds — and that includes EE Savings Bonds! If you've been doing this, you need to file amended tax returns to get a refund of the excess taxes you've been paying.

In our planning practice, we often find that many people overpay their taxes needlessly because they fail to understand our tax laws and they don't obtain proper counsel.

The Call Feature, or Heads They Win — Tails You Lose

Most muni bonds are *callable*, which means that the government which issued the bond, at its option, can *redeem the bond* (i.e., give you your money back) before it matures.

Say the government issues a bond at 10% and interest rates later drop to 4%. The government would save a lot of money if it were to cancel all those 10%'ers, return principal to the investors, and issue fresh bonds at the new current rate of 4%.

In other words, if you bought that 30-year bond expecting to enjoy 10% interest for many years to come, you could find yourself getting all your money back much sooner, which would force you to reinvest at the new lower rates. As a taxpayer, you'd be happy to see your government save money by refinancing its debt at lower rates, but as an investor, you'd be quite annoyed.

Of course, if interest rates rise from 10% to 15%, the government will not call the bonds. Thus, investors would be left with a bond that pays 10% while new investors buy new bonds that pay 15%. In other words, when it comes to callable bonds, heads the government wins — tails you lose.

Are Tax-Free's a Better Buy than Taxables?

Now that you understand how tax-free income works, answer this question: Which is better, a CD paying 7% or a tax-free bond paying 5.5%?

It's a tough question, because the CD's rate is *before* taxes, while the muni's rate is *after* taxes — an apples-to-oranges comparison. We need an apples-to-apples comparison, and that means we need to determine the muni's *taxable-equivalent yield*. Here's the formula:

$$\frac{\textbf{Muni Rate}}{\left(\textbf{100} - \substack{\textbf{Your} \\ \textbf{Tax Rate}}\right)}$$

When calculating the taxable-equivalent yield, be sure to include state income taxes. Figure 3-1 shows you the TEY you need to earn, depending on the current muni rate and your tax bracket.

The Triple Threat Against Muni's

It's worth noting that while the Supreme Court has upheld the tax exemption for muni bond interest many times over the past 150 years, in recent years the federal government has succeeded in making small inroads against the tax-free status of municipal bonds.

Muni Tax Threat #1

The first occurred in the Tax Reform Act of 1986, when the federal government declared that certain tax-free bonds, known as Industrial Development Bonds, are not entitled to tax-free status. IDBs essentially are corporate bonds issued in the name of a state government, which states allow to induce big companies to do business in otherwise economically-depressed areas. Since the proceeds of the bond offering are for the benefit of the company and not the state, the Supreme Court agreed with the federal government that tax exemption is not required. Although IDBs typically are offered to institutional investors, individual investors need to be aware of them ...and steer clear.

TAXABLE EQUIVALENT YIELDS

If your Federal Tax Rate is... ▼

...and your municipal bond's tax-exempt rate is...

	4%	5%	6%	7%	8%	9%	10%	11%	12%
15%	4.71	5.88	7.06	8.24	9.41	10.59	11.76	12.94	14.12
28%	5.56	6.94	8.33	9.72	11.11	12.50	13.89	15.28	16.67
31%	5.80	7.25	8.70	10.14	11.59	13.04	14.49	15.94	17.39
36%	6.25	7.81	9.38	10.94	12.50	14.06	15.63	17.19	18.75
39.6%	6.62	8.28	9.93	11.59	13.25	14.90	16.56	18.21	19.87

...then this is what you must earn from a taxable investment in order to obtain the same after-tax return.

For an investor in the 28% federal tax bracket, buying a 6% muni is equivalent to buying a CD that pays 8.33%. The muni advantage gets even better when you factor in state income taxes.

FIGURE 3-1

Muni Tax Threat #2

The second inroad came in 1991. That's when the federal government began requiring taxpayers to declare on their tax returns how much interest they receive from municipal bonds. Many are concerned that Uncle Sam wants this data for only one reason: So the feds can see exactly how much revenue they're losing from muni bonds. Until 1991, no studies had been done, so nobody was sure of the exact amount of interest paid by municipal bonds. There is concern that there will be renewed attempts to terminate munis' tax-free status. While this situation is not something I'd lie awake at night worrying over, you should be aware of it because such a change would drastically reduce the value of muni bonds.

Muni Tax Threat #3 — the biggest risk of all

Congress is considering a complete overhaul of the tax code. Half a dozen proposals have been offered: a flat tax, value-added taxes, consumption taxes, and more. Each of these proposals would have the same effect on municipal bonds: They would eliminate the tax advantage that muni bonds currently enjoy, and if that advantage disappears, muni bonds could face losses of 20% or more.

Remember that the primary benefit of owning muni bonds is based not on fundamental economic principles, but rather on tax law: Muni bond interest is free of federal and state income taxes merely because somebody says it is. And nowhere is it written that "somebody" might not change their mind. Indeed, if the tax advantages of muni bonds are legislated away, muni bonds stand to lose 20% or more of their value, almost overnight. Here's why this could happen:

Say muni bonds currently yield 5.5% and 30-year U.S. Treasuries yield 7%. The T-bond is more profitable — but only on a pre-tax basis. After paying taxes (assuming a 31% federal income tax bracket), the T-bond nets only 4.83%. That's less than the muni. So even though the muni rate is lower than the T-bond's rate, current tax law makes the muni the better buy.

This, again, is why muni bonds are so popular. But many of the tax proposals before Congress would remove the tax advantage that muni's enjoy. If that happens, muni's will lose their popularity as well.

For example, one flat tax proposal would exempt from taxes all investment income. This means all investments would enjoy the tax-free status that muni's alone currently hold. If that happens, a 5.4% muni would lose 20% of its value in order to equal a 6.7% Treasury, since both would have the same tax treatment. That means the market value of the muni would drop 20% if this law is enacted. Chapter 14 explains further why bond values fluctuate.

The flat tax is not the only threat. Other bills would tax all investment income — including muni bond interest. Although this is the opposite of the flat tax proposal, the effect is the same: It "levels the playing field" — to the detriment of muni bonds.

And some even are pushing for the complete elimination of the federal income tax — including repeal of the 16th Amendment itself. This camp, which favors a sales tax or value-added tax, also exempts investment income, again removing the tax advantage that muni bonds currently enjoy and again causing a 20% loss in the value of muni bonds.

Will any of these proposals become law? Frankly, I see lots of reasons for doubt, including:

- Losing their tax-exempt status means states will be forced to increase the rates they offer on their muni bonds. To pay for this increase in borrowing costs, state and local governments will have to raise income and property taxes. Once people realize this, support for tax reform could fade.

- The proposals would do away with tax deductions for mortgage interest and property taxes (the latter of which would increase as noted above), making homes less affordable. Foreclosures will rise and home values will drop — as much as 25% according to some economists — followed by a severe recession affecting home builders, real estate agents, mortgage companies, and settlement firms.

"Taxes grow without rain."
—Jewish proverb

- Ditto for the millions of people who work directly or indirectly in the tax and accounting field, for elimination of our current, complex tax code would put all these folks out of work, with significant implications for the overall economy. Clearly, many voters will not remain quiet once they realize what tax reform really means.

- In addition to the real estate and accounting fields, many other special interest groups would be hurt by tax reform. Wait for the lobbyists to get involved.

- Public policy makers don't want a flat tax. After all, the tax code offers one of the most effective ways for the government to execute its social agenda. Does the government want to provide low-income housing? Then offer a tax credit to developers. Want to rebuild inner cities? Establish tax-free enterprise zones. Need to preserve historic buildings? Create a Historic Rehabilitation Tax Credit. Need to employ disadvantaged, inner-city youth? Give employers a Targeted Jobs Tax Credit. Want to discourage car buyers from choosing autos that get low gas mileage? Assess a gas guzzler's tax. The tax code is filled with rules that encourage society to act in certain ways, and a flat tax eliminates this critical tool. Policy makers know that — and they don't like it.

- While Congress can choose to stop taxing other investments, many will challenge — in court — Congress' ability to tax muni bond interest. Indeed, as we've seen, muni bond interest is tax free because of a Supreme Court ruling, not because of legislation.

During President Clinton's first year, health care reform seemed a sure thing, but it died and has not resurfaced. The same easily could happen here. After all, a flat tax was first proposed by Congress in 1967, during the Johnson Administration.

Despite these doubts, there remains real concern about the safety of muni bonds and muni bond mutual funds. As long as these uncertainties exist, your portfolio probably should not contain them.

Tax Threats Aside, Might Municipal Bonds Make Sense For You?

The higher your combined federal/state income tax bracket, the more sense it makes for you to invest in muni's instead of CDs. Or so the logic goes. Tax-free bonds are very popular because they have little default risk and, on an after-tax basis, they earn considerably more than CDs.

And individual investors aren't alone in their love for muni's. Wall Street loves muni bonds, too. Eager to demonstrate their abilities, brokers are quick to show that clients, on an after-tax basis, earn more in a 5.5% tax-free bond fund than in a 7% CD. And the higher your tax bracket, the more compelling this argument.

Thus, financial advisors routinely tell their clients to move from taxable to tax-free bonds and bond funds. This idea is so ingrained that no one challenges it.

Until now.

Even ignoring the major risk posed by the flat tax proposals, I dispute the notion that municipal bonds are better for investors than taxable bonds. Consequently, it is my contention that municipal bonds and muni bond funds are among the most over-sold investments in America today.

The rationale for muni bonds goes like this: Interest paid by a 7% taxable bond is subject to tax; interest from a 5.5% muni bond is not. To fairly compare them, as we've seen, one must focus not on the taxable bond's 7% rate, but on it's after-tax rate of 4.62%, since the muni fund's rate of 5.5% is itself (being tax-free) an "after-tax" rate.

> *"The tax-exempt privilege is a feature always reflected in the market price of municipal bonds. The investor pays for it."*
> —Justice Louis D. Brandeis

Thus, it is easy to see that the muni bond's 5.5% beats the taxable bond's 4.62% (assuming a 28% federal income tax bracket and 6% state bracket). These results are illustrated in Figures 3-2 and 3-3: Figure 3-2 shows that $10,000 invested in a 7% taxable bond fund[4] for 20 years would be worth $24,677 after taxes, while Figure 3-3 shows that this same investment in a 5.5% muni bond would be worth $29,178. These results support the conventional wisdom that tells people to buy municipal bonds and muni bond funds instead of taxable bonds and taxable bond funds.

TAXABLE BOND FUND
AFTER TAXES

year	start value	x yield 7.00%	− fed tax 28%	− state tax 6%	= end value
1	$10000	$700	$196	$42	$10462
2	10462	732	205	44	10945
3	10945	766	215	46	11451
4	11451	802	224	48	11980
5	11980	839	235	50	12534
6	12534	877	246	53	13113
7	13113	918	257	55	13718
8	13718	960	269	58	14352
9	14352	1005	281	60	15015
10	15015	1051	294	63	15709
11	15709	1100	308	66	16435
12	16435	1150	322	69	17194
13	17194	1204	337	72	17988
14	17988	1259	353	76	18819
15	18819	1317	369	79	19689
16	19689	1378	386	83	20598
17	20598	1442	404	87	21550
18	21550	1509	422	91	22546
19	22546	1578	442	95	23587
20	23587	1651	462	99	24677

Account Value: **$24,677**

FIGURE 3-2

STATE MUNI BOND FUND
TAX-FREE

year	start value	x yield 5.50%	− fed tax 0%	− state tax 0%	= end value
1	$10000	$550	$0	$0	$10550
2	10550	580	0	0	11130
3	11130	612	0	0	11742
4	11742	646	0	0	12388
5	12388	681	0	0	13070
6	13070	719	0	0	13788
7	13788	758	0	0	14547
8	14547	800	0	0	15347
9	15347	844	0	0	16191
10	16191	891	0	0	17081
11	17081	939	0	0	18021
12	18021	991	0	0	19012
13	19012	1046	0	0	20058
14	20058	1103	0	0	21161
15	21161	1164	0	0	22325
16	22325	1228	0	0	23553
17	23553	1295	0	0	24848
18	24848	1367	0	0	26215
19	26215	1442	0	0	27656
20	27656	1521	0	0	29178

Account Value: **$29,178**

FIGURE 3-3

But the conventional wisdom is wrong. When you invest in taxable bonds, bond funds, and CDs, you owe taxes on the interest you earn. You report the interest on Schedule B of your tax return, and this either simply reduces the refund you otherwise would receive, or increases the amount you owe.

If it reduces your refund, the IRS sends you a check smaller than what you otherwise would have received. But if you owe money, you simply (albeit grudgingly) write a check to the IRS for the amount due.

---

[4] For simplicity's sake, this example assumes use of municipal bond mutual funds, with all interest reinvested at the same rate. A more complete discussion of mutual funds can be found in Part V.

And that's the key: In our 200+ collective years of practice as financial planners and investment advisors, having worked with thousands of clients and managing hundreds of millions of dollars in assets, *we have never seen a client sell a bond or liquidate a bond fund in order to raise the cash needed to pay the taxes that Schedule B says are owed.* Instead, every client pays the tax from another source: either by offsetting the tax against other deductions on the tax return, or by using other assets, such as cash from their checking account, or both.

And by not turning to the bond or bond fund itself, *the interest earned stays invested,* where it is allowed to compound, earning even more interest the next year. The results can be seen in Figure 3-4: By ignoring the tax implications, that 7% taxable bond fund in 20 years will be worth $38,697 — or 36% more than the muni fund!

> *"The difference between death and taxes is that death doesn't get worse every time Congress meets."*
> —Anonymous

TAXABLE BOND FUND
PAYING OUT OF POCKET

year	start value	X yield 7.00%	− fed tax 0%	− state tax 0%	= end value
1	$10000	$700	$0	$0	$10700
2	10700	749	0	0	11449
3	11449	801	0	0	12250
4	12250	858	0	0	13108
5	13108	918	0	0	14026
6	14026	982	0	0	15007
7	15007	1051	0	0	16058
8	16058	1124	0	0	17182
9	17182	1203	0	0	18385
10	18385	1287	0	0	19672
11	19672	1377	0	0	21049
12	21049	1473	0	0	22522
13	22522	1577	0	0	24098
14	24098	1687	0	0	25785
15	25785	1805	0	0	27590
16	27590	1931	0	0	29522
17	29522	2067	0	0	31588
18	31588	2211	0	0	33799
19	33799	2366	0	0	36165
20	36165	2532	0	0	38697

Account Value: $38,697

FIGURE 3-4

The results are clear: In the end, you will have more money if you choose an investment that forced you to pay taxes than if you choose an investment that is more "tax efficient" — or in this case, tax-free.

How can this be? Because the notion of "taxable equivalent yield" ignores human nature. Muni bonds make sense if you pay the tax by liquidating your account, but in the real world, people don't do that. And all the financial planning formulas and testing models ignore the most important element affecting your personal finances: your lifestyle. Perhaps we should call this approach "real world yields."

Should you sell your muni fund and replace it with a taxable bond fund? This 5-question review will help you decide:

1) **Are you in the 15% federal income tax bracket or lower?** If you are, you are better off in taxable's than in tax-free's.

2) **Do you have muni bonds or bond funds in an IRA or other tax-qualified account?** If you do, you're making a terrible mistake. (See Chapter 61 for more.)

3) **Do you rely on your investment interest for current income?** Muni bonds are ideal for clients who need current income, so if you receive your interest or dividends in cash and if you are in a high tax bracket, owning muni bonds is probably the right strategy.

4) **Do you have a well-balanced portfolio?** Muni bonds do have their place in a diversified portfolio (see Chapter 44), even though you might be reinvesting your interest and dividends. That's because muni bonds offer shelter from some risks that are present in other investments, and risk-adjusted return can be more important than return alone.

5) **Do you reinvest the interest you earn from muni bonds?** If you do, then you should not invest in muni bonds or muni bond funds.

When it comes to successful money management, you must recognize that **The Rules of Money Have Changed,** and you cannot rely on the old way of doing things — no matter how ingrained those habits have become. If you bought muni bonds or muni bond funds, you need to reconsider that decision.

Insured Municipal Bonds

Some 42% of all the muni bond issues outstanding are insured. Many people feel buying insured bonds is smart investing, when in reality it's nothing more than smart marketing by Wall Street. Here's why:

When a stockbroker cold calls Mrs. Glidlick to pitch her a bond, his biggest challenge is to overcome her fear of default risk. Above all else, she wants safety. So, naturally, when he invites her to buy the muni, Mrs. Glidlick's first question is, "Is the bond *insured?*"

She asks this question because she's been trained by the banks to seek FDIC coverage, and the broker desperately wants to say, "Yes!" The fact that the bonds might be *guaranteed* is irrelevant to her, because she is not familiar with this concept (but you are!). But, she can visit her money at the bank every day and see the gold FDIC sticker on the bullet-proof glass. To her, that's safety. Thus, Mrs. Glidlick wants to know if the broker's muni is insured like her bank account.

Enter the world of *insured municipal bonds.*

The broker can say "yes" thanks to outfits like the Municipal Bond Insurance Association, which controls 44% of the insured muni market, and AMBAC, the second-largest insurer of muni bonds. In its sales literature, MBIA says if a muni defaults, it will reimburse investors, and the cost for this protection is about five dollars per thousand dollars of bond principal.

In other words, insuring a bond that pays 5% interest would cost you ½ of 1% per year. That doesn't sound like much — until you realize that it's equal to 10% of the total interest you are due from the investment. That's a pretty steep price to pay for insurance, especially considering that the only way the insurance can pay off is for the government that issued the bond to go broke first. In 1991, MBIA collected more than $150 million in premiums, yet in nearly 20 years has paid only a handful of claims.

Maybe it's fortunate that MBIA has not had to pay many claims: Remember when I told you that FDIC has only pennies for every hundred dollars that it insures, and how that figure made FDIC look woefully unable to meet a string of bank failures? Well, MBIA isn't much better off — it has only $2.72 in capital for every $100 it backs!

Even if MBIA was called upon to pay a claim, the payoff would not be what most investors would expect: MBIA does not promise to repay your principal should a bond default. Instead, it will simply pay you the interest the bond should have been paying; you'll have to wait until the bond's normal maturity date to get your money back — and that could take decades.

The whole idea of insured muni bonds is ridiculous. Not only are you cutting your interest rate from, say, 5% to 4.5%, but the entire premise suggests that MBIA is stronger than the government that issued the bond in the first place! Now think about it: If Idaho went broke, what would that mean for the economy as a whole? Could an insurance company possibly be stronger and safer than a government? I don't think so, and neither should you. Avoid insured municipal bonds.

Chapter 10 - Zero Coupon Bonds

To understand zeros, let's look more closely at their name. *Coupon* means "interest rate." The name derives from a time when coupons were attached to bond certificates. Each coupon represented six months' worth of interest, so twice each year the bond holder would clip one coupon from the certificate and take it to the bank, which would redeem the coupon for cash. Thus, the word *coupon* became synonymous with "interest rate."

Therefore, "zero coupon" means "zero interest." Why would anybody buy a bond offering zero interest? The answer is found in its price. Recall that all bond certificates feature a *face value*. Many people think the face value refers to the price of the bond when you buy it. Not true: The face value refers to the amount the issuer must pay when the bond matures (at the maturity date, which also is displayed on the face of the certificate). Thus, a bond's *face value* is not necessarily the same as its *price*.

This is why people are willing to buy zeros, or bonds with "no interest": You buy them for a price substantially below their face value (this is known as a *discount*). At maturity, the issuer pays you the full face value, and the difference between what you paid and what you receive back is equal to the interest you should have earned during the life of the bond but didn't.

The Most Common Zero of All

You're more familiar with zeros than you realize, because the most common zero is a U.S. Savings Bond. EE Bonds, after all, do not pay any interest. Instead, you buy a $100 bond for $50 — half the face value — and when it matures, Uncle Sam pays you $100. The extra $50 that you get back at maturity is equal to what you should have earned in interest but didn't. That's all there is to zeros.

Despite their simplicity, many people are confused about how much interest they earn from Savings Bonds. That's because the rates vary, depending on when the bond was purchased. And the 1994 General Agreement of Tariffs and Trade, known as the GATT Treaty, made the biggest changes of all. Here's the truth about interest rates on U.S. Savings Bonds:

- Savings bonds you bought before GATT became law are not affected. That means you continue to earn a rate based on the rules that were in effect when you bought your bond.

- Savings bonds you buy now, but which you hold for at least five years, also are not affected by GATT.

- Only those bonds you bought since GATT became effective in May 1995, and which you hold for less than five years, are affectedby GATT. Under prior rules, bonds held less than five years received a minimum of 4% interest annually. GATT eliminated this floor and replaced it with a new market-based rate, similar to that which is in place for those who hold their bonds for more than five years.

Because there is no floor to this market-based rate, it is possible that savings bonds held for less than five years could pay no interest. But for that to happen, all interest rates throughout the economy also would have to be at zero, a scenario which is highly unlikely to occur.

Four Reasons Why Zeros are Losers

Many financial planners (but not those at my firm) love to sell zero coupon bonds, usually for college planning purposes. If you have a baby and want to start saving for college, planners often will tell you, zeros are very convenient and safe. Just buy a bond, toss it into your safety deposit box, and at maturity in 18 years, it will be worth thousands — and in the meantime you don't have to fuss with certificates, interest checks, or other details. Because many zeros are government bonds, they also are safe from default risk.

It's worth noting that although many people buy U.S. Treasury zeros, the U.S. government does not issue them. Instead, they are created and manufactured by Wall Street brokerage firms. The brokers take ordinary Treasury Bonds and split them in two, giving the interest to one investor and the principal to another. The principal portion is the zero. You can buy such versions as LYONs (Liquid Yield Option Notes), TIGRs (Treasury Interest Grantor Receipts), STRIPS (Separated Treasury Receipts of Interest & Principal Securities), and ZEBRAs (Zero Equivalent Bond Rate Accumulators). By the way, you can also buy PIGs (Passive Income Generators), and Bunny

Bonds (which pay interest in the form of more bonds instead of cash), but as you might expect, nobody on Wall Street has issued a BEAR.

> Do you realize what this means? Zero coupon bonds are derivatives! A derivative is an investment whose existence is based on the existence of another investment. In this case, a U.S. Treasury led to the creation of a STRIP. Yet, STRIPs are just as safe as the Treasuries themselves.
>
> Keep that in mind next time you hear that derivatives are dangerous. Many are, it's true, but then again, many aren't. Some actually are quite tame, despite fierce names like LYONs and TIGRS.

Problem #1: The Return is Roughly the Same as Treasuries

And on an after-tax, after-inflation basis, that return is not good enough. For a recap of this discussion, turn to Chapter 2.

Problem #2: Zeros are Much More Volatile than Other Bonds

Prices for zeros are much more volatile than ordinary bonds because zeros don't pay current interest. Here's a horror story to illustrate:

In the early '80s, an investor bought a 7-year zero coupon bond issued by Braniff Airlines. The bond's yield to maturity was 10%, about the same as other rates at the time. But in the 6th year, Braniff went broke, and the bond became worthless. Because the investor hadn't received interest each year, he not only lost his $10,000, he lost the interest that had been accumulating inside the bond as well.

You see, if you own an ordinary bond, at least you'll get a check for the interest on a regular basis. Had my client owned a regular Braniff bond, he'd have received checks during the six years equal to 60% of his investment. Instead he got nothing. This makes zeros much riskier than ordinary bonds.

Problem #3: Phantom Income

Even though you don't receive a check each year for the interest you've "earned," you must pay taxes as though you did. This is known as *phantom income*. Here's the IRS' rationale:

Say a zero-coupon bond is issued with a face value of $100 and a maturity date of 10 years from now. You pay $50 for the bond, and in 10 years you are to receive back the face value of $100. You earn $50 in interest, and it is paid to you at maturity in one lump-sum.

Zeros are technically known as OID bonds, for *Original Issue Discount,* and the tax you pay each year is based on *OID Interest.*

Since you are earning $50 in interest over a 10-year period, the IRS contends that you are earning $5 per year, even though you don't physically receive the interest in cash each year. Thus, if you were to sell your bond after one year, you would receive $55, rather than the $50 you paid. The IRS therefore concludes that since the bond has grown in value, in effect you have earned interest, and therefore you must pay taxes on this interest. This is *phantom income*: You must pay taxes on income you didn't get.

Let's get back to our Braniff investor. Not only did he lose his investment, he was paying taxes every year on the interest he never got. (In the year the bond became worthless, he was able to declare it as a loss on his tax return — small consolation!)

Problem #4: Zeros are Callable

In itself, a zero that's callable doesn't seem to be any worse than any other callable bond. But because buyers of zeros toss their certificates into safety deposit boxes, they often aren't informed when the bond is called. One of my clients had a zero, which she bought in 1970. We quickly discovered that the bond had been called in 1984, and she never knew it. Since bonds stop paying interest when they are called, I had to inform her that her bond hadn't earned any interest for the last 12 years!

Three Reasons Not to Take Physical Possession of Certificates

This is why I discourage clients from taking physical possession of certificates. Had she allowed her broker to keep the certificate for her, the broker would have notified her when the bond was called. Clients who want possession of certificates think their investment is safer; not only is this *not* true, but by taking the paper, you're creating new headaches, to wit:

Possession Problem #1: You've Got to Keep Your Certificate Safe

Certificates are money and must be safeguarded like cash. They are very difficult to replace if lost or stolen.

Possession Problem #2: You Become Responsible for Monitoring any Activity in the Bond

You must track receipt of interest checks as well as call actions and defaults. That's your broker's job, but he can't perform these services unless you let him hold the bond for you in your brokerage account.

Possession Problem #3: You Must Return Your Certificate to Your Broker When You Want to Sell or Redeem it, Anyway

Most brokers won't sell your bond until you deliver it to them. If the bond has been damaged (torn, stained, water damaged, or altered), your broker may reject it, forcing you to get a replacement certificate, which can take months. You can't sell the bond in the meantime.

To avoid worries that your broker might go broke or steal your bond, simply confirm that your broker is covered by the Securities Investors Protection Corporation. Coverage is provided up to $500,000 ($100,000 in cash and $400,000 in securities), and virtually all major securities firms carry supplemental coverage to protect each client up to $25 million. So, when it comes to the safe keeping of certificates, keep yours with your broker, not with you.

> SIPC, which is the brokerage industry version of FDIC, protects your account in case the brokerage firm collapses. SIPC *does not* protect you against investment losses, and many people have been fooled into buying investments they otherwise would not have bought because fast-talking brokers told them SIPC guarantees you against investment losses. It doesn't.
>
> And, yes, SIPC is about as well-funded as FDIC. (See Chapter 6 for more.)

In fact, I predict that the government will abolish the production of physical certificates in favor of electronic transactions. All that paper is expensive to print and maintain, and it provides many opportunities for fraud. Soon, you'll be required to keep securities with your broker, so you might as well start now.

Chapter 11 - Bond Ratings

There's never any question about the safety of U.S. Government Securities, but what about little county governments and corporate bonds? To help investors distinguish the Braniffs from the General Electrics, Wall Street rates the financial stability and default risk of companies and municipalities, as well as the bonds they issue. Standard & Poor's and Moody's are the two major bond rating agencies. Although there are subtle differences, their scales are very similar, with important distinctions between investment-grade and speculative-grade bonds.

The highest rating is AAA (S&P) and Aaa (Moody's). Don't demand a AAA rating: Even General Motors is only AA-rated. In fact, only 21 companies on the Fortune 500 are AAA. Any company or bond rated BBB/Baa or above is considered investment-grade. Anything BB/Ba or below is speculative-grade (also known as junk bonds).

Just as you shouldn't overstate the importance of a AAA rating, don't overemphasize the ratings themselves, either, because companies and municipalities pay to be rated. (If you pay for your rating, you might cancel if you receive a poor grade. Maybe that's why the top rating is AAA instead of A: This way, to the uninitiated, an A rating sounds better than it is.)

Figure 3-5 shows two bonds, each with an interest rate of 8.4%, and each with a face value of $10,000. Bond A's price is the same as its face value. Therefore, the yield is the same as the rate: 8.4%.[5]

But Bond B is much lower-rated. It too has a face value of $10,000. To compensate you for the higher risk of default, you demand a higher profit. To get it, you buy this bond for just $7,356, substantially below its face value. You still receive $840 in interest each year because that is what the certificate says it pays (8.4% on $10,000); The certificate doesn't know — or care — that you paid only $7,356 for it.

In other words, the B-rated bond earns $840 on a $7,356 investment, and this translates to an annual yield of 11.4% — or 3% more than the AAA-rated bond. As you can see, the greater risk produces a greater return.

At least it's supposed to. This leads us to the story of RJR Nabisco.

---

[5]For more on rate vs. yield, see Chapter 13.

BOND RATINGS

	Rating Descriptions	Standard & Poor's	Moody's	Face Value	Rate	Current Price	Yield	
	Highest Score	AAA	Aaa	$10,000	8.4%	$10,000	8.4%	Bond A
		AA+	Aa1					
	Very Strong	AA	Aa2					
		AA-	Aa3					
		A+	A1					
		A	A2					
		A-	A3					
		BBB+	Baa1					
	Adequate	BBB	Baa2					
		BBB-	Baa3					
		BB+	Ba1					
	Least Speculative	BB	Ba2					
		BB-	Ba3					
		B+	B1					Bond B
	Speculative large uncertainty or major risk exposure	B	B2	$10,000	8.4%	$7,356	11.4%	
		B-	B3					
		CCC	Caa					
	In Payment Default	CC, D	Ca, C					

INVESTMENT — GRADE (rows AAA through BBB-)

SPECULATIVE — GRADE (rows BB+ through CC, D)

FIGURE 3-5

91

Chapter 12 - Event Risk

In 1988, Nabisco was one of the largest, best-known companies in America, makers of Oreos Cookies, Ritz Crackers, Lifesavers, and Camel cigarettes. Worth $22 billion with no debt, Nabisco was rated AAA and considered "too big" to be taken over by corporate raiders. After all, who could possibly raise enough money to buy the company? Thus, it was felt Nabisco could go about its business immune to the takeover artists of the '80s.

Until KKR came along.

In 1988, Kohlberg, Kravits and Roberts decided to buy Nabisco. Based on current stock prices, KKR calculated that it could buy Nabisco for $22 billion, then sell off the pieces of the company for a total of $26 billion — giving itself a profit of $4 billion in the process.

So, armed with $5 million of its own capital, KKR borrowed $26 billion from banks and investors around the world, using Nabisco itself as collateral for the loans. This is the same way you buy your home: With a little money down, you borrow a huge sum by posting the home as collateral. If you default on the loan payments, the bank becomes owner of your house.

> *"When a fellow says, 'It ain't the money but the principle o' the thing,' it's the money."*
>
> —Abe Martin

Of course, there were a couple of interesting differences between what you do to buy your home and what KKR did to buy Nabisco.

If you are like most borrowers, your lender requires that you put down at least 10% of the value of your home. For KKR, this would have meant a down payment of $2.2 billion — yet they were able to get financing by putting down only $5 million. That's like buying a $400,000 house with a cash deposit of *ninety-one dollars!*

Also, KKR actually managed to borrow $4 billion *more* for Nabisco than it was worth — as though you could borrow $432,000 to buy that $400,000 house!

By posting Nabisco as collateral, Nabisco became obligated for the debt. In other words, KKR saddled a debt-free company with $26 billion worth of debt — $4 billion more than the entire company was worth!

When KKR announced the takeover on Monday, October 24, 1988, S&P and Moody's immediately cut Nabisco's rating to B from AAA. Thus, Nabisco, which closed on Monday as AAA, opened on Tuesday as a B!

Return now to Figure 3-5, and you'll see that AAA bonds (such as Nabisco's before the takeover) were trading at full face value, or $10,000 for a $10,000 bond. But B-rated bonds were trading for just 73 cents on the dollar, or $7,356 for a $10,000 bond. In other words, if you owned a Nabisco bond — which you bought for safety — you opened the newspaper on Tuesday to discover that your bond had lost 27% of its market value — literally overnight!

KKR's takeover made Metropolitan Life Insurance Company very upset. MetLife had invested $117 million in Nabisco bonds. The takeover presented Met with a $32 million loss! MetLife sued KKR, but the New York Superior Court threw the case out, ruling in essence that when you pay your money, you take your chances.

This is *Event Risk*, defined as an occurrence within a company that is both unexpected and beyond the control of management, yet which produces an adverse effect on the value of the company's securities.

Can you think of other examples of event risk? How about:

- Johnson & Johnson's Tylenol poisonings

- The Dalkon Shield

- Mansville's asbestos crisis

Note that an airline crash is not event risk. While such an event can and often does adversely affect an airline's stock, such an event is a known risk of that business and, therefore, does not meet the definition of event risk.

So as you consider any investment, think not only about the things you know can go wrong, but about the things you haven't thought of, which could go wrong as well.

Chapter 13 - Rate, Yield, and Total Return

Say you put $10,000 into an 8% CD that matures in 10 years. How much money will you earn? It depends.

If you earn *simple interest*, the bank pays you $800 per year, and you'll have $18,000 in 10 years ($800 interest per year for 10 years is $8,000, plus your original $10,000). Thus, simple interest means there is no compounding, and therefore the *rate* and the *yield* are the same. In this example, both are 8%.

But what if the bank compounds your interest on an annual basis? If so, at the end of 10 years you would have $21,589 — not $18,000. Thus, an 8% CD compounded annually over 10 years *yields* the same as an 11.6% CD that does not compound. Therefore, the more often your interest is compounded, the more money you will earn, as the table below shows. That's why an investment's *yield* is more important than its *rate*.

THE MORE FREQUENTLY YOU COMPOUND THE MORE MONEY YOU MAKE

$10,000 Invested for 10 Years at 8%

Amount Invested	Annual Rate	Time	Compounding Frequency	Ending Value
$10,000	8%	10 years	simple interest	$18,000
$10,000	8%	10 years	annually	$21,589
$10,000	8%	10 years	quarterly	$22,080
$10,000	8%	10 years	monthly	$22,196
$10,000	8%	10 years	weekly	$22,241
$10,000	8%	10 years	daily[6]	$22,253

FIGURE 3-6

Therefore, don't assume one investment will earn more than another just because its rate is higher. Be sure to consider the frequency of compounding as well, for that will determine the *yield*, which is the true determinant of how much interest you will earn.

---

[6]Also known as "continuous compounding."

What's the True Yield?

So, fine, the yield is more important than the rate. But what exactly is a bond's *true* yield?

Say a broker offers to sell you a $10,000 bond that matures in seven years, pays 10.5% interest and is callable in two years. The broker tells you the price of the bond is $11,284.

If you asked him, "What's the yield?," he could say the "nominal yield" is 10.5%. *Nominal yield* (also known as *coupon*) is the stated rate of interest that is printed on the certificate itself.

Or, the broker could reply that the "current yield" is 9.3%. *Current yield* adjusts the rate of interest by the actual purchase price. Since you are paying $11,284 for a bond that pays $1,050 in annual interest, simple division shows you are earning 9.3%.

Less likely, the broker could say that the "yield to maturity" is 8.26%. *Yield to Maturity* is the effective interest rate you get if you hold the bond until it matures in seven years.   It reflects the fact that you paid $11,284 but will receive back only the $10,000 face value at maturity, incurring a loss of principal of $1,284.

Least likely is that the broker will tell you that the "yield to call" is only 4.25%. *Yield to Call* recognizes that this bond could be called — meaning you might get your capital back in as little as two years. If that were to happen, you would get only two years' worth of interest payments instead of seven. And, like the *yield to maturity* calculation above, you will receive back only the $10,000 face value, not the $11,284 you paid. *Yield to Call* is the worst-case scenario for this bond — and the one most likely to occur.

So which is the true yield? Well, it depends[7] on your point of view. Technically, they all are.

Therefore, the broker hasn't lied when he quotes a yield of 10.5% — he just isn't telling you the whole truth, either. This is why buying an investment based on yield is extremely difficult. It's dangerous, too, because for all its varieties, *yield* says nothing about *total return*.

---

[7]Aren't you getting tired of seeing this answer?

Yield vs. Total Return

We have learned that the same rate compounded at different intervals produces different yields, and that you should therefore focus on yield, not rate.

Now you can forget about yield, too.

Instead, favor *total return*. Here's why: In all our examples so far, both the rates and yields shown have assumed that your principal remained unchanged. This is the case for CDs, but what about investments whose principal value can fluctuate, such as stocks? In such cases (and as you'll learn, this applies to virtually every investment *except* bank accounts and CDs) you must adjust the yield by any increase or decrease in the value of your original principal. Making such adjustments, known as a gain or loss, produces the *total return*, and it is the only figure that counts when trying to determine the return of an investment.

For example, suppose you invest $10,000 in a stock which pays an 8% dividend. After one year, your investment would be worth $10,800 (ignoring compounding). But suppose the stock's value increased by 5% during the same period, or $500. Therefore, your investment is really worth $11,300, and that means your *total return* — the dividends *plus* the increase in your principal's value — is 13%, far superior to the stock's 8% dividend alone. Likewise, if your investment had lost 5% of its value, your total return would have been only 3%.

Therefore, total return is your income (dividend or interest) plus or minus changes in the value of your original investment. Since CDs never change in value, its yield and total return always are the same, but that's not true for other investments. That's why you must never buy investments based on their yield, for those with the highest yields often have the lowest total returns, and since it's the total return that matters, a high yield is irrelevant.

Those who chase yields — meaning those who buy investments only because they offer high yields or rates of interest — do so out of greed, and greedy people get what they deserve.

Chapter 14 - Interest Rate Risk

So far, we've learned about a variety of risks: default risk, liquidity risk, inflation risk, tax risk, and event risk. Yet perhaps worse than any of these is *interest rate risk*. Without question, interest rate risk causes more people to lose money than any other type of investment risk. So pay particular attention to this chapter!

Harry is home having dinner when the phone rings. It's a cold-calling stockbroker. (They know when you're likely to be home!) The broker says, "Harry, instead of keeping your money in the bank at 3% interest, I can give you a bond issued and guaranteed by the U.S. Government, which pays 8% interest annually, pays that interest on a monthly basis — just like a Social Security check — is free from state income taxes, and is liquid at all times. Harry, what I'm offering you is safer than the bank, earns more interest than the bank, is as liquid as the bank, and lowers your taxes. What do you say? Can I put you down for $10,000?"

> *"Sometimes your best investments are the ones you don't make."*
> —Donald Trump

Pretty appealing pitch, isn't it? And as you've been learning, everything the broker has said is true: Government bonds are safer than banks, they pay higher interest rates, they are lower in taxes, and you can sell your bond whenever you want.

However, the liquidity part of that pitch is a bit weak — and is the cause of more investor losses than anything else on Wall Street. Here's how it works:

Say Harry accepts the pitch and invests $10,000 to buy that 30-year government bond with its 8% interest rate and $10,000 face value. Let's further say that two years later he decides to sell his bond, because he needs the cash to buy a car. Let's also say that during this time, interest rates have changed, and the government is now issuing new bonds with new 10% interest rates.

Enter Jane, another investor. She is interested in buying the same type of bond that Harry happens to be selling. This presents Jane with a choice: She can buy either Harry's government bond from Harry, or she can buy a brand new one from the government. Since both have a face value of $10,000, which one will she buy: Harry's, offering a rate of 8%, or the new government bond which offers 10%?

It should be obvious that Jane will buy the new government bond, which pays 2% more than Harry's bond. Simple enough.

But this next question is a bit more difficult: What must Harry do to convince Jane to buy his bond instead of the government's? He cannot change the interest rate of his bond. After all, that's set in stone — 8% is printed right on the certificate itself.

The answer: Since he can't increase the rate of his bond, *Harry must lower the price.* He must sell his bond for less than its $10,000 face value.

How much less? Well, in this example, for Jane to make as much money on Harry's bond as she would have earned on Uncle Sam's bond, she must buy it for $8,000. In other words, paying $8,000 for a $10,000 bond at 8% is equal to paying $10,000 for a $10,000 bond at 10%.

In this example, Harry must sell his bond for $2,000 less than what he paid for it! Try to explain to him how he managed to lose 20% of his money in a *government-guaranteed* investment!

This phenomenon is called *interest rate risk*, and as I said, it is the biggest cause of investor losses in the world. It is also very confusing to new investors, so follow this explanation carefully.

As interest rates change in the economy, the value of existing bonds will change as well — but in the opposite direction. The ratio is roughly 1 in 10, i.e., for every 1% change in interest rates, there is a corresponding 10% *opposite* change in prices. Thus, Harry found that when rates *rose* 2%, his bonds *fell* 20% in value.

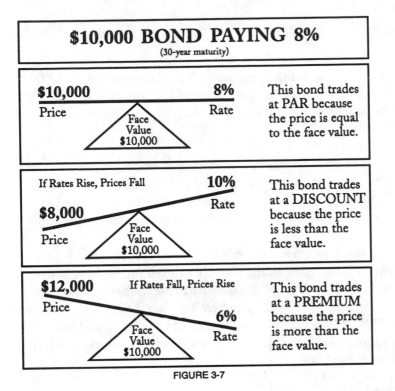

FIGURE 3-7

Picture a seesaw with interest rates on one end and bond prices on the other; as one side rises, the other falls. Therefore, had rates fallen to 6% instead of rising to 10%, Harry would have been able to sell his bond to Jane for 20% *more* than he paid instead of 20% *less*. Thus, as a result of interest rate risk, bond holders can make a lot of money, or lose a lot of money. It all depends which way interest rates go.

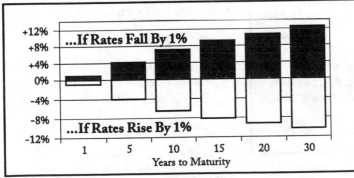

You can use this advice the next time you take a cruise: Always rent a cabin near the center of the ship; since the bow and stern rock with greater severity, you're more likely to get seasick if you're out at the extremes. Investing can produce similar results: The further out (in time) you go, the more volatility and nausea you might experience.

WHAT HAPPENS TO THE PRICE OF AN 8% BOND

...If Rates Fall By 1%

...If Rates Rise By 1%

Years to Maturity

FIGURE 3-8

Also, the longer a bond's maturity, the more extreme its swings in value. A 30-year bond fluctuates much more than a 1-year bond, as Figure 3-8 shows.

How to Beat Interest Rate Risk

Have you been able to figure out how Harry can avoid losing $2,000? It's easy: All he has to do is *keep his bond!* He loses money only if he sells; if he keeps his bond to maturity, the government will pay him the full $10,000 amount.

Remember: The government's "full faith and credit guarantee" is only for the "timely payment" of interest and principal. That means Uncle Sam will pay interest *on time* to whomever owns the bond, and *at maturity* will return principal to whoever owns the bond at that time.

The government also says its bonds may be bought and sold prior to maturity, but is silent regarding the buy and sell prices, leaving investors to negotiate the price of the security between themselves. This is where the phrase *negotiable security* comes from: All stock and bond prices are negotiable between buyers and sellers.

This also explains why the New York Superior Court ruled against MetLife in its suit against KKR. The court noted that the bonds, although reduced in market value, continued to pay interest as before, and if MetLife simply held the bonds to maturity, it would receive back 100% of its investment. Like telling the doctor your arm hurts when you "go like this," the court told MetLife, don't go like that! Keep your bond until maturity, and you don't have to worry about interest rate risk![8]

If you think Harry's predicament is merely hypothetical, recall the bond market of early 1993. Long-term interest rates had dropped to their

---

Bond buyers are never happy people. Consider Harry, golfing with his buddies, happy in the knowledge that he's earning 8% interest. Then his golf partner mentions he just bought a 10% bond. Suddenly, Harry's not happy. "Bert's getting 10% and I'm only getting 8%," Harry says to himself. So he goes home, calls his broker and says, "Sell my bond and get me one paying 10%!" His broker replies, "Okay, Harry, but if you sell your bond, you'll lose 20% of the value." Suddenly, Harry's not happy again.

If he keeps his bond, he earns only 8%, or $800 on his $10,000 investment, while his buddy Bert earns 10%. If Harry sells his bond, he loses $2,000 — 20% of his investment — and if he reinvests the remaining $8,000 into that new 10% bond, his income will still be only $800 — exactly where he is today. No matter what Harry does, he's stuck.

Bond buyers are never happy people.

---

[8]MetLife had other concerns due to accounting rules affecting insurers, but that's not relevant here.

lowest levels in 27 years, but in 1994 they rose 2.75%. That corresponded to a 27.5% *loss* for bond holders — the worst one-year loss in bond history; estimates put total investor losses at $1.5 trillion. In fact, it was the first time bonds posted a negative total return in modern times — all due to interest rate risk.

This means you should buy only those bonds which feature a maturity date you can tolerate. Don't buy a 30-year bond for your child's college education, unless your kid plans to attend college in his or her 30s!

It is because of interest rate risk that bond yields don't tell the whole story. Follow Edelman's Rule #1: Never, never, never, never, never, never, never buy an investment based on *yield*. Look at any personal finance magazine or the business section of any newspaper and you'll see ads proclaiming high yields, but none of these ads adjust their yields for any gain or loss in market value. Figure 3-9 shows that while a bond's income remains constant over time, its liquidation value fluctuates wildly.

IF YOU BOUGHT A 30-YEAR GOVERNMENT BOND IN 1965 FOR $10,000...

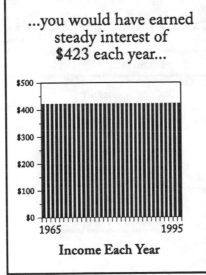

...you would have earned steady interest of $423 each year...

Income Each Year

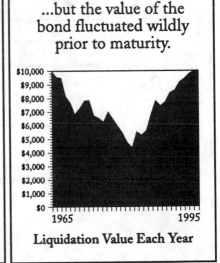

...but the value of the bond fluctuated wildly prior to maturity.

Liquidation Value Each Year

FIGURE 3-9

HEADS THEY WIN, TAILS YOU LOSE

What Happens to Bonds if...

	Your Bonds	Meaning	This is Known As
...Rates Fall:	will be called	You get your principal back, and are forced to reinvest at new, low rates.	Call Risk
...Rates Rise:	will continue to pay to maturity	You will continue to earn interest, but at less than currently available rates. If you sell, you will not get back 100% of your investment.	Opportunity Risk

What Happens to Ginnie Maes if...

	Then	Meaning	This is Known As
...Rates Fall:	The underlying borrowers will refinance early, speeding up return of capital to you.	You'll get your money back sooner than expected, forcing you to reinvest at new low rates.	Prepayment or Maturity Risk
...Rates Rise:	The underlying borrowers will delay or slow down repayment, extending the life of the security.	You won't get your money back as soon as you expected, and the delay could be decades.	Extension Risk

FIGURE 3-10

This volatility provides opportunity for high-risk speculators and gamblers to try to guess which way interest rates will move next. Thus, it is in the bond market that you'll find the biggest institutional players, not in the stock market. Indeed, while $7 billion worth of stocks trade each day in the U.S., $43 billion worth of bonds are traded. And while stock prices move by eighths, or 12.5 cents, bonds move by *basis points*. Each basis point is just $1/100th$ of 1%.

> Institutional investors will buy a bond at 7.34% and sell it at 7.32%. Why bother trying to capture a measly two basis points ($2/100ths$ of 1%)? Well, if you were trading $300 million in principal, those two basis points would translate to $60,000 — or nearly three times the annual salary of the average U.S. worker. Not bad for a few minutes' work.

Should You Buy Bonds?

So before you buy bonds, ask yourself if you think interest rates are headed up or down over the next couple of years. After all, rates can do only one of three things:

- go up

- go down

- stay the same

If rates rise, your bonds lose value. If rates fall, your bonds grow in value. If rates stay the same, the bond's value stays the same. Thus, only one of these three scenarios — rising rates — places you in jeopardy.

If you believe rates are likely to rise, does this mean you should not buy bonds? Not at all. First of all, you're probably wrong (simply because most investors are; as Barron's put it, "If the majority were right, the majority would be rich."). Second, bonds are a cornerstone of any diversified portfolio, as we'll explore later, and besides, there are two very effective strategies you can use to protect yourself against interest rate risk.

The first strategy, as we've discussed, is simply to hold any bond you buy until it matures. The problem with this is that it forces you to keep a bond whose rate may be lower than those now available in the marketplace.

Using Gold to Beat Interest Rate Risk

The second strategy, although it might sound strange, is to buy gold. Ordinarily, gold is a very silly investment. It is highly volatile and very speculative: The only reason investors buy it is because they think someone else will pay more for it in the future than they pay today. That's a foolish bet.

Furthermore, gold doesn't pay dividends, and while one share of stock can split, becoming two shares, your ounce will never become two ounces. Thus, gold is a silly investment. However, there is a demonstrated relationship between gold prices and bond prices. Think about it: Gold hit its all-time high of $800/ounce in 1980, at the same time interest rates reached their all-time high. What caused gold and interest rates to be so high? Why, none other than our old nemesis, inflation.

Inflation makes gold prices rise. In fact, gold prices merely reflect inflation: A hundred years ago, a $20 gold piece (one ounce of gold) would have bought a fine quality man's suit. Today, that gold coin — one ounce of gold — is worth at this writing about $400, and it still buys a quality suit. Clearly, gold prices move with inflation: When inflation was high in the '80s, gold prices were high. When inflation fell, gold prices fell as well.

So gold and inflation are related, just as we have learned that interest rates and inflation are related. Do you see the connection? Both gold and interest rates have a *positive correlation* to inflation (meaning when inflation rates rise, gold prices and interest rates also rise).

Now recall the relationship between interest rates and bond prices. That's an *inverse correlation*. When interest rates rise, bond prices fall.

Let's put it all together: When inflation rises, gold prices rise and interest rates rise. But as interest rates rise, bond prices fall. Therefore, inflation causes gold prices to go up and bond prices to go down. Thus, we can see clearly the inverse relationship between gold prices and bond prices. And, it's again a 1 in 10 ratio: A 1% change in bond prices often reflects a 10% change in gold prices — in the other direction.

> *"A gold mine is a hole in the ground with a liar on the top."*
>
> —Mark Twain

Therefore, whenever we buy bonds for a client, we seek to place one-tenth or so of that investment into gold. If we put $10,000 into bonds, for example, we'd recommend $1,000 or so into gold. Note that we are not buying gold because we think it might go to $1,000 an ounce; Rather, we buy gold because we're *afraid* it's going to $1,000 an ounce — for that would mean inflation has jumped and our clients' bond values are falling.

GOLD vs. BONDS
1975-1994

Performance of gold and bond prices at selected intervals

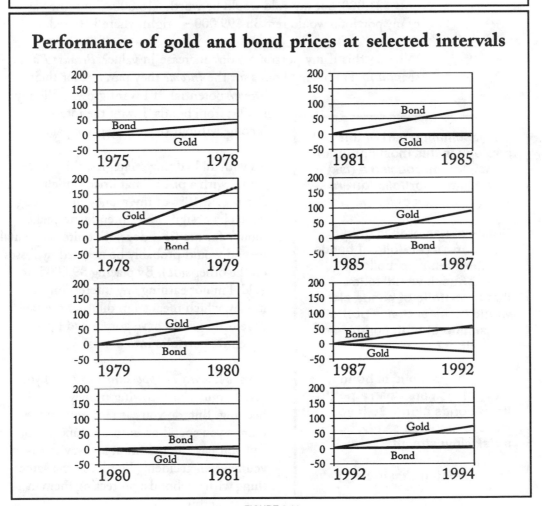

FIGURE 3-11

Reducing Risk Via Hedging Strategies

Gold, therefore, is a *hedging strategy*, also known as insurance: I am protecting myself in case interest rates move against me. I don't care what happens to the price of gold, because that's not why I bought it. Rather, I am more concerned with the money I placed in bonds, because I have ten times as much in bonds as in gold.

Let's look at an example. Say I create a portfolio with a total investment of $99,000, consisting of $90,000 in bonds and $9,000 in gold. If rates rise 1%, my bonds should fall 10%, and if bonds fall 10%, then gold should rise 100%. Thus, my bonds would now be worth only $81,000, but my gold would be worth $18,000. Thus, the value of my portfolio would remain $99,000 — right where I started.

Why do this if my portfolio won't increase in value? *Because I don't want it to.* I'm buying bonds for the *income* they pay, not for their *growth* potential. If I want growth, I'll buy stocks; from bonds, I want the interest income without risk to my principal.

As with all hedging strategies, this one comes with a price. That price is the fact that I've placed 10% of my money into a hedge, which by design is not intended to make money for me (if it does, it's quite accidental — and would probably be negated by losses on the other side). By placing $9,000 into gold, I'm not earning any interest on that money, which means I'm diluting the rate of return I would have gotten had I placed my entire portfolio into bonds.

This is known as *opportunity cost*, and you could argue I'm throwing money away by hedging. But, do you earn interest on the money you spend on auto insurance? No. But you pay the premium anyway in case you have an accident. I'm doing the same thing with my bonds: protecting them in case something goes wrong. Thus, this

---

The fascinating part of this strategy is this most important principle: *Introducing a risky asset into a portfolio lowers the overall risk of the portfolio.*

Bonds are safer than gold. Therefore, a portfolio of bonds is safer than a portfolio of gold. Thus, it would follow that a portfolio of bonds alone would be safer than a portfolio consisting of both bonds and gold, right?

Wrong. A portfolio of bonds and gold is safer than a portfolio of bonds alone. So if you want to increase *safety,* **buy a** *risky* **investment.**

Try explaining *that* **to Harry.**

strategy means I will not earn as much money as I could, but then I am not taking as high a risk, either. As with all investment strategies, there are tradeoffs, and you must decide which tradeoffs are worthwhile and acceptable.

Also, please note that since I'm buying gold only as a hedge for my bonds, I would sell the gold when I sell the bonds. I don't need one without the other.

It also needs to be stressed that this strategy is not a sure thing, although Figure 3-11 shows it has worked remarkably well since the U.S. left the gold standard in 1972. This prior success notwithstanding, gold is subject to a variety of non-inflationary factors, including political turmoil and the laws of supply and demand. Therefore, there can be no assurance that this strategy will work in the future as it has in the past.

> **How do you buy gold?** We buy it for our clients through mutual funds, which we'll cover in more detail in Part V. If you prefer, you can buy bullion, gold coins, or the shares of gold mining companies. But you'll discover that gold mutual funds do all of these, and much more effectively and conveniently than you could on your own. Also, owning gold via mutual funds alleviates the need for you to worry about safe-keeping.

For more on hedging strategies, see Chapter 20.

"With money in your pocket, you are wise and you are handsome and you sing well too."
—Yiddish Proverb

Part IV
Equities

Part IV — Equities

Overview - Growth After Income

Equity means ownership. For example, if you own shoes worth $20, your equity in them is $20. Thus, when you *own* something, you have *equity* in it. When you have ownership in a company, your equity is your *share* of the company, which is represented by a *stock* certificate (those who *lend* companies money get *bond* certificates).

"There is no security in this life. There is only opportunity."
—Douglas MacArthur

Thus, ownership = equity = shares = stock, and you'll find that the financial world uses these terms interchangeably.

As we've learned, stocks are higher in risk than bonds. With stocks, we don't know how much money we're going to earn (if any), and we don't know if we'll ever get our money back.

As Figure 4-1 shows, people are willing to take this risk because the odds are stacked in your favor: The most you can lose is 100% of your investment, but your gains are potentially unlimited.

WHY INVESTORS TAKE THE RISK

Potential Gain: *Unlimited!*

The best stocks 1987-92

Company	5-year price change
PacifiCare Health	3,047%
United Healthcare	2,789%
US Healthcare	1,700%
Home Depot	1,507%
Blockbuster	1,464%
Conseco	1,357%
Cracker Barrel Country Stores	1,237%
Stewart & Stevenson	1,082%
Thorn Apple Valley	1,004%
Harley-Davidson	950%

Potential Loss: *Amount You Invested*

The worst stocks 1987-92

Company	5-year price change
Continental Airlines	-99%
Circle K	-99%
Ames Department Stores	-99%
National Convenience Stores	-98%
Rexene	-98%
Wang Laboratories	-96%
GlenFed	-94%
Meritor Savings Bank	-94%
Hadson	-94%
New Valley	-93%

FIGURE 4-1

Chapter 15 - Four Benefits of Owning Stock

Indeed, smart investors happily take the bad with the good. If you owned equal amounts of the 10 best and the 10 worst stocks of the five-year period ending 1992, you'd be rich — despite the fact that half the stocks you bought became virtually worthless.

But stock ownership goes beyond that. People invest in stocks for several reasons, so let's look at them in detail.

Benefit #1: Stocks Can Grow in Value

Figure 4-2 shows the performance of the S&P 500 Stock Index from 1926 to 1995.

A $10,000 investment on January 1, 1926, would have grown to $482,872 as of December '95. That's an average annual rate of appreciation of 5.7%.[9]

CAPITAL APPRECIATION OF THE S&P 500 STOCK INDEX
1926 — 1995

Average Annual Return: 5.7%
Ending Value of a $10,000
Investment : $482,872

$510,000
$410,000
$310,000
$210,000
$110,000
$10,000

1926   1995

Reflects growth of the S&P without dividends

FIGURE 4-2

---

[9]Some cautions: Throughout this book, you'll see many references to the past performance of various investments over a variety of time periods. Often, these results are displayed graphically in a "mountain" chart like the one on this page. This information is intended for discussion only. Please remember that **past performance is no indication of future success,** and none of the charts you see here is intended to suggest that your experience will be the same.

Also, please note that although the S&P's average annual appreciation was 5.7%, in no year did it actually generate that exact return — just as no family in America has 2.3 children, although that's how many kids are in the "average" U.S. family. Choosing an investment because you expect it to earn a return based on its historical average almost certainly will lead to disappointment — or worse. So, please use all the "mountain" charts in this book solely for what they're intended: as discussion guides only.

Benefit #2: Stocks Can Generate Income

As shown in Figure 4-3, that same $10,000 invested in 1926 earned dividends worth $235,965 through 1995. That's an average annual income from dividends of 4.6%. Notice how much more stable this mountain is compared to the first. That's because stock dividends are much more reliable than stock prices.

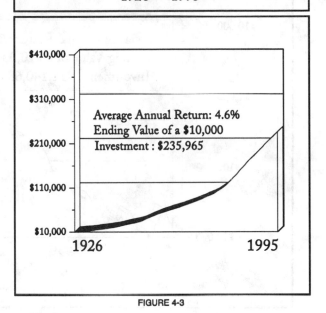

DIVIDEND INCOME OF THE S&P 500 STOCK INDEX
1926 — 1995

Average Annual Return: 4.6%
Ending Value of a $10,000
Investment : $235,965

FIGURE 4-3

Therefore,

$482,872 from growth in value
+ $235,965 from dividends
$718,837 is your *total return*, right?

Wrong!

Instead of $718,837, you'd have $11,140,684.

> When banks pay income, it's called *interest*.
>
> When stocks pay income, it's called a *dividend*.

How can the sum be greater than the two parts?

The answer, of course, is based on the power of compounding. By reinvesting your dividends back into stocks, you own more shares, which generates more income, which generates more shares, and so on.

TOTAL RETURN OF THE S&P 500 STOCK INDEX
1926 — 1995

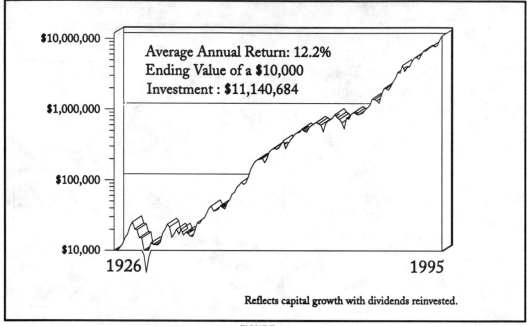

Average Annual Return: 12.2%
Ending Value of a $10,000
Investment : $11,140,684

Reflects capital growth with dividends reinvested.

FIGURE 4-4

Thus, as we discussed earlier, the most important number is the total return, not just growth and not just dividends. No investment in this century has generated a higher average annual total return than stocks.

All mountain charts — those you see in this book and elsewhere — always assume dividends are reinvested, unless it says otherwise.

Benefit #3: Stocks are a Hedge Against Inflation

By 1995, due to inflation, you would have needed $86,949 to buy what you could have bought with $10,000 in 1926. If your money was in the stock market, this would be no problem for you, for $10,000 invested in 1926 would have been worth $11,140,684 by 1995, or 130 times as much as the rate of inflation.

Benefit #4: Stocks Offer Three Tax Advantages

To understand them, let's compare the results of investing in stocks with that of investing in CDs.

Tax Advantage #1: You Pay No Taxes on Capital Gains Until You Sell

As we've learned, investors make money two ways: from growth and income. Income, whether interest or dividends, is taxable as ordinary income in the year it is earned. Thus, if you earn $800 from a CD, you pay taxes on that interest. Ditto for stock dividends. In both cases, this is true even if you reinvest the interest or dividends.

But if you own an investment which grows in value, the growth is considered to be a *capital gain*, and you do not have to pay taxes on capital gains until you sell the investment. Thus, if you buy a stock for $10,000 and it grows in value to $10,800, you do not have to pay taxes on your $800 gain until you sell. So the first tax break is that *capital gains are tax-deferred until you sell.*

Tax Advantage #2: Your Capital Gains Tax Rate Might Be Lower than Your Income Tax Rate

This tax break comes when you finally do sell: Under current tax law, the maximum tax rate on capital gains is 28%. Interest and dividends, though, always are taxed at your top income tax bracket, which could be as high as 39.6%. So, the second tax break is that *you may pay lower taxes on capital gains than you do on interest and dividends.*

Tax Advantage #3: Capital Gains Pass to Heirs Free of Capital Gains Tax

Say you invest $10,000 in stocks and watch them grow to $25,000. Say you then die. Since you never sold the stocks, you never paid the capital gains tax. Say further that your kids (or other heirs) inherit the stocks. When they sell them, they will not pay a tax on the capital gains that were produced during your lifetime, either. So, the third tax break is that *capital gains pass tax-free to heirs at death*.

> **Thinking of giving assets to your children? If you sell stocks you own and give them the proceeds, you'll have to pay taxes on your capital gain. Giving them the stocks directly won't help, either, for *they'll* have to pay the capital gains tax when *they* sell the stock. This is because whenever you give assets away while you are alive, the recipient receives your *cost basis* [the amount you originally invested] along with the asset. Therefore, when the recipient sells the asset, the recipient will have to pay the same capital gains tax that you would have had to pay.**
>
> **On the other hand, if you give the stock to the recipient as an inheritance [*inheritances* are gifts from people who have died], the recipient's cost basis is updated to the value of the asset as of your date of death. Thus, leaving stocks to your kids *after* you've died gives them a *stepped-up* cost basis. That means they do not have to pay capital gains taxes on the profit you accumulated in your lifetime. (There might still be an estate tax due, but we'll cover that in Chapter 73.)**
>
> **Thus, there's no tax break in giving away appreciated stocks to children while you're alive.**

To summarize, the three tax benefits of owning stocks are:

1. You don't pay taxes on capital gains until you sell;

2. When you sell, capital gains are taxed at a lower rate; and

3. You can pass capital gains to heirs tax-free at death.

Chapter 16 - Stocks: an Indication of the Nation's Financial Health — Sometimes

Buying stock is good for you, and it's good for the country, too, for it provides industry with the capital it needs to build business, which creates jobs. But owning stocks is risky, so Congress provides these tax benefits to encourage you to buy them. Still, what good are tax benefits if you lose your money in a stock that goes bust?

For example, look at Oracle Systems. In 1990, the day Oracle reported record revenues (up 54% from the previous year), Wall Street responded by knocking down the price of Oracle's stock by 31%. Why would the stock go down 31% the day the company reported a revenue gain of 54%?

The answer is that Wall Street had expected Oracle to do even better and was disappointed at the "meager" results reported by the company.

That might sound strange, but this is the most fundamental aspect of investing in the stock market, and it is in direct contrast to how you run your daily life. As individuals, we tend to focus on today. How was your day at school? When does the meeting start? How's traffic?

The TV news is great at telling us what happened today, but rarely does Tom Brokaw tell us what's going to happen tomorrow.

B.C. JOHNNY HART

By permission of Johnny Hart and Creators Syndicate, Inc.

The Three Types of Economic Indicators

The financial markets operate exactly the opposite. Rather than focusing on today, Wall Street looks to tomorrow. This is why the stock market is called a "leading economic indicator," as opposed to a lagging or coincident indicator.

Economic Indicator #1: Leading

A leading indicator tells you what is *going to happen*. For example, people who want to build homes first must apply for a construction permit. Therefore, the number of permit applications that are filed serve as a leading economic indicator, for this tells us how many homes *will be built*. If you own a lumber yard, a big increase in the number of permit applications would tell you to increase your inventory in preparation for an increase in lumber sales. Maybe you'd better hire more employees, too, to help you handle the new business. You don't need the extra inventory or staff today, but this leading indicator says you soon will.

Economic Indicator #2: Coincident

If you later learn that housing starts have increased recently, you know those homes *are under construction*, which means builders by now have bought all the lumber they need. Thus, you lumber yard owners had better stop ordering wood, for the recent wave of new business has reached its crest. Thus, construction starts is a *coincident indicator*, for it tells you *what is happening now*.

Economic Indicator #3: Lagging

And if you learned that sales of new homes have reached their seasonal high, you'd know that many homes *were built*. Thus, new home sales is a *lagging economic indicator*, for it tells you *what has happened*. If you owned that lumber yard, it's probably time to lay people off and hold a big sale to get rid of excess inventory.

It's important that you understand the concept of economic indicators, because that will help you understand the stock market. The market, as I mentioned, is a *leading* indicator. When you hear how the market "did" today, the stock market is not telling you how the U.S. economy *was*, nor how it *is*. Rather, the stock market is telling us how the economy *is going to be*, i.e., how much money Wall Street expects companies to make in the future.

These predictions generally are focused six to nine months in advance. Thus, a report that a company's stock is "up" (i.e., it's price is higher than it was) doesn't mean the company is making more money today than it was yesterday. Rather, it means Wall Street expects that the company will be earning more money in six or nine months than it earns now. And if a stock goes "down" today, Wall Street expects the company to make less money in the future than it does today.

> A client once called me, saying he wanted to buy stock in a certain company. When I asked why, he said the firm had just launched a new product. "I bet they're going to make a lot of money with this product," he said, "So I want to buy the stock."
>
> I agreed with him. "You're absolutely right," I said. "You should buy the stock — last year!"
>
> If you try to act on today's news, you're too late. Wall Street is way ahead of you, and there's little chance you'll catch up.

Because stock prices are based on the future, you cannot buy stocks based on what's happening today in business, politics, or society. Those who do soon discover they're too late. This is why you should ignore the "Buy Now!" tips often found in the personal finance press: They're constantly telling you what's hot *now*, but by the time you read it — after it's been written, printed, and distributed, it's usually too late.

One of my favorite calls to my radio show occurred in mid-1991. Debbie was a sincere but thoroughly exasperated woman. "I just don't understand this!" she gasped. "When the economy was going strong in the 1980s, the stock market crashed, yet while we're in the midst of this terrible recession, the stock market is reaching new all-time highs!"

"What's going on?" Debbie demanded. "Has the financial world gone mad?"

Not at all. What Debbie didn't understand is that Wall Street talks in "future-speak." Stocks crashed in 1987, not because the economy had suddenly turned bad, but because Wall Street believed the economy was *going to become* bad.

And the recession in 1990 proved Wall Street right. Then, in 1991, as the recession reached its peak, the stock market reached new all-time highs, in direct contrast to what Debbie thought the market should do. After all, how could stocks make money in the middle of a recession?

The answer, of course, is that there's a big difference between a company's stock and the company itself. On October 19, 1987, General Motors stock dropped 27%. But was GM any different from the day before? Of course not. Thus, you'll often discover that stock prices take on lives of their own — much to the consternation of a company's management.

Why aren't today's stock prices always in sync with a company's current value? Look at it this way: Say General Motors announces it is going to launch a new type of automobile — one that gets 1,000 miles to the gallon. Clearly, such a product would be fabulously popular — and GM would make a fortune. That means the value of the company would rise.

But to build this car, GM must construct a new factory that will take years and cost billions. For now, that means GM will not be making huge profits. No matter: Since investors are expecting profits to come in the future, they price the stock today *as though those profits are already being realized.* If GM later fails to earn that profit — say, if the technology proves faulty — GM's stock price will drop back to its former levels.

Thus, while it can take a company months or years to produce a profit, investors can price the stock today in anticipation of those profits. If investors do not believe the company will be profitable, that also will be reflected in today's stock price.

I hope that by now you are beginning to understand how Wall Street prices stocks. I use the word *beginning* because you might have the impression, from what I've written, that the stock market works in an efficient, orderly manner. Unfortunately, it's not so simple, because Wall Street is sometimes (often?) just plain wrong, while at other times, it can't make up its mind.

In fact, an old joke says the stock market has predicted 18 of the last seven recessions — meaning that just because Wall Street *thinks* something is going to happen doesn't mean it *will* happen. Oracle is a perfect example. If Wall Street is always right, how could it have *overestimated* its projections of Oracle's profits by so much? And if Wall Street knew the recession was coming, why did it lower stock prices in 1987 — four years too soon? (Because its call was so premature, Wall Street was obliged to return prices to its pre-crash level, only to initiate a second price correction in the form of the mini-crash of 1989.)

As a well-known money manager once told me, "I correctly called the Crash of '87, but I called it five years early."

Stocks Anticipate the Economy

Indeed, stock prices do anticipate both recessions and recoveries. As Figure 4-5 shows, the stock market has fallen as early as 12 months before the nation entered a recession, and regained its strength up to eight months before the rest of the nation.

While I've been using the phrase "Wall Street" both indiscriminately and in the singular, the financial markets actually consist of several hundred thousand analysts, researchers, statisticians, economists, mathematicians, computer scientists, physicists (yes, physicists), brokers, and traders from around the world — not to mention investors! So don't be lulled into a false feeling that "Wall Street" is a single unit. Not only is it not single, its players are not even homogenous. With so many people offering so many opinions, it's actually hard to believe that Wall Street is able to make any predictions with accuracy.

STOCK PRICES FALL FIRST AND RECOVER FIRST

The Dow Jones Industrial Average and Recessions

Recession Starts	Dow Peaked	Dow Lead (months)	Recession Ends	Dow Bottomed	Dow Lead (months)
Dec. 1948	May 1948	7	Dec. 1949	June 1949	6
July 1953	Jan. 1953	5	May 1954	Sept. 1953	8
Aug. 1957	July 1957	1	Apr. 1958	Oct. 1957	6
Apr. 1960	Jan. 1960	3	Feb. 1961	Oct. 1960	4
Dec. 1969	Dec. 1968	12	Nov. 1970	May 1970	6
Nov. 1973	Jan. 1973	10	Mar. 1975	Dec. 1974	3
Jan. 1980	Jan. 1980	0	July 1980	Apr. 1980	3
July 1981	Apr. 1981	3	Nov. 1980	Aug. 1982	3
July 1990	July 1990	0	Mar. 1991	Oct. 1990	5

FIGURE 4-5

Stock Market Indexes

To keep track of all these players, you need a scorecard, and Wall Street has produced lots of them. The best-known is the Dow Jones Industrial Average, which is an *index* consisting of 30 stocks, each representing a different industry. But there are more than 2,000 stocks listed on the New York Stock Exchange and more than 20,000 in the country.

If you wanted information about a group numbering 20,000, how accurate do you think your information would be if you only asked the biggest 30? Not very accurate, especially if you compared the results to a survey which asked 500 people, or 5,000. Obviously, the broader the base, the more accurate the data.

That's why many Wall Street professionals pay closer attention to the Standard & Poor's 500 Stock Index and the Wilshire 5000 than they do the Dow. The point is that you should not make buy or sell decisions simply because of what you hear about an index. Just because the Dow drops, for example, doesn't necessarily mean your stocks are down (unless, of course, you happen to own the same 30 stocks that comprise the index).

International Stocks

Everything we've discussed about stocks thus far has been focused on the U.S. But there's a strong case for investing in stocks internationally as well.

NON SEQUITUR WILEY

©1994 Washington Post Writers Group. Reprinted with permission.

TOTAL VALUE OF STOCKS WORLDWIDE

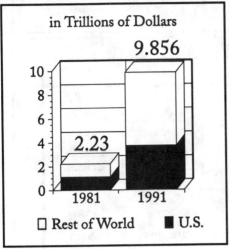

in Trillions of Dollars

FIGURE 4-6

In 1981, the world's market capitalization — the value of all stocks worldwide — was $2.23 trillion, and the United States accounted for about 50%. Today, world market capitalization has tripled to about $10 trillion, and the U.S. has only a 33% share.

Many view this as evidence of America's decline in power, but that's not the case. In 1981, the U.S. was worth half of $2.2 trillion, or $1.1 trillion. In 1995 the U.S. was worth a third of $10 trillion, or about $3 trillion. In other words, the U.S. economy doubled in size. Although its share of the world's wealth declined in percentage terms, we must keep in mind that the pie is much bigger than before.

It's because this pie is growing so rapidly that we need to place some of our investments internationally. While the U.S. economy

TOTAL VALUE OF STOCKS WORLDWIDE

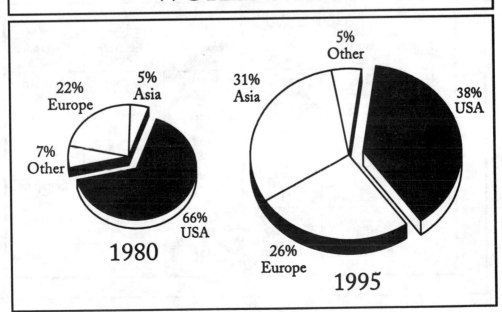

FIGURE 4-7

TOP PERFORMING MARKETS IN THE WORLD

Year	1st	2nd	3rd	4th	5th
1980	Italy +81%	Hong Kong +73%	Malaysia +63%	Austria +55%	U.K. +41%
1981	Sweden +38%	Denmark +25%	Malaysia +18%	Japan +16%	Spain +12%
1982	Sweden +24%	USA +22%	Neth +17%	Germany +10%	Belgium +10%
1983	Norway +82%	Denmark +69%	Australia +56%	Sweden +50%	Neth +38%
1984	Hong Kong +47%	Spain +42%	Japan +17%	Belgium +13%	Neth +12%
1985	Austria +177%	Germany +137%	Italy +134%	Switzerland +108%	France +83%
1986	Spain +123%	Italy +109%	Japan +100%	Belgium +81%	France +79%
1987	Japan +43%	Spain +38%	UK +35%	Canada +15%	Denmark +14%
1988	Belgium +55%	Denmark +54%	Sweden +49%	Norway +43%	France +39%
1989	Austria +105%	Germany +47%	Norway +46%	Denmark +45%	Singapore +42%
1990	UK +10%	Hong Kong +9%	Austria +7%	Norway +1%	Denmark 0%
1991	Hong Kong +50%	Australia +36%	USA +31%	Sing/Mal +25%	New Zealand +21%
1992	Hong Kong +32%	Switzerland +18%	USA +7%	Sing/Mal +6%	Neth +3%
1993	Hong Kong +116%	Malaysia +110%	Finland +83%	New Zealand +69%	Singapore +67%
1994	Finland +52%	Norway +24%	Japan +21%	Sweden +18%	Ireland +14%
1995	Switzerland +43%	Sweden +37%	USA +34%	Spain +28%	Netherlands +25%

FIGURE 4-8

doubled in the past 15 years and remains the largest in the world, the rest of the world quadrupled in the same period! As explained more thoroughly in Chapter 51, *percentages* are the key to your financial success, not *dollars*.

Look at Figure 4-8, which compares the percentage performance of the U.S. stock market against the stock markets of other nations. Since 1980, our market has been in the top five only four times — during the biggest bull market in our nation's history!

This is further evidence that **The Rules of Money Have Changed**, and we must respond by investing some of our money overseas.

Some people think I'm suggesting fly-by-night outfits. Quite the contrary. I'm not talking about tossing money into some jungle venture accessible by dirt roads. Rather, I'm suggesting that you invest your money in the biggest, safest, most successful, diversified, and technologically-advanced companies in the world — the "bluest" of the "blue chip" stocks — the same kinds of companies you like here in the U.S. I merely suggest you do the same overseas.

It's easy to do. In fact, it's hard *not* to. For example, if you wanted to invest only in the safest, strongest, highest quality companies, and your search was limited to the U.S., you would omit:

- 7 of the world's 10 largest **financial** companies
- 7 of the world's 10 largest **insurance** companies
- 7 of the world's 10 largest **utility** companies
- 8 of the world's 10 largest **appliance** companies
- 8 of the world's 10 largest **auto** companies
- 8 of the world's 10 largest **chemical** companies
- 8 of the world's 10 largest **electronic** companies
- 9 of the world's 10 largest **machinery** companies
- 9 of the world's 10 largest **banks**

You've heard of the Fortune 500 — the largest companies in the United States. But have you looked at the Fortune *Global* 500 recently? Only 151 of them are U.S.-based companies (more than any other nation — but still only 30% of the total).

THE WORLD's
LARGEST COMPANIES

Only 30% are based in the United States

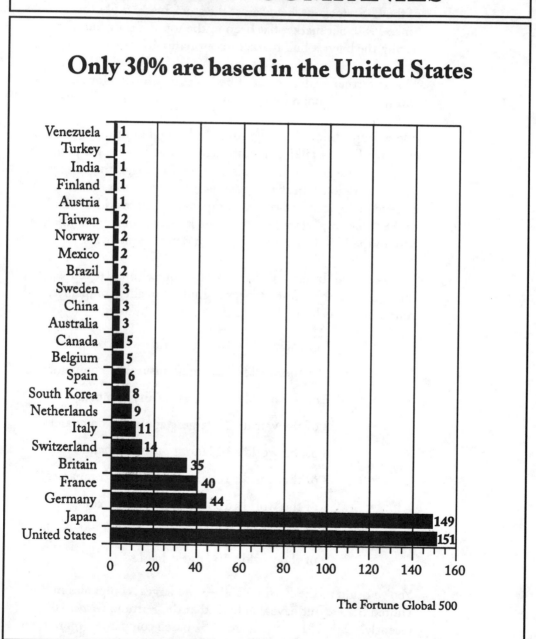

The Fortune Global 500

FIGURE 4-9

Let's talk in more practical terms. Do you use any of the products listed below?

DO YOU USE ANY OF THESE PRODUCTS?

- ❏ Alpo Dog Food
- ❏ Dannon Yogurt
- ❏ Glidden Paint
- ❏ Libby's Vegetables
- ❏ Mott's Apple Sauce
- ❏ Ponds Cold Cream
- ❏ Ball Park Franks
- ❏ Close-Up Toothpaste
- ❏ Dove Soap
- ❏ Hills Bros. Coffee
- ❏ Q-Tips Swabs
- ❏ Stouffers Dinners
- ❏ Contadina Sauce
- ❏ Frigidaire Appliance
- ❏ Ragu Tomato Sauce
- ❏ Vaseline
- ❏ Carnation Milk
- ❏ Cup-a-Soup
- ❏ Friskies Cat Chow
- ❏ Weed Eater

FIGURE 4-10

Each is manufactured by a foreign company. Don't get depressed that foreign companies sell lots of products in the U.S., though, because the U.S. does the same thing in other countries: 76% of Exxon's sales occur outside the United States, as do 64% of Coca-Cola's and 39% of Ford's. It is not a matter of whether you *like* being part of a global economy, only whether you'll *make money* from it.

The Risks of Investing Internationally

Say you want to own stock in Sony, the biggest consumer electronics company in the world. Sony's stock trades in Tokyo, not New York. Thus, to buy Sony stock, you must convert your U.S. dollars into Japanese yen before you can buy the stock on the Tokyo market.[10]

U.S. CORPORATIONS WITH BIG FOREIGN REVENUES

Company	Percent of Revenue Earned Outside the United States
Exxon	76%
Mobil	68
Coca-Cola	64
Colgate-Palmolive	64
IBM	62
Citicorp	53
Dow Chemical	52
Johnson & Johnson	50
3M	49
Procter & Gamble	46
duPont	45
Xerox	44
Goodyear	43
Woolworth	42
Ford Motor	39
General Motors	32
Sara Lee	31
Philip Morris	27

FIGURE 4-11

[10]And before some of you start yelling, "Hey! What about ADRs!", let me just say that (a) American Depository Receipts essentially make the currency conversion for you, and (b) keep in mind that this is an introductory-level book, not an intermediate-level one. So, shaaaaddup.

Therefore, you are subject not only to stock market fluctuation, which is perhaps the most well-known of all investment risks, you're also subject to foreign currency exchange rate fluctuation, which causes the value of the dollar to change relative to the yen. Should the dollar move against you at the same time the stock moves against you, your losses can be twice as bad as they otherwise would have been. Figure 4-12 shows the dual impact of changes in stock prices and currency prices. Thus, even if the stock makes money, you still could lose money if the dollar moves against you.

COMBINING CURRENCY CHANGES WITH INVESTMENT RETURNS

If the total return based on foreign currency is this...	...but the change in the foreign currency vs. the U.S. dollar is this...								
	20%	15%	10%	5%	0	-5%	-10%	-15%	-20%
	...then the total return for the U.S. investor (in U.S. dollar terms) is this:								
20%	+44%	+38%	+32%	+26%	+20%	+14%	+8%	+2%	-4%
15%	+38%	+32%	+27%	+21%	+15%	+9%	+4%	-2%	-8%
10%	+32%	+27%	+21%	+16%	+10%	+5%	-1%	-7%	-12%
5%	+26%	+21%	+16%	+10%	+5%	0	-6%	-11%	-16%
0%	+20%	+15%	+10%	+5%	0	-5%	-10%	-15%	-20%
-5%	+14%	+9%	+5%	0	-5%	-10%	-16%	-19%	-24%
-10%	+8%	+4%	-1%	-6%	-10%	-15%	-19%	-24%	-28%
-15%	+2%	-2%	-7%	-11%	-15%	-19%	-24%	-28%	-32%
-20%	-4%	-8%	-12%	-16%	-20%	-24%	-28%	-32%	-36%

If a foreign stock you own rises 15%, but that nation's currency falls 15% against the dollar, your total return would be -2%.

FIGURE 4-12

HOW TO CALCULATE U.S. RETURNS FROM A FOREIGN INVESTMENT

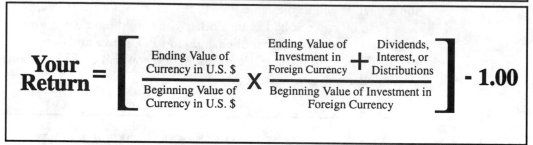

$$\text{Your Return} = \left[\frac{\text{Ending Value of Currency in U.S. \$}}{\text{Beginning Value of Currency in U.S. \$}} \times \frac{\text{Ending Value of Investment in Foreign Currency} + \text{Dividends, Interest, or Distributions}}{\text{Beginning Value of Investment in Foreign Currency}} \right] - 1.00$$

FIGURE 4-13

The Weak Dollar vs. Strong Dollar

You often hear that "the dollar is down" or "the dollar is up." What exactly does that mean, and is it good news or bad news?

The dollar going down against a particular foreign currency means that the foreign currency now buys more dollars than before. This increases the rate of return that foreigners earn on their purchases of U.S. investments and products, because they can buy more without actually spending any more of their own currency. The dollar going up is just the opposite: Like inflation, it causes foreigners to pay more for U.S. products and it lowers their returns from U.S. investments.

So is a declining dollar good or bad? Again, it depends.[11] If you are an American consumer trying to buy a product made overseas, a declining dollar is bad, for it will take you more dollars to buy that item. But if you are an American manufacturer who sells products overseas, the declining dollar is good, because your product is now cheaper for foreigners to buy, and thus your sales are likely to increase.

This is why the government finds it so difficult to develop and execute monetary policy. If the administration supports a strong dollar, foreigners will not invest in the U.S. (which upsets U.S. business and Wall Street), but foreign goods become cheaper (which pleases U.S. consumers). That dynamic explains why the President (*any* president) cannot make everybody happy.

---

[11]Sorry.

Chapter 17 - Three Ways to Buy Stocks

Method #1: Full Service Brokers

If you call a broker at a full-service firm and say, "I have $10,000 to invest: What should I do?," she'll tell you! These folks monitor and evaluate stocks constantly, and it's their job to provide clients with investment advice. If you need such assistance, you should use a full-service broker.

Full-service brokers will charge you a transaction expense — typically 1.5% of the investment amount. And that's each way, meaning you pay 1.5% when you buy a stock and another 1.5% when you sell it, for a total cost of about 3% (sometimes more, sometimes less, depending on how many shares you are buying, the price of each share and how frequently you trade; prices vary from firm to firm).

Method #2: Discount Brokers

If you know you want to buy a particular stock and all you need is someone to get it for you (*execute the trade*), you may want to use a discount broker, whose transaction fees will be less — maybe a lot less. But if you call a discounter and say, "I have $10,000 to invest: What should I do?," he'll tell you to call a full service broker!

Discount brokers do not provide investment advice, nor do they provide you with a specific representative — someone with whom you can establish a relationship. All you'll get is a toll-free phone number to use when placing an order, like buying out of a catalog.

So, if you need help in choosing and monitoring investments, use a full-service broker. If you don't need the help, use a discounter and save some money.

> **In defense of brokers everywhere, please observe this rule of etiquette: Do not ask for advice from full-service brokers, then buy their recommendations from discount brokers to save money. It's rude.**

How to Lower Your Costs When Buying Stocks

Always buy in *round lots*, meaning 100-share increments. Anything other than 100 shares is an *odd* lot, and you will be penalized for trading in odd lots (with the New York Stock Exchange trading 400 million shares a day, trading 12 shares is considered a nuisance.)

The first penalty: When you're buying you must pay $1/8$ (12.5 cents) per share more for your stock than it's worth, and when selling you receive $1/8$ less. The second penalty: Your trade will not be executed as quickly as a round lot. While this delay isn't something most investors notice, it could make a big difference in the price.

> **Say you order 150 shares of a stock. Is your trade a round lot or an odd lot?**
>
> **Actually, both! Your broker will execute two trades, one for 100 shares (a round lot) and one for 50 shares (an odd lot).**

This ¼ round-trip surcharge is in addition to the *spread*, which all stock investors pay. The spread is the difference between a stock's buy price and its sell price. Typically $1/8$ to ¼, the spread is the fee charged by the trader who executes the order that your broker placed for you.

Say you ask a broker for the price of a stock and he replies, "Ten, ten and a quarter." He means that someone who buys the stock will pay $10.25, while someone who sells the stock will receive only $10. The difference — 25 cents — is pocketed by the trader.

Most brokerage firms also have other fees, such as annual account fees, transaction fees, and other costs. At least one national firm charges a $4.50 fee each time you trade, while another levies a $50 charge when you close your account.

Investors are willing to pay these fees because they believe their profits will outweigh the costs. If you pay fees totaling 3% of your investment, you must earn 3% just to break even. Thus, you must consider costs as you invest.

Not long ago, I ran into a old friend of mine. He was one of the sharpest brokers I ever worked with — he once won the National Options Trading Championships — and he told me he had just created a new computer model for trading in options. Options are a (usually) speculative form of derivative where huge trading costs usually require significant profits just to break even. (This is why most brokers who trade options do it for their clients instead of themselves. Clients may or may not make money, but the brokers are certain to profit from commissions).

Anyway, my friend told me that mathematical tests of his model, using historical market data from the '70s and '80s, showed he would have made incredible amounts of money. Thus, my friend was now looking for investors to help him finance the further development of his model.

"What do you need investors for?" I asked. "Why don't you just start trading for real?" And he replied, "Because my model doesn't take commissions into consideration. Once I do, the trading costs are so high that I can't figure out how to make money with this thing!"

Remember that when people brag about how much money they're making, they're often not calculating their performance *after fees*. Remember, it's not how much you make, but how much you keep that counts!

> *"The Broker's Creed: Never in doubt, sometimes in error."*
> —Anonymous

Method #3: Buying Stocks without a Broker

The third way to buy stock is directly from companies offering a *Dividend Reinvestment Plan*. DRPs are available from about 1,000 companies — typically large companies like IBM and General Motors. The best part is that DRPs usually are free and the company will reinvest your dividends into more shares, also at no charge. (Brokers cannot reinvest dividends for you.) But DRPs have their problems, too.

Five Disadvantages of DRPs

If you know you want IBM, you can buy it directly from IBM. There are disadvantages, however:

- you must execute all transactions via mail, which takes time;

- restrictions usually apply, such as the amount you are permitted to invest;

- not all companies offer DRPs;

- many DRPs are beginning to charge fees, negating the primary benefit of using them; and

- you are forced to work individually with each company whose stock you buy, and the paperwork can become overwhelming. The same is true for the tax-reporting and record-keeping requirements, often making DRPs more trouble than they're worth compared to simply working with discount brokers.

Still, if you want to purchase DRPs, you can find a complete list of them at your local library.

Chapter 18 - Real Estate Investing

Real estate allows you to diversify your investments beyond the "paper" markets of stocks and bonds into hard or "real" assets. There is one clear advantage, as you can see from Figure 4-14: Real estate is much less volatile than stocks and bonds.

The reason is simple: It's easy to sell paper assets (just phone your broker), but selling real property takes a great deal more time. This reduced liquidity helps stabilize prices in the real estate market.

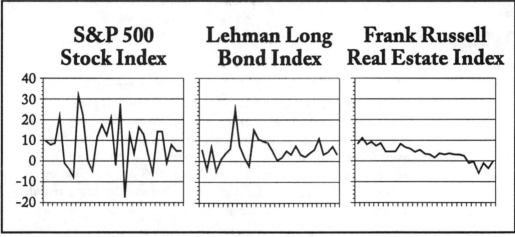

VOLATILITY OF ANNUAL RETURNS
1979 — 1995

FIGURE 4-14

But stability is a double-edged sword: While prices are more stable than stocks and bonds, your ability to get out of a bad investment is equally reduced. That means you could be stuck with a property you don't want, but which you can't sell — and you're stuck with the carrying costs in the meantime, such as mortgages, taxes, utilities, maintenance, repairs, and security. All these negatives conspire to establish real estate as a very risky investment, and one to engage in only after you already own cash, bonds, and stocks (or mutual funds of bonds and stocks), and even then only if you have the financial (and emotional) resources to withstand a worst-case scenario.

So why buy real estate? Like stocks, real estate can produce income and grow in value, and those can be reasons enough to invest.

But forget about real estate's oft-cited third benefit: tax savings. There aren't any long-term tax advantages to owning real estate that you don't also get from stocks. While it's true that owning investment real estate allows you to depreciate the property, depreciation only increases your ultimate capital gain, as we discussed in Chapter 15. As for the deductions you get from all the expenses you incur from owning and maintaining the property, realize also that each dollar in deductions saves you only 20 or 30 cents in taxes. You're still losing 70 or 80 cents in the process. So if you're going to buy real estate, do so for income and growth, not for tax benefits.

The biggest problem with real estate is that buying it is not a simple prospect. Rental property requires a large cash outlay, often beyond the ability of most investors. And let's not forget the Hassle Factor.

The Hassle Factor

You'll never get a phone call in the middle of the night because something went wrong with the stock you own, but people who own rentals face all kinds of management problems. You have to find tenants, which takes time and costs money, and then you must hope your tenant pays rent on time and doesn't trash the place. You'll get phone calls at odd hours because the heater's not working, or the refrigerator has gone bad. So get ready, because buying a rental means you become a *landlord*.

You Need Strong Cash Reserves If You Rent

Investors who own rental properties should maintain at least 12 months' worth of the rental's mortgage payments in cash reserves, in case the tenant fails to pay rent. Here's the worst case I've seen: A client owned a rental property, and the tenant didn't pay rent. In his state, eviction couldn't occur for 90 days. On the 89th day, the tenant filed for personal bankruptcy, putting a stay on eviction procedures. The personal bankruptcy lasted nine months, during which time my client was unable to evict the tenant (who still was not paying rent).

Finally, after a year and again facing eviction, the tenant vanished, and my client discovered that he had taken with him the washer/dryer, refrigerator, and dishwasher. There were holes in the walls, cigarette burns in the carpet, and broken doors. All told, my client had to spend $10,000 repairing the house before he could rent it again. This took two more months, for a total of 14 months with no rental income plus $10,000 in repair costs.

I cite this story not to dissuade you from owning rental property, for many people do so with great success. My point, rather, is that bad things can happen, and as with all financial planning, you need to be prepared for the worst (and then hope it never happens!).

So, if you're going to invest in real estate, you need to buy several properties (for diversification). Make sure they are income-producing to reduce your monthly cash outlays, and to provide you a hedge against the risk that the properties might not grow in value but fall instead. Don't buy raw land, and never borrow money to invest in real estate.

Your Home is Not a Real Estate Investment

By the way, your home is not an investment. It's a place to live. Therefore, you should buy your home because you love the house, you can afford it, and it is close to schools, shopping, work, and relatives — not because you think the house will grow in value over time.

If your home does grow in value, that's only a coincidence. Homes are not *expected* to grow in value beyond the rate of inflation — unlike stocks, which are expected to grow faster than inflation. Besides, when you move, the next house you buy will cost more, so the fact that yours grew in value will be meaningless.

Still, many a homeowner has been known to make the claim, "My house is the best investment I ever made!" What utter nonsense. Whenever I find someone who says that, I find that (a) their home is the *only* investment they ever made or (b) they don't live in Texas, Florida, New England, Colorado, California, or half a dozen other areas of the country.

Even if you were lucky enough to live in Washington, D.C. or the New York City area (where home values did remarkably well in the 1980s), your home still failed to be "the best investment" ever.

Consider the facts: Say you bought your home in 1980 for $150,000 and sold it in 1990 for $500,000. Wow! That represents a gain of 233%. Anybody would have to admit that that's a pretty darn good return, and because my firm is headquartered in the Washington, D.C. area, lots of my firm's clients enjoyed such growth, leading to the sentiment that buying a house was their best investment.

But was it really? During the same period, the Dow Jones Industrial Average grew from 800 to 3,000 — a gain of 275%. Thus, the stock market performed even better than the real estate market.

So why does everybody think real estate is the greatest investment?

The answer is found not in the *asset* my clients bought, but in the way they bought it. When they bought that $150,000 house in 1980, they didn't pay cash. They put down only $15,000 and they financed the rest. Thus, they watched their $15,000 cash investment produce a profit of $350,000 — and *that's* a total return of 2,333% — far outpacing the measly 275% earned by the stock market.

But this is not being fair. You were willing to buy your house with borrowed money, but you would never buy stocks with borrowed money. Yet if you did, your stocks would have performed just as amazingly as your house!

In other words, it wasn't the real estate that produced such high returns, it was *the leverage* that did it. You borrowed somebody else's money, paid them a small amount for the privilege, and then invested it for huge profits. Lots of stock investors do that all the time (it's called a margin account) and it's highly speculative, because you must repay the loan even if the stocks go down in value.

As I explain in Chapter 58, I have no problem when clients borrow money to buy a home, but I refuse to allow them to borrow money to buy stocks or other investments. That includes real estate.

Why is it okay to borrow money to buy a home but not to invest in real estate? Because your home is not a real estate investment. Rather, it's a place to live.

Never Borrow Money to Invest in Real Estate

If you're going to invest in rental property, pay cash for it.

This will come as heresy to real estate investors, who know that fortunes are made through leverage. You buy a townhouse for $100,000 with only ten grand in cash. Then, after you get a tenant to pay rent equal to your mortgage payment, you wait for the property to appreciate. When the townhouse's market value hits $150,000, you borrow another $30,000 from the increased equity and use *that* money to buy *three more* $100,000 properties — using $10,000 as down payments for each one. Rent each as before, and after each property gains an additional $50,000 in value, you sell out, pocketing a cool $250,000 — on your original $10,000 investment!

Of course, that's assuming things go according to plan. But life has a way of, *ahem*, not cooperating. Perhaps the best illustration comes by way of my client, Jason.

Jason bought a house for $150,000. As the market took off, he watched the value of his home grow in just two years to $300,000. Thus, Jason decided to buy more real estate to cash in on all the profits. "The money's just waiting to be made!" he gushed.

Jason, who had borrowed $120,000 to buy his first house, obtained a home equity loan for $100,000 more and used it to buy a $200,000 townhouse. Jason's monthly mortgage payment on the rental was $755; add taxes, insurance, and maintenance and repairs, and Jason discovered that he needed to charge $1,000 in rent just to break even on his costs. No problem; finding a tenant would be as easy as placing an ad in the classifieds.

Or so he thought. After six weeks, Jason finally rented his property for $700 — $300 less than his monthly expenses. (He didn't know that rental properties are routinely vacant 25% of the time.) He covered the mortgage out of his own pocket during this time.

But Jason was not worried about his "negative cash flow." He figured, "I'm getting tax benefits here, so I'll recover some of the losses on my tax return." Besides, he added, "with the house growing in value so rapidly, I'll more than make up the difference."

Then his tenant failed to pay rent one month, and the next month's check bounced — which caused Jason's mortgage check to bounce. Jason got rid of the tenant, but he remained liable for the rental's mortgage payments as well as those on his own home. He was fast running out of cash, so Jason found himself with a choice: Either sell the property or risk defaulting on the rental's mortgage. If the latter occurred, it would ruin his credit rating. Reluctantly, Jason chose to sell the property.

Unfortunately, the economy had turned. The result: Jason sold the townhouse for $180,000 — $20,000 less than he had paid. Factoring in his expenses (not to mention the 3 a.m. phone calls because the furnace was not working) Jason lost more than $25,000.

That's why you should buy investment properties for cash: If you lose your tenant, at least you have no risk of defaulting on a mortgage.

This is also why you must add and maintain at least 12 months' worth of rental income to your cash reserves for each property you own, just in case your investment doesn't go according to plan.

Chapter 19 - Collectibles

Collectibles include coins, stamps, artwork — even 1960s-era lunch boxes! One of my clients collects Japanese swords, another, comic books and baseball cards. Collectibles consist of all kinds of things.

The most commonly discussed advantage to collecting is anonymity. With no government supervision or reporting mechanism, no one knows what you buy, the price you pay, or when you sell. This is quite different from dealing with registered securities: When you sell stocks and bonds, the IRS is informed about the transaction.

> As a professional advisor, I remind you that tax law requires you to declare capital gains on the profits you earn when you sell collectibles. However, the burden of honesty is on you.

The Four Problems with Collectibles

Assuming you do pay taxes on your profits, what's the big deal in owning collectibles? Sure, they can grow in value, but so can every other equity investment — stocks, real estate, even gold. And if growth is your sole motivation (excluding love for your collection), I challenge you to find any collectible that earned more money in any given time period than the best stock of that same period.

So don't kid yourself: You're not going to find instant wealth through collectibles. But what you will find are four problems.

Problem #1: No Buyer Protection

The anonymity of collecting can work against you. If you want to buy stock, you are guaranteed your trade will occur at the fair market value. But if you buy a piece of art, who's to say you're paying a fair price? And who's to say you're getting the original and not a worthless copy?

"I started out with nothing. I still have most of it."
—Michael Davis

Problem #2: You are Responsible for Safekeeping

If your collectible gets damaged or lost, the value is gone. You don't
have to worry about that when you buy stock.

Problem #3: Lack of Liquidity

You can sell your stock virtually whenever you want. But who's to say
you'll find someone to buy your record collection?

Problem #4: You'll Never Sell

Yet the biggest problem with investing in collectibles is best demonstrated by one of my clients, a wine collector. At our first meeting,
he gave me a list of his assets, including his $40,000 wine collection.
When I asked, "When do you plan to sell your wine?," he replied,
"Sell it? I'm going to drink it!"

Well, if he's going to drink it, it's not an asset! And that's the attitude
I find among collectors. They fall in love with their collections. They
won't sell any of it. People generally don't get too emotionally attached to their Treasury bills, but they do get attached to their
autographed Spiderman comic book.

Here's the bottom line: If you want to be a collector, recognize that it is a very high-risk venture. To succeed, you must approach it like a hobby. How do you know which coin is most likely to grow in value? Which baseball card is the best buy, or fairly priced? Like any hobby, you need to get immersed in the subject. You can't just go to a weekend card show and pick up something, or you'll get ripped off: You'll pay $15 for something worth only $5. You must be serious about what you are doing.

If you are serious, you can have fun at the same time. But over the next 20 years, I'm not sure you'll make any more money than if you were to just buy stocks and stock mutual funds instead.

Chapter 20 - Hedge Positions

You may have noticed that this book is devoid of exotic investments, also known as speculation. That's because I'm not one to recommend that you engage in speculative trading activity, or that you buy overly risky investments.

However, as we discussed in Chapter 14, a speculative investment might succeed for the very reason a safer investment fails. Therefore, to protect the safer investment, we also should own some speculative ones. Let's examine the risks your investments could face and how speculative investments might protect you against them.

Risk #1: Inflation

We saw in Chapter 14 how inflation directly hurts bonds, because inflation causes interest rates to rise, and rising rates cause bond prices to fall. Gold, though itself a very speculative investment, tends to rise with inflation, and thus can be an effective hedge for your investment in bonds.

Risk #2: Recession

Another potential problem is recession, a period in which the economy is not growing. During recessions, stocks and bonds fall in price. However, recent recessions have been brought on by shortages (real or perceived) in consumable goods. Thus, while stock and bond prices fell, gasoline prices rose, as did the prices of many other commodities. Therefore, maintaining a position in natural resources — such as oil & gas, minerals, forest products, and others — makes sense. You can buy these types of investments in a variety of ways, such as through mutual funds, stocks of companies that operate in these industries, and even directly through commodities trading.

"When you bet on a sure thing — hedge!"
—Robert Half

Risk #3: Lack of Confidence

In Chapter 5, you learned that consumers believe issuers when they say that stock and bond certificates have value. But if consumers were to lose that faith, paper assets would not be worth the, uh, paper they're printed on. Therefore, it makes sense to possess hard assets as a hedge against paper ones. The most common hedges are real estate, gold, and other precious metals.

> **Sorry, jewelry doesn't count. The markup prohibits you from selling at a profit, and most jewelry is not investment grade. Like a home, buy jewelry because you love it, not because it's protecting your Treasuries.**

Risk #4: Collapse of the Dollar

When the dollar dumps, you'll be glad you own foreign currencies, which you can do directly or through mutual funds.

Risk #5: Stock Market Crash

If you think the stock market is going to go down — or if you just want to protect yourself in case it does — consider two strategies: selling short (defined in Chapter 23) or options trading (discussed below). Although a complete discussion of options is beyond the purpose of this book, you should be aware that options can be defensive. Following is one such example.

How to Boost Your Stocks While Lowering Your Risk

Options are derivatives and most people think these are highly speculative, with fortunes gambled in all-or-nothing stakes. While that is true for many derivatives, there are some that actually increase safety. Such is the case with a little-used options strategy called Covered Call Writing.

CCW is a conservative strategy designed to reduce risk and increase income when investing in stocks. Briefly stated, stock options are contracts in which you buy or sell the right to buy or sell. (Read that again; it sounds redundant, but it isn't.)

We're interested here in low-risk "Covered Call Writing." Here's how it works: Say it's August and you buy 300 shares of XYZ stock at the price of $48 per share. XYZ pays a quarterly dividend of 50 cents per share. Therefore, if the price never moves, you'll earn 4.2% per year.

At the same time, you would participate in Covered Call Writing. To do so, you would "write three January 50 Calls." This means you are selling ("writing") the right for someone else to buy the stock from you (they can "call" it away) between now and the third Friday of January at the specified price of $50. (All contracts expire the third Friday of the month.)

Each contract represents 100 shares, hence three contracts. The buyers pay you a fee (called a "premium") of $3.50 per share, or $1,050. (The premium is based on the amount of time until expiration and the spread between the current price and the "strike price", in this case $50. Therefore, the premium changes constantly.)

Assuming you don't cancel this out, only two things can happen next: The contract will get exercised (meaning your stock will be sold as agreed for $50) or it will expire worthless in January. Either way, you keep the $1,050.

Let's look closer at what happens in each case.

If the option is exercised:

Naturally, no one would exercise an option to buy your stock at $50 if the price stays at $48. Therefore, the buyer of the option is betting XYZ will rise above $50 by late January. If it does rise, say to $53, he can buy your shares for $50 and immediately sell them for $53, profiting $3/share.

If this happens, you've sold them for $50, $2 per share more than what you paid for it. That's a gain of $600, or 4.2%. Add the $1.00/share in dividends you received, plus the $3.50/share premium, and you've made 13.5% in less than six months. Total annualized return: 27%.

If the option expires:

If the price fails to climb above $50, the options will not be exercised. Therefore, you will still own the stock in February. Then you sell another option, and earn another $1,050. Keep repeating this process and, including dividends, your total annual return will be 18.75%.

Clearly, this strategy can yield big rewards. Among the advantages are: 1) you are establishing a profitable sell price the day you buy the stock. If exercised, you are guaranteed a profit; 2) you reduce risk because the premium in effect reduces the price you paid for the stock; and 3) your annual yield is boosted far above that of the dividend alone.

However, there are other considerations. For one, you are limiting your potential profits. No matter how high the stock rises, you won't sell for more than $50. You can solve this problem by buying your option back, in effect canceling it out. You would do this if you later think the stock will dramatically rise and you don't want to miss the gains to be made. (This is "buying a January 50 call.")

Also, you have not reduced the risk that your stock may drop in price. The only certainty is, should XYZ drop $25, your option will not be exercised — a small consolation. To protect yourself, you may "buy a January 45 put" giving you the right to sell your stock for $45 ("put" it to someone else). This is the opposite of what we've reviewed here, and is designed to minimize losses, rather than protect gains.

Because of the potential for price drops, you should choose a high quality, blue-chip stock that fits your budget, and which offers a stable trading range, solid fundamentals, high dividends, and good growth potential.

Keep in mind the figures shown exclude commissions, which will reduce your total return. Also, dividend and option income is taxable.

Covered Call Writing is not a reason to own stocks, but the strategy might be of help to those who already own them. Prior to opening an account, you must receive and are urged to read "Characteristics and Risk of Standardized Options," which is published by the Options Clearing Corporation in cooperation with the NASD and all major U.S. stock exchanges. The booklet is available from any broker or financial advisor.

Part V
Packaged Products

Part V — Packaged Products

Chapter 21 - The Four Problems You Encounter When Buying Investments

In Parts III and IV, we learned about the many types of investments that are available to you. In this part, we're going to revisit those investments, but in a slightly different way. Why? Because although many of the investments we've discussed are neat ideas, buying them is sometimes easier said than done. Let's examine why.

Problem #1: Lack of Affordability

Many of us don't have $10,000 to invest — let alone a quarter million. You might have only $100, and try finding investments you can afford with that amount — or a broker willing to help you.

Because of what investments often cost, millions of people avoid the investment world. By not buying stocks and bonds, though, companies have trouble raising the cash they need to build factories, which in turn would create jobs and boost the economy. Thus, lack of affordable investments not only is a problem for investors, it's a problem for our nation.

Problem #2: Lack of Liquidity

Perhaps you like the idea of investing in a Ginnie Mae,[12] and you've got the $25,000 needed to buy it. But say you later need $2,000 unexpectedly. This would present you with a problem, for you can't sell a piece of your Ginnie Mae; you'd have to sell the whole bond. So although investments are liquid, they're not as flexible as savings accounts.

---

[12]See Chapter 8.

Problem #3: Inability to Achieve Diversification

Say you want to invest $10,000 in stocks. As we covered in Chapter 17, you should buy stocks in 100-share increments, and with many stocks priced in the $100/share range, that means you can buy the stock of only one company. That's risky, for the best way to invest safely is to buy many stocks instead of just one.

Therefore, it would make a lot more sense to own 20 or 30 stocks instead of just one, but it's hard to diversify with just $10,000. This is why you should not buy individual stocks unless you can invest at least $250,000. Why? Because one round lot (100 shares) at $100/share will cost you $10,000. And since diversity demands that you buy at least 25 stocks, you need $250,000. Few of us have a quarter of a million dollars to put into the stock market.

Problem #4: You Have Little or No Assistance

Let's say you have a sufficient amount of money with which to invest. Which will you choose? With more than 20,000 stocks and hundreds of thousands of bonds available, which should you buy? And once bought, when should you sell? If you're like most people, you'd be better off hiring a professional money manager to make those decisions for you — if you could afford one.

Chapter 22 - How to Beat the Four Problems

Be sure you read the previous chapter before you read this one.

In the Crash of '29, the problems cited in the previous chapter became so overwhelming that millions of investors fled the markets, leading to the Depression. To bring individual investors back, Congress needed to fix the four problems, and it did so with the Investment Company Act of 1940.

The Act allowed Wall Street to create new kinds of companies for the sole purpose of helping consumers invest — in other companies! Individuals buy shares in these investment companies, which then hire managers to buy dozens of stocks and bonds. The profits (or losses!) of each company are then distributed to their respective investors on a pro-rata basis. So, if an investment company has assets of $1 million, of which $5,000 is yours, you would receive $5,000/1,000,000ths of the profits or losses. That's all there is to it.

INVESTMENT COMPANIES ARE POOLS OF MONEY

$100 $25,000 $500

$100,000

$4,000,000

1. Assets are placed into pool by investors.
2. Manager of the pool buys investments.
3. Results are distributed pro-rata to investors.

FIGURE 5-1

The Four Benefits of Investment Companies

Thus, you can beat the four problems cited in Chapter 21 by investing in investment companies. By doing so, you'll enjoy these benefits:

Benefit #1: Affordability

You can join most investment companies with as little as $100, and you can add to your account whenever you want, with amounts as little as $25. Investing in stocks and bonds is now within reach of almost everyone.

Benefit #2: Your Money is Liquid

Since you own shares of the investment company instead of owning individual stocks or bonds, you can sell pieces of your investment any time you wish, simply by selling your shares of the investment company. Thus, if you've invested $5,000, you can sell, say, $200 if that's all the cash you need at the moment. You can't do that with individual securities.

Benefit #3: Diversification

Placing your money into an investment company means you own a small piece of hundreds of individual stocks or bonds instead of just one stock or one bond. Like 12 placing eggs in 12 baskets, you have better protection against something going wrong with one of the eggs.

Benefit #4: Professional Management

Investment companies are operated by professional money managers, and if you are like most Americans, you will earn much more money by relying on their expertise than trying to choose from the thousands of stocks and bonds all by yourself.

In fact, if you've ever lamented the fact that you, as one of the "little guys," can't compete with the big institutional money managers, now you can: Just hire one to work for you — by placing your money with an investment company.

Chapter 23 - The Most Common Type of Investment Company

You're a lot more familiar with investment companies than you may realize. Although the Act created three types of investment companies, the most common is an *open-end fund*, which you know under its more familiar name, "mutual fund."

That's right: Plain ol' mutual funds are really investment companies, and this explains why mutual funds have become the most popular way Americans invest. (It also explains why my previous chapter's description of investment companies sounded so familiar.)

When the law was created in 1940, 68 funds held $400 million in assets. Today, more than 6,000 funds hold more than $2.8 trillion in assets. Yet, the irony is that nobody reading this book owns a mutual fund. In fact, no investor anywhere owns a fund. No one has, and no one ever will.

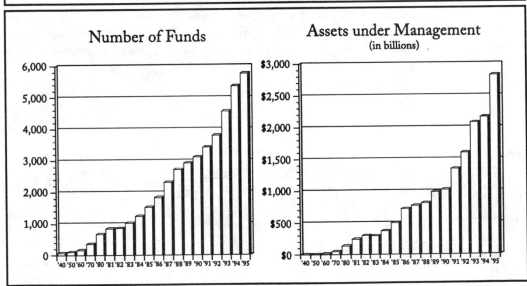

THE SOARING POPULARITY OF MUTUAL FUNDS

FIGURE 5-2

Mutual Funds are Not Investments

Rather, mutual funds simply are a *method through which people invest*. People call my firm all the time asking, "What are your mutual funds paying?" The truth is that mutual funds don't "pay" anything!

People also say, "I don't like mutual funds because they're risky." But there's no such thing as a "risky" fund. Nor has anyone ever lost money in a mutual fund. Mutual funds are not good, and they're not bad.

A mutual fund, in fact, is merely a mirror – a reflection of something else. Thus, if you invest in a mutual fund that invests in stocks, you own stocks, and you are as likely to make money or lose money as any other person who invests in stocks.

In fact, you can use mutual funds to buy virtually any kind of investment: stocks, bonds, government securities, real estate, gold and other precious metals, international securities, foreign currencies, natural resources, hedge positions, even CDs and money markets. You can find funds that engage in virtually any type of trading activity, including options and futures contracts, derivatives, and even selling short.[13]

Technically, mutual funds are called *open-end* investment companies because they forever buy and sell their shares. In industry jargon, mutual funds *sell* shares to the public (and they will do so forever, because they have an unlimited supply of shares to offer), and when you want your money back, the fund will *redeem* them for you (and they will accept redemptions forever — or, rather, for as long as there are shares to redeem).

---

[13]Short-selling is a bet that a given stock will decline in value rather than rise. When selling short, the potential gain is limited, but potential losses are unlimited — making short-selling extremely speculative.

SHOE JEFF MacNELLY

Reprinted by permission: Tribune Media Services.

The price of a fund always equals the value of whatever it owns. The price is called the NAV, for *net asset value*. (If it seems obvious that the fund's NAV[14] would equal the value of the fund itself, stay tuned; You'll later discover another type of investment company where this is not true.)

The Biggest Myth About Mutual Funds

When you mention the words "mutual fund," most people think of stocks. But the truth is that mutual funds do not always invest in stocks. In fact, most mutual funds invest in government bonds — either U.S. or municipal. If this surprises you, revisiting our earlier manufacturing lesson (Chapter 5) should help you understand.

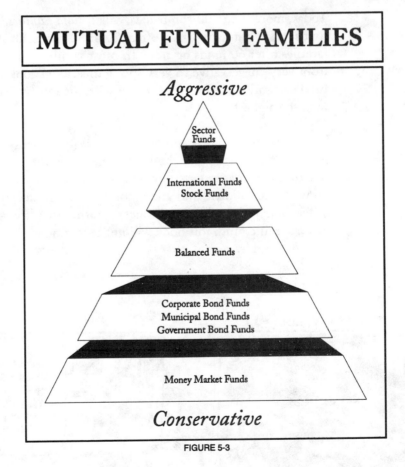

MUTUAL FUND FAMILIES

Aggressive

Sector Funds

International Funds
Stock Funds

Balanced Funds

Corporate Bond Funds
Municipal Bond Funds
Government Bond Funds

Money Market Funds

Conservative

FIGURE 5-3

---

[14]That's enayvee, not nah-v.

Like any manufacturer, Wall Street seeks to make products that consumers will buy. Above all else, what do most people want from their investments? *Safety*. Since government bonds are the safest investment, consumers seek them above all others — which is why Wall Street manufactures government bond mutual funds more than any other kind of fund.

Yet you rarely hear about government bond funds. All those financial magazines and investment newsletters brag about the "Hot Mutual Funds to Buy Now," but only the riskiest of investments (stocks, gold, real estate, international securities, and other equities) can achieve such lofty returns. And sure enough, when you look at the lists of top performers, the riskiest funds are always the ones listed. Thus, for many people, mutual funds have become synonymous with stocks, even though stock funds represent only 36% of the mutual fund universe.

Today, more than 400 companies, called *fund families,* sponsor mutual funds. Each family typically offers 20 or 30 funds, although the largest families offer 60 funds or more. In most families, the choices range from very conservative to very speculative. Let's look at these basic fund categories one by one, starting with the lowest risk and ending with the highest.

The charts that follow represent the average performance of all mutual funds in the category, for the 10-year period ending 1995, according to Morningstar as reported by Ibbotson & Associates, and assuming reinvestment of dividends and ignoring taxes. In keeping with my goal of teaching you fundamental concepts rather than trying to get you to buy a specific fund, this book will not recommend that you buy any specific fund by name.

NON SEQUITUR   WILEY

©1994 Washington Post Writers Group. Reprinted with permission.

U.S. Government Securities Funds

For the 10-year period ending in 1995, U.S. Government Securities Funds have averaged 7.8%; $10,000 would have grown to $21,214. Look closely at Figure 5-4: Can you see the Crash of '87?

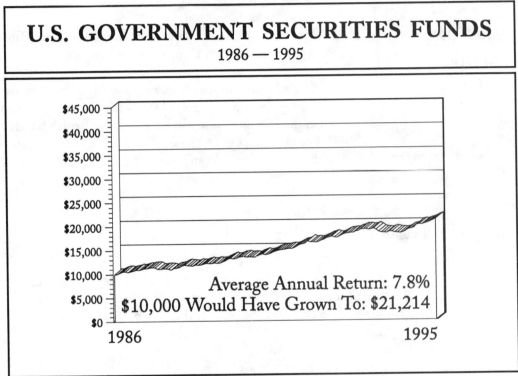

U.S. GOVERNMENT SECURITIES FUNDS
1986 — 1995

Average Annual Return: 7.8%
$10,000 Would Have Grown To: $21,214

FIGURE 5-4

Of course not — the stock market crash had no effect on government bonds!

Just as there are several types of government securities, there are several types of government securities funds as well, including:

- **Ginnie Mae funds.** Since Ginnie Maes are the most popular of all government bonds, it follows that Wall Street would offer funds that invest exclusively in them. These are typically the highest-yielding government funds, with equally high volatility due to interest rate risk.

> *"If you put your money where you mouth is, you will look very funny to other people."*
> —Winston Groom

- **Adjustable Rate Mortgage funds.** These feature lower yields and lower volatility.

- **Zero-Coupon funds** (also known as "Target Maturity" funds). These funds only buy zero-coupon bonds.

- **Short-Term funds.** These buy Treasuries that mature in less than three years.

- **Intermediate funds.** Treasuries bought by these funds typically mature in three to seven years.

- **Global Government funds.** These funds buy bonds from governments around the world. If rates are rising in the U.S. but falling in England, the British bonds could be the better investment, and these funds can buy accordingly. Watch out for currency risk in addition to interest rate risk.

Municipal Bond Funds

The next step up in risk takes us to municipal bonds. The average rate of return in our 10-year snapshot was 8.1%; $10,000 would have grown to $21,827. Like before, the Crash of '87 is invisible on this chart.

Muni funds include:

- **Money Market funds.** These funds are a tax-free alternative to bank savings accounts.

- **Single-State funds.** These funds invest exclusively in the bonds from one state, so that investors who live in those states can avoid state income taxes as well as federal income taxes. (Other muni funds buy bonds from many states, forcing investors to pay state income taxes on their interest. Single-state funds avoid this problem — but their yields often are less. You must calculate the taxable equivalent yield [Chapter 9] to determine which is best for you.)

- **Puerto Rico funds.** As a territory, not a state, obligations of Puerto Rico are obligations of the federal government. Thus, the interest is free of state income taxes as well as federal income taxes, and all Puerto Rico G.O.s carry a AAA bond rating. But Puerto Rican bonds are burdened with an unfair reputation, which forces Puerto Rico to offer higher interest rates — to entice investors to buy what are perceived to be "riskier" bonds than those available from the states. It's silly (maybe sad), and smart investors can take advantage of this discrepancy — especially those who live in states which do not exempt the interest on their own bonds.

- **Insured Muni funds.** All the muni bonds in these funds carry insurance from MBIA, AMBAC, or another insurance carrier.

- **High-Yield Muni funds.** It's almost an oxymoron that a government-guaranteed bond can be considered "junk", but Wall Street frowns on states which are not prudent with their finances. Most of the bonds in these funds are revenue bonds, which carry no government guarantees. Still, defaults are rare, and the extensive diversification helps further to absorb the risk.

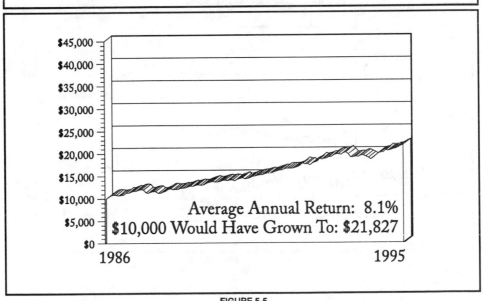

MUNICIPAL BOND FUNDS
1986 — 1995

Average Annual Return: 8.1%
$10,000 Would Have Grown To: $21,827

FIGURE 5-5

High-Yield Corporate Bond Funds

Next, we find high-yield corporate bond funds, which have a 10-year track record of 9.5%; meaning $10,000 would have grown to $24,807 over the past 10 years. There are three kinds of corporate bond funds:

- **Short-Term** and **Intermediate** funds, both of which buy high quality bonds; and

- **High-Yield** funds, buy long-term bonds of low quality (i.e., junk).

In my opinion, junk bond funds were created for only one reason: so Wall Street can make money selling them. Their primary selling point is the yield, but this contradicts Edelman's Rule #1: Never, never, never, never, never, never, never chase yield.

Those who chase yields *always* get what they deserve.

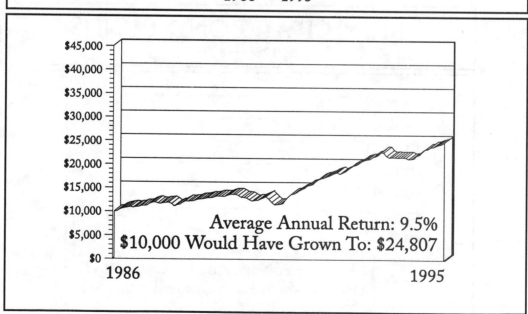

HIGH-YIELD CORPORATE BOND FUNDS
1986 — 1995

Average Annual Return: 9.5%
$10,000 Would Have Grown To: $24,807

1986   1995

FIGURE 5-6

The History of Yield-Chasing

Ever since your granddaddy was a little boy, bank accounts never paid more than 5%. In fact, for much of this century, banks paid only 2% or 3%. There was virtually no difference in rate from one bank to another, and thus few options for savers.

Until 1974, that is, when Congress deregulated money rates and allowed the securities industry to create money market funds. (Banks were prohibited from offering these new products.)

As interest rates climbed with inflation in the late '70s, these new money funds began to offer rates as high as 14%, and consumers flocked to them. For the next six or seven years, savers enjoyed the high rates and safety offered by these money funds, and Americans slowly became spoiled — even dependent — on them.

By the early '80s, as interest rates started back down, so did the money fund yields. As rates dropped to 8% (only half as good as before but still much higher than banks), yield-addicted consumers longed for the "good old days" of the inflationary '70s.

Seeing the demand, Wall Street offered the first U.S. Government Securities mutual fund. By investing primarily in Ginnie Maes, the highest-yielding government security, this fund dazzled investors with yields once again around 13%. Thus, as money fund yields dropped, investors switched their assets into Ginnie Mae funds. What could be wrong with that? These savers had been using money funds ever since they were created, and nobody had lost money. (Like bank accounts, money funds feature a stable NAV of $1; since the share price never moves, all the fluctuation is in the yield, which changes daily.)

> **For millions of investors, Ginnie Mae funds were a lesson learned too late. For others, it was a lesson not learned at all.**

While there was little practical difference between savings accounts and money funds, this was not true when savers moved from money funds to Ginnie Mae funds. And few were prepared emotionally or financially for what was about to happen.

As we learned in Chapter 14, Ginne Maes (like all bonds) rise in value when interest rates are falling. And that's what happened in the early-to mid-'80s. Interest rates fell from 1980 to 1986. To restore their fallen yields, owners of money funds switched to Ginnie Mae funds, where they got back their higher yields, along with the added bonus of capital gains (which occurred because interest rates continued to drop). Thus, everyone was happy.

Until 1987.

By then, long-term rates, which had reached their low of 7%, began climbing upward. As rates went higher, so did the yields on Ginnie Maes. But as you know by now, yield doesn't tell the whole story. So although the yields grew, the value of Ginnie Maes fell. By 1988, U.S. Government Funds were facing negative total returns — investors actually were losing money in what they thought were "government-guaranteed investments"!

To boost this declining performance, some funds even began trading in options in a futile effort to artificially boost the yield, but as rates continued to rise, this only increased their losses. Thus, the fun and easy profit of government bond funds was gone, and having realized the limitations of these investments, Wall Street stopped trying to make them something they weren't.

Today, government bond funds are dull, boring investments, with good but not great yields, and a new emphasis on maintaining a stable NAV. This is fine for savvy investors who know how to separate good investments from bad, but what about the yield-hungry neophytes?

Never one to pass up a sale, Wall Street came through once again, this time with corporate bond funds. As we learned in Chapter 11, yields on AAA-rated bonds are similar to the yields of government bonds, while junk bond yields are much higher to compensate investors for the higher risk.

Thus, Wall Street didn't bother creating funds that consist of bonds issued by Ford and General Electric. What would be the point? With little risk of default, yields on those bonds were about the same as Treasuries. Since investors weren't happy with the yield available from government paper, they certainly wouldn't be interested in the yield of high-grade corporates, either.

But junk bonds were another story. Because these companies had one foot in bankruptcy court, they offered investors obscenely high yields — 18% was common. Armed with these great yields, junk bond funds hit the market in 1987 (with euphemistic names like "High Yield" instead of "junk") and attracted huge amounts of money in very short periods. Once again, everything went well — until interest rates started rising again in 1989. But this time, it was worse than the two earlier episodes of rising rates.

In the past, losses were incurred only because of interest rate risk. This time, though, investors had to contend with credit risk in addition to interest rate risk. When interest rates rose, the increased borrowing costs forced many companies out of business, leaving their investors holding worthless bonds. While a holder of government bonds can ride things out until rates come back down or until the bonds mature, owners of junk bonds enjoyed no safe harbor. When the companies went broke, the bonds defaulted and investors discovered their money was gone. That had never happened with their bank accounts or their government bond funds.

Needless to say, the yield-chasers fled junk bond funds, most of them never to return. Today's junk bonds are a ghost of their former selves: Yields have returned to more realistic (but still high) levels, and most of the worst junk has long since defaulted. What's left probably will survive to maturity. But don't tell that to those who invested in junk bonds in the '80s, for they have long since fled. But where did they go?

You can find the yield-chasers hanging around one of Wall Street's latest enticements: *collateralized mortgage obligations*. CMOs, at one point the hottest product on the Street, are *derivatives*, because they owe their existence to (are "derived from") something else. In a CMO, Wall Street literally "invents" a security, much the same way the government invented mortgage bonds in the '60s.

NON SEQUITUR   WILEY

©1994 Washington Post Writers Group. Reprinted with permission.

Did you see the *"60 Minutes"* report a few years ago about Denver's default on some industrial development bonds? *"60 Minutes"* interviewed a retired widow who had invested her life savings — $40,000 — in these bonds. The bond's yield was 18% (at a time when bank accounts were paying 8%) before they went bust. So *"60 Minutes"* put this teary-eyed widow on TV, and she won the sympathy of everyone watching.

Except me, for this lady didn't always have tears in her eyes. Earlier, her eyes were filled with dollar signs. When her broker offered those high-yielding bonds to her, her only question was, "How many can I get?"

Well, she got all she wanted — and as much as she deserved.

I know this sounds cruel. I know there's a lot more to the

It's one thing to create a bond backed by mortgages (since the mortgage itself is backed by a house — an appreciating asset), but it's quite another to create a bond where the collateral is of less certain value. Indeed, some amazing things are being collateralized today. Like automobile loans.

It works like this: A bank issues thousands of auto loans, holding each car's title as collateral (if the borrower fails to pay, the bank repossesses the car.) In the latest fad, a bank packages together thousands of these loans, then sells the package to Wall Street. Since the interest rates for auto loans typically are higher than mortgage rates, Wall Street can re-sell them to investors at higher yields than mortgage bonds.

That sounds okay in theory, but these products are so new that nobody knows for sure what will happen if borrower defaults exceed expectations. You could find mutual funds owning a lot of cars.

Even more bizarre are derivatives that secure credit card debts. By doing with credit card balances what they did with auto loans, Wall Street's newest CMO touts the highest yields available (since credit cards charge 18% to 21%), but look out below!:

- there's no collateral to go after, should cardholders default on their debt;

- nobody knows what will happen when interest rates rise (will it force a new wave of defaults?); and

- nobody knows what will happen when rates fall.

The bottom line: Stay tuned for a replay of the junk bond market.

Those who spent the last 15 years chasing yields have had a rocky ride — far rockier than their counterparts in the stock market. And that's the irony: The yield chasers wanted safety above all else, and safety is the one thing they never got. But investors in the stock market, who gave up the holy grail of safety, enjoyed higher returns and much less volatility — even considering the Crash of '87.

Remember, if you chase yield, you deserve what you get.

If you insist on buying junk bonds, please at least buy them through mutual funds. When the widow's story broke on *"60 Minutes"* (see sidebar), my colleagues and I (naturally) reacted with the same horror as the rest of America.

We quickly analyzed our clients' mutual funds to learn if any of them owned these bonds, and we discovered that one of the funds we'd recommended to clients did own these bonds. However, our initial shock quickly evaporated. Why? Because the fund had $8 billion in assets, with several thousand bonds in the portfolio. The Denver bonds represented two-tenths of one percent of the portfolio, which meant that when the bonds defaulted, a given client's account which had been worth $10,000 was now worth $9,999.80.

And that's not all. Despite the default, the fund's dividend had remained intact because all the other bonds in the portfolio were unaffected by the Denver bonds' collapse. Thus, the fund earned in the month of the default only two-tenths of a percent less than it should have earned. Thus, our

story, such as the fact that the broker should not have let her place such a high percentage of her net worth into one invest-ment; that the city of Denver had a responsibil-ity to bring to the market only bonds that were viable; and that inflation and its attendant higher costs of living forced her to seek higher returns so she could pay her bills.

I'm aware of all that. But I'm equally aware, having worked with thousands of individual investors, of two other points:

First, *she was greedy*. Nothing else can explain why she would place all her money into those bonds. Investing some money, even a lot of money, was the fault of an overly-aggressive salesman. But *all* her money could only be her own greedy fault; and

Second, *it's your money, honey*. Despite the prom-ises a broker might make, you are ultimately respon-sible for your actions, and you are the one who must live with the results.

Like I said, I know this sounds cruel. But some-times, life is.

clients who owned this fund didn't notice that they owned the Denver bonds, nor that the bonds had defaulted, because they owned a highly diversified bond fund instead of just one bond.

Thus, while the widow should not have bought junk bonds in the first place, life would have been much kinder if she had at least put her life savings into a *fund* of junk bonds. That way, if one bond were to default, she would have been insulated.

And insulation you'd need. Although the average yield on junk bond funds in the '80s was 16%, the average annual return was only 12%. What happened to the other four percent? It was lost through bond defaults. In other words, so many of the bonds went broke that the defaults reduced the total return.

By the way, can you see the Crash of '87 in Figure 5-6? Not yet! We're still dealing with the bond market, and it was the stock market that crashed. (The drop you see is not the stock market crash of 1987. It's the junk bond collapse of 1990!)

Balanced Funds

Of all mutual fund categories, the next is the most unique and the least understood of all — and a favorite of mine and my colleagues. Unlike all other mutual funds, which invest exclusively in one asset class or another (such as government securities funds or stock funds), a balanced fund invests a portion of its assets into each of the four major asset classes: cash and cash equivalents, government securities, corporate bonds, and corporate stocks. Thus the name "balanced": The theory is that if one asset class were to fall in value, another would rise to compensate, thus giving you a "balanced" rate of return.

Because balanced funds do not place all their assets into any one asset class at any one time, they generally are considered to have the lowest level of risk of all mutual funds. But be careful when selecting a balanced fund: Only 200 or so exist, although a lot more claim the title. Funds similar to balanced funds are:

- **Asset Allocation funds,** which allow the fund manager to move between asset classes, often without limitation. Some invest in foreign stocks, bonds, currencies, and precious metals, in addition to the four traditional asset classes of a balanced fund. (True balanced funds, by contrast, must maintain certain minimums in the basic four asset classes at all times.) Asset allocation funds can be surprisingly volatile, for the manager is able to make aggressive "bets" as to which asset group is poised to do best. If he bets wrong, you've got a problem.

- **Growth and Income funds,** which split the assets between only two assets groups (stocks and bonds) instead of all four. Generally, these funds make more money in good times and lose more in bad times than balanced funds, but their average returns over long periods are not very different.

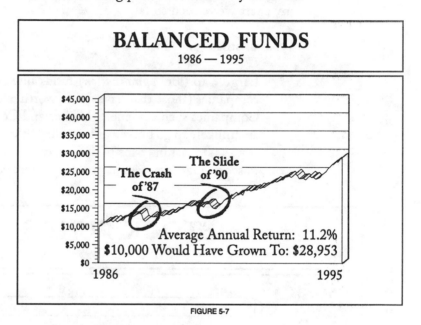

BALANCED FUNDS
1986 — 1995

The Crash of '87

The Slide of '90

Average Annual Return: 11.2%
$10,000 Would Have Grown To: $28,953

1986　　　　　　　　　　1995

FIGURE 5-7

- **Equity Income funds** create the most confusion. People often choose these funds for diversity, thinking they are getting stocks (*equity*) and bonds (*income*). Actually, that's not what the title means; "Equity" indeed means "stock", but "income" in this case means "dividends," not "bonds." Thus, these funds buy stocks which pay dividends (as opposed to stocks which do not pay dividends). These funds are not nearly as diversified, or as low in risk, as you might think.

Balanced funds averaged 11.2%; $10,000 would have grown to $28,953. Take a close look at Figure 5-7. You can see the Crash of '87, because balanced funds have a portion of their assets in stocks, and that portion got walloped in the crash.

Stock Funds

Stock funds' average rate of return was 14.5%; $10,000 would have grown to $38,720. On Figure 5-8, the Crash of '87 is easy to spot, isn't it?

The Crash's dramatic effect on stock funds forces us to recognize that most well-known of all risks: market, or price, risk. As you know, and as the chart confirms, stocks and stock funds are very sensitive to this risk. Indeed, this mountain chart contains more peaks and valleys than any chart we've seen so far.

Types of stock funds include:

- **Large Cap** (for *capitalization*) **funds** buy stocks of large companies (those that have or are worth a lot of money). Companies such as General Motors and Colgate-Palmolive are unlikely to go broke, and that makes them safer than other stocks (at least in terms of default risk), but they are less likely to score huge increases in profits in short periods, either.

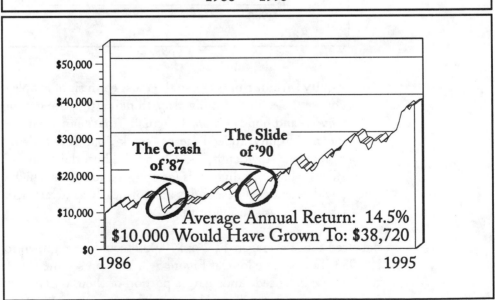

FIGURE 5-8

- **Small Cap funds** buy stocks of smaller companies. Such lesser-known firms have a greater risk than large caps of going broke, but they have greater potential for profit, too.

- **Dividend Yield funds** (also known as Equity Income Funds, discussed earlier) buy stocks which pay dividends. Close cousins are **Rising Dividend** funds, which buy stocks whose dividends are expected to increase.

- **Option Income funds** sell option contracts against the stocks they buy. This strategy boosts the fund's income above that generated by dividends alone, but it also places a ceiling on the potential gains the fund can earn in any particular stock. (See Chapter 20 for a description of how these options work.)

- **Sector funds** buy stocks of only one industry, such as airlines, computers, or biotechnology. These are extremely speculative, for Wall Street can be very harsh to individual sectors even when the overall market is rising.

- **Index funds** attempt to replicate a market index such as the Dow Jones Industrial Average or the S&P 500.

The Truth About Index Funds

Because index funds get a lot of attention in the press, it's worth taking a closer look. Proponents of index funds like to cite studies showing that most professional money managers (including those who manage mutual funds) did not beat the indexes in the 1980s. Therefore, the argument goes, you should invest in index funds because they make more money than other types of stock funds.

Furthermore, proponents argue, since index funds simply buy whatever stocks are contained in the index, the services of a professional manager are not required. Therefore, the cost of owning index funds is lower than the cost of owning other stock funds, and this savings translates to still higher returns for the investor.

However, these are weak positions. In fact, there are four good reasons to reject index funds in favor of other types of stock funds.

Four Arguments Against Index Funds

Argument #1: Buyers of Index Funds are Guaranteed to Earn Less Than the Index

This is because an index is a mathematical theory, not a real product. Therefore:

- an index doesn't pay commissions, but index funds do; and

- an index doesn't pay taxes, but you do.

Thus, if you invest in index funds, you *cannot* do as well the index. But if you're going to take the risk of the stock market, you should want at least the *opportunity* to beat the index, and index funds deny you that opportunity.

Even if you were able to match the performance of the index by buying an index fund, all that means is you would equal the Dow Jones Industrial *Average*, or comparable gauge. Do you really want to be *average*? Most Americans want to excel — or at least be above-average — but that can never happen if you invest in an index fund.

Argument #2: The Primary Argument for Supporting Index Funds is Flawed

Although it is true that many stock funds failed to beat the S&P 500 in the 1980s, it is wrong to conclude that this is always true. In fact, to fully understand this issue, we must look more closely at the 1980s — and at the 20th century as a whole.

Throughout most of the 20th century, small stocks outperformed large stocks. Since there are a lot more small stocks than large stocks from which to choose, and since they tend to do better than large stocks, most money managers buy small stocks. Therefore, for most of this century, money managers generally have outperformed the S&P 500 Stock Index.

But not in the 1980s. Not only did the stock market grow at a much faster pace than ever before, large stocks generally did better than smaller stocks. And it is large stocks which make up the indexes (remember, of 20,000 stocks traded in the U.S., the Dow Jones Industrial Average consists only 30 of the largest companies; the S&P 500 holds only 500 of the biggest). Therefore, most funds in the 1980s did not do as well as the Dow or the S&P 500. But it is wrong to assume that this aberration is the norm, and equally wrong to make an investment decision based solely on the performance of the stock market in that decade.

To prove this point, look at the example provided by 1993: Of 1,557 stock mutual funds monitored by CDA/Weisenberger, 1,066 — or 68.5% — beat the S&P 500.

Argument #3: The Index Fund Boosters are Wrong Even if They're Right

Let's assume indexers are right when they say most funds fail to beat market indexes. Even if that premise is correct, their conclusion remains wrong, for index funds also fail to beat the indexes. Therefore, their conclusion does not solve the problem. The correct solution, then, is to *buy a fund that does beat the market*. Even the indexers admit such funds exist, and they're not hard to find.

Argument #4: Index Funds are Riskier Than Professionally-Managed Stock Funds

Index funds are as volatile as the stock market itself. But many professionally-managed stock funds enjoy lower risk, thanks to the investment styles of the portfolio managers controlling those funds. Thus, many stock funds can produce the desirable result of superior returns with reduced risk — something no index fund can match.

So when offered the opportunity to buy an index fund, Just Say No.

International Funds

International stock funds have averaged 12.2%; $10,000 would have grown to $31,709.

Types include:

- **Global funds** buy stocks from nations throughout the world.

- **International funds** buy stocks from all nations except the United States. Choose these (instead of global funds) when you also buy a U.S. stock fund, to avoid creating redundancy in your portfolio.

- **Single Nation funds** buy stocks from only one country.

- **Regional funds** buy stocks from a single continent or region, such as Europe, the Pacific Rim, or Latin America.

- **Sector funds** buy stocks of specific industries from foreign nations.

Never Invest in Funds That Exclusively Buy Foreign Bonds

While you also can find international funds that buy bonds, they are a bad bet. Bonds are supposed to be safer than stocks, but buying foreign bonds subjects you to the same foreign currency risk as foreign stocks. Thus, if you're willing to expose yourself to foreign currency risk, you might as well give yourself the opportunity to enjoy the potential gains, and that means you should choose stocks when investing overseas, not bonds.

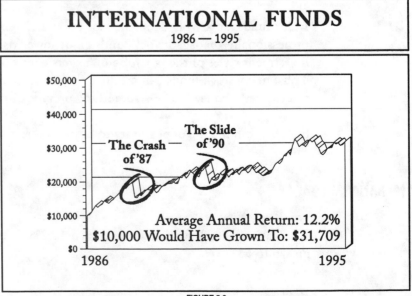

FIGURE 5-9

Indeed, some of the most ironic investments in the market are international government bond funds. With the pitch of buying bonds issued only by the strongest governments in the world, these funds appeal to conservative investors, yet they gyrate wildly in the foreign currency markets.

How Mutual Funds are Taxed

Mutual funds earn dividends and capital gains, and as they do, they periodically distribute them to shareholders. These distributions are subject to taxes each year — dividends at ordinary income tax rates, and capital gains at capital gains tax rates.

You Are Overpaying Taxes on Your Mutual Funds

I'll bet this is true even for those who automatically reinvest their distributions.

The IRS contends that once you earn a dividend or capital gain, it is your choice to reinvest it or not. Since most investors reinvest their distributions, *millions of mutual fund investors overpay the taxes due on their mutual funds.*

Here's how it happens: Let's say Casey invests $10,000 into a bond fund that pays an 8% annual dividend, or $800. Casey automatically reinvests this $800 and the fund gives him more shares. At tax time, Casey must pay taxes on the $800 he earned that year.

If Casey were to do this for five years, he would earn a total of $4,000 in dividends (I'm ignoring compounding to keep this example simple), and he'd pay taxes each year along the way. At the end of the five years, his fund would be worth $14,000 (his original investment of $10,000 plus the $4,000 in dividend reinvestments). Thus, if Casey were to sell his fund, he would receive a check for $14,000. Therefore, he would owe nothing in taxes because he had already paid them.

But many fund investors blow it. They forget they've paid taxes each year on the dividends; when they sell their fund and get their check for $14,000, they also get from the fund an IRS Form 1099 stating that amount (it's called *gross proceeds*). They dutifully give the 1099 to their tax preparer who asks, in an effort to determine the profit they earned (and thus the tax owed), "How much did you invest in this, anyway?"

And they say, "Ten grand," and the tax preparer records that they made a profit of $4,000, includes it on their Schedule D, and they end up paying taxes on that profit all over again! This sounds preposterous, but I can assure you it is perhaps the most common tax mistake made by mutual fund investors.

Do you see the trap? Most investors think the "amount invested" is the amount of money they sent to the fund. But the IRS says all reinvested dividend and capital gain distributions count as "investments," too. Therefore, when Casey's accountant asked how much Casey invested, Casey's answer should have been $14,000 — not $10,000!

You can avoid this problem simply by following these steps:

- Keep all your mutual fund statements, and

- When your tax preparer asks you a question, *don't answer*. Instead, give your preparer the statements you collected. (Casey's reply should have been, "How much did I invest? I don't know. That's what I hired you for! Here — take my statements and figure it out yourself!")

If you prepare your own taxes, be aware of this trap.

There actually are four ways to calculate gains and losses: FIFO, by trade lot, by average cost single method, and by average cost double method. Which you choose matters only if you sell shares at different intervals. If you sell your shares all at once, as Casey did in our example, none of this is important.

FIFO, or First In-First Out, assumes you sell first the shares you bought first. "By Trade Lot" means you pick which shares you want to sell. Under the Average Cost Single Method, you figure the tax on the average cost and the average profit from all your trade lots. Under the double method, you separate the trade lots into two groups — those held less than one year and those held more than one year.

If you sell shares at different times, the method you choose can reduce your taxes, and once you pick a method, you cannot change it for that particular investment, so talk with your financial or tax advisor before you start selling.

Chapter 24 - Closed-End Funds

The second product created by the Investment Company Act of 1940 was a *closed-end fund*. Unlike open-end funds, which offer an unlimited number of shares forever, closed-end funds sell only a certain number of shares, and when they're gone, they're gone. Shareholders who wish to sell cannot return their shares to the fund like mutual fund owners. Sellers instead must seek buyers on the New York Stock Exchange.

This accounts for the most fundamental difference between open-end and closed-end funds: Because you sell your shares to another investor instead of the fund, the price is determined by negotiation. And that means the price agreed upon could be different from the fund's actual NAV.

And, in fact, it usually is. Closed-end funds routinely trade 10% to 20% *below* their NAVs. This is not a criticism of such investments, simply a fact. But what is a criticism is the sales pitch that I've seen brokers use to get people to invest in closed-end funds.

"You can get $10,000 worth of stock for just $8,000!," is how the pitch goes, with the implication that one day the fund will trade at the net asset value of $10,000, giving the investor a profit of $2,000.

The pitch would be fine if it were true, but it's not. It's normal for closed-end funds to trade at discounts, and because it is unlikely for them to rise to their NAV, it is unethical for brokers to suggest otherwise. It is also foolish to buy these funds on such assumptions.

Many closed-end funds invest in foreign countries, which means they face more risks than open-end stock funds, including both currency risk and — because they invest in only one country — sector risk.

Chapter 25 - Unit Investment Trusts

The final product created by the Investment Company Act of 1940 was the *Unit Investment Trust*. UITs were created to solve a problem faced by the Act's other two types of funds: the absence of a maturity date.

Remember that those who own individual bonds can avoid interest rate risk simply by holding their bonds until maturity, at which time they will receive back 100% of their investment, regardless of the current level of interest rates.

But owners of the Act's first two investments (mutual funds and closed-end funds) do not have that luxury. Because they own funds containing hundreds of bonds instead of individual bonds themselves, there is no single maturity date. Thus, when one of the bonds in the portfolio matures, the portfolio manager uses the money to buy another bond. Therefore, open-end and closed-end funds never mature, and the only way to get your money back is to sell your shares. This means you always are subject to interest rate risk.

This problem is solved by UITs. Here, the manager buys hundreds of bonds, as do its fund cousins. But here, each bond is selected for similar maturity dates and interest rates. Thus, when a given bond matures or is called, your pro rata share of the proceeds is returned to you. Thus, while you can sell at any time (subject to interest rate risk as with the others), you also have the ability to wait for the UIT to mature.

That's the good news about UITs. The bad news is that while mutual funds and closed-end funds offer both the triple benefits of diversification, professional selection, *and* professional management, UITs feature *only* diversification and professional selection. There is no professional management, for once the bonds are purchased they simply are held until maturity.

Chapter 26 - Wrap Accounts

A relatively new invention, wrap accounts are an attempt to solve conflict of interest, one of the oldest problems on Wall Street. After all, since your broker earns a commission every time you trade, is he telling you to sell XYZ and buy ABC because it's good for you, or good for him? Investors lie awake at night fretting over this question.

Wall Street's first solution was private money management. Instead of taking recommendations from your broker, your broker would take instructions from a professional money manager, to whom you would pay a flat fee of 3% per year. The manager would issue buy/sell recommendations to your broker, who would execute the transactions as before.

This eliminated conflict of interest because the broker did not order trades but merely executed them, and since the money manager earned the same fee whether he ordered many trades or few, he had no incentive to trade unnecessarily.

But this solution created a new problem: In addition to paying your broker 3% per year for executing trades, you were now *also* paying 3% to your money manager. You had to earn 6% just to break even!

Enter the *wrap account*.

Introduced in the early 1980s and now available at virtually every brokerage and planning firm in the country, wrap accounts offer the same private management and trade execution as before — but now for just half the cost. (Typically, the manager gets 60% of the fee, and the brokerage firm shares the remaining 40% with the broker.)

The minimum account size is $100,000, although competition is starting to lower that figure, and investors with large amounts often can negotiate lower fees. Today, nearly $100 billion is invested in wrap accounts, and four brokerage firms have 60% of the market:

- Smith Barney   29%
- Merrill Lynch   18%
- Paine Webber   7%
- Prudential   6%

Wrap accounts make sense for the same reason that mutual funds do: Most investors would be foolish to try investing on their own because of their lack of experience, knowledge, or the time that's required to achieve success. It's often equally foolish to blindly accept the recommendations of a stockbroker, who often is little more than a salesperson on commission. (Remember, stockbrokers are hired by brokerage firms to *sell*, not to *analyze*, and asking most brokers to manage a stock portfolio is like asking a car salesperson to repair a transmission.)

But asking your broker to help you find qualified managers, whether they work at a private money management firm or a mutual fund, makes perfect sense. In fact, placing your money with a private manager is no different than using a mutual fund: After all, who do you think manages a mutual fund? A money manager, of course! And just as private managers pay brokers and planners part of their fees to bring them business, funds do as well.

Of course, there are differences between funds and private managers. For one thing, you can't brag to your friends on the golf course that you, *humph*, "hired" a mutual fund. After all, any soul with a hundred bucks can do that. But private managers require a minimum of $100,000, so the mere mention that you've hired a manager carries with it the implicit statement that you're, *ahem*, RICH!! And while mutual funds simply send you quarterly statements in the mail, private managers often give you a gold-embossed leather binder with your name on it. *Wah hoo!* If you're lucky, they may even buy you dinner. *Hubba Hubba!*

But aside from these differences, you'd be hard pressed to find any other material differences between so-called "private" managers and those who manage regular ol' mutual funds.

The Wrap vs. Fund Debate

If there's little difference, why are firms encouraging their brokers to sell wraps instead of funds?

The answer can be traced to the Crash of '87. Before then, wraps were little used. But investors in the Crash's aftermath, worrying whether stocks will continue to fall, *simply stopped trading*. (I'll bet you did, too, if you owned stocks back then.)

And what happened when investors stopped trading? Brokers and their firms stopped earning commissions! This soon plunged the nation's brokerage firms into a severe recession, well ahead of the rest of the country.

But brokers who had placed clients into wrap accounts were sitting pretty. Although trading activity was reduced dramatically, the wraps were still earning their daily fee of 0.008219% (that's 3% per year).

Soon, all brokerage firms saw the light: By moving clients into wrap accounts, they were assured of collecting management fees whether clients traded or not, whether markets crashed or not. Indeed, fees have proved to be a much more stable source of revenue than commissions, and everyone on Wall Street is jumping on the bandwagon.

If you don't believe me, try this little test: Call a brokerage firm and ask the receptionist to connect you to the best broker in the firm. He'll say okay, then connect you to the *Broker of the Day* (the one randomly assigned to receive all incoming calls that day). When the Broker of the Day answers, say, "I have $10,000 to invest in stocks for the long term. What do you suggest?"

Odds are high she'll recommend a stock mutual fund, since you can't buy many individual stocks with just ten grand. Ask her to mail you information, then hang up.

Thirty minutes later, ask a friend to do the same thing with the same firm. When they get connected to the same broker, have your friend say the following: "I have $100,000 to invest in stocks for the long term. What do you suggest?"

Odds are high that this same broker will now suggest a wrap account.

10 Reasons to Avoid Wrap Accounts

But if a fund was good enough for the client with $10,000, why is it not good enough for the one with $100,000? "Because mutual funds are for little investors," the broker will answer. "You don't need them when you've got large assets."

Yet just the opposite is true, because the more you invest, the less mutual funds cost (as we'll see a few pages from here). Therefore, it can be argued that *small* investors are the ones who are ill suited for funds, not *large* investors, because small investors pay higher fees.

Proponents of wrap accounts also claim that investors can influence a wrap manager's selection decisions. Thus, if you don't want to invest in tobacco companies, you can tell your manager to avoid those stocks. In a mutual fund, since your money is commingled with everyone else's, you do not have this opportunity.

But I don't see this as an advantage. After all, you're hiring the manager to buy stocks for you because you lack the expertise. Why, then, would you want to tell the manager what to include or exclude? It doesn't make sense!

If that weren't enough, here are eight more reasons why wrap accounts are not preferable to mutual funds:

1. **You can't easily track your performance** until your manager sends you a statement, something most do only four times a year. But mutual fund prices are published in newspapers every day, making your monitoring efforts much easier;

2. **The paperwork and tax reporting requirements are huge.** Every time your manager buys or sells a stock, you get a confirmation in the mail. This makes for one elaborate IRS Schedule D when you prepare your tax return, too. Mutual fund owners do not have these problems;

3. **The fees you pay are not always tax deductible.** You must itemize the fees you pay in a wrap account as a miscellaneous deduction on Schedule A, and deductibility is allowed only to the extent that total Schedule A expenses exceed 2% of

your Adjusted Gross Income. As a practical matter, this means most investors cannot deduct their wrap fees. Mutual fund owners do not have this problem because all fund fees are built into the NAV; fund fees therefore not only are 100% tax-deductible, you get the deduction automatically when you report sales on Schedule D. Wrap account holders get nothing without a lot of work;

4. **There are no standard reporting requirements for wrap accounts.** Although managers are supposed to comply with AIMR Performance Measurement Standards, they are not legally required to do so. Some managers report their performance before fees are deducted, while others report performance for only certain portfolios or clients. Both tactics distort the truth, and investors can find it difficult to compare one manager with another. This problem does not exist for mutual funds, which follow standardized rules regarding value and performance calculations;

5. **Most wrap account managers fail to seek "best execution" on behalf of their clients, and the Securities and Exchange Commission is investigating.** By law, money managers have a fiduciary responsibility to the client, meaning they must place the client's interests ahead of all others. One obligation is to seek "best execution" for clients: Managers by law must execute trades with the brokers who offer the lowest commissions. But this rarely happens; Managers almost always place their trades with the broker who brought them the account.

   This coziness between manager and broker is very controversial, and the SEC is investigating. Furthermore, the SEC has noted that many wrap accounts are nothing more than "unregistered mutual funds," and it has proposed rules that will force many wrap accounts to either substantially change the way they operate or get out of business;

6. **You get one heckuva lot of mail,** as your broker sends you paperwork every time a trade is executed in your account. You'd better keep, sort, and organize all of it if you hope to be able to prepare your taxes accurately;

7. **You must sign a contract** that could be difficult to terminate if you decide to cancel. Many contracts require you to pay hefty fees if you cancel, or levy other restrictions you don't find with mutual funds; and

8. **Wrap accounts are expensive.** Paying 3% per year is an exorbitant cost for professional advice — especially compared to mutual funds, as we'll see next.

Please think carefully before you invest in a wrap account.

Chapter 27 - Mutual Fund Charges and Expenses

All mutual funds charge an annual fee to their shareholders, called the *annual expense ratio*. While fees range from 0.2% of assets to 12%, most funds charge 1.5% to 2.5% each year. The annual expense ratio is assessed daily. Thus, if a fund's cost is 2% per year, the fund will deduct 0.005479% each day.

It is through this fee that funds recover their operational, administrative, and management costs, and while all fund investors pay the fee, most are unaware of it because the fee does not appear on client statements. To determine the fee, read page 2 of the fund's prospectus.

Because of the fee, a fund which reports a gain of 10% actually earned more than that. The reported return is *after* the annual expense ratio is deducted. All funds operate in this manner.

In a seminar last year, as I was discussing this subject, a woman in the audience strongly disagreed with me.

"I don't pay any fees in my mutual fund," she said.

And I replied, "You mean they work for free? They answer their phone, mail you information, and pay postage all at no charge?"

"That's right," she said. "I don't pay any fees for my funds. They're all no-load and they don't cost me a thing."

I hope you see her error: She was confusing *loads* with the annual fee. The two are separate, and it's the load that gets all the publicity. What, then, does *load* really mean?

The Four Types of Mutual Fund Loads

It's simple: The load refers not to the annual fee but to the *sales charge*, and there are four kinds.

Sales Charge #1: Front-End Load

Also known as Class A shares, you pay a fee when you invest, up front. Unlike the expense ratio, which is paid every year, a front-end load is paid only once, when you invest money. There is no fee for reinvesting dividends or capital gains, and you can withdraw your money at any time without charge (at the then-current value, of course, which may be higher or lower than the amount you invested). Although the legal maximum is 8.5%, virtually all equity funds charge 5.75% or less, and bond funds charge 4.75% or less.

> If you invest $100 in a Class A fund, you pay the load, and if you invest another $100 next month, you pay another load — but only on the new deposit; the money already in the account is not charged a second time.
>
> So don't bother trying to invest $100 today and $10,000 tomorrow, hoping to avoid the fee on the second deposit. That trick won't work. In fact, on Wall Street, no trick ever works — so please forget about trying to outclever the system. You won't succeed.

Furthermore, front-load funds offer several discounts:

- **Breakpoints** essentially are volume discounts; the more you invest, the lower the load. While an equity fund's maximum charge might be 5.75%, discounts often start at $25,000. Big discounts typically apply if you invest $100,000, $250,000, or $500,000, and most funds waive their loads entirely for those who invest $1 million or more.

- **Rights of Accumulation** give you a discount based on the total amount of money you invest not just in that fund, but in any fund in an entire fund family. Thus, if you are investing $5,000 in a fund but previously have invested $20,000 in other funds of the same family, you are entitled to the $25,000 discount level on the $5,000 investment you are making today. You also are permitted to add up all the investments made by members of your household for purposes of calculating the biggest ROA discount.

- **Letter of Intent.** If you open an account today with a small amount but plan to invest more within the next 13 months, you are entitled to the breakpoint today, thus giving you a discount on today's investment even though you have not yet invested enough money to actually qualify for it. (If you fail to fulfill your LOI, the fund will retroactively collect the higher fee from your account.)

- **Free transfers.** All fund families allow investors to move money between funds with no additional load (although a small transfer fee — and taxes — might apply) provided the money stays in the same family.

Five Common Broker Tricks

Federal rules require all front-end load mutual funds to automatically award the above discounts to investors. However, the higher the load, the higher your broker's commission. Therefore, make sure you're working with an ethical broker.

Trick #1: Splitting Registrations to Avoid Breakpoints

Instead of opening a joint account with husband and wife for $250,000, the broker opens two accounts, one in each name, for $125,000 each. This avoids the $250,000 breakpoint, meaning you pay a higher load and the broker gets a higher commission. *It's illegal.*

Trick #2: Failing to Award Rights of Accumulation

An investor who already has a large account in a fund family opens a new, small account for her children, but the broker fails to apply the discount to the new account, which you're entitled to by virtue of the existence of the larger account. *It's illegal.*

Trick #3: Failing to Disclose Letter of Intent Availability

A broker allows a client to open an account with a small amount, knowing that the client intends to add to the account within 13 months, but does not execute the trade with the proper LOI discount. *It's illegal.*

Trick #4: Recommending an Investment Amount Slightly Below a Breakpoint Level

A broker tells a client to invest $95,000 into a fund, failing to disclose that if the client were to invest just $5,000 more, the entire investment would receive the $100,000 discount level. (Quite often, due to the discounts, investing $100,000 can cost less than investing $95,000.) *It's illegal.*

Trick #5: Churning

This is when a broker encourages a client to sell a fund from one family for the purpose of buying a second fund from another family, without any economic or fundamental justification to support the recommendation. The broker simply wants the client to incur a second load, so he can earn a second commission. *It's illegal.*

If you think any of these tricks have been played on you, don't panic. Having once supervised a sales force of 63 stockbrokers, I can say that if indeed a mistake occurred, it's almost always an honest mistake. All you need to do is bring the matter to your broker's attention, and your account will be quickly corrected. If your broker does not cooperate, notify the branch manager or the fund directly. The law is on your side, and you'll have no problem getting it fixed. The last thing your broker wants is for you to contact the federal regulators, for any of the above violations could cost brokers their licenses.

*"The most dangerous untruths
are truths moderately distorted."*
—Georg Christoph Lichenberg

When Tricks are Really Treats

Furthermore, there can be very good reasons why it might appear you have overpaid when in fact your broker actually is working for your best interests. Indeed, as an arbitrator with the NASD, I can assure you that what might appear to be a rule violation often turns out to be a generally-accepted practice which is acceptable to regulators. Two common examples include offering funds from several families and recommending that a client move assets from one fund family to another.

Such recommendations could make sense when the advisor determines that a client needs to place some assets into, say, both a bond fund and a stock fund. No one fund family offers the best funds in all asset classes, so most advisors recommend funds from several families when recommending several funds.

Although this might deprive you of the discounts that may be available through Rights of Accumulation, the recommendation nonetheless can be acceptable, for it emphasizes *performance* over *fees*. After all, higher costs certainly are worthwhile if it reasonably can be expected to produce a higher return. If your broker or planner instead placed primary emphasis on the *family* instead of the *fund*, you might wind up with second-best (or worse) funds.

Just as Ford gave us both Mustangs and Edsels, fund families have their winners and losers. No single fund family has the best funds in every category. So to get the best funds, you often must choose funds from different families, and while this strategy might increase cost, it also can result in higher profits.

Sales Charge #2: Back-End Load

Also known as rear-load, reverse load, or Class B shares, these funds don't charge you a load when you invest. Instead, reverse loads collect their money in two ways:

- A 12(b)1 fee, named after the rule that allows it, is usually 0.75% per year. In most funds, this extra fee vanishes after seven years; and

- A surrender fee on withdrawals, typically 5% or 6% in the first year and declining 1% per year until it vanishes in the 6th or 7th year. Each deposit receives its own "clock."

Technically called a *contingent deferred sales charge*, reverse load funds offer several features to minimize the fee. For example:

- you are permitted to withdraw dividends and capital gains at any time with no charge;

- many funds allow you to withdraw each year up to 12% of your investment at no charge; and

- for liquidations beyond these amounts, the fund assumes you are withdrawing the oldest shares first, thus paying the lowest fee possible.

> Here's an example of how the CDSC might work: Say you invest $1,000 and after three years the fund has grown to $1,100.[15] If in that third year you were to withdraw $600, the first $100 of the withdrawal would be at no charge, because the surrender fee does not apply to profits. The remaining $500 would be subject to a 3% fee (the surrender charge in the third year). Thus, your total cost for withdrawing $600 in this example is $15.

Sales Charge #3: Level-Load

Also known as Class C shares, these do not charge a front-load or a back-load. Instead, the fund adds a 12(b)1 fee, usually 0.75% per year. Unlike Class B shares, where this extra fee disappears after seven years, Class C shares maintain this additional cost as part of the fund's annual expense ratio, for as long as you own the fund. Although the total annual fee is no higher than the reverse load, there is typically only a 1% surrender fee which disappears after 12 months.

> Many funds which claim to be "no load" are not. Ignore the advertising and look carefully at the prospectus to see if loads exist.

Sales Charge #4: No-Load

In these funds, you don't pay a front-end, reverse, or level load.

---

[15]Okay, that would be a lousy fund. But work with me here, people.

Comparing Loads

For comparison, figures 5-11 and 5-12 ignore taxes and assume equal annual expense ratios and a 10% annual return for 10 years.

COMPARING FEES

No-Load Method

Year	Amount	Sales Charge NONE	Net Invested	10% Growth	12(b)1 Fee (none)	Ending Value	Surrender Fee (if applicable)
1	$10,000	-	$10,000	$1,000	-	$11,000	-
2	$11,000	-	$11,000	$1,100	-	$12,100	-
3	$12,100	-	$12,100	$1,210	-	$13,310	-
4	$13,310	-	$13,310	$1,331	-	$14,641	-
5	$14,641	-	$14,641	$1,464	-	$16,105	-
6	$16,105	-	$16,105	$1,611	-	$17,716	-
7	$17,716	-	$17,716	$1,772	-	$19,487	-
8	$19,487	-	$19,487	$1,949	-	$21,436	-
9	$21,436	-	$21,436	$2,144	-	$23,579	-
10	$23,579	-	$23,579	$2,358	-	$25,937	-

Front End-Load Method

Year	Amount	Sales Charge 4.75%	Net Invested	10% Growth	12(b)1 Fee (none)	Ending Value	Surrender Fee (if applicable)
1	$10,000	($475)	$9,525	$953	-	$10,478	-
2	$10,478	-	$10,478	$1,048	-	$11,525	-
3	$11,525	-	$11,525	$1,153	-	$12,678	-
4	$12,678	-	$12,678	$1,268	-	$13,946	-
5	$13,946	-	$13,946	$1,395	-	$15,340	-
6	$15,340	-	$15,340	$1,534	-	$16,874	-
7	$16,874	-	$16,874	$1,687	-	$18,562	-
8	$18,562	-	$18,562	$1,856	-	$20,418	-
9	$20,418	-	$20,418	$2,042	-	$22,459	-
10	$22,459	-	$22,459	$2,246	-	$24,705	-

FIGURE 5-10

COMPARING FEES

Rear-Load Method

Year	Amount	Sales Charge NONE	Net Invested	10% Growth	12(b)1 Fee (0.75%)	Ending Value	Surrender Fee (if applicable)
1	$10,000	-	$10,000	$1,000	($83)	$10,918	($500)
2	$10,918	-	$10,918	$1,092	($90)	$11,919	($400)
3	$11919	-	$11,919	$1,192	($98)	$13,013	($300)
4	$13,013	-	$13,013	$1,301	($107)	$14,207	($200)
5	$14,207	-	$14,207	$1,421	($117)	$15,510	($100)
6	$15,510	-	$15,510	$1,551	($128)	$16,933	-
7	$16,933	-	$16,933	$1,693	($140)	$18,487	-
8	$18,487	-	$18,487	$1,849	-	$20,336	-
9	$20,336	-	$20,336	$2,034	-	$22,369	-
10	$22,369	-	$22,369	$2,237	-	$24,606	-

Level-Load Method

Year	Amount	Sales Charge NONE	Net Invested	10% Growth	12(b)1 Fee (0.75%)	Ending Value	Surrender Fee (if applicable)
1	$10,000	-	$11,000	$1,000	($83)	$10,918	($100)
2	$10,890	-	$11,979	$1,089	($90)	$11919	-
3	$11,859	-	$13,045	$1,186	($98)	$13,013	-
4	$12,915	-	$14,206	$1,291	($107)	$14,207	-
5	$14,064	-	$15,470	$1,406	($117)	$15,510	-
6	$15,316	-	$16,847	$1,532	($128)	$16,933	-
7	$16,679	-	$18,347	$1,668	($140)	$18,487	-
8	$18,163	-	$19,980	$1,816	($153)	$20,183	-
9	$19,780	-	$21,758	$1,978	($167)	$22,035	-
10	$21,540	-	$23,694	$2,154	($182)	$24,056	-

FIGURE 5-11

As you can see, the results are as follows:

Year	Value After 10 Years
No-Load	$25,937
Front-Load	$24,705
Rear-Load	$24,606
Level-Load	$24,056

It's clear from this example that, all others factors being equal,[16] the no-load fund is the most profitable choice. But of the remaining three, which is best?

WHICH TYPE OF LOAD PRODUCES THE HIGHEST PROFITS?

Clearly, there's not much difference among them, but if you think the front load fund is best, beware: We're looking at 10-year results. If you examine different time intervals, the answer changes.

	The Most Profitable	Middle	The Least Profitable
1	Level	Front	Rear
2	Level	Front	Rear
3	Level	Rear	Front
4	Level	Rear	Front
5	Level	Rear	Front
6	Rear/Level (tie)		Front
7	Rear/Level (tie)		Front
8	Front	Rear	Level
9	Front	Rear	Level
10	Front	Rear	Level

FIGURE 5-12

[16]And they never are.

193

As you can see, "best" is determined by how long you stay invested. Since we don't know how long that will be (despite your intentions), it is impossible to tell which share class (A, B, or C) will prove best for you. Because the differences are so small, and because you really can't be sure how long your money will stay invested, simply choose the version you like best; the economic difference between the three versions is so slight you needn't worry about making the "wrong" choice.

> It is inappropriate to ask a stockbroker for advice regarding no-load funds. By doing so, you're asking the broker to work for free, and that's rude: If you ask a waiter to bring you food, you had better be prepared to pay for the service — regardless of how the food tastes. (If you don't want to pay the service charge, go to a fast food joint and save the 15%.)

Why Pay a Load at All?

But let's return to the bigger question: Since the no-load clearly is best, regardless of how long you invest, how can you explain the fact that 78% of all mutual fund owners buy load funds?

Many people think — and lots of brokers argue — that paying a load is worthwhile because load funds earn higher returns, which more than compensate you for the fees you incur.

Nice theory, but dead wrong.

The truth is that *loads have absolutely no effect* on investment performance. The 1995 *Forbes* Honor Roll list of the best mutual funds contains 8 no-load funds and 12 loads, and the book "*The 100 Best Mutual Funds You Can Buy*" contains 40 no-loads and 60 loads.

Loads do not affect performance because the load is merely a marketing expense.

Remember we talked about the manufacturing process? All products must be sold — even (especially?) mutual funds — and funds accomplish this in various ways. Some families distribute their funds through stockbrokers, whom they compensate by paying commissions. Such funds charge loads — up front, reverse, or level — which they in turn give to the broker. (You could bypass the broker when buying A, B, or C shares by going directly to the fund, but you'll still pay the fee because it is assessed by the fund, not the broker.)

No-loads sell their products via advertising in newspapers, magazines, and direct mail. This is why they do not charge a load: By selling directly to investors, they skip the broker and hence the load they would have paid him or her.

Buying a load fund from a broker is the same as buying an airline ticket from a travel agent. Whichever way you buy your ticket, the price is the same. When you let a travel agent place the order for you, the airline rebates a portion of the ticket price to the agent, just as load funds rebate a portion of the load to the broker.

If air fares are the same, why not buy directly from the airline? Because the travel agent knows you like aisle seats and non-smoking hotel rooms near the elevator. He'll help you find the best route, handle reservations, and even courier your tickets to you — all for free! Hotels, car rental companies, and airlines pay travel agents to perform these services — so they don't have to! But either way, using or not using a travel agent will have no effect on your air fare, nor on whether your plane leaves on time.

Just as tickets bought from travel agents can't determine the quality of the flight, paying loads won't get you a better fund. There is, in fact, only one legitimate reason for paying loads: to provide compensation to the person assisting you.

In accepting this compensation, your advisor (whether a stockbroker, financial planner or other advisor) cannot promise performance. But she can promise — and you should demand — a high level of service. In addition to helping you select funds that are appropriate for you, your broker should monitor them for you and advise you when you should sell due to changes either in the economy or in your personal circumstances. Your advisor should handle all record-keeping and tax-reporting for you as well.

In fact, the Mutual Fund Forum, a trade organization representing load mutual funds, says a professional advisor will:

- understand individual financial needs and help investors formulate long-term investment goals and objectives;

- help the investor develop realistic expectations by discussing the risks and rewards of investing;

- match individual goals and objectives of the investor with appropriate mutual funds;

- continually monitor the individual's mutual fund portfolio and keep the investor apprised of any pertinent changes;

- conduct a regular review of the investor's financial status to ensure proper positioning of the mutual fund portfolio; and

- help investors "stay the course" of their long-term investment programs.

If you are not receiving these services, then you're not getting what you're really paying for. (For more on choosing an advisor, see Part XII.)

Thus, if you know how to analyze and select funds, and if you have the time and ability to monitor them and handle your own tax reporting, then you probably should buy a no-load fund. In fact, that's who no-loads are for: the do-it-yourselfer, because in practice, "no load" really means "no help."

Assuming you work with an advisor, it doesn't really matter whether you choose Class A, B, or C, for the economic difference is statistically insignificant over time. The choice basically is whether you want to pay when you buy, pay (maybe) when you sell, or pay a little bit annually.

This is why loads are irrelevant to investment performance: Funds hire portfolio managers to manage their assets, and these managers are not concerned about whether a given fund is load or no-load. Such issues are marketing decisions, not investment management issues.

As Michael Lipper of Lipper Analytical Services, a major mutual funds rating organization, told *Business Week:* "If it's a period shorter than five years, I'd pay attention to the sales charge. If it's beyond five years, I would look at it but not be terribly influenced."

Chapter 28 - Annuities

How you would like to invest in mutual funds without paying taxes each year on the profits you earn? Enter the *variable annuity* — the best product since mutual funds.

Here's how it works: Instead of opening a mutual fund account, you turn to an insurance company, which sponsors variable annuities. Each annuity offers "subaccounts" managed by a mutual fund family. These subaccounts closely mimic the fund family's mutual funds, and you can choose the ones you want.

Variable annuities derive their name from the fact that the return you earn *varies* with the performance of the subaccounts you choose. If you choose the stock subaccount, your account will rise and fall with the stock market; if you invest in the bond subaccount, your account will reflect the performance of the bond market.

The Power of Tax-Deferred Growth

Why bother inserting an insurance company as middleman? Because under current tax law, money placed in an insurance contract grows *tax-deferred*, meaning you don't pay taxes on your earnings until you withdraw your money. And money that grows tax-deferred grows more quickly than money that is taxed annually, as Figure 5-13 demonstrates.

THE POWER OF TAX DEFERRED GROWTH

$50,000 invested at 8% assuming a 28% tax bracket and full withdrawal after 30 years.

value after lump-sum withdrawal
value before withdrawal ⇨

$600,000
$400,000
$200,000
$0

5yrs 10yrs 15yrs 20yrs 25yrs 30yrs After-Tax Value

☐ Earnings Taxed Annually at 28%
■ Earnings Not Taxed Until Withdrawal

FIGURE 5-13

Annuity marketers love to produce charts like 5-13, but there's a big difference between theirs and the one you see here: They always compare the tax-deferred's high point of $503,000 with the taxable's end value of $268,295. But this is an apples-to-oranges comparison, for the taxable investment is net of taxes while the tax-deferred is not. They like to brag that the tax-deferred investment produces a net profit 906% higher than the taxable investment, but that's not true. After paying the taxes that have been deferred, the after-tax profit is $326,256, meaning that the true increase in profit is 653%, not 906%.

Still, this remains a solid improvement and confirms that annuities are worthy of investment, but it's not quite as dramatic as annuity marketers would lead you to believe. That's why you must never take charts and statistics at face value (even those in this book!). Be sure to examine who's behind the numbers, and what their agenda might be.

Should You Defer Taxes Even If You Expect Rates to Rise?

Many investors question the viability of tax-deferred strategies, given today's relatively low tax rates. Besides (knowing Congress), rates could well rise over time. Therefore, why defer paying taxes when future tax rates will be higher?

That's a valid question, and the answer is this: Even if rates rise, tax-deferral remains a winner. Look at Figure 5-14, which assumes $100,000 is invested at 10% annual interest for 10 years. This example assumes that tax rates will rise during this period, from 30% to 50%.

In this example, the taxable account pays taxes annually while the tax-deferred account defers taxes. If you completely liquidate both accounts in the 10th year, the net value of the taxable account (which paid taxes at ever-increasing rates each year) would be $174,026, while the tax-deferred investment (which paid no taxes during the 10 years but then paid all its taxes at the top rate of 50%) has a net after-tax value of $179,687 — $5,661 *more* than the taxable account. Thus, the tax-deferred annuity comes out (slightly) ahead.

CATHY CATHY GUISEWITE

WHY DEFER TAXES IF RATES ARE LIKELY TO RISE?

$100,000 invested at 10% for 10 years in a rising tax rate environment

Year	Tax Rate	Value of Taxable Account	After-Tax Yield	Value of Tax-Deferred Account	After-Tax Yield
1	30%	107,000	7.0%	110,000	10%
2	30%	114,490	7.0%	121,000	10%
3	35%	121,931	6.5%	133,100	10%
4	40%	129,246	6.0%	146,410	10%
5	45%	136,354	5.5%	161,051	10%
6	50%	143,171	5.0%	177,156	10%
7	50%	150,330	5.0%	194,817	10%
8	50%	157,846	5.0%	214,353	10%
9	50%	165,739	5.0%	235,794	10%
10	50%	174,026	5.0%	259,374	10%

If you withdraw a lump sum:

Gross Value of Tax Deferred Fund	$259,374
Original Principal	$100,000
Taxable Profit	$159,374
Less 50% Tax	($ 79,687)

Net Value of Taxable Fund **$174,026**

Net Value of Tax-Deferred Fund **$179,687**

If you take a 10% income stream:

Net Value	$174,026		Net Value	$259,374
Income	x 10%		Income	x 10%
	17,400			25,937
Less 50% Tax	(8,701)		Less 50% Tax	(12,968)
Net Annual Income	$8,701		Net Annual Income	$12,968

FIGURE 5-14

199

But this assumes you liquidate in the 10th year — and that's highly unlikely. More likely: You'll want to receive income from the investment on a regular basis. Assuming you withdraw 10% per year from the current balance, you'll receive from the taxable account (after paying taxes) $8,701, but the tax-deferred investment will give you $12,968 — *a 49% increase in after-tax income* compared to the taxable account!

No matter how you calculate it, tax deferral makes a lot of sense, and the power of tax-deferred annuities can't be ignored.

Variable annuities are a great deal — so great, in fact, that Congress is losing tens of millions of dollars in tax revenue, because many who otherwise would invest in mutual funds are buying annuities instead. For this reason, I expect Congress to disallow them before the end of the decade.

It won't be the first time Congress has eliminated tax-favored investments: Single premium whole life was outlawed in 1982 and significant restrictions were placed on IRA contributions in 1986. In both cases, Congress allowed existing accountholders to keep their accounts; new accounts simply were forbidden (this is called *grandfathering*).

Thus, if annuities are right for you, you should buy them while you can.

An Investment That Can Rise But Never Fall

If tax-deferral isn't enough, how would you like to invest knowing your account can only rise, never fall? Sound intriguing? Here's how it works:

Say you place $100,000 into a variable annuity, choosing the annuity's stock subaccount. Let's further say your timing isn't exactly wonderful: The day after you invest, a major stock market crash cuts the value of your account to $75,000.

If you withdraw the $75,000, you'd lose $25,000. Instead, you should withdraw $74,000, leaving $1,000 in the account. The reason: The annuity guarantees to give you:

- what you invested minus withdrawals, or

- the current value,

whichever is greater.

Your investment ($100,000) minus withdrawals ($74,000) is $26,000; The current value is $1,000. Therefore, the insurance carrier owes your beneficiary the greater of the two, or $26,000.

Variable annuities also periodically reset the minimum value of your investment for purposes of calculating the above. In other words, every five or seven years or so, the annuity carrier will set the *current value* as the *new minimum* below which you cannot fall.

Thus, if you invest $100,000 and it later grows to $150,000, the latter amount becomes the basis for the minimum guarantee. It the account later falls to $125,000, the contract guarantees you the $150,000 value.

One Piece of Fine Print

How do you benefit from this can't-lose guarantee? It's easy: All you have to do is **DIE!**

Remember, the guarantee is from an *insurance company!* So although this guarantee is excellent, it comes with, um, a fairly significant piece of fine print.

Thus, most folks should not be impressed with this "no-loss" guarantee, but for some people it is worthwhile. Take elderly retirees with lots of money in CDs, for example. Such folks are not spending all their money and they know they never will. Rather, they intend to leave their money to their grandchildren for college.

Because they want nothing to happen to their money, the grandparents put everything into CDs. They should consider an annuity's stock subaccount instead: Because of the no-loss guarantee, the worst thing that could happen is that the account will be worth at their death exactly what it is worth today, even if the stock market crashes in the meantime. But assuming stocks perform as well in the future as they have in the past, the account should be worth substantially more than if they invest the money in CDs.

Fixed Annuities

Some people don't like the "variable-ness" of annuities. They want the security of a fixed rate of return, like they get from CDs. To meet this demand, insurers offer *fixed annuities*.

Check out these ads (I've hidden the names), which appeared in trade magazines read by insurance agents. In both cases, agents earn higher commissions than the investors earn in

interest! The annuity on the left pays agents a 10% commission, while the annuity on the right pays 8.5% — plus *free steaks! Variable annuity sponsors don't play these ridiculous games.*

As much as I love variable annuities, I hate fixed annuities. Under the law, fixed annuities are considered insurance products and are sold by insurance agents. Variable annuities, on the other hand, are considered securities products, and those who offer them must possess both a federal securities license and a state variable life license. This subtlety makes all the difference.

Under insurance law, money you give to an insurance company is commingled with the general assets of that company. Thus, if the carrier goes broke, your money is lost with it. But because variable annuities fall under federal securities rules, money you invest in a variable annuity is segregated from the assets of the insurance carrier. Thus, even if the insurance company goes broke, your money remains safe.

> **If you insist on buying a fixed annuity, buy a variable annuity instead and select the fixed subaccount. You'll get the fixed return you want and the safety you need.**

Remember when Executive Life of California Insurance Company went broke? People who owned its fixed annuities received letters saying they might never get their money back. People who owned Executive Life's variable annuities, however, were not affected by the carrier's troubles. Not only did their money remain available, it continued to grow in value. That's a big difference in safety. That's why I don't like to recommend fixed annuities.

In fact, the only people who do routinely recommend fixed annuities are insurance agents who are not licensed to sell variable annuities.

How to Move Fixed Annuities to Variable Annuities

If you own an annuity and want to know whether it is fixed or variable, try one of the following:

- Call your agent and ask.

- Call your insurance company and ask.

- Look at your contract for the word "fixed" or "variable." You'll find one or the other.

- Look at your most current statement. If it says you will earn a specific rate of interest over the next several months or year, you have a fixed annuity.

If you discover that your annuity is fixed, you easily can transfer the money inside it to a variable annuity with no tax consequences by executing a *Section 1035 Exchange*. This section of the tax code allows tax-free exchanges between annuities, provided the assets are transferred directly from one insurance company to another.

To execute a 1035 exchange, simply sign a form available from any variable annuity carrier. Be aware that although 1035 exchanges avoid tax liabilities, you might incur a withdrawal fee for leaving the fixed annuity. Contact your fixed annuity carrier to be certain, or ask the insurance agent who sold it to you.

Annuity Charges and Expenses

Almost all annuities are offered on a Class B basis, as discussed in Chapter 27, although some Class C versions are being introduced.

The IRS has a say, too. In exchange for not taxing you each year, any withdrawals you make prior to age 59½ are subject to a 10% IRS penalty. Thus, annuities are intended as long-term investments.

This applies to both fixed and variable annuities. In addition, variable annuities also incur the following expenses:

- **an annual contract fee** which ranges typically from $30 to $75 per year, depending on the size of your account;

- **the annual expense ratio** of the subaccount. Since variable annuities are managed by mutual fund families, you'll incur their annual costs as well (see Chapter 26); and

- **an annual mortality charge** of 1% to 2% per year to compensate the insurer for the death benefit guarantee it provides.

Because of the additional costs, many assume they will earn more in mutual funds than in annuities. But consider the following:

- you must pay taxes **annually** on the profits you earn in a mutual fund, but you don't with the annuity. This tax-deferral can more than compensate for the additional cost, as long as you keep the variable annuity for five years or more;

- **you can lose money in the mutual fund,** but the annuity offers a minimum guarantee. Thus, you receive a benefit in exchange for the additional cost; and

- perhaps most importantly, **the assumption itself has not always proven valid.** In 1991, for example, Lipper Analytical Services reported that, net of all costs, the average stock mutual fund gained 35.21%, while the average variable annuity stock subaccount gained 36.25%. Thus, the annuity average actually *beat* the fund average by 1.04%, defying expectations of reduced performance. (There are several theories as to how this occurred. I favor the theory that people who invest in annuities, considering their surrender fees and tax penalties, do so for the long term. Thus, redemption requests are minimal, and the subaccount managers know it. Therefore, while mutual funds must keep a portion of their assets in cash to handle redemption requests, annuity managers can invest a higher percentage of the annuity's assets. By putting more of the money to work, they can earn more — thus helping to compensate for the higher costs.)

Warning: Annuities Contain Two Tax Traps

There are two tax traps with annuities that you must beware:

Annuity Tax Trap #1: Withdrawals are Income

If you liquidate an annuity or receive income from it, the proceeds are taxed at ordinary income tax rates, as opposed to the potentially more favorable capital gains tax rates.

Annuity Tax Trap #2: No Step-Up in Basis

This will affect your children more than you: Annuities do not enjoy a stepped-up basis at death, which we discussed in Chapter 15. This means your children could incur significant tax liabilities — equal, in fact, to the tax savings you enjoyed during your lifetime. The bottom line is that the tax break provided by annuities is *deferral*, not *exemption*. *Someone* (eventually) will pay taxes on the profits you earn in your annuity — if not you, then your heirs.

In my experience, most clients are unconcerned by this, or rather, they are more concerned (and rightfully so) in ensuring that they will have sufficient income throughout their lifetime. Possible adverse tax implications for heirs are a secondary consideration.

"There is nothing more demoralizing than a small but adequate income."
—Edmund Wilson

Chapter 29 - Real Estate Limited Partnerships

As discussed earlier, real estate should be part of your overall investment mix. Unfortunately, it requires a lot of cash and can cause considerable headaches from The Hassle Factor (see Chapter 18).

These concerns led to the creation of limited partnerships. It has been said that limited partnerships consist of investors who have the money and the general partner who has the experience. Later, the general partner has the money and investors have the experience.

Well, maybe not always. Certainly, a lot of people lost a lot of money through partnerships in the 1980s. This has led to the bad name given these products. But blaming investment losses on partnerships is like blaming the bottle for killing you instead of the poison you drank from it. The truth is that partnerships have been known to be profitable.

Partnerships are similar to closed-end funds: Rather than buying property on your own, you pool your money with other investors (known as limited partners), and a manager (the general partner) buys property, then manages and eventually sells the property, returning to investors their pro-rata share of the proceeds. Limited partnerships can be formed to buy any type of investment, such as oil wells or railroad cars, but most deal with real estate.

How did this simple concept cause so many people to lose so much money? As with most strategies, there was nothing wrong with the concept; It was the *implementation* that ruined the deal. To see how partnerships work, and what went wrong, let's return to the late 1970s.

A Trip Through Time

Have you ever noticed that physicians often work in the same building? Here's why: Doctor Billem needed office space. So, he formed a partnership with 19 other physicians, each putting up $50,000 ($1 million total); Each owned 5% of the partnership. The partnership is *limited* because Dr. Billem's liability is limited to his $50,000 investment. (Unlike a *general partnership*, where all partners have unlimited personal liability for any losses the partnership incurs.)

Actually, the doctor didn't put up $50,000 in cash. Instead, he got a bank loan at 10% interest (a $5,000 annual cost). The partnership, flush with $1 million raised from the doctors, then borrowed an additional $1 million from the bank. With $2 million, the partnership bought land and erected a building, and the doctor, with only $5,000 cash-out-of-pocket, now owns a 5% interest in the partnership, valued at $100,000.

During the two years it takes to complete the building, the partnership spends most (maybe all) of its money in construction costs. These losses pass through the partnership to the partners (including Dr. Billem), who claim the losses on their tax returns. Thus, over two years, he spends $10,000 in loan interest payments but gets perhaps $70,000 in tax deductions. At his 70% marginal tax bracket, this saves him $49,000 in federal income taxes. Not bad for a $10,000 investment.

And it gets better. When the building is complete, Dr. Billem moves in. As a tenant, he pays rent to the partnership, and since rent is a routine office expense, it is tax-deductible. Furthermore, as one of the building's owners, he receives his rent back as a cash distribution from the partnership — tax-free due to interest and depreciation allowances.

Thus, Dr. Billem pays rent and gets a tax break on one hand, and gets his money back — along with a second tax break — on the other hand. Not too shabby!

The Tax Reform Act of 1986 killed all these games. But in doing so, the Act didn't simply tell partners such as Dr. Billem that they weren't allowed to build more buildings in this fashion. No, the Act changed the rules *retroactively*. Thus, the tax deductions Dr. Billem had previously taken were reclaimed, so that back taxes were due in full — with interest and penalties. Dr. Billem went from owning a shrewd investment to owing hundreds of thousands of dollars!

And all the other real estate investors got skinned with him. Before TRA, developers who wanted to borrow billions to erect buildings (not knowing if anyone would move in, and not caring either, since the tax savings were worth five or six times their investment), found money readily available from banks. Tenants were irrelevant in this game, and the banks knew it.

But when the tax law changed, these builders found themselves with buildings they couldn't fill — and losses they couldn't deduct. With no tenants, the builders had no rental income, and with no income, they couldn't make their loan payments. The banks foreclosed.

But banks don't want buildings. They're in the banking business, after all, not the real estate business. They want cash so they in turn can pay interest to their depositors. Forced to foreclose on defunct developers, the banks became reluctant owners of see-through buildings (so-called because without any tenants you could see in one window and out the other side), and banks started to lose money themselves.

This (admittedly oversimplified) explains the S&L crisis of the '80s.

The problem was not the partnerships, nor was it real estate. Rather, the problems were caused by investors borrowing too much money and relying too heavily on tax benefits instead of pure economics. Through *leverage* Dr. Billem borrowed $100,000 he didn't have, and his profits were dependent on tax law.

Unfortunately, as he learned too late, there is nothing natural about tax law. *What Congress giveth, Congress may taketh away.*

As with all packaged products, the key to success is not found in the product packaging but in the underlying asset. If you want to own real estate but don't have enough money to buy your own, partnerships can be acceptable alternatives — if done correctly.

What To Do If You Own a Busted Partnership

If you own a partnership that has gone bust, guess what you need?

Another partnership! Under the Tax Reform Act of 1986, partnership losses are considered *passive*, which you cannot deduct against *active* income, such as income from your job. So, you need to buy another partnership that generates *passive income*, to use to offset your passive losses. Such partnerships are called PIGs, for *passive income generator.*

Try telling people who've lost money in one partnership that what they need is another one! It's not the sort of recommendation that usually goes over very well.

Chapter 30 - Real Estate Investment Trusts

REITs (pronounced reets) are similar to partnerships, with one major difference: REITS trade on the New York Stock Exchange, allowing investors to buy and sell whenever they want. Investors in limited partnerships can't do this; Once you invest in an LP, you can't get your money back until the general partner sells the properties (which won't happen for 10 years or more).

So the good news is that REITs are liquid. But that's also the bad news. For *being able* to sell means investors *do* sell. The result: Shares in REITS trade with the same volatility as stocks. In the Crash of '87, for example, REITS lost 30% of their value just like the stocks trading on the NYSE.

If you think about it, it was illogical for REITS to fall during the Crash. After all, REITS invest in real estate, not stocks. But when investors are panicking, logic has no place. So investors who choose real estate to divorce themselves from the volatility of the stock and bond markets quickly discover that REITS fail to achieve that objective.

The bottom line is that while you should invest in real estate, we have found no truly efficient, effective way to do so. Be aware of the problems of each method, choose the version that you regard to be the "least evil" and invest only a small percentage of your total assets in this asset class.

Part VI
The Best Investment Strategies

Part VI — The Best Investment Strategies

Overview - Combining Growth and Income

Up to this point, I've focused on teaching you how different kinds of investments work, including their risks and fees. Now we're going to focus on how to develop successful investment strategies using those investments. By the end of this part, you'll be able to answer the two most difficult questions all investors ask: Where should I invest my money, and when is the best time to invest?

Chapter 31 - Safe or Risky?

If you were to put your 6-year-old's education fund entirely into one investment, knowing that your child will not be able to attend college if you lose the money, would you invest in the stock market?

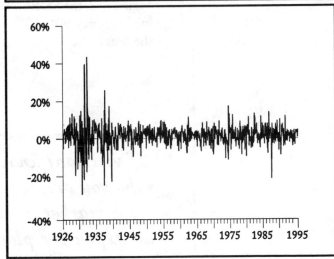

MONTHLY RETURNS OF THE S&P 500

FIGURE 6-1

Most people (including you, probably) would say "no" because the stock market seems so uncertain, risky, and volatile.

This attitude is supported by Figure 6-1, which displays the monthly performance of the S&P 500 Stock Index since 1926. Over the past 68 years (816 months), the market made money in only 60% of the months. Although these are good odds from a gambler's perspective, few parents would take such a "gamble" with their kid's college education.

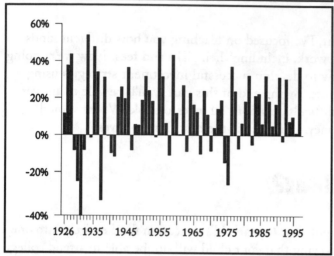

ANNUAL RETURNS OF THE S&P 500

FIGURE 6-2

But see in Figure 6-2 how the stock market did over one-year intervals: Stocks now made money 70% of the time. Is this success rate high enough for you to invest in stocks?

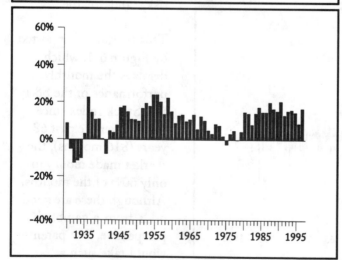

5 YEAR RETURNS OF THE S&P 500

FIGURE 6-3

How about five-year intervals? In the 64 rolling five-year periods since 1926, shown in Figure 6-3, the S&P 500 made money 90% of the time.

"If you don't know who you are, the stock market is an expensive place to find out."

—George Goodman

10 YEAR RETURNS OF THE S&P 500

FIGURE 6-4

15 YEAR RETURNS OF THE S&P 500

FIGURE 6-5

In every 10-year interval, the S&P 500 made money 96% of the time. In fact, in every 15-year interval and beyond, the stock market made money 100% of the time.

Yet most people don't see it this way. They fret over what the market is doing today, even though the market is focused on tomorrow. "Should I get in now or wait?" the multitudes ask. "If things are going well, I'll get in, but if things are going bad, I'll stay out." That attitude will cause you to lose lots of money, because as we will learn in Chapter 32, the stock market is focused on the future, not the present. Therefore, your investments must be based on where you're *going*, not on where you *are*.

Thus, the key is not *when* you invest in the stock market, nor *which* stocks you buy. The key is *how long* you invest. We can convert something as risky and uncertain as stocks into a safe, predictable investment.

217

Chapter 32 - World Events Will Not Destroy Your Investments

Those who focus on today's headlines always make bad investment decisions. The news is filled with doom and gloom, and as we hear about today's crisis, we develop a pessimistic attitude. That discourages us from investing.

Yet it can be argued that a time of crisis is exactly the best time to invest. Although this is the opposite of when people want to invest, history proves it is the best time. And since our nation is always suffering from one major crisis or another, it's always a great time to invest!

Indeed, as Figure 6-6 shows, markets consistently go up, despite the crisis du jour. In fact, from 1940 through 1995, the market went up 77% of the time — despite some pretty awful problems.

Yet most investors dismiss this logic and instead act emotionally. It's a recipe for investment disaster.

"Successful investing is anticipating the successful anticipations of others."
—John Keynes

WORLD EVENTS DO NOT DESTROY STOCKS

The S&P 500 Went Down in Only 13 Years Since 1940

Year	Event	S&P 500
1940	Germany invades France	-9.78%
1941	Pearl Harbor	-11.59
1942	Gas rationing begins	+20.34
1943	War escalates	+25.9
1944	Consumer good shortage	+19.75
1945	Roosevelt dies	+36.44
1946	Labor strife	-8.07
1947	Cold war begins	+5.71
1948	Berlin blockade	+5.5
1949	Russia explodes A-bomb	+18.79
1950	Korean conflict begins	+31.71
1951	Korean conflict	+24.02
1952	Government seizes mills	+18.37
1953	Russia explodes H-bomb	-0.99
1954	McCarthy hearings	+52.62
1955	Eisenhower falls ill	+31.56
1956	Suez canal crisis	+6.56
1957	Russia launches Sputnik	-10.78
1958	Recession	+43.36
1959	Castro seizes power	+11.96
1960	Russia downs spy plane	+0.47
1961	Berlin Wall erected	+26.89
1962	Cuban missile crisis	-8.73
1963	Kennedy assassinated	+22.8
1964	Gulf of Tonkin	+16.48
1965	Civil rights unrest	+12.45
1966	Vietnam war	-10.06
1967	Race riots	+23.98

Year	Event	S&P 500
1968	USS Pueblo seized	+11.06
1969	Japan is new economic power	-8.5
1970	N. Vietnam invades Cambodia	+4.01
1971	Wage and price freeze	+14.31
1972	Record US trade deficit	+18.98
1973	Mideast oil crisis. Long gas lines	-14.66
1974	Deep recession in US & Europe	-26.47
1975	Recession deepens	+37.2
1976	Gold prices plunge	+23.84
1977	Trade wars loom	-7.18
1978	Interest rates surge	+6.56
1979	Inflation & oil prices skyrocket	+18.44
1980	American hostages in Iran	+32.42
1981	High unemployment	-4.91
1982	Worst recession in 40 years	+21.41
1983	Interest rates fluctuate	+22.51
1984	Deficit goes over $200 billion	+6.27
1985	Record number of S&Ls fail	+32.16
1986	Tax Reform Act of 1986	+18.47
1987	Stock market tumbles	+5.23
1988	Fear of recession	+16.81
1989	Invasion of Panama	+31.49
1990	Iraq invades Kuwait	-3.17
1991	The Gulf War	+30.55
1992	Civil War in the Balkans	+7.67
1993	The Great Flood of 1993	+9.99
1994	Worst bond market ever	+1.31
1995	Oklahoma bombing	+37.43

FIGURE 6-6

Chapter 33 - Focus on the Hill, Not the String

People fear the stock market because stock prices are volatile. Prices can fall, and people fear falling.

Yet, this fear is misguided. By focusing on the daily ups and downs of the market, people forget the more important point: Stocks rise more than they fall. Imagine a boy walking up a steep hill while playing with a yo-yo.

If you focus on the yo-yo, you'll become obsessed with its wild gyrations — while ignoring the fact that the boy is steadily climbing higher. True, the yo-yo will always reach a low point, but each low point will be higher than the last low point, because the boy is now on higher ground. So it is with the stock market.

BORN LOSER ART SANSOM

Reprinted by permission of Newspaper Enterprise Association, Inc.

Chapter 34 - Understanding Volatility

Risk is the basis for volatility: Indeed, in its most elementary definition, "risk" simply refers to the degree to which the future value of your money may differ from the present value of your money. The greater the difference, the greater the risk. This difference is expressed by the term *volatility*.

A 30-day T-bill carries no volatility: One dollar invested in a T-bill always is worth one dollar. But one dollar invested in stocks can rise or fall dramatically. Therefore, stocks are considered to be much riskier than T-bills.

However, volatility is not a reason to *avoid* stocks any more than it is a reason to *own* them. Rather, volatility is merely a *characteristic* of stocks. Prices go up, and prices go down. And they do that a lot. As Figure 6-7 shows, the average spread since 1940 between the S&P 500's highest prices of the year and the lowest is 22.4%. That's extreme volatility. Yet all these gyrations have occurred on an upward slope. So, you need to focus not on the daily activity of the market, but on its long-term trend.

"According to my calculations, the stock market should go up, down, up, down, up, down, up, down, up, down, then up."

ANNUAL MARKET VOLATILITY OF THE S&P 500

Spread Between the Year's High and Low, 1940-1995

1940	34.7%	1959	12.5	1978	20.7
1941	25.9	1960	14.4	1979	14.6
1942	26.7	1961	23.2	1980	35.4
1943	24.9	1962	30.5	1981	20.2
1944	13.9	1963	17.9	1982	33.1
1945	28.9	1964	13.4	1983	22.1
1946	30.8	1965	12.7	1984	14.2
1947	16.7	1966	24.9	1985	25.7
1948	20.8	1967	19.3	1986	22.1
1949	21.4	1968	21.1	1987	40.3
1950	20.4	1969	17.4	1988	15.6
1951	14.2	1970	29.7	1989	26.6
1952	14.1	1971	15.0	1990	22.1
1953	16.0	1972	15.8	1991	29.0
1954	36.8	1973	26.4	1992	11.2
1955	29.2	1974	46.4	1993	9.3
1956	14.3	1975	30.9	1994	8.9
1957	23.0	1976	17.0	1995	32
1958	31.2	1977	16.9		

Avg: 22.4%

FIGURE 6-7

If you think 22.4% is a lot of fluctuation, remember that's just the *average*. For truly extreme volatility, look at the S&P during and after a *crisis*. As Figure 6-8 shows, in the five weeks following every major crisis since the Korean War, stocks dropped an average of 16%. At that rate, stocks would be completely wiped out in just eight months.

That's enough to scare anyone.

STOCKS DURING AND AFTER A CRISIS

Crisis	Drop in S&P 500	Next Six Months	Next Year
Korean War	15% in 5 weeks	31%	36%
Sputnik	10% in 3 weeks	8%	30%
Steel Price Roll Back	20% in 8 weeks	11%	24%
Liquidity Crisis	12% in 4 weeks	16%	42%
Arab Oil Embargo	17% in 9 weeks	-1%	-28%
Nixon Resignation	19% in 5 weeks	30%	27%
Hunt Silver Crisis	12% in 4 weeks	26%	29%
Financial Panic	26% in 3 weeks	7%	16%
Gulf War	12% in 3 weeks	11%	25%
Average	**16% in 5 weeks**	**15%**	**22%**

FIGURE 6-8

But if those crises caused you to sell in a panic, you'd have made a big mistake. Because in the six months following each crisis, those same stocks gained an average of 15%, and 22% in the year afterward.

Remember, the stock market is a yo-yo. It drops fast and hard, and it rises equally so. Ignore the short-term or momentary fluctuations, for they have little impact over long periods.

So if you want to achieve investment success, all you need to do is think of stocks the same way you do puppies.

Why Do People Love Puppies?

After all, most people don't like stocks, but almost everyone loves puppies. Yet all puppies pee on the rug. While this is not something people enjoy, it's not a reason to avoid buying puppies, either (okay, maybe it is).

You should have the same attitude regarding stock market volatility. You are not buying stocks because you like volatility, but rather *in spite of it*.

Don't let volatility scare you away from stocks. If you do, you'll miss wonderful opportunities.

Chapter 35 - Following Your Emotions is a Sure Path to Failure

Investor losses almost always begin with emotions. To illustrate, let's return to 1972.

The Dow is at 700. Over the next 10 years, America will face runaway inflation, Watergate, the resignation of the President, two recessions, an oil embargo, 18% interest rates, and hostages in Iran.

CHART OF EMOTIONS

You Get In

You Get Out

FIGURE 6-9

Let's move forward to 1982. The Dow is still at 700! Not only is nobody making money in stocks, it's hard to remember the last time anybody did. All this gloom and doom led *Business Week* to publish its now-infamous cover story entitled *"The Death of Equities."*

As we move into the 1980s, we find big differences from the '70s. Our hostages come home. Interest rates come down. The recession is over. And everywhere you turn, people are talking about stocks again: On the bus, at the watercooler, during dinner parties, people are talking about the money they are making in the market, and each evening's newscasts announce "yet another all-time high" for stocks.

All of which lead you to a new emotion: **Hope.** Hope that the market will keep going up. By 1986, after the Dow reaches its all-time high of 2700, hope is replaced by yet another emotion: **Greed.** "Look at all the money they're making," you say to yourself. "I've got to get in on this."

> It sort of makes you ask the question, "Should I stay out of the market and watch it go up, or should I get in and make it go down?"

So you invest in stocks in early 1987, just in time to catch the market's peak in August. By September, with the market down 5%, your greed is replaced once again by hope: This time saying, "I hope it goes back up!"

But on October 19th, stocks drop 12% in a single day (they're now down 35% from their August 22 high) and hope quickly converts into the strongest of all emotions: *FEAR.* In a panic, you sell, leaving you to ponder how you managed to lose money during the biggest bull market in the history of the United States. This is why you've got to quit drawing conclusions from the evening news. All they do is report on what has happened, and you can't make money *after* you hear the news, because the news will elicit an emotion from you, and that emotion is certain to send you in the wrong direction.

Indeed, if we follow our emotions, we're going to do the exact opposite of what we're supposed to do, for the simple reason that half of all the people who invest in the stock market are dead wrong.

The Odds are 50/50 That You're Dead Wrong

Don't believe me? Ask yourself: If you wanted to sell a stock, to whom would you sell it? To *Somebody Else*, right? Well, one of you is dead wrong — we just don't know which one! After all, the stock is going to go up or down — so one of you has to be wrong!

In other words, the proper way to buy stocks is completely opposite from the way you buy everything else. For example, have you bought a TV lately? How about a car, dishwasher, or other major item?

When you made that purchase, did you buy from the same manufacturer as you did before? If so, no doubt the reason was because you had great success with it. And you fully expect your future experience to match your past experience.

But did you select your new car *only* because your last one was good? No, not you. You're too smart for that. No, you spent a weekend at the library reading *Consumer Reports*, and you interviewed all your friends and co-workers to learn their experiences. Then, once you settled on the brand and model, you shopped all over town looking for the best deal — eventually driving 200 miles to save thirty bucks.

Does this sound familiar?

Sure it does. Yet, you'll throw five grand at a stock because on the bus to work, you overheard some guy — who you don't even know — talk about it.

Admit it. When it comes to investing, *you act emotionally.*

You must recognize that relying on past performance and product reviews — which is how you buy ordinary products — does *not* apply to the stock market. In fact, so basic is this principle that the U.S. Securities and Exchange Commission requires every prospectus to proclaim in bold print that:

"PAST PERFORMANCE IS NO INDICATION OF FUTURE SUCCESS."

It doesn't say *"not much indication"* or *"sometimes not any indication"* or *"just a little indication."* It says **NO INDICATION.** The past is completely irrelevant: Just because money did well when invested in one way at one particular time does not mean money invested in that same way at another time will perform as it did before. In fact, you can guarantee yourself that it won't, for the simple reason that the economic circumstances of the past are not the same as those of today — and those of today will not be the same tomorrow.

Ohmigawd, It's Snowing!

While in the midst of a crisis, one frantic client called me. "The market's down 12% in just this month!" she cried. "At this rate, I'll be broke in a year!" True, I calmly explained to her, if stocks continued to go down at their current rate, she'd soon lose all her money.

©1996 Tribune Media Services
Reprinted with permission.

Eric & Bill

"Let me remind you that past performance is no guarantee of future results."

But I also noted that it was February, and a large snowstorm had dumped two feet of snow on the ground in less than a week. At this rate, I told her, she could expect to be buried under 35 feet of snow by July. "That's silly," she replied. "It'll be done snowing by then. Things will have changed a lot by July."

My point exactly.

Yet the market's snowstorms cause people to panic. In a panic, people throw away all their goals but one: safety. Forget about college, forget about retirement, the heck with taxes, *I want my money to be safe!*

As I've shown you throughout this book, any time you focus on safety instead of performance, you are sure to fail financially. In fact, people who focus on safety are at the greatest risk of being bamboozled. Witness *Money* magazine's March 1994 cover story, "8 Investments That Never Lose Money." The stock market had recently plunged, rising interest rates had sent bonds plummeting, the dollar was fading against the yen, so *Money* came to the rescue with a list of eight investments that "never lose money."

By the end of the year, six of the eight did.

Beware those who make claims about safety. Investing is about performance, not safety, and volatility is your traveling companion.

"8 INVESTMENTS THAT NEVER LOSE MONEY"

Money Magazine's March 1994 Cover Story

	Subsequent Performance March 1 - December 31
CGM Mutual	-9.85%
Dominion Resources	-6.55%
Gillette	+22%
Hershey	-3.17%
Investment Co. of America	-2.5%
Merrill Lynch Capital A	-4.89%
Sentinel Balanced	-2.98%
Unilever NV	+5.76%

FIGURE 6-10

Chapter 36 - Standard Deviation

Say an investment's rate of return fluctuates, or *deviates*, each year. If its rate of return were to *routinely* deviate, this deviation would become *standard*. Hence the term "standard deviation."

The standard deviation is the amount of swing in performance that an investment can be expected to have from year to year. The standard deviation is an investment's "average variation from the average return." The higher the standard deviation, the greater the volatility, and therefore the greater the risk.

> If you want to get rid of a cold-calling broker, ask, "What's the standard deviation?" They'll never call you back, fearing you know more than they do!

This is a difficult concept, so let's try an example. Say Fund ABC has earned an average of 8% per year over the past 10 years, with a standard deviation of 6. Statistically, there is a 67% probability that returns will fall within 1 standard deviation, and a 95% probability that returns will fall within 2 standard deviations. Thus, 67% of the time, Fund ABC earned between 2% and 14%, and 95% of the time, the fund earned between -4% and 20%.

This explains why neophyte investors so often get what they don't expect. The amateur, who expects Fund ABC to earn 8% (since that's the average annual return), is shocked when the fund loses 2%. But the astute investor knows such a result in any one year is quite possible, based on knowledge of standard deviation.[17]

To carry it a step further, it is highly unlikely that a fund's return in any one year will be exactly the average. Rather, it always will be either higher or lower than the average.

Thus, standard deviation teaches us to look beyond the "average annual return" figures that are touted by stockbrokers and mutual fund advertising.

---

[17]Standard deviation is not without its flaws. The biggest problem is that it punishes funds for *overperformance* just as much as for *underperformance*. Yet, most investors don't mind making money nearly as much as they hate losing money. This introduces *semivariance*, a variation of standard deviation which places greater emphasis on downside volatility than upside volatility. But that, and its offspring *lower partial moment*, is rather complex stuff, not suited for a basic book like this. Forget I mentioned them.

The Tortoise and the Hare

Compare the two investments below. Assuming you knew in advance that they would perform as shown, which would you choose?

Year	Tortoise	Hare
1	+10%	+18%
2	+10%	+32%
3	+10%	+11%
4	+10%	-17%
5	+10%	+10%

FIGURE 6-11

Most would choose the hare, believing it produces a higher rate of return, and indeed, that's exactly how most people choose their investments: by focusing on returns and ignoring risk. Such a strategy usually fails, as it does here, for the tortoise makes more money than the hare.

> I know you don't believe me, so get a calculator to prove it to yourself.

Not only does the tortoise make more money, it does so with far less risk: The hare's standard deviation is 17.85, while the tortoise's is zero. That means you can be 95% certain that the tortoise in any one year will earn 10%, while the hare could lose 25%!

Since we don't know when real losses will occur, it's better to invest like the tortoise. Yet, if these were two mutual funds, personal finance magazines and the hare itself (in advertisements and direct mail) would brag about the year when it gained 32%, and investors would have been enticed to buy it. The tortoise, meanwhile, would have gotten little or no press attention.

Is 20% Really Better Than 10%?

In fact, it's the funds you *don't* hear about — the ones that *don't* make it to #1 — that really are the best choices.

For example, given the one-year performances of two funds below, which would be ranked #1?

Year	Fund A	Fund B
1	+20%	+10%

The answer is Fund A, of course. But what if the following occurs in the second year?

Year	Fund A	Fund B
1	+20%	+10%
2	+0%	+10%
Total	+20%	+20%

Both A and B now display a two-year total return of 20%, but as you can see below, an investor would have made more money in Fund B.

	Fund A	Fund B
Initial Investment	$1,000	$1,000
Value After Year 1	$1,200	$1,100
Value After Year 2	$1,200	$1,210

Yet, you would have been more likely to invest in Fund A, because its marketing literature would have bragged about its performance in Year One.

Thus, you need to keep in mind that there is a big difference between investment returns and investor returns.

Standard deviation reveals a fund's true level of risk. Look at Figure 6-12: It clearly shows the volatility of international stocks. Because of this volatility, my colleagues and I rarely recommend that clients place more than 15% of assets into this asset class, and depending on the client, we may recommend much less (maybe even zero). Yet investors who fail to examine standard deviation often place too much money in risky investments, with correspondingly disastrous results.

STANDARD DEVIATION
1986-1995

U.S. Government Securities Funds	6.25
Municipal Bond Funds	6.97
Corporate Bond Funds	14.13
Balanced Funds	10.52
Stock Funds	13.54
International Stock Funds	21.11

FIGURE 6-12

Chapter 37 - Why Funds Make Money But People Do Not

Although most stock funds have made a lot of money over the years, many of the people who bought those funds actually managed to lose money. Let's examine how.

Morningstar, one of the best-known mutual fund research and rating services, analyzed the asset growth and total returns of 219 stock funds, tracked over a five-year period ending May 31, 1994.

Morningstar compared each fund's average annual return, which it called the *investment return*, with the return on the average dollar that was actually invested, which it called the *investor return*. The investment return, then, is the total return of the fund while the investor return is the return that people actually earned based on when they bought and when they sold.

The study's average annual investment return over the five years was a positive 12.5%, but the average annual investor return was a negative 2.2%. How could investors have lost money when the investments themselves made money?

The answer is simple. Investors bought their shares after hearing that the funds did well (meaning they bought when the price was high) and then panicked during market declines, thereby selling when the prices were low. When the market picked up again, investors jumped back in.

Buying high and selling low is the exact opposite of what you're supposed to do: You need to stick it out, for that is the only way to earn high consistent returns. Panicking only causes you to lose.

And the longer you hold your investment, the more time you have to catch up to the average investment return. The secret to investment success, then, is to buy quality investments and hold them for many years — especially through bad or declining markets and periods of uncertainty.

Intellectually, that's easy. The challenge is to control your emotions, which tempt you to buy or sell at exactly the wrong time.

One of the most successful mutual fund managers in the business once told me, "My goal is to place in the top 25% each year, because if I do that, my 3-year ranking will place me in the top 10% and my 5-year ranking will be in the top 5%. That's because so few funds are consistently in the top 25%." Yet, he lamented, many investors pass his fund by because each year he's only in the top quartile, and there's nothing glamorous about that. Smart investors know better.

The year 1991 provides an excellent illustration. The S&P 500 gained 25.8% that year, but it's a fair bet that few investors enjoyed those profits. Why? Take a look at the figure below.

As you can see, the market gained 13% in the first six weeks of the year. Imagine! Thirteen percent in just six weeks! At that rate, the market would be up 112.7% for the year!

And by mid-February, that's exactly what the TV newscasters and financial press were telling us. Upon hearing this news, lots of folks cashed in their CDs, and bought stocks and stock mutual funds. Then they just sat back and waited for the profits to come rolling in. And they waited. And waited. And waited.

They waited for 10 months. And virtually nothing happened.

Indeed, by mid-December the S&P 500 stood at 377.70, barely higher than mid-February's level of 369.02. That represented a dismal gain of just 2.4% — well below what investors could have earned virtually anywhere else — even in dull CDs. Disgusted, investors sold their shares and returned to the bank. Hey, at least they'd get 5% in a certificate of deposit.

And sure enough, no sooner had the masses given up hope, the stock market took off. From December 11 to the end of the year, the market skyrocketed, with the S&P gaining 10.4% in just two weeks. For the year, the market posted a gain of 25.8%, one of the most impressive yearly performances in Wall Street history. But while the market made tons of money, many investors didn't, for almost all of the gains for the entire year occurred in just eight weeks — the first six and the last two. The masses, desperately trying to catch the wave, weren't even in the water when the tide came in.

Some people, though, did enjoy all the profits of 1991. They were the folks who had invested in 1990 and were still invested in 1992.

Chapter 38 - Beta

Another tool Wall Street uses to evaluate mutual funds is *beta*, which is the amount of volatility a mutual fund experiences relative to the stock market as a whole.

A fund with a beta of 1 is deemed to have the same risk (i.e., volatility) as the S&P 500. Thus, a fund whose beta is 2 is twice as volatile as the S&P, while a fund whose beta is 0.5 is half as volatile. In practice, this means if the S&P rises 10%, a fund whose beta is 2 would be expected to rise 20%, while if the S&P falls 10%, the fund would be expected to drop 20%.

> If you know the Greek alphabet, you must be figuring, hey, if there's a beta, there's gotta be an alpha. After all, would you start a list with the letter "B"?
>
> *Alpha,* also called the Jensen index, measures the return produced by the fund's manager, as opposed to the return produced by the overall market. A positive alpha means the manager brought value to the fund.

Know Beta for What It Isn't

Although beta is a popular tool, it is often misunderstood. Here are two points to remember about beta.

Point #1: Beta Does Not Predict Fund Profitability

Just because higher-beta funds rise faster in up markets than lower-beta funds, don't be fooled into thinking higher-beta funds always make more money than lower-beta funds. Beta does not predict future circumstances. Rather, it merely suggests how a given fund is likely to perform if those circumstances exist. It could very well be that actual circumstances will favor low-beta funds.

Point #2: Beta Compares Fund Performance to the U.S. Stock Market

Betas are available for all mutual funds, including bond funds, international funds, even gold funds. However, be careful to use beta only when comparing funds that invest in U.S. stocks. Otherwise, you could draw the wrong conclusion. For example, the beta of the average international stock fund is .64. This suggests that international stock funds are very low in volatility, but you know that's not true.

R-Squared (R^2)

To determine whether a fund's beta is reliable, examine the R-Squared (R^2). An R^2 of 100 means all movements of the fund are due to movements in the market. The lower the R^2, the less impact the market has on the fund's movements, and the less relevant are beta and alpha.

> If that cold-calling cowboy wasn't scared off when you asked about standard deviation, start talking about R^2. You'll hear a dial tone real quick!

One Beta I Really Like

As you'd expect, research shows that the average beta of all stock funds is 1 (after all, the average of all stock funds is by definition the market average). However, the average beta of balanced funds is 0.65 — or roughly 35% less than stocks.

Now recall what we learned in Chapter 23: For the 10 years ending December 31, 1995, balanced funds produced an average annual return of 11.2% and stocks returned an average of 14.5%. In other words, balanced funds earned 77% of the return of stock funds but took only 65% of the risk to do it!

This strikes me as an excellent risk-to-reward relationship and explains why I'm such a big fan of balanced funds.

Chapter 39 - Portfolio Optimization vs. Maximization

A maximizer's primary goal is to earn as much as possible. To her, any risk is acceptable. Optimizers, by contrast, want to earn as much as possible *relative to the risk they must take to get there*.

My firm's planners are optimizers. Our clients might be able to earn higher returns elsewhere, but it's unlikely they'll do so on a risk-adjusted basis. Still, for those who are purely performance-motivated, our style may be too boring.

This is not a right-or-wrong issue. That's why, when you're interviewing planners or brokers, you should ask if they consider themselves to be a maximizer or an optimizer, and you need to make sure their answer matches your attitude.

For more on developing an Optimal Portfolio, see Chapter 45.

Chapter 40 - The Rankings Trap

All this explains why you must never invest in a mutual fund simply because of the rankings published in some personal finance magazine. Yet many investors do. But if you misuse the rankings, you could wind up with disastrous results.

Indeed, when reviewing recently published performance statistics, many fund owners ask, "Why aren't the funds I own listed as the best?"

This question implies that you *should* be able to choose the one fund out of 6,000 that will produce the highest return. Such a feat not only is impossible, it's the wrong reason for choosing a fund. Still, used properly, rankings can be helpful in monitoring and comparing funds. Here, then, are tips about rankings.

Tip #1: Last Year's Winners Rarely Repeat Their Performance

How mutual funds perform in one year has little to do with how they'll perform the next, which is why every prospectus states:

"PAST PERFORMANCE IS NO INDICATION OF FUTURE SUCCESS."

Yet, millions of investors ignore this advice and dump huge amounts of money into funds simply because the fund was at the top of some magazine's list.

Witness the Oakmark Fund. It had a mere $8 million in assets when it was introduced in 1991. After it was ranked #1, investors started pouring money in. By December 1992, assets had ballooned to more than $320 million, and by December 1993, assets had skyrocketed to more than $1 billion (that's *billion*).

The same thing happened to the Lexington Strategic Investment Fund, named the #1 fund of 1993 with a whopping 263% profit. The fund had assets of only $8 million in January 1993, but had $90 million just one year later — an 11-fold increase. What happened?

Hearing of the fund's great performance, investors rushed in, expecting Lexington to make as much money in 1994 as it did in 1993.[18] But was that a reasonable expectation? Hardly: Lexington had one of the worst track records in the industry! Indeed, an investment of $10,000 in 1983 was worth only $409 in 1993 — even including 1993's outstanding performance!

Indeed, Lex's average annual return for the 10-year period of 1984-1993, at 14%, sounds fine, but the average annual return from 1983-1992 (which omits 1993's huge return) was *negative* 11.9%. That's why the fund, which had $173 million in assets in 1984, only had $8 million by January '93!

Lex's story is not isolated. Rather, it's the norm. Consider this:

- Of all the funds in the SEI Equity Universe that placed in the top quartile from 1981 to 1985, 52% placed in the bottom two quartiles in the following five-year period. Likewise, of all the funds that placed in the worst quartile in the first time period, 50% placed in the top two quartiles in the second time period.

- Of all the funds rated five-stars by Morningstar from 1991 to 1993, 63% earned less than the average fund in subsequent time periods.

- Of all the funds that were top-ranked by Lipper in the five-year rolling periods from 1984 to 1993, 42% fell to the bottom two ranks in the following period. Similarly, 36% of the funds that were bottom-ranked later performed in the top two ranks.

- In the 10-year period after being named to the 1980 Forbes Honor Roll, the funds on the list earned 20% below the S&P 500. The 1981 Honor Roll performed 26% worse than the average and the 1982 Honor Roll performed 27% worse.

Clearly, just because a fund is "tops" at one time does not mean it will be "tops" at another. The reason is because the time periods themselves are completely arbitrary.

---

[18]It's true. Lex started the year with $8 million. Based on it's 263% gain, Lex should have ended the year with $29 million. Instead, it had $90 million. Where did the other $61 million come from? From new investors, of course.

Why Do Rankings Always Track the Calendar?

Do you only invest on the first day of a month and sell on the 31st? Rankings always assume you do. But then, they have to choose *some* start and stop dates, and besides, what difference does it make which dates are used? If you think it makes no difference, think again. Take the Bull & Bear Special Equities Fund, for example. The fund's average annual return over the five-year period ending October 1, 1995, was an impressive 18.3%. But look at its five-year record ending August 1, 1995, instead. By starting and stopping the five-year clock two months earlier, the fund's average annual return drops from 18.3% to a dismal 5.2%. That's a pretty incredible difference.

So you tell me: Is that a great fund or a terrible one? Think about that the next time you pick up the current copy of some consumer magazine. Maybe you'll catch the October issue and buy the fund; maybe you'll read the August issue and avoid it.

Be a smart investor and ignore the fact that somebody happens to rank a fund #1 for some arbitrary period of time.

Tip #2: Do Not Focus on the Rate of Return

If last year's winner (Fund ABC) earned 100%, but this year's winner (Fund DEF) earned only 50%, that means ABC is a better fund, right?

Wrong. This year's economy is different from last year's; thus, you should expect fund performance to mirror those differences.

Therefore, what matters is how a fund does in a particular time period as compared to similar funds *in that same period*. Relativity is the key, not isolated statistics.

Tip #3: Disregard Short Periods

The longer the period, the more accurate the ranking. Not only is quarterly performance data meaningless, few professionals make decisions based on even one-year periods. Statistically, the most meaningful data is derived from 10-year intervals or longer.

This is why the SEC requires funds to advertise 10-year performance data; left on their own, funds certainly would promote shorter intervals if it made them look better (and it often does).

Yet, although 10-year data is more important, the personal finance press usually tout one-year and three-year data; Many even list 90-day results (a notable exception is *Forbes*, which displays readings not merely by years but also by up-markets and down-markets, which transcend the calendar).

As a former journalist in the financial trade press, I can tell you that many publishers tout 90-day returns merely because they have subscriptions to sell. They need something new to say each issue just to stay in business. Thus, what's important to the media is not necessarily important to investors. (This also supports the argument against buying last year's winners: Every quarterly list contains names that are different from before. The names on each list constantly change, proving the impossibility of predicting next quarter's winning funds.)

Tip #4: Be Sure You Use Valid Rankings

More than two dozen publications rank funds, and many are flawed. Some forget that mutual funds have different objectives, which will produce different rates of return. It is ridiculous to compare stock funds to bond funds, yet many rankings do. Be certain you are comparing apples to apples, as a review of *risk* is as important as one of performance. Others rank only a few hundred funds — sort of like saying the Washington Redskins had the best record in '94, which is true if you ignore the 28 teams that did better.

Used properly, rankings can help you select funds that:

- demonstrate consistent long-term performance that is competitive with other funds in the same category;

- offer volatility equal to or below that of others; and

- based on your outlook, are positioned to perform favorably over the next five years or beyond, interim fluctuations notwithstanding.

Keep these points in mind the next time you review the rankings, and you'll be a happier, more successful investor.

Chapter 41 - Do You Need to Pick the Best Fund?

Although I've given you valuable tips in using rankings, I really believe that the whole concept is somewhat flawed. People turn to rankings with the false hope (expectation?) of finding the "best" fund, because both fund advertising and the personal finance press give the impression that you had better choose the best fund or risk losing all your money.

IS CHOOSING THE WORST REALLY SO BAD?

Performance of Mutual Funds by Category
1985-1994

	Best	Worst	Average
U.S. Government Securities Funds	9.4	6.1	8.2
Municipal Bond Funds*	14.0	7.4	11.4
Corporate Bond Funds	11.4	7.0	9.5
Balanced Funds	14.8	6.1	11.4
Stock Funds	19.9	6.4	13.0
International Stock Funds	22.2	10.7	15.1

Average Annual CD Rate for Period: 6%

*Adjusted for taxable equivalent yield, based on 28% federal income tax bracket. (See Chapter 9)

FIGURE 6-14

"It is better to be approximately right than precisely wrong."
—Warren Buffett

That's nonsense, and I'm here to tell you that you can relaaaaax. Although it's always desirable to pick the "best" fund, don't be overly concerned about the need to do so. Because, in fact, picking the best fund is really not that important. Not only is it nearly impossible to do, even picking the worst isn't so bad.

Look at Figure 6-14, which shows the average annual return for the best, worst, and average funds in each category for the 10 years ending 1994. In the balanced fund category, for example, even the worst earned 6.1%, while the best averaged 14.8%. So if you're worried that you'll never be able to pick the best fund, relax: It's not a winner-take-all contest. The truth is you don't have to pick the best fund, for even picking the worst — in any category — produced better returns over the last 10 years than the 6% average annual return that CDs provided.

Chapter 42 - The Computer vs. The Money Manager

In a study of money manager performance, researchers asked managers to program a computer with their investment style, and then they compared the performance of the computer's buy/sell decisions with that of the managers themselves. Guess who won?

The computer, every time. Why? Because the computer didn't wake up in a bad mood or second-guess itself. To understand this, say you're buying a stock at $20 a share. At what price will you sell?

...

I bet you haven't thought of a price. So, go ahead and think of a price before continuing. I'll wait.

...

Okay, now you have a price in mind. I'll bet your price is *higher* than $20. Am I right?

Hasn't it occurred to you that maybe, *just maybe*, the price might go *down*? That's the first problem with investors: They never think their stock will go down. After all, they say, "Why would I buy it if it's going to lose money?"

That's why you must establish *two selling prices* whenever you buy a stock: one that's higher than your buy price, and one that's lower.

You Greedy Pig

By the way, I bet your sell price was $30, wasn't it? That's a 50% gain over your buy price! You greedy pig![19] You've been happy with a 4% return from your bank account, but you now demand 50% from the stock! That doesn't make any sense! Remember: Bulls and bears both make money, but pigs get slaughtered.

---

[19] I don't even want to comment on those of you who set $40 as your sell price.

Let's be reasonable about this. Let's establish $18 and $24 as our sell prices; that would be a 20% gain while limiting losses to 10%. Thus, when your broker calls to say your stock has hit your sell price of $24, guess how you will respond?

You'll say, "It's doing great! I don't want to sell now! It's going to $30! Hold on to it!" Greed has taken over.

And indeed, the stock will go to $27, then $28, back to $22, and you'll end up selling at $18. You'll manage to lose 10% of your investment — and then complain that stocks are too risky.

Stocks are not the problem — you are the problem, because you let your emotions get in the way.

When you buy an investment, determine when you're going to sell — either a price (such as $50 per share) or a time (when my son goes to college). And when your sell point is reached, _SELL!_ And the simple way to avoid driving yourself crazy is to follow Edelman's Rule #2: Once you sell an investment, *you no longer may look at the price in the newspaper.* Observe this rule or you will drive yourself crazy.

I often get questions on my call-in show from people thinking of refinancing their mortgage. "The rate is 8.5%," they say. "Should I take it or wait for the rate to drop to 8%?" I have no answer because they're asking the wrong question!

The right question is: Are you happy with the rate currently available? If you are, take it. If you're not, don't take it. Trying to catch the top or bottom of any market is a fool's game.

Chapter 43 - The Theory of Market Timing

The stock market's century-long upward curve is filled with many short-lived peaks and valleys. Rather than holding stocks for decades (which forces you to experience the market's declines as well as the surges), wouldn't it be smarter to be in stocks only when prices are moving upward?

Market timers say yes, you should invest at the low, ride the wave up and get out at the top, before the market goes down. Then, simply wait on the sidelines (in cash) for the market to hit another low, then jump back in, and ride the next wave to the next high. Simply repeat this process of buying low and selling high, and you'll become fabulously rich.

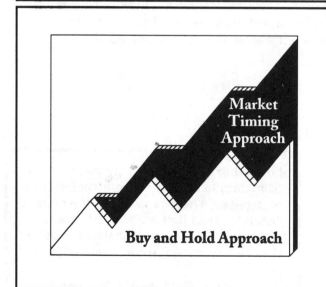

FIGURE 6-15

Very appealing pitch, isn't it? Don't worry if you don't know how to do it, for lots of Wall Streeters will do it for you — for a fee, of course. According to *Forbes*, one million people spend $500 million a year subscribing to newsletters which offer market timing advice, and millions more have invested billions in accounts managed by money managers who buy and sell stocks based on timing strategies.

There's only one problem with market timing: *It doesn't work.*

Why not? *Because nobody knows how to do it!*

For example, if you had invested in the S&P 500 on March 31, 1990, and sold on March 31, 1995, you would have earned an average of 9.5% per year.

During these five years, the stock market was open 1,264 days. If you were out of the market for just 10 days — the 10 days in which the S&P made the most money — how much of your five-year profit do you think you'd have missed?

An incredible 65%. That's right: 65% of the total profit that was earned by the S&P over five years *occurred in just 10 days*. A person who missed those 10 days would have earned 3.3% per year instead of 9.5%.

And if you skipped the 20 biggest days, not only would you have missed all of the market's five-year gain, *you actually would have lost 5.5% of your money per year over the entire five year period.*

If this shocks you, read on, for this is not an aberration. In the 744 months between 1926 and 1987, where stocks averaged 9.5% per year, 61% of those months were profitable. Yet, if you took away the top 50 months — just 6.7% of the total — your total return would have been zero. *Removing 6.7% of the time eliminates 100% of the profits.*

Think about it. How often does the nightly television news start with a story about "today on Wall Street?" Rarely, because on a typical day, the stock market is quite boring. But when the market does move — watch out! Market moves are rare but dramatic, and that's why the stock market is news only a few times each year.

That's why market timing fails. Prices move so rapidly — often for no apparent reason and with no warning — you can't react in time.

Hundreds of articles and studies over the past century, from economists and money managers, in government, academia, and business, *unanimously agree that market timing does not work.* In fact, the only people who endorse the concept are those newsletter writers, stockbrokers, financial planners, and money managers who make money by convincing you to try it.

And this raises another major point about taking advice from people: Are they telling you to do something because it's good for you or good for them? What exactly is their motivation? All too often, sellers of financial advice make more money getting you to do something than if they had done that very thing themselves.

I assure you: Rarely do the brokers who pitch market timing actually do it with their own money, and if they do, they certainly are not making very much money at it — for if they were, they'd be so busy managing their own money they wouldn't waste time trying to get your money from you.

There can be no other conclusion. Let's face it, people in my profession are not exactly known for their charity. They're in this business to make a buck. And once enough bucks are made, they're off to the Hamptons.

> *"Wall Street's graveyards are filled with men who were right too soon."*
> —William Hamilton

Thus, if market timing really worked, these guys certainly would have made enough money from their own account by now that they could kick back and relax. Yet they're still plying their wares to an unsuspecting public.

Forget about the argument that market timing is so new that timers haven't had enough time to earn the millions they fully expect to earn — suggesting that you need to get in now before the rest of the world finds out about their success. This argument is nonsense because market timers have been around as long as the markets themselves — like fleas on a dog.

In fact, if you were a market timer, and you *knew* your system worked, how much money would you put into your strategy? All you've got, I'm sure.

Say you were around in 1926 and you had a system that you *knew* would correctly time the market. How much money would you have invested? Ten dollars? A hundred? A thousand?

The truth is, if you began in 1926 with one hundred dollars, and were shrewd enough to be in the market each month stocks made money and were out of the market each month stocks lost money — so that your account only went up, never down, every month over 66 years — guess how much money you'd have had by 1992?

Your $100 would have grown to more than $26 billion — that's *billion* with a "b." If you started with $10,000, you'd now have $2.6 *trillion* — nearly enough to pay off the national debt. Microsoft's Bill Gates would look downright poor by comparison, with his measly $0.015 trillion (that's $15 billion, okay, not so poor).

> *"An economist is an expert who will know tomorrow why the things he predicted yesterday didn't happen today."*
>
> —Laurence J. Peter

The awesome power of this number is so enticing, so compelling, that market timers use it as an inducement to sell their services. Imagine! If your timing efforts produced only a fraction of these results, you'd be fabulously rich beyond your wildest dreams! So, c'mon! Let's give it a try!

Yeah, right.

The problem is that market timing is not like the lottery. At least with the lottery, you know *someone* is going to win — maybe even you, although with odds of 4 million to 1, you're more likely to get hit by lightning. But market timers offer no such odds. *Nobody* wins with market timing — except the con artist selling it to you. After all, if they were so sure about their abilities, why don't they do it with their own money instead of trying to collect 3% in annual fees from you?

Indeed, the Forbes 400 — a list of the wealthiest people in America — features no market timers. Not on the current list, nor any previous list. You'd think that with all the people selling timing services, *somebody* by now would have amassed billions. So the fact that no timer has ever made the list ought to tell you something.

By contrast, though, #1 on the Forbes 400 is none other than Warren Buffett, the most successful investor in America, and arguably in American history. How did he amass his $16 billion? By buying stocks such as Coca-Cola, Geico Insurance, Gillette, American Express, The Washington Post Company, Solomon Brothers, and Disney, and holding onto them for decades.

Yep, the timers are absent from the Forbes 400, but the buy-and-holders are well represented.

Why Market Timing Fails

Market timing fails for the simple reason that *you must be right twice* in order for it to work. (At least with lottery tickets, you need to be right only once.)

The best example comes by way of Gertrude. Watching a presentation I once gave at the World Bank, she stood up and proudly announced to everyone, "I called the "Crash of '87!" She then proceeded to tell us her story (whether we wanted to hear it or not):

"I knew the market was going to crash," she said, "so I called my broker on October 4 and told him, 'Sell everything!' And he sold all my stocks and moved all my money into a money market fund. He thought I was crazy — everybody thought I was crazy — but I sure had the last laugh on the 19th!"

Gertrude has been telling this story to everyone within earshot since 1987, recalling with great fanfare how she got out when the Dow was at 2600 and laughing heartily when the crash knocked the Dow down to 1800 in a matter of days. She gleefully talks about all the money her friends lost when they didn't listen to her.

> *"All you need is look over the earnings forecasts publicly made a year ago to see how much care you need to give to those being made now for the next year."*
> —Gerald M. Loeb

When she took a breath, I asked Gertrude, "When did you get back in?"

Her smile disappeared. She sat down, mumbling, "I never did. My money is still in cash."

So the truth came out. Gertrude was proud that she called the market once and avoided the market's losses when the Dow dropped from 2600 to 1800. Other folks, not as smart as Gertrude, saw their investments fall from 2600 to 1800. Today, though, those same people (yes, they're still holding on) find that their investments have risen back up with the Dow, which by the spring of 1996 surpassed 5600. Gertrude, though, is frozen in time, her money still sitting in money markets as it has since the Dow was at 2600. She can't get back into stocks, she says, until the market falls back to where it was when she got out. She could be waiting a long, long time.

Clearly, Gertrude did not do herself any favors. As she learned, *being right once is not enough*. It's not enough to know when to get out; you also must know when to get back in, or you'll find yourself worse off than if you had never gotten out in the first place.

That's why market timing fails: One wrong will undo many rights. I find Gertrude so fascinating because she fully expected to be right, and she was indignant when nobody would believe her. But why should her friends believe her? After all, she's just one person with an opinion. Would you liquidate all of your investments just because a friend told you to?

Maybe it would depend who the friend is.

If your friend is Gertrude, no thank you. But what if your friend was an economist at the Federal Reserve Board? Certainly the forecasts issued by the Fed each February and July ought to be pretty darn good. After all, because it controls interest rates, the Fed (theoretically at least) is in the position of being able to influence the very events it is predicting. So it would follow, then, that the best predictions ought to be coming from the Fed's own forecasts.

Here's the story of a broker who attracted new clients by demonstrating his ability to pick winners every time.

How did he do it? Each month, he'd mail letters to 100 prospective clients. Fifty of the prospects would receive a letter saying they should sell a particular stock; the other 50 would get a letter advising they buy that same stock. Naturally, one of the letters would prove correct. So, the next month, to whichever group had received the "correct" letter, the broker would mail a second letter. These 50 letters would again contain a recommendation pertaining to a specific stock, and again, 25 would be told to buy and 25 would be told to sell.

In the third month, the 25 prospects who had received the second "correct" letter got one more, half again containing buy recommendations and half touting sells. In the fourth month, the broker would call the dozen remaining "correct" prospects, and tell them the following:

"Look, I've told you to do something three times in a row. I was right every time, but you didn't listen to me. Now, I'm giving you another recommendation right now, and if you don't take it, you'll never hear from me again." Every prospect would sign up.

This sales pitch is illegal, and when he was found out, the broker was barred from the securities industry.

> *"Money isn't everything, as long as you have enough."*
> —Malcom Forbes

Yet, according to a study of the accuracy of Fed predictions of Gross Domestic Product from 1980 to 1994, conducted by the Fed itself, the Fed never made a correct prediction. Yup, they scored a big fat zero. Nada. Nothing. Zilch.

If the Fed itself can't make accurate predictions, is it any wonder that Gertrude can't? Would *you* care to try?

Would an Advance Score Card Make Any Difference?

For the sake of argument, let's assume for the moment that market timing works. In fact, let's go the timers one better and pretend we know *in advance* what will happen in the short-term. Would it make any difference in the long-term?

Let's say it's August '87, three months before the Crash, and you're about to invest for five years. You must choose a money manager and *stick with whomever you choose*. Which group of managers will you choose:

(a) those who are destined to make money in the Crash of '87, or

(b) those who not only will lose money in the Crash, but will lose more than the average.

Although those in group (a) clearly make more money over the next three months than those in group (b), that's not the case over the next five years. According to the *Hulbert Financial Digest*, money managers who made money in the Crash of '87 earned an average of just 1.4% in the five years following the crash, while managers who lost money during that period earned, as a group, an average of 5.1% in the following five years. Thus, even picking the right group in the short-term would have led to failure in the long-term. Which is more important to you — long-term or short-term?

> *"Even when the experts all agree, they may well be mistaken."*
>
> —Bertrand Russell

What If You Switch Managers Every Year?

Okay, you say, the above example is fine, but it's pretty unrealistic. After all, who says you've got to stick with the same manager every year? Why not just move from manager to manager each year based on their track records? After all, the above example demonstrates that at least one group of managers did manage to prosper in the Crash.

True, but the above example also assumes you were able to identify that group of managers *before* the fact — which is as impossible as picking next year's Super Bowl winner. But the point is well taken anyway. So let's try another example.

Since we can't predict who will do well in the coming year, we'll do the next best thing: Each January 1, we'll switch our account to the #1 money manager of the *previous* 12 months. After all, this is how millions of investors pick their mutual funds. They buy some magazine, check the rankings for last year's winners, and promptly buy those funds.

> *"I don't have a clue which direction the next 10% or 15% price movement will take the market. But I know with certainty which direction the next 100% movement will take it, and that's all that really matters."*
>
> —Nick Murray

Let's say we do the same thing. According to the *Hulbert Financial Digest,* in the period of 1981 to 1992, switching annually to the *best* manager of the previous 12 months would have given us a total gain of 51.2% (an average annual rate of return of 4.7%).

On the other hand, if we had switched each year to the *worst* manager of the previous 12 months, we would have earned a total gain of 220% (an annual return of 20%). Meanwhile, if we had just bought the S&P 500 itself and held on, our gain would have been 308%, an average annual return of 28%.

The correct conclusion, then, is that *nothing beats the buy-and-hold strategy.* Even making the right timing choice is not as good as making no timing choice. Invest your money into a broadly-diversified group of mutual funds and leave them alone.

When the Pros Try Timing

I'm not saying you shouldn't engage in active trading or market timing just because you can't do it as well as the typical Wall Street pro. I'm saying they can't do it, either.

If you want proof, look at the U.S. Trading and Investing Championships, sponsored by the Financial Trading Association, staged annually since 1983. Although open to all investors, most entrants are professional stockbrokers. The contest challenges these pros to see how much money they can make in short periods of either four months or one year. Since the pros are trading for their own account (not for their clients) and since they're investing real money (not computer models), there's no doubt everybody is trying their best.

The results? According to the FTA, of the 3,500+ entries from 1983-1990, only 22% made any money at all. Only a handful managed to keep pace with or exceed the S&P 500.

These results are not a phenomenon. Rather, they're quite common. As Mark Hulbert, editor of the *Hulbert Financial Digest*, has written in *Forbes* magazine: "Most active traders are losers... trading is costly. It is so costly that the average investor is almost guaranteed to lag the market unless he or she follows a long-term investment strategy."

Please pay attention to this. Don't trade actively. Instead, change your investments as often as you change televisions. When properly selected, your TV ought to last years — and when you finally do replace it, odds are good it's because your circumstances have changed, not because the TV broke. So, pick your investments like you would a TV — with a lot of care and a plan to hold on for a long time.

> *"God created economists to make weather forecasters look good."*
> —Anonymous

> *"The first principle is that you must not fool yourself — and you are the easiest person to fool."*
> —Richard Feynman

Chapter 44 - Diversification: The Key to Your Investment Success

Am I saying all your money should be in stocks or stock funds? Of course not. Nobody should subject all their money to just one risk.

While it's easy to understand why people don't like risk, in truth there's nothing wrong with placing your money at risk; in fact, it's impossible *not* to, for even bank accounts place you at risk, if only due to taxes and inflation. Thus, every investment choice involves risk. The key, then, is knowing which risks are appropriate.

Most people are willing to gamble small amounts of money, as the popularity of lottery tickets, casinos, and football pools attests. Gamblers know they can't earn big money unless they're willing to take big risks. The secret, then, is to learn how to take risks properly.

So let's learn how to do that. Say you have $25,000 to invest for 25 years. If you choose a 5.25% CD, your account would grow to $96,621 (ignoring taxes).

On the other hand, let's say you split your $25,000 evenly into five piles as follows:

- With the first pile, **you buy 5,000 lottery tickets,** and like almost everyone else who plays the lottery, you lose it all. Thus, after 25 years, the ending value of this $5,000 is zero.

- With the second pile, **you bury it all under your mattress.** Thus, by earning no interest for 25 years, this $5,000 remains $5,000.

- With the third pile, **you open a bank savings account** at 2% interest, where it grows to $8,240 over the next 25 years.

- With the fourth pile, **you buy a U.S. Treasury earning 7%.** This pile grows to $28,627.

- And with the fifth pile, **you invest in the stock market,** and although the average stock fund earned 14.5% over the past 10 years, we'll say yours performed below average, earning only 12% per year. At that rate, your $5,000 will grow to $98,942.

255

In total, you have $140,809 — $44,188 *more* than if you had invested the entire amount in a CD — even though you lost *all* of the first pile, earned *nothing* on the second, invested in bank accounts with the third, super-safe government bonds with the fourth, and "gambled" in the stock market only with the last fifth. How can this be?

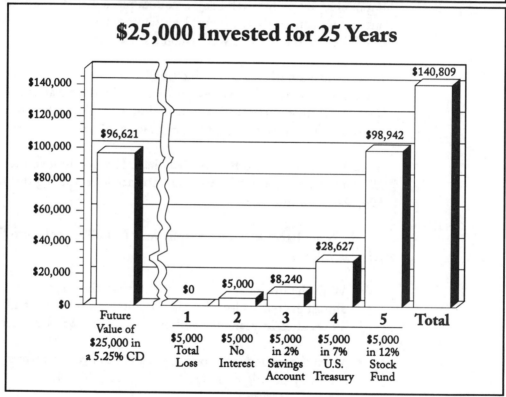

DIVERSIFICATION vs. BANK CDs

$25,000 Invested for 25 Years

FIGURE 6-16

This result is possible thanks to *diversification*. This simple principle recognizes that the maximum loss of any investment is limited to the amount you invest, but the maximum gain is unlimited — as Einstein showed us in Chapter 3. Thus, the profits from earning 12% on the fifth pile more than compensate for the losses incurred in the first pile. Even though part of your money might go down in value and other parts may earn less than acceptable returns, only one small part of your money needs to earn above-average returns to make your overall return far higher than if all your money had been placed into just one mediocre (but safe!) investment.

And that's the key: Diversification allows to you take small, calculated risks, and the key to achieving personal financial success is in knowing how to do this. As General George Patton put it, "There's nothing wrong with taking risks. That's quite different from being rash."

But successful risk-taking means you must be *willing* to take financial risks. Most Americans are unwilling to do so. By emphasizing safety, they lock themselves into low returns, which leads to financial failure. In fact, many people fail financially not because they take too much risk with their money, but because they take *too little* risk with their money.

Note: This example, which uses five categories invested in equal amounts, is not intended to serve as an actual investment model. My firm, for example, routinely creates portfolios using eight or nine major asset classes with different amounts placed in each, and we don't use mattresses or lottery tickets.

> **Do not make the mistake of Mr. Anderson. He came to my firm as the unhappy owner of five mutual funds, into each of which he had placed 20% of his money for diversity. Yet, each one had lost money. Not only that, each had lost roughly the same amount of money. Upon inspection, we discovered that all five funds were invested in U.S. government bonds! That's not diversity — that's redundancy! Naturally, when interest rates went up, his funds all went down. And this guy couldn't figure it out. "How could all five funds lose money?" he demanded. "Mutual funds are awful!"**

Asset Allocation

How do we create proper diversity? Through *asset allocation*. This concept focuses on the forest, not the trees, and its premise is supported by a landmark study published in *Financial Analysts Journal*. By examining the performance of 82 large pension plans over a 10-year period, the study sought to explain why one institutional money manager makes more money than another.

The study found that 93.6% of the difference in performance from one plan to another was due to asset allocation, not investment selection. Thus, what matters is not which stocks you buy, but what portion of your total assets you place into stocks. Thus, investors who devote all their attention to figuring out which stocks or funds to buy are missing the point — as are the magazines and newsletters that proclaim with each issue, "Hot Stocks to Buy Now!"

Here's how asset allocation works, using a hypothetical example solely to demonstrate the concept, as shown in the figures below.

ASSET ALLOCATION

You start with equal amounts...	...so that your pie looks like this:
	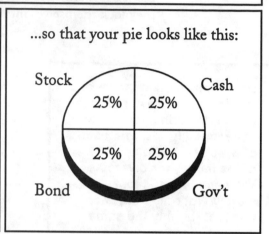
FIGURE 6-17	FIGURE 6-18

This model uses four major asset classes: cash, government securities, bonds, and stocks, and to keep things simple, we're splitting our assets equally into each of the four categories.[20]

Asset allocation acknowledges that higher-risk asset classes are expected to grow more quickly than lower-risk ones. On that premise, we would expect stocks to be our fastest-growing group. If this happened, we would later find that we no longer have equal amounts in each asset class: Since our stocks made more money than the other investments, stocks now hold 38% of our total assets instead of the original 25%, and the weightings of other asset classes have changed based on their performance as well.

As Chapter 51 explains, think in percentages, not dollars: While the pie's value changes with time, the percentage is always 100%. With stocks now 38% and cash only 15%, we find that our model has fallen

---

[20]This example is not intended to serve as an actual allocation model. In a real model, we might add real estate, international investments and foreign currencies, natural resources, precious metals, and other hedge positions, placing more money in some categories than in others based on the client's circumstances, objectives, liquidity needs, and risk tolerances.

out of balance. Thus, to restore the pie to its original shape, we need to rebalance the portfolio. We do this by reallocating the assets: we sell enough of the stocks and bonds to bring them each back down to 25%, and use those dollars to buy more of the cash and government bonds to bring each of them up to 25%. This will return the model to its original proportions.

ASSET REALLOCATION

Some assets will grow faster than others...   ...so you reallocate the assets...

...to restore the new pie...   ...to the original formula.

FIGURE 6-19

In other words, asset allocation requires that you *sell your winners* — the ones that made the most money — and *buy your losers* — the ones that made the least money (or perhaps even lost money).

I'll bet you're thinking, "Is Edelman crazy?"

Not at all. Think about it: If you spend your investing career "selling winners" and "buying losers," you will become very, very wealthy.

Asset allocation succeeds because it forces you to do the very thing you don't want to do. Emotionally, you want winners, not losers. If stocks are doing much better than bonds, you'll want stocks. After all, you ask, why on earth would you want to sell the great stocks and put the money into the rotten bonds?

Because you *don't want to buy winners.*

If you're buying winners, that means they've already made money, and you thus would be buying after the fact. But *selling* a winner means you made money with it — and that's the whole point to investing, isn't it?

There is no "is."

When people tell me they love their investments, it always is because those investments have made money (nobody ever loves an investment that has lost money). This creates a trap, for there is no present tense in the world of investing.

At no time will you ever own an investment that is doing great. You might have an investment that *has* done great, or one that *will be* great, but that's it. This is very different from one that *is* great.

And just because it *has been* great doesn't mean it *will be* great. Remember: on Wall Street, there is no "is."

Thus, *you want to buy losers,* or more accurately, it doesn't matter if it was a loser *before* you bought it. All that matters is that it becomes a winner before you sell it. But if you act emotionally, you'll fail. You'll buy more stocks — "They're making so much money!" — and you'll sell your government securities — "Those dogs! I want to dump them!" In other words, you'll want to buy and sell based on past performance, even though PAST PERFORMANCE IS NO INDICATION OF FUTURE SUCCESS.

Please realize that in this example, my concern is not that I think stocks are no longer a good investment. Instead, my concern is that having 38% of the money in stocks is too high a percentage (according to our hypothetical example's circumstances, risk tolerance, and financial objectives). Thus, the decision to reduce exposure to stocks is a financial planning issue, not an investment outlook issue.

You see, if you don't reallocate, eventually you will own nothing but stocks. You'll find that you have 100% of your money in just one asset class, and you will have abandoned the concept of diversification.

> Of course, in the real world, you might not want to reallocate your assets back to the original model. Over time your health, income, marital status, and other circumstances could change, and these changes could require a change in your model portfolio.

How Often Should You Reallocate?

Aside from changes in your personal circumstances, this does raise an interesting question: How often should you rebalance your portfolio? Many academicians have tried to answer this question, using computer models back-dated to 1926. Researchers have focused on chronology (meaning you rebalance the portfolio at certain time intervals); weightings (you rebalance whenever any asset class gains or loses a certain percentage); or a combination of the two.

The conclusion is that there is no conclusion: Like the search for Pi, no one has been able to determine the most effective and efficient rebalancing program. (If someone had found the formula, you'd have heard about it by now.) Instead, researchers have discovered that different methodologies produce similar results, provided each methodology is applied consistently. In other words, the key to successful rebalancing is to establish your parameters and stick with them.

For example, you might choose to rebalance your portfolio every two years. Or perhaps, whenever one asset class increases or decreases 20% from its initial weighting. Or perhaps some combination of the two. The design is not as important as the implementation: Changing your methodology or failing to execute it on schedule will reduce the effectiveness of this strategy.

Chapter 45 - Developing an Optimal Portfolio

Most neophytes think they must choose between investments that are safe, but which earn low returns, or those that are risky but which can earn high returns. Broadly speaking, this means investors often feel they must choose between stocks and bonds.

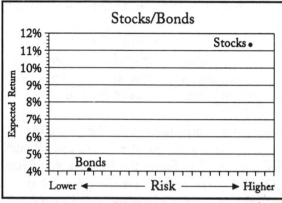

FIGURE 6-20

As you've learned in this book, bonds are safer and, on average, earn less than stocks. Therefore, it holds that Portfolio A, consisting of 100% bonds, is safer than Portfolio B, which is 100% stocks. It also holds that A makes less money than B. Thus, a chart of these facts would look like Figure 6-20.

Therefore, you would conclude that any portfolio containing a combination of stocks and bonds must fall somewhere between these two points.

But it doesn't work out that way. As you see in Figure 6-21, which reflects market performance from 1926 to 1995, a blended portfolio of 20% stocks/80% bonds actually is lower in risk than a portfolio of 100% bonds — and it earns more money, too. How can this be?

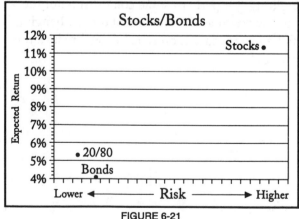

FIGURE 6-21

The answer lies in the fact that all investments contain risks. But not all investments face the same risks.

For example, the biggest risk facing bonds is interest rate risk (Chapter 14). Stocks are not as sensitive to this particular risk as bonds. Therefore, if you owned a portfolio that was 100% bonds, and you wanted to reduce interest rate risk, you could do so by moving some of your money, say 20%, away from bonds. Moving that money protects that 20% from interest rate risk, and if you moved that money to stocks, you'd be increasing your return at the same time, since stocks earn more than bonds. Therefore, a portfolio that contains some stocks is actually safer than a portfolio that does not.

This is the same principle as that used in Chapter 13 to demonstrate that gold can reduce the risk of owning bonds.

PORTFOLIO OPTIMIZATION

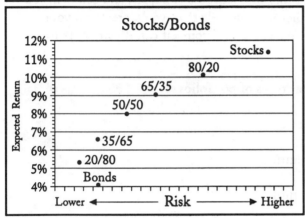

FIGURE 6-22

OPTIMIZING BETWEEN U.S. AND INTERNATIONAL STOCKS

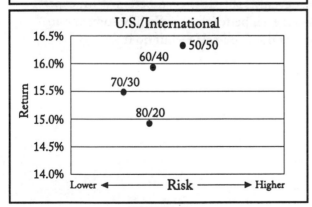

FIGURE 6-23

Figure 6-22 shows the risk/ return of a variety of portfolios, based on their holdings of stocks and bonds. As shown, a portfolio of 20% stocks/80% bonds is lowest in risk. But which is the *optimal* portfolio? Recall that an optimal portfolio is one which earns the highest returns *relative to risk*.

The answer is the portfolio containing 35% stocks/65% bonds. Why? Because it has virtually the same risk as the portfolio of 100% bonds, but its return is nearly 75% higher.

Similar results can be found comparing U.S. stocks with international stocks, as Figure 6-23 shows.

This discussion is not intended to suggest that you should build a portfolio consisting of just two asset classes. The point is that you can build a portfolio that is safer and more profitable by investing in many asset classes than you can by investing in only one asset class. Indeed, *introducing a risky asset into your portfolio reduces the overall risk of that portfolio.* Put another way, , if you want to lower your overall investment risk, invest in something risky.

And you don't have to be a rocket scientist to do it, either. Although professional advisors like me and my colleagues are expert at Modern Portfolio Theory and other sophisticated concepts, and can help you build more efficient allocation models than you'll create on your own, even simple models you create yourself can do wonders for your portfolio.

After all, there are four types of portfolios...

- low risk/low return

- low risk/high return

- high risk/low return

- high risk/high return

...and the best one is low risk/high return. Indeed, as seen in Figure 6-24, simply splitting your assets equally among cash, bonds, and stocks goes a long way toward achieving that goal, and using five asset classes, again just evenly split, does even better. With expert guidance, you can obtain even better results. So hire someone to show you how to do it, or do it yourself — but do it.

DIVERSIFICATION PROVIDES HIGHER RETURNS WITH LESS RISK
1972-1992

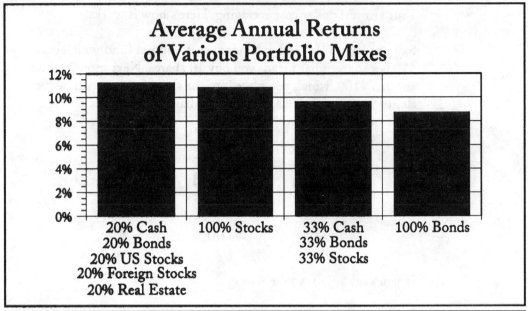

Average Annual Returns of Various Portfolio Mixes

20% Cash
20% Bonds
20% US Stocks
20% Foreign Stocks
20% Real Estate

100% Stocks

33% Cash
33% Bonds
33% Stocks

100% Bonds

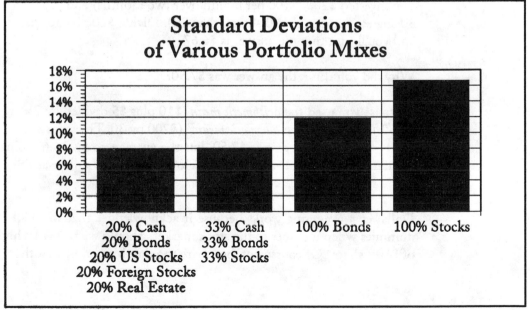

Standard Deviations of Various Portfolio Mixes

20% Cash
20% Bonds
20% US Stocks
20% Foreign Stocks
20% Real Estate

33% Cash
33% Bonds
33% Stocks

100% Bonds

100% Stocks

FIGURE 6-24

265

Chapter 46 - Dollar Cost Averaging

So far, we've been talking about investing as though you had a large sum of money to invest right now. Maybe you don't. Instead, maybe you have only a few dollars to put away each month.[21]

Your answer: dollar cost averaging. Here's how it works.

Say you have $100 and you buy a stock mutual fund which costs $10 per share. That means you buy 10 shares. Next month, you save another $100, which you place into the same fund, only now the shares are just $5. Thus, you buy 20 shares. What's the average price of all your shares?

Month	Amount Invested	Price Per Share
1	$100	$10
2	$100	$5

If you said $7.50, you're wrong.

You invested $200 ($100 per month over two months) and you own 30 shares (you bought 10 shares, then 20). Divide $200 by 30 shares and you'll find that the answer is $6.67.

Why did you think the answer was $7.50?

Because you used the *arithmetic mean* ($10 plus $5 divided by 2 = $7.50.) But I used the *harmonic mean*[22] ($200 by 30. Thus we're both right — the average *price* is $7.50, but the average *cost* is $6.67. Since the harmonic mean always produces a lower number than the arithmetic mean, *you have a built-in profit!*

Dollar cost averaging works because it acknowledges that we're all dummies when it comes to the stock market. Should we buy at its high of $10 a share? Of course not, but we're too dumb to know that the

---

[21]If you don't think you can even manage that, see Chapter 49 to learn how.
[22]Don't get too excited — you learned about both of these in grade school.

current price is destined to be the high, so we buy it. Thus, dollar cost averaging protects you by saying, "Okay, you dummy, if you insist on buying at $10 a share, I'm not going to let you buy very much."

Later, when the price goes down to $5 a share, DCA says, "Hey, you dummy, now's the time to buy!" so it forces you to buy lots of shares. In other words, DCA has you buy relatively few shares when the price is higher and more shares when the price is lower, thus giving you the average lowest cost. And since the average lowest *cost* is lower than the average lowest *price*, you're in a great position to enjoy a profit.

Investors are a funny lot. When the price of their favorite ice cream drops 50%, they load up, but if the stock market cuts the price on their favorite stock — in essence, putting it on sale — they figure there's got to be something wrong, so they return the shares they previously bought!

Thus, dollar cost averaging succeeds because you buy fewer shares at higher prices and relatively more shares at lower prices. To make it work for you, simply invest a specific amount of money at a specific interval. Perhaps $100 per month, $25 per quarter, or a $2,000 IRA each year. It does not matter as long as you are consistent. Be sure to invest at each interval regardless of what the stock market is doing at the moment.

In fact, dollar cost averaging helps you overcome your fear that you'll invest at the top of the market. If you had invested $1,000 in the S&P 500 on January 1 of every year since 1965, you'd have earned an average annual return of 11%. But if you got really lucky and were able to make your investments on the one day each year when prices were at their lowest, you'd have averaged 11.7% instead. But, knowing your luck, it's more likely that you'd have picked the worst day to invest each year. If so, your average annual return would have been 10.6%.

As you can see, it doesn't much matter when you invest when you dollar cost average. It only matters that you *do* invest and that you *stay invested.* "Timing" doesn't matter — "time in" does.

"Common sense is genius dressed in its working clothes."
—Ralph Waldo Emerson

267

Two Problems and Two Tips with Dollar Cost Averaging

There are two problems with trying to implement dollar cost averaging correctly — and you're the cause of both of them (what else is new?).

Problem #1: When the Price Goes Down, You Won't Want to Buy More

"Why should I keep buying this dog?," you'll ask, allowing your emotions to defeat you. Therefore, when dollar cost averaging, follow Edelman's Rule #2: Never follow the price in the newspaper; it will only upset you and prevent you from doing what you need to do to achieve financial success. Just buy your shares and ignore the rest.

Problem #2: You May Fail to Follow Through

It is vital that you *stick to your plan*. Too often, people simply forget to keep it up, what with life's everyday hectic schedules and all. *Don't let anything stop you from fulfilling your DCA obligation on schedule.*

To help you establish a successful DCA strategy, be sure to follow these two important rules:

Like everybody else, our clients too have difficulty keeping up with dollar cost averaging. To help them, we created a free service called The S.M.A.R.T. Plan.™

Through The S.M.A.R.T Plan,™ we mail an invoice each month to our clients. It's not an actual bill, but it looks like one. The invoice reminds them to send money to their mutual fund account. Each client chooses the amount to be displayed on the invoice, but they are not required to respond, although of course, it's in their own best interest to do so!

Thus, when our clients are busy paying their phone bill and sending in their mortgage payment, seeing this invoice reminds them to "pay themselves first." Our clients love this service, because it helps them stick with their financial plan. After all, *Saving Monthly Accumulates Rewards over Time.*

Tip #1: Use Stock Mutual Funds, Not Individual Stocks

Do not use individual stocks or you run the serious risk of mistakenly engaging in the dangerous practice of *dollaring down* instead of dollar cost averaging.

Case in point: On a tip from his uncle, one of my clients once bought a stock at $6/share. When the stock later dropped to $4, he bought more.

> You don't need my firm's S.M.A.R.T Plan,™ to enjoy the benefits of dollar cost averaging. Just sign up for Automatic Checkbook Debiting with your favorite mutual fund. Through ACD, the fund each month will withdraw a pre-authorized amount from your bank checking account and deposit that money into your fund account. All you need to do is remember to record the transaction in your checkbook.

("If I liked it at six," he figured, "I ought to love it at four!") When it dropped to $2.50, he bought more, and more still when it dropped to $1. Soon after the stock became worthless, *Forbes* ran a story disclosing that the stock was an alleged front for the Mafia. By that time, my client had lost $33,000.

You see, when a given stock begins a significant sustained downward spiral, there's often a good reason — with no assurance that the price will ever recover.

Yet for dollar cost averaging to succeed, the price must recover. This is why you'll have better success with DCA via a mutual fund instead of via specific stocks, because if a given stock is on a permanent downward trend, the fund manager can dump the stock and replace it with another. Thus, although a given stock might never recover, the fund can, preserving DCA's effectiveness.

Tip #2: Choose the Most Volatile, Speculative Investment You Can Find

The best choice for DCA, and this might surprise you, is a fund whose price tends to swing to great highs and lows. Ordinarily, we'd dismiss funds with such high betas (Chapter 38) as too risky, but when you're using DCA, this risk plays to your advantage.

Why? Because DCA's success is based on the efficient accumulation of shares. That means you need an investment which can drop in price, for the bigger the drop, the more shares you accumulate and the better your efficiency. After all, if you use a bank account, dollar cost averaging won't make any difference.

> Why do so many people fail financially? Because they fail to follow successful strategies like dollar cost averaging. The president of one of the largest mutual fund companies in the nation once told me that of his fund family's four million shareholder accounts, only 65,000 were adding money to their fund on a regular basis.

Thus, you should choose an investment (such as a U.S. or international stock fund) which experiences dramatic swings in value. If you are using DCA in such a fund, you'll actually celebrate when the stock market crashes! My clients who were dollar cost averaging during the Crash of '87 certainly did: Since these investors were buying each month anyway, the 30% drop in stock prices gave them the chance to buy on sale! When the market later recovered, they made a bundle. (Remember, the only people who get upset during market crashes are those who are selling — not those who are buying!)

Two Other Forms of Averaging

There are two other ways you can average your investments: income averaging and value averaging.

Taking Risk with Income, Not Principal

Some people just can't bring themselves to invest in stocks. If that describes you, consider income averaging. Through this method, you invest your money in super-safe U.S. Government Securities. Then, simply invest the monthly interest into a stock mutual fund. This way, your principal remains safe and sound, and your income will be invested in stocks via dollar cost averaging.

Naturally, this strategy is not as effective as investing the principal itself in stocks, but it's a good compromise for safety-conscious investors.

Value Averaging

This is actually a more effective strategy than dollar cost averaging, but I don't emphasize value averaging because most people cannot stick with it.

Unlike dollar cost averaging, where you invest a *specific amount* at a specific interval, value averaging has you buy a *specific number of shares* at a specific interval.

For example, you might buy five shares of a stock mutual fund each month. If the fund's share price is $10, you'll invest $50 that month. If the share price rises to $15, you'll invest $75 the next month, but if the price falls to $5, you'll invest only $25.

If you run some models of value averaging on a computer spreadsheet, you'll see that it produces more efficient returns than dollar cost averaging. The problem, though, is that you may be required to invest a sum that exceeds your ability at any given interval, and if you can't fulfill the obligation, you destroy the strategy. For example, if the share price jumped in a short period, you might not have the money that's suddenly required. Another problem is that although you're able to invest $50, you only invest $25 one month because the share price dropped. Not investing when you have the ability to do so is a waste of opportunity.

Therefore, I and most planners tend to favor dollar cost averaging, for you can more likely fulfill its requirements than you can those of value averaging. Dollar cost averaging also is easier because you send in the same amount each month. With value averaging, you have to track your investment to determine how much money you are supposed to send in.

So if you're a diehard, try value averaging. If you're a scaredy-cat, use income averaging, but if you're just like me, you'll use dollar cost averaging.

Chapter 47 - When is The Best Time to Invest?

Given $100,000 to invest, should you slowly invest that money over a period of time or simply invest all at once as one lump sum?

To understand the answer, realize that dollar cost averaging (Chapter 46) is intended for the *accumulation of assets*, not the *distribution of assets* already accumulated. Studies have shown that the investor who invests all at once makes more money than investors who DCA their way into the market.

> *"The only absolute safe way to double your money is to fold it once and put it in your pocket."*
>
> —Frank McKinney Hubbard

This should be no surprise to you; After all, the entire benefit of *averaging* means that by default, you are guaranteed *not* to receive the *lowest* cost available, which in turn means you will not receive the highest returns, either. Since stock prices historically have an upward bias, the *sooner* you invest, the more money you will make, and dollar cost averaging delays that effort.

People who try to DCA large sums into the market soon learn why their strategy doesn't work: By investing $100,000 over a one-year period, they invest just $8,333 in the first month. That means they *didn't* invest $91,667. What will they do with that block of cash in the meantime?

It sits in cash, earning 4% interest — hence the problem. Although you lower your risk by dollar cost averaging, you also lower your return. Therefore, the best time to invest is when you have the money! (After all, if you don't have any money, it's a pretty lousy time to invest, eh?)

This also means you should invest *as soon as you do have the money*. People sometimes tell me they're saving $25 per month in a bank account. "As soon as it grows to $5,000, I'll buy a mutual fund," they say. If your money is sitting in a bank at only 3% per year, do you realize how long it will take $25/month to grow to $5,000? Don't wait: Invest your money effectively *now*.

Though all this sounds fine, you're probably unconvinced, because you know that with your luck, the stock market will crash the day after you invest your life savings.

So please don't misunderstand me. I said to invest all your money at once, not invest all your money *into stocks* at once. The proper way to invest a lump sum is to invest it all at once — but into a highly diversified portfolio. Revisit Chapter 44.

Chapter 48 - Investing for Current Income

You may have noticed that all my strategies thus far assume you are investing for the future. But what if you need income now? This is a common problem for retirees, and here's your answer.

If you are retired, or about to be, keep in mind you still need to diversify because you still need at least some growth. In fact, a big mistake investors make is to focus too much attention on retirement. As a financial planner, I really don't care that you might be nearing retirement, and neither should you.

After all, retirement is a lifestyle issue, not an economic one (unless you have failed to make the proper preparations). Indeed, entering retirement doesn't mean you will stop eating.

My point is that being retired does not mean your life is over — although it once did. For most of our nation's history, people never retired. Instead, they died. Of course, this is no longer true: When you retire at 65, you can expect to live another 20 or 30 years. That means if you're 60, you need to be just as concerned about inflation as someone who is 30.

Yet most retirees and pre-retirees believe their only worry is *safety*. Wrong! You should be worrying that you'll be able to afford food after inflation erodes your income in the years to come. You don't want to run out of money before you run out of life.

Yet most people don't see it this way: By focusing exclusively on safety and their need for *current* income, they ignore — even sacrifice — *future* income by placing all their money into CDs.

Recall the retirees we described in Chapter 6. Over 14 years, their CD income was cut 74% while the cost of living grew 51%, leaving them with an income of $465 when they needed $2,666. Indeed, inflation and a large drop in interest rates have created a true crisis for Americans who depend on investment income.

The solution to this crisis is a *Systematic Withdrawal Program*, and it's available with virtually every mutual fund. Here's how it works:

Invest in a fund (balanced funds are my favorite for this strategy) and reinvest the dividends and capital gains. Believe me, you don't want them: They come only occasionally, and the amount changes frequently with fluctuations in interest rates and the fund's performance.

Instead, tell the fund you want to make withdrawals on a systematic basis each month, equal to the rate of 7.5% per year (or any rate you choose; you can increase or decrease the rate at any time, although clearly the more you withdraw, the higher the risk that you may begin to withdraw your own principal).

> *"The difference between rich people and poor people is where they sign their checks. Poor people sign the front. Rich people sign the back."*
> —Ric Edelman

On $100,000, a 7.5% income stream would be $7,500, or $625 a month, and your check will arrive like clockwork every month, just like a Social Security check.

Figure 6-25 shows the results of a Systematic Withdrawal Program using the average balanced fund for the period 1986-1995. (This hypothetical example relies on the average results of the universe of balanced mutual funds in existence for the 10-year period ending December 31, 1995. There is no assurance these results will be repeated.)

The $100,000 investment distributed $7,500 per year, yet 10 years later, the value of this hypothetical account had grown to $216,475.

Not only did you get a stable income, but after 10 years, you would have been able to adjust your income to begin taking 7.5% from the current value of $216,475. Thus by boosting your annual income to $16,236, *you would have kept pace with the cost of living.*

Contrast this to a series of 1-year CDs: They would have paid only $64,000 during the 10 years, the ending value would have remained $100,000 and the income in 1995 would have been just $5,810.

Two important points about this strategy: First, note that during this period, the account value fluctuated dramatically. In this example, the account fell in value twice — in 1987 and 1990. But so what? Your income remained stable (which is the primary concern of retirees), and over the entire period, the account grew.

Second, the tax implications are confusing. Although you received checks totaling $7,500 per year in our example, this is not necessarily the amount on which you paid taxes. Instead, taxes are due on the fund's dividend and capital gain distributions, which you voluntarily reinvested, and this figure might have been higher or lower than the income stream you received. (Remember: You always pay taxes on dividends and capital gains, whether you receive them in cash or reinvest them back into the account.)

If you — or your parents or relatives — are upset that today's CD rates are only a fraction of what they used to be, consider this outstanding alternative.

SYSTEMATIC WITHDRAWAL PROGRAMS

Assuming a $100,000 investment on January 1, 1986...

Year	...invested in a 1-year CD:		...invested in the Average Balanced Fund receiving monthly income equal to 7.5% per year on a systematic basis:	
	You would have received annual interest income of...	...and the Year-End Value of your CD would have been:	You would have received annual income of...	...and the Year-End Value of your fund would have been:
1986	$7,020	$100,000	$7,500	$133,240
1987	$6,920	$100,000	$7,500	$129,245
1988	$7,920	$100,000	$7,500	$137,513
1989	$9,700	$100,000	$7,500	$156,717
1990	$8,630	$100,000	$7,500	$148,591
1991	$6,570	$100,000	$7,500	$179,546
1992	$4,050	$100,000	$7,500	$185,009
1993	$3,320	$100,000	$7,500	$198,027
1994	$4,060	$100,000	$7,500	$184,646
1995	$5,810	$100,000	$7,500	$216,475
Total Income:	**$64,000**		**$75,000**	
Ending Value:	**$100,000**		**$216,475**	

FIGURE 6-25

Chapter 49 - Three Ways to Create Savings

Maybe you're finding it hard to save. That's not uncommon, for even those who are free of debt sometimes find it difficult to save money. Many people spend all their money each month, and they can't (or won't) change their spending. If that describes you, the following strategies will help.

Savings Creator #1: Pay Yourself First

Let's begin by accepting two facts. Fact One: you spend all your money every month, and have nothing left to save. Fact Two: You can't change Fact One.

Fine. I won't argue with you.

> *"A billion dollars doesn't go as far as it used to."*
> —J. Paul Getty

Instead, let's just make a subtle change in *how you pay your bills*. Currently, you deposit your paycheck into your checking account, and then you start writing checks. If you're like most, you pay the mortgage first, then car payments and other loans, followed by the phone bill and utilities. You save the credit cards (if any) for last, because the amount you pay to them is directly related to how much is left in your checkbook after all the other bills are paid.

So, you send minimal amounts to each credit card company and by the time you're done, your checkbook balance is at or near zero. And while you promised yourself that you'd save some money this month (like you promise yourself every month), you now discover (as always) that there's nothing left to save. In fact, you barely had enough to pay the bills themselves.

Without realizing it, you are treating yourself as a creditor — albeit a benign creditor. You want to pay this fellow named Yourself, but you know Yourself will never hassle you for the money, so it's okay to miss a few payments — or ignore Yourself altogether. Thus, you pay Yourself last each month, which all too often translates into not paying him at all.

To fix this, you must pay Yourself first — before you pay any other bills. By writing a check to Yourself for $25 or $50 (or whatever), you are certain that you will have paid Yourself — before your checkbook runs out of money.

And if you're concerned that you will run out of money, don't fret — because you're going to run out of money anyway (you always do, right?). At least, this way, you'll run out of money *after* you've paid Yourself. And that's the point.

Savings Creator #2: Your Future in a Peanut Can

Try using a trick my big brother Brad taught me when I was eight years old: Stop spending coins; spend only paper currency.

It's easy: Just put the change you collect each day into a piggy bank (I still use the Planters Peanuts can that Brad gave me) and you'll save $20 a month or more — and double the savings if your spouse does likewise, even more if you get the kids involved. Then deposit the money into your mutual fund account.

Who says saving money is hard?

Savings Creator #3: Spend Your Way to Wealth

Many people fail to save because they simply don't want to stop spending. Fine. Keep spending. In fact, I want you to.

Just change what you spend your money on:

"It's better to live rich than to die rich."
—Samuel Johnson

- Instead of buying a bottle of ketchup, buy Heinz stock.

- Instead of buying a gallon of gas, buy stock in Exxon.

- Instead of a six-pack of soda, buy shares of Coca-Cola.

- That new lawnmower? Try stock in John Deere instead.

So go ahead and spend your money. Spend as much as you want. But instead of buying things that later will have no value (like an empty ketchup bottle or a vacation), or virtually no value (like costume jewelry, clothing, or furniture) make sure the things you buy will retain and even grow in value.

Remember: Life is a series of choices. I'm not telling you to stop spending money, merely to choose *how* you spend it.

Once you get into this habit, you'll develop as much excitement buying investments as you currently do buying clothes. The reason that this is a foreign concept for you is that you have never bought anything that has retained it's value — except maybe your house. But once you start to buy things that rise in value, you'll never look back. If you think shopping is fun, wait until you start shopping for things that make money for you. Now, *that's* shopping!

"Take care of the pence, for the pounds will take care of themselves."
—Philip Dormer Stanhope

Chapter 50 - How to Prepare for Economic Collapse

You may have noticed that all the advice in this book is based on the simple premise that the world is not going to come to an end. But for all the pessimists, doomsayers, conspiracy theorists, and other partypoopers who disagree with me, for those who truly believe (or who merely occasionally ponder the notion) that the entire federal system is about to collapse, let me offer you the steps you should take to prepare:

1. Immediately sell all investments: stocks, bonds, government and municipal securities, mutual funds, company retirement plans, IRAs, and stock options. Close all bank accounts and empty out any safety deposit boxes. Cancel all insurance policies and obtain any cash values from such policies now.

2. Quickly sell your home and all other real estate.

3. Place one-quarter of your assets in cash (U.S. currency), using small denominations — nothing larger than twenties. Keep substantial amounts of cash with you at all times. Bury the remainder in several geographically-distinct places, each at least 10 miles from another.

4. Place one-quarter of your assets in the currencies of Switzerland, England, Germany, France, and Japan. Keep a substantial amount of these currencies with you at all times. Bury the remainder alongside your U.S. currency.

5. Place one-half of your assets into gold coins (using the American Eagle, Canadian Maple Leaf, or South African Krugerrand) or bullion (using coins, wafers, and kilobars [32.15 ounces]. Avoid bars [at 400 ounces, they're too big]). You also can use silver ingots if you wish. Keep a substantial amount with you at all times. Bury the remainder alongside your cash.

6. Quit your job. The paycheck you get will be no good anyway.

7. Buy a house with surrounding property in the mountains, selected with the following criteria:

    - difficult to find, more difficult to see, most difficult to reach
    - at least 100 miles from any government office or military base
    - reliable, independent, and water source on the property
    - easily defended

8. Build several escape routes and hidden entrances/exits/hiding places on the property, along with traps and mines to keep intruders and trespassers at bay.

9. Buy at least one all-terrain four-wheel drive vehicle, one motorcycle for each person in your group, and two German shepherds (male and female). Stock lots of fuel and spare parts for the vehicles and biscuits for the dogs.

10. Load up on survivalist gear: clothing, weapons and ammunition, drypacked foodstuffs; electrical generators, lamps, two-way and ham radios, emergency medical kits, tools, and rations. Also: complete reference books covering the fields of botany, medicine, mechanical engineering, warfare, construction, farming, psychology, pharmacology, and sociology. Also almanacs, encyclopedias, and while you're at it, novels, too, for leisure time might be high. Books on tax law will not be required. A Bible, Koran, or Torah is highly recommended.

11. Hope to hell you're right, for if you're not, you'll look awfully silly.

BROOM HILDA   RUSSELL MYERS

Reprinted by permission: Tribune Media Services.

Part VII
The Best Financial Strategies

Part VII — The Best Financial Strategies

In this part, you will learn:

- How to get out of debt

- Whether to buy or lease your next car

- How to pay for college

- Whether parents of young children should work

Chapter 51 - How to Get Out of Debt

I'm going to show you how to get out of debt and increase your ability to save. But first, let's see how people get themselves into debt in the first place.

Is money a problem for you? Here are some warning signs, courtesy of the Consumer Credit Counseling Service:

- an increasing amount of your net income is going to debt payments

- you pay only the minimum amount on loans and credit cards

- you've reached your limit on credit cards

- you pay bills with money that was intended for other things

- you use credit cards to pay for things that you used to pay for with cash

- you often pay bills late

- you delay or omit visits to the doctor or dentist because money is tight

- you get calls from collection agencies regarding unpaid bills

- you work overtime or a second job to raise cash to pay bills

- losing a job would create instant financial trouble

- money is a constant concern to you

If any of this hits home, you need to read this chapter.

Don't Spend Tomorrow's Income Today

Nobody intends to become debt-ridden, but at some point in your life you may turn around and say, "Gee, how did I accumulate all this debt?" It starts very innocently.

You see, none of us are born in debt. We start life with a clean slate. But then we make bad decisions, or we fall into traps, and the most common trap people fall into is committing themselves to a future lifestyle that is predicated on their current lifestyle.

> *"A family budget is a process of checks and balances; the checks wipe out the balances."*
> —**Arthur Langer**

Here's a great example. Debbie is 23 and lives with her parents. She earns $23,000 a year. Her parents cover her basic living expenses, although Debbie chips in $500 every month.

Recently, Debbie's old clunker died and she needed a new car to get to work. She intended to buy a Ford Escort for about $12,000, but the salesman talked her into buying a hot new Mustang for $23,000. Well, we can't really blame the salesman — Debbie loved sitting behind that wheel. And considering her income and expenses, as the salesman showed her, Debbie easily was able to afford the 'stang. So she bought it, financing $20,000. Her payment is $445 a month for five years.

By committing herself to this payment for the next five years, she will not be able to move out of her parent's house. Consider the figures: Her after-tax income is about $17,000, or $1,400 per month.

BABY BLUES   KIRKMAN & SCOTT

Reprinted with special permission of King Features Syndicate.

From this, Debbie has obligated herself to $445 for the car payment, plus another $150 per month for insurance, gas, and maintenance — a total of 43% of her income! That leaves her with only $805, and that's not enough to rent an apartment and pay for food, clothes, furniture, and utilities — plus entertainment expenses.

Today, Debbie doesn't mind. But what about three years from now? She has made a decision today that commits her income for the next five years. This not only means she must continue to earn at least as much in the future as she earns today, she must actually *increase* her earnings if she wants to improve her lifestyle.

And since she has already committed $595 toward her automobile expenses for the next five years, and another $500 to her parents in lieu of rent, her discretionary income is reduced to just $305 per month. So guess what happens when she decides to rent a house at the beach for a week with her girlfriends next summer? Debbie runs out of money — not because she doesn't have any money, but because she has already committed the money she has.

> *"Just as soon as people make enough money to live comfortably, they want to live extravagantly."*
> —Anonymous

So, to get by, Debbie starts to pay for gasoline with a credit card. When it is time for fall clothes and Christmas shopping, she uses the credit card some more. Soon, she discovers that she's built up thousands of dollars in credit card charges. When the bill arrives each month, she find herself unable to pay it off because her money already has been spent.

It's very easy to fall into this trap, and newlyweds are caught all the time. My clients Darren and Barbara asked me if they could afford to buy a $225,000 house, and after reviewing their situation I told them they could, but only if they were willing to become "house poor." They'd have to use all their current savings and investments to get into the house, and then, even after considering both their incomes, they'd be stretched each month to pay for the mortgage and related costs. Thus, I told them, they could afford the house *if* they both continued to work and *if* their future expenses and income both remained unchanged.

Because I didn't say "no" outright, they were excited. "But," I was quick to remind them, "you don't have children yet."

Too often, I have seen couples experience radical changes when a baby comes. But by purchasing such an expensive home — by committing such a large amount of their income to maintaining that home — they essentially were making decisions today that would affect (haunt?) them in the years to come.

Therefore, I advised them to buy a less expensive home, one that did not place such financial restrictions on them for the next 30 years. I cautioned that by doing it their way, in the best case they'd be house poor and in the worst case they'd lose their home. They rejected my advice. Six years later, after two children, they lost the house and divorced. (For more on the notion of working while raising young children, see Chapter 54.)

Expenses Should Be Adjustable Over Time

If you want to avoid the debt trap, keep your fixed expenses as low as possible. Don't obligate yourself to long-term expenses, such as "buy now, pay later" deals. That way, if your income or lifestyle changes, you will be able to handle the change financially. Debbie and Darren & Barbara failed to do this.

"Budgeting: A method of worrying before you spend instead of afterward."
—Anonymous

But let's say you have succeeded on this point. Let's say you haven't made commitments for income you haven't yet earned. Thus, when your expenses go up or your income goes down, your lifestyle can change accordingly. Congratulations — but don't skip the rest of this chapter yet.

There's still one more trap awaiting you: You must be willing to make that lifestyle change when the time comes. Being *unwilling* to change is as deadly as being *unable* to change.

The best example I can offer is Lon and Gretta. When they married, Lon was 42 and Gretta was 39, and she became (rather unexpectedly) pregnant at 41.

From the time she was 18 until her marriage, Gretta had been on her own. She owned a condo, and enjoyed an excellent career. She earned $60,000 and, with no family, was able to live quite comfortably.

> *"Money is better than poverty, if only for financial reasons."*
> —Woody Allen

Lon was in research, with an income not as high as Gretta's. He too owned a home, and after the wedding, they sold their houses and together bought a bigger, more expensive home. Still, not much changed for them financially. Their joint income allowed them to live pretty much as before.

Then they had the baby, and six months later, Lon was let go after his firm lost a big grant. This forced the family to rely solely on Gretta's income for a time. Soon, Lon was back at work, although at a lower salary. Although things should have worked out, by the time they came to my office, Lon and Gretta owed $30,000 to credit cards.

Although they had not fallen into the trap of spending money they hadn't yet earned, they had fallen victim to the second trap: They each continued to spend as they always had, without regard for their new and different circumstances.

Indeed, they acted as though they were still "single and free." Gretta would think nothing of spending Saturday at the mall. Lon, too, regularly indulged himself. A car buff, he was forever under the hood, installing some new gizmo or other he bought at the local speed shop.

Yet they never adjusted their spending to reflect their new family obligations. So while they incurred new expenses with the house and the baby, they still maintained their *previous* spending habits. And while they easily could have paid for their new lifestyle or their old one, they couldn't afford both simultaneously.

Thus, Lon and Gretta continued to use their credit cards as each had done for the past 20 years. But now, instead of being able to pay them off each month as they'd always been able to do, balances started accumulating. At thirty thousand, it occurred to them that something was wrong. But they weren't sure what. After all, they hadn't been doing anything new or different. They had always spent money, and their incomes had always been enough to cover it. So *spending* couldn't be the problem. What, then, could it be?

This is the trap many people get into. We are so used to supporting only ourselves that we become used to instant gratification. We don't have to worry about feeding or clothing others, and since we earn our own money, we don't have to ask others for permission before we spend it. We've got ready access to cash that we're not afraid to spend. And since all our friends are just like us, it seems both easy and right.

Then one day you find yourself in your mid-40s with a spouse, a house, and kids — and lots of debts. Make sure you don't commit tomorrow's income today, and when your life changes, make sure your spending habits change with it.

Getting Out of Debt is Like Losing Weight

Now that you understand how people get into debt, let's focus on how to get out of it. In fact, it's a lot like losing weight.

The problem with trying to lose weight is that nature abhors a vacuum. Most people who eliminate (or sharply reduce) eating from their daily activities don't replace it with anything. That goes against nature, for if you don't fill the void, nature will fill it for you.

You know the drill: People who lose weight focus all their attention on *the food they're not eating*. So as soon as they reach the weight they wanted, guess how they celebrate? By going out to dinner!

I find the same problem with clients who are trying to get out of debt. Many people who want to eliminate their debt or save money try to do so by *not spending* — and as soon as they reach their goal, they reward themselves by, you guessed it, *shopping* — putting themselves right back where they started.

SALLY FORTH   HOWARD & MACINTOSH

Reprinted with special permission of King Features Syndicate.

So if you want to get out of debt, the first thing you must realize is that "getting out of debt" is the wrong goal. For one thing, it's not fun. Getting out of debt means you can't spend money, and that's no fun for the same reason dieting is no fun (for dieting means you can't eat, or at least you can't eat the stuff you want to eat, or in the quantities you want to eat it).

So we need to set the right goal. And that means we must learn about goal-setting.

The Four Steps to Properly Setting Goals

First, set a positive goal for yourself. "I will save to buy a home" is a positive goal, while "I will not spend money" is a negative goal. By focusing on the positive, you'll quit spending money because you'll be so focused on your goal that you won't notice you've stopped spending money.

Second, set a date for achieving your goal. A goal is not a goal until you set a date for it. Having lived in the Washington, D.C., area for 15 years, I've always planned to go inside the Washington Monument. But I never have, just as New Yorkers never visit the Statue of Liberty! Why not? Because I have never set a date. We have too many things to do in our lives, and therefore only those with deadlines ever get accomplished.

So set a date for achieving your goal, and make sure your date is attainable. If it's not, you'll become discouraged and quit. But don't set a date so far away that achieving it is pointless. "I want to be debt free by the time I die" is a silly deadline, because you won't be able to enjoy the benefits of achieving that goal.

And don't worry about missing your deadline, either. One of my clients is 35 and a self-made millionaire. When I congratulated him on his success, he replied, "What success? I failed miserably! My goal was to be a millionaire by age 30 — I didn't make it until I was 34!"

If you aim at the eagle, you'll bag the pheasant, and you won't eat crow.

Third, write it down. Until you see your goal in front of you, it's not real. Tape your goal onto your bathroom mirror, your refrigerator door, your car's steering wheel, and your PC's monitor. Keep reminding yourself of your goal. One client of mine kept a picture of his dream house above his television. Another, who wanted to buy a Jaguar, bought a Matchbox version for five bucks and kept it in his pocket. His co-workers regularly saw him playing with it at his desk. (Today, he drives the real thing.)

> **"Whoever says money can't buy you happiness doesn't know where to shop."**
> **—Anonymous**

Dartmouth polled their graduating class of 20 years ago, asking one question: Have you established a specific written life goal plan? Only 3% of the graduates had done so, but when the college compared the net worths of the graduates, it discovered that the 3% who had created a written plan for themselves were, in the aggregate, worth more money than the remaining 97% put together.

And fourth, stay focused. Keep your goal in front of you. If your goal is to buy a home, tour model homes. Read *House and Garden*, *Architectural Digest*, and similar magazines. Design your own floor plan. By immersing yourself in your goal, you'll find it easy to stop spending money, because you won't regard it as "not spending." You'll regard instead it as "preparing to spend my money on something *really special*."

> **"Obstacles are things a person sees when he takes his eyes off his goal."**
> **—E. Joseph Cossman**

Focus on the benefits you'll derive by reaching your goal, not on the sacrifices you're enduring. If you can't perceive the benefits, you won't achieve your goal, and even if by some chance you do reach your goal, you won't sustain your victory.

Keep all this in mind as I show you the mechanics of getting out of debt, for if you simply follow the steps I outline for you, you won't do yourself any good. Oh sure, following my plan will get you out of debt — but it won't *keep* you out of debt. Only you can do that.

Set your goal, give yourself a deadline, write it down, and stay focused. You'll be amazed how far this will take you.

Where to Start Your Journey

What's the first thing you do when driving to a place you've never been? *You look at a map.* And where's the first place you look? *Where you are.* Only after finding your current location do you then seek the place you're trying to reach. By comparing the two, you can figure out how to get there.

And that's the first thing you've got to do with your debts: You must become an expert on *where you are.* Do you know *exactly* how much money you owe and to whom you owe it? Can you tell me the cost of that debt — the interest rate and minimum payment?

Too often, people in debt have no idea how much they owe. If you don't know the details, you can't fix it. Telling your mechanic that the car doesn't work is not much help. He's got to know exactly where the problem is — before he starts repairs. Similarly, if you don't have a firm grasp of exactly what you owe, to whom you owe it, and what the payment terms are, forget about trying to eliminate your debts. So let's start there.

It's simple to do. Just take a sheet of paper and make four columns. In the first column, list the name of each creditor (who it is you owe). In the second column, list the amount you owe to that creditor. Third, state the interest rate each is charging you, and fourth, state the minimum payment you must make each month. Do this before continuing. I'll wait.

...

Now that you have your list, I'll bet you wrote them down as you thought of them, in random order. So let's do it again, this time in order. Which creditor will you place at the top of your list? When I ask that question in my debt management seminars, most participants think the first debt to list is the one with the highest balance.

Wrong.

When making your list, show first the creditor which charges you *the highest interest rate.* Place the 21% credit card above the 18% credit card, which appears above the 14% card and so on — even if you owe more to the 14% card than to the 21% card.

> I hope seeing all your debts listed on a sheet of paper makes you realize that you need to pay off those debts. If you keep going into debt, you might set a new record. In our firm, that record is held by a client who has $170,000 in credit card debts. His minimum payment is $12,000 per month!

How long will it take you to become debt-free? For most people, at least as long as it took to accumulate the debt. So if you've been increasingly in debt for five years, plan on taking five years to get out of debt.

If that surprises you, remember that you can jump into a hole faster and easier than you can climb out of one, and if that discourages you, remember to focus on the benefits, not the costs, and forget about quick fixes. There is no such thing.

And you can forget about "credit doctors" or other marketers who claim they can "fix" your credit record for you. Such pitches are a scam. There is nothing anybody can to do repair a bad (but accurate) credit record — except you, by following the methods I'm outlining for you here. No quick fixes, no magic solution.

I'm addressing these credit repair outfits in a sidebar because that's all the attention they're worth.

Management Before Elimination

I emphasize the *rate* instead of the *balance* because we have to stop the bleeding before we can cure the patient. You're not going to get rid of your debt overnight, and until you do, additional interest charges are accruing. Therefore, you must reduce the speed with which interest charges are accumulating, and that means we have to focus on the debt that's charging you the highest interest.

And, in case I need to say it: While we're working on eliminating your debts, do not add to them.

Now that you have listed all your debts in the proper order, look at column four: the minimum monthly payment. Each month, make certain you pay the minimum payment to each creditor. Never skip a payment and always send at least the minimum. If you don't, the creditor will make a note in your credit file, and this will haunt you when you try to buy a house or a car. Make sure you stay current. I cannot overemphasize the importance of this.

After you pay the minimum to each creditor, devote all your remaining money exclusively to the creditor that charges you the highest rate. Do not spread this money evenly among all the debts. Instead, send whatever you have left entirely to the most expensive creditor. After you finish paying off that creditor, go down your list to the next-highest creditor, again devoting all resources (beyond the minimum payments) to that creditor until that debt too is gone, and keep repeating this process until they're all gone.

Empty Your Bank Account

To accelerate this process, withdraw any money you have in the bank and send it off to the creditor at the top of your list.

If this advice shocks you, please understand that it makes absolutely no sense to have money in the bank earning 3% while you have debts that cost 18% or 21%. While you're at it, liquidate any other assets you have, such as savings bonds, stocks, mutual funds, even baseball cards.

> **Liquidate all your assets, with one exception: Do not liquidate your IRA or company retirement accounts. The tax penalties would be so high and you would be jeopardizing your future retirement to such an extent that it's not worth it.**

"But if I close my bank account, I won't have any money," you might be complaining. Well, I've got news for you: *You don't have any money now!* You just don't realize it. And if you're worried about needing cash in the event of an emergency, let me ask you: What do you think a credit card is for?

Why bother paying more than the minimum to *any* card, when paying the minimum is so much easier? Besides, paying the minimum will eventually pay off the balance, right?

Right. But the key word there is *eventually*. Say you've got an 18% credit card with a balance of $1,800. If you pay only the minimum each month, it will take you nearly 14 years to eliminate the debt. But if you pay just $10 more per month, you'll get rid of the debt in less than four years — saving you 10 years and $1,400 in interest!

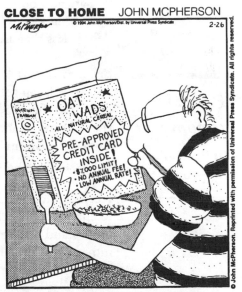

CLOSE TO HOME JOHN MCPHERSON

Yet another example of the credit card companies' aggressive attempts to attract new card-holders.

Love Your Credit Card

"I had plastic surgery last week. I cut up my credit cards."
—Henny Youngman

I love credit cards. What I don't like is credit card debt. Credit cards are wonderful cash management tools, and I encourage you to obtain one and keep it with you. If the car breaks down during a road trip, you can pay for repairs and overnight lodging. If Aunt Ida needs you to care for her, you can buy a plane ticket to see her right away.

So I have no problem with credit cards. What I have a problem with are people who don't pay them off every month, and with people who own assets that produce lower returns than the cost of the debt, when they should be selling the assets to eliminate the debt.

Get Out of Debt By Getting Into Debt

Next, go borrow some more money.

And get as much as you can — provided that (a) the amount of money you are now borrowing is not more than the total amount of debts you already have; and (b) the interest rate you'll have to pay on this new debt is less than the rate you're currently paying.

"Practice economy at any cost."
—Anonymous

See how this trick works? Say you owe $5,000 to an 18% VISA card. Maybe you can get a new VISA card from another bank that charges only 14%. Take $5,000 from the new card to pay off the balance on the old card — and in essence, you'll cut your interest rate to 14% from 18%. Do this as often as you can to reduce your interest charges while you're working to eliminate the debts themselves.

Keep in mind that this is just a temporary solution. The real goal is to eliminate the debts, not merely reduce their cost. And be sure you understand the terms of your new card: Many card issuers offer introductory rates to get you to switch, but these "teaser rates" often last only a few months, after which time the rate rises dramatically — perhaps to a rate even higher than the rate you're currently paying. In other cases, the low rate applies only to new purchases, not to existing balances that you transfer from another card. Execute this strategy carefully, or you'll defeat the purpose.

Next, Focus on the Cause

Now that you've stopped adding to your debts, reduced their interest charges, and begun a plan to eliminate them, we can focus on what caused all this debt in the first place.

And guess what the cause is? *It's you.* You are the cause. You are the problem. Remember the Newmans from Chapter 1, and how they were spending their money? Like them, too many of us let our spending habits get us into trouble.

The most astonishing aspect about the Newmans' is that their daily spending represented 3% of their total annual income. To understand the importance of this, consider John D. Rockefeller. When he died in 1937, how much money did he leave behind?

All of it!

Do you get the point? You were trying to guess how much money he had in dollar terms, because that's how you're used to dealing with money. But where money is concerned, *dollars* are irrelevant. To succeed financially, you must think in terms of *percentages*.

Thus, when Rockefeller died, he left "all of it" behind, or 100%. Rockefeller had 100% of his money, just as you have 100% of yours. The reason this is so important: *Amounts* constantly change, but *percentages* never do. The amount of money varies from day to day, but the percentage never does: You always have 100% of your money.

This is why you have the same assets as Rockefeller: He had 24 hours a day, just as do you, and he had 100% of his money, just as you have 100% of yours.

By the way, Rockefeller had $900 million when he died in 1937, the equivalent of about $12 billion today, or three times as much as Ross Perot.

If you don't earn interest on your money today, you've given that day away forever. And if you earn a lower interest rate today than you should have earned, you have given that away as well — forever.

If you want to make your finances very simple, just think of all of your money as 100 *per cent*. Through your entire life, you will have only 100 of these cents, and you will never get more, so spend them with care.

297

Where Does Your Money Go?

So start thinking about it. What will you do with your 100 pennies? The first thing you do is something you'd rather *not* do: pay taxes. That costs you about a third of your pennies, leaving you with 67.

Finished with the taxman (or should I say he's finished with you), you first need shelter. Lop off 28% of your income for housing. That leaves you with 39 pennies.

Next comes food, on which the average family spends about 18% of income. You're down to 21 pennies — and you're still naked!

> *"My problem lies in reconciling my gross habits with my net income."*
> —**Errol Flynn**

So let's buy some clothes. Seven pennies ought to cover that. Now, you need to get around town, so siphon off 11 pennies for transportation-related expenses. You've got three left.

What's going on here? You've got only three pennies left and you haven't had any fun yet! (You also haven't paid for insurance, utilities, or your kids' education, either, but I won't mention those because I don't want you to get discouraged.)

And with *their* precious three pennies left, the Newmans chose to buy candy bars and coffee! So, the next time you think spending fifty cents on a soda won't make any difference, think again.

SALLY FORTH   HOWARD & MACINTOSH

Reprinted with special permission of King Features Syndicate.

You Make Plenty of Money

Please don't try to tell me you're in debt because you don't make enough money. You already make as much money as it takes to become financially successful. You simply are not using your resources wisely. Life is all about choices, and if you are in debt, I'm willing to bet it's because you made some bad choices. You spent every tax refund you ever got — often before you got it. Every time you got an increase in salary, you upgraded your lifestyle. And while it's true that this new income allowed you to handle the new payments, it also did two more things: It forced you to maintain your income stream so you could keep paying for these new financial obligations, and since the new income was pre-allocated, you were prevented from saving it or from using it for other purposes in the future.

> Just to prove I'm not totally heartless, I will admit that there is one legitimate cause of indebtedness that is beyond one's control: huge medical bills resulting from health problems.
>
> But that's about it. Being out of work doesn't qualify, which will annoy those reading this who have been downsized in the past few years. While I agree that a person might be facing some serious economic challenges after being let go rather unceremoniously, that's not an excuse to be in debt. You should have been accumulating savings while you were working, and maintaining cash reserves to tide you over (at least for a time), and your lifestyle should not have been relying on your full income stream. In other words, loss of your job should be a difficulty — not a disaster.
>
> If this scenario has happened to you, I'm sorry. And if it hasn't (yet), be forewarned so you can be prepared.

If you think you're not rich because you never had the opportunity to become rich, look elsewhere for sympathy. Why do I say this? Because in a study by the Employee Benefit Research Institute, 70% of non-retired Americans say they could reduce their expenses in order to save for retirement, but only 18% say they are very likely to do so. Apparently, living well today is more important to most of us than living well tomorrow.

Indeed, say you go out for dinner and a movie twice a month, spending $75 each time. That's $1,800 a year. If you instead saved that money over 30 years at 10% per year, you'd have $339,073! Yet, according to EBRI, restaurant meals "are no longer considered luxuries, but a standard part of the middle-class lifestyle."

So, please, don't tell me you don't make enough money. The truth is you simply *spend* too much money.

Track Your Expenses

What all this leads to is the need to track your expenses. You've got to determine where you are spending your money, because until you know where your money is going, you won't be able to stop it from going there.

I want you to track your expenses so that you can see how you are spending your money. I am convinced that once you see how you are spending your money, you will quickly and easily fix the areas that need improvement. And you'll be able to do all this without having to create — or live with — a budget.

There are two ways to track your expenses. One way is fast but hard; the other is slow but easy. The choice is yours. The fast/hard way is to spend a weekend going backward in your checkbook and through your credit card statements for the past six months. It's hard, because you'll work all weekend, and you'll have gaps, particularly regarding the cash you spent, but by Sunday night you'll be ready to go to the next step.

> **Forget about budgeting, for you won't do it even if I tell you to. There's probably nothing more tedious, or less effective, because budgets only reflect how you *think* you'll spend your money, not how you really *do* spend your money. After all, how often does life go according to plan? So forget the dreaded "B" word.**
>
> **See? There's good news after all!**

The other way is slow/easy, and here you start to track all your expenses for the *next* six months. It's very easy to do, for you just record expenses as they occur. It takes very little effort, but it's slow: It'll take you six months to complete the process. The choice is yours.

PC or No PC

If you have a computer, you can do this with Quicken, Managing Your Money, Microsoft Money, or any similar software package. You also can use a spreadsheet program such as Excel or Lotus. *This is not an excuse to buy a personal computer, nor does it dismiss those who don't have one.* Tracking expenses is just as easy with an ordinary pencil and paper, so don't think you need to spend two grand on a PC to get started, or that you can't get started because you don't have a PC.

If you have a PC, follow the instructions provided by the software. I'll explain how to do it here for those using paper, which is how my wife Jean and I did it when we started to get our financial life in shape.

But first, starting now, *you may no longer spend cash.* To effectively track spending, your money must leave a paper trail, and cash leaves no trail. Therefore, you must use checks and credit cards only. I'll talk more about how to properly use credit cards later in this chapter.

To begin, draw on your paper a series of columns (you'll probably need 20 or so, maybe more).

In the first column, list to whom you wrote each check. In the next column, write down the dollar amount of the check. For each of the next 20 columns (or more if needed), assign a spending category — one each for FOOD, CLOTHES, AUTO, UTILITIES, and as many other categories as you wish. Then list the amount shown in column two under the appropriate category.

For example, say you spent $157.99 at the grocery store. In the first column, you'd write the name of the store. In the second column, you'd write "$157.99" and then you'd move to the FOOD column, where you'd again write "$157.99." See Figure 7-1.

TRACKING YOUR PERSONAL EXPENSES

Paid To	Amount	Food	Clothes	Gifts	Auto	Travel/ Enter.	Phone
Grocery Store	157.99	157.99					
AT&T	21.21						21.21
Ford Motor Credit	236.49				236.49		

FIGURE 7-1

I don't care what your categories are, provided that each is meaningful to you, and that you use the category consistently. For example, where will you show money spent on dinners at restaurants? Will you list it under FOOD or ENTERTAINMENT, or perhaps DINING OUT or something else? For some people, UTILITIES is sufficient, while others set separate categories for TELEPHONE, ELECTRICITY, WATER, and GAS.

The choice is yours; Just make sure you are consistent with where you place the expense. Also try to ensure that each category is not so broad it is used too often nor so limited that it is seldom used. For example, CLOTHING is fine, but creating three categories —CLOTHING-HIM, CLOTHING-HER, and CLOTHING-KIDS might enable you to determine more easily where the money is really going. But I once had a client who showed a category of "Clothes, William, Socks, Blue." Another client not only listed ENTERTAINMENT, she showed the name of the movie, gave a review, and listed that she bought a KitKat and Junior Mints. Both of these people are a little nuts.

Okay, they're a *lot* nuts. Don't go crazy with this. Just make sure your categories make sense to normal people. Below is a list of categories to help you get started:

EXPENSE CATEGORIES

Household
Mortgage/Rent
Association Fees
Utilities
Phone/Cable
Food
Child Care
Private School
Clothing
Maintenance

Charitable
Church Dues
Tithe
Donations

Transportation
Auto Loan/Lease
Fuel/Oil
Public Transit
Parking/Tolls
Repairs/Maintenance
Registration Fees

Health Medical
Professional Fees
Drugs/Medicine

Debt Service
School Loans
Personal Loans
Credit Cards

Insurance
Life
Health
Disability
Long-Term Care
Auto
Home
Personal Property

Gifts
Birthdays
Anniversaries
Holidays

Savings/Reserves
Auto
Home
College
Retirement
Special Events

Recreation
Club Dues/Fees
Movies
Vacation
Dining Out
Lessons/Camp
Hobbies

Legal & Accounting
Retainers
Tax Preparation

Miscellaneous
Barber/Beautician
Professional Dues
Subscriptions
Pet Care
Domestic Help
Child Allowances
Dry Cleaning
Alimony
Child Support
Toiletries
Parental Care

FIGURE 7-2

What to Do When an Expense Extends to More Than One Category

Often, you'll need to itemize your spending. Say you spend $300 at a department store, buying a variety of items. Write the name of the store in column one, "$300" in column two, then split the total among the various categories appropriately. See the example in Figure 7-3.

TRACKING YOUR PERSONAL EXPENSES

Paid To	Amount	Food	Clothes	Gifts	Auto	Travel/ Enter.	Phone
Grocery Store	157.99	157.99					
AT&T	21.21						21.21
Ford Motor Credit	236.49				236.49		
Macy's	300.00		225.00	75.00			
Cash	190.07	18.76			46.31	125.00	

FIGURE 7-3

Do this for all your spending each month, and then total each column at the bottom. This will show you not only your total spending for the month, but how much you spent in each category.

Once you have produced dollar totals for each column, you need to convert the dollars to percentages, so you can see what percentage of your total spending occurred in each category. To do this, divide each column's dollar total into the total dollars you spent (the figure at the bottom of column two). See Figure 7-4.

TRACKING YOUR PERSONAL EXPENSES

Paid To	Amount	Food	Clothes	Gifts	Auto	Travel/ Enter.	Phone
Grocery Store	157.99	157.99					
AT&T	21.21						21.21
Ford Motor Credit	236.49				236.49		
Macy's	300.00	225.00		75.00			
Cash	190.07	18.76			46.31	125.00	
Total	905.76	176.75	225.00	75.00	282.80	125.00	21.21
Percent	100%	20%	25%	8%	31%	14%	2%

Example: $\dfrac{176.75}{905.76} = 20\%$

FIGURE 7-4

When you're done, all the categories should add up to 100% — and this is how the Newmans discovered that 3% of their income was going to coffee and candy bars. And you'll be just as shocked about how you're spending your money as the Newmans were shocked about how they were spending theirs, and that's how you'll fix it.

You'll see that you are spending incredibly high percentages of your income in completely foolish places, and you won't tolerate it. Instead, you'll stop. But until you go through this process, you won't know whether the amount you're spending in a given area is too much or too little.

Where Americans Spend Their Money

According to the federal government's Consumer Expenditure Survey:

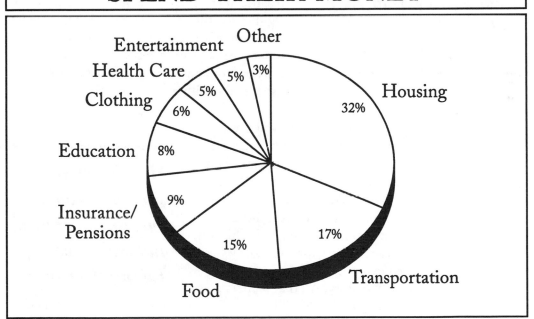

WHERE AMERICANS SPEND THEIR MONEY

FIGURE 7-5

How to Handle Credit Card Purchases

Most of us use credit cards often. Although you write a check to "VISA" or "DISCOVER" or whatever, that obviously doesn't reflect what you bought. Therefore, you must break down the invoice, itemizing the bill across the many categories you've established.

But what if you're only making a minimum payment, or if you already had a balance, added to it, and now are making only a partial payment? It can get confusing, and here's how to solve that problem: Go get a new credit card.

> **Yes, go get another card. How many debt counselors advise people that they need to get *more* credit cards to help them get out of debt!**

"Never borrow money except for a primary residence, education, or emergency health problems."

—Old South saying

I want you to get a new card because I want you to stop using all your existing credit cards. By placing all your new charges on the new card, you'll be able to track them each month. And make sure you pay off the balance in full every month. If you won't be able to pay off the balance at the end of the month, you have no right to use the card now. Remember, a credit card is merely a way for you to use the bank's money for 28 days instead of your own. If you can't pay for an item with cash, then you can't use the card, either.

By using the new card, you're not using the old ones — but you still have balances on them. That means you need a category called DEBT SERVICE. And as you make payments to those old cards, this is where you list the payment. This way, you can ignore what the money was used to buy. Those purchases are ancient history; All that matters now is paying off the debt.

"It takes time to succeed because success is merely the natural reward for taking the time to do anything well."

—Joseph Ross

Two Tricks to Help You Pay Off Your Cards Each Month

If you are concerned that you don't have the discipline to pay off the balance in full each month, get an American Express card instead of VISA, Mastercard, or Discover. American Express is a charge card, not a credit card. Amex does not charge interest. Instead, you MUST pay the full balance every month.

> **The truth is, if you don't have the self-discipline to pay off your credit card every month, I'm not sure this chapter will help you very much. You know carrying a monthly balance is stupid, and if you do it anyway...well, there's not much I can do for you if yer gunna ackt stoopid.**

Here's another trick that might help you pay off the balance each month: Every time you use your new credit card, immediately write a check payable to VISA (or whomever) for the amount you just charged. If you spend $35 at a store and put it on VISA, write a check for $35 to VISA right away. Then put the check in your drawer, and when the bill shows up, just slip the check into the envelope. You will have already debited your checking account, so the money is already there to cover the bill when it arrives.

If You Must Spend Cash

Sometimes spending cash is unavoidable, so if you must spend cash, get a receipt so you can remember what to record later. Just write "cash" in column one (like when you wrote a check to "Visa") and itemize by category where the money went. Thus, if you withdraw $100 from the ATM machine, you'll need to record what you spent that money on — whether it was a pack of gum (FOOD), a parking meter (AUTO), beer with the gang after work (ENTERTAIN-MENT), or all three.

CALVIN AND HOBBES   BILL WATTERSON

Two "Unexpected" Expenses You Must Expect

When I ask participants in my debt management seminars to list categories of spending, they're real quick to offer food, shelter, clothing, transportation, education, travel, entertainment, and a few others. But there are two categories no one ever mentions, and I think this helps explain why you're in debt.

Unexpected Expense #1: Repairs

When I see that people have credit card debts, I ask why. And they often reply with something to the effect of, "Well, the car broke down. It cost $800 to fix. As soon as I get out from under that, I'll be okay."

And they work real hard and they pay off $100 a month until they get rid of that bill, and guess what happens next? The roof leaks. Or their son falls on the playground and breaks his arm. Or the washing machine dies. Let's face it: Life happens. Yet when things happen, people feel shocked, as though they didn't know things happen.

If you think occurrences like these are unexpected, you're deceiving yourself. Things are great until the car breaks down. Things are great except you owe $500 in taxes. Things are great until the basement floods. *Things are great until the next thing happens.* Time, a great physicist once said, is just one damn thing after another.

You just bounce from one crisis to another, like the guy who's always losing 10 pounds. He loses 10 pounds but then it's Thanksgiving. So in January he loses 10 pounds again, then it's Easter. Afterward, he loses 10 pounds, and it's Father's Day. He loses 10 pounds and goes on vacation. It's just a vicious circle, and we find our debt clients running round and round all the time. They're constantly going from "I paid off my credit cards" to "I owe $2,000" because they don't recognize that expenses in the UNEXPECTED category occur all the time. While it's true we don't know what the expense is, when it will occur, or how much it will cost, we should acknowledge that *something* will occur — and it's going to cost us money.

> *"Earn a little, and spend a little less."*
> —John Stevenson

This is why you can't track your expenses for just one month. You must do it for six months because you might go several months without an incident. And if you have a crisis that costs you several hundred dollars every four or five months — and you do, as tracking your expenses will reveal for you — you'll learn that you must set aside enough money on a monthly basis to prepare for it. So set a new category for yourself called UNEXPECTED.

Unexpected Expense #2: Gifts

Haven't you heard of Christmas or Hanukkah? Every December, people are overwhelmed by the money they spend on presents. Then they get to January and say, "Thank goodness that's over," and they spend the next six months paying off the bills. Come November, they get shocked all over again.

It's easy to prepare for the costs of gift-giving: Just look at last January's credit card bills and checkbook — because you're going to do it again this year!

And while we're on the subject, does anybody you know have a birthday? If you're not anticipating birthdays, anniversaries, graduations, confirmations, weddings, births, and other milestones in the lives of those you love, you're just adding to the "repair bill crisis" that is certain to hit you.

Control Yourself

After completing their six-month review, many people show me their results and lament all the money they spend on gifts. "But I've got no choice," they say. "I've got a large family and we're very close," implying they are forced to spend hundreds or thousands of dollars every year.

FRANK & ERNEST   BOB THAVES

WHILE MY LEFT BRAIN WAS WORKING OUT A SENSIBLE BUDGET FOR THE MONTH, MY RIGHT BRAIN ORDERED A GIANT PIZZA!

E-mail FandEBob1@AOL.COM

THAVES 10-11
© 1994 by NEA Inc.

Nonsense. If you are deep in debt, you have no business spending money you don't have on gifts that people don't need. You can bake cookies or rely on a hobby to make them a gift. Write a check to the American Cancer Society and tell the family that you've done so in their name.

Do you think I'm being cheap? Hey, I'm talking about *survival* here. If you were rich, yes, I'd say you were cheap. But since you're broke, I'd say you are prudent. And if your family — the people who know you best and love you most — can't support you in your efforts to improve yourself financially, then shame on them.

Have you ever heard the phrase "the rich get richer and the poor get poorer?" It's true, because the rich keep doing the things that got them rich, while the poor keep doing the things that got them poor.

Indeed, being "poor" is a state of mind. But being "broke" is just a temporary financial condition. People who are poor stay poor; They won't bother to read this book or seek to improve their lot in life. But you're not poor, you're just broke — as evidenced by the fact that you are reading this chapter. And although you're broke at the moment, that will change because of your desire and your effort.

Don't be SNIOP

And frankly, you shouldn't care if your sister thinks you're cheap. Because if that's what she thinks, then she's not much of a sister.

Don't let the attitudes of other people drag you down or dissuade you from achieving your goals.

Don't be SNIOP'd. Don't be Susceptible to the Negative Influences of Other People. Think about it the next time your co-workers invite you out for a drink after work. You know that if you go, you'll spend fifteen or twenty dollars. You want to go with everyone, it's fun, it helps with office politics, and so on, but you also know you'll spend twenty bucks you don't have.

You need to excuse yourself from going. "I'm really tied up. I have other plans." (Your "other plan" is to become wealthy.)

But they'll use peer pressure. You know what I'm talking about. So you give in, telling yourself you won't spend much. But the night goes on, and sure enough, you've spent $20. Congratulations: You've been SNIOP'd.

You need to put a steel rod in your back and say "I CAN'T MAKE IT." If they criticize you, or talk about you, or hassle you about not joining them, please realize that this is their problem, not yours. If you allow yourself to be caught up in their game, you'll never get anywhere financially. This is often hard to do, but it's a critical element to eliminating your debt.

If you're wondering how it is that your friends, neighbors, and co-workers can afford to go out for dinner, buy fancy cars, take frequent vacations, dress their kids with the latest fashions, and decorate their home so extravagantly, here's the answer: They can't.

These people are seriously in debt. Look, you know what they earn — about the same as you. And you know you can't afford it. That means they can't afford it, either. But your neighbors are so busy keeping up with each other that it's hard to tell. Remember: You can see their clothes, their house, their car and their vacation photos, but you haven't seen their credit card statements or bank accounts. Don't assume that since they're doing it, (a) it can be done, and (b) you ought to be doing it, too.

Why? Because the truth is, (a) it *can't* be done, (b) *they* shouldn't be doing it, and (c) you shouldn't be trying, either.

Without question, you will experience the feeling of being SNIOP'ed. "No way," you're saying. "Not from my friends." Wanna bet? You'll find it's like crabs in a barrel. As soon as one crab starts to crawl out, another will reach up and pull it back down. If you're not prepared psychologically for this to occur, you will get SNIOP'd for sure.

Virtually All Your Expenses are Optional

George and Monica came to me several years ago. At the time, they had a combined annual income of $120,000, yet owed $22,000 to credit cards, and they were adding debt at the rate of $2,000 per month (they were obtaining a new card every month). Despite their high income, they were spending considerably more than they were earning.

When we reviewed their situation, I discovered that a lawn service visited their home twice a month, at $85 per visit. I told them to cancel the service, and George replied, "But our lawn will look terrible if we do that! We must keep this expense."

I also noticed that they subscribed to cable TV, including every premium channel — a monthly cost of $69! I told them to cancel cable. Monica gasped. "There will be nothing for us to watch! We can't cancel cable!"

I'm sure you'll agree with me that a lawn service and cable TV are optional, yet neither George nor Monica understood this. Both these expenses are optional, just as — pardon me for shocking you — virtually *all* your expenses are optional.

Health club membership? Optional.

Entertainment? Optional.

Telephone? Optional.

Clothes? Most of it — or more accurately, the total money you spend on it — is optional.

Food? Again, mostly optional. Oreos, I regret to inform you, are not mandatory.

Are you getting my point? Almost everything you spend money on is optional! So don't tell me, "I gotta do this, I gotta do that." Sometimes, though, you'll find that you've been spending money on a certain item or in a certain way for so long that by now, not only can't you remember when you *didn't* spend money like that, now you think you *must*. Again, let me repeat: *Cable TV is optional*. Hard to believe, but true.

You *can* stop spending your money on things that in the bigger picture really don't matter. You *can* change it. You *can* fix it. You *can* stop it.

Don't feel locked in or trapped, because you are not. True, there are some expenses that you cannot change easily or quickly. Once you buy a car, you're stuck with the payments. But most of your spending is much more flexible than you might think at first. You are in more control of what's happening around you than you realize. But you've been SNIOP'd for so long you've forgotten that you do have a choice about how you spend your money.

The bottom line is that you got into debt because of your *attitude*, not your income. And it is your attitude about money that must change first, or changes in income won't matter.

As it didn't for George and Monica. By refusing to change how they spent money, they sought other solutions for their debt. And they found one: the equity in their home. They owed $150,000 on their $200,000 home, so from the $50,000 in equity, they borrowed $25,000 and used that money to pay off their credit cards. Problem solved, right?

Wrong: Within a year, their credit card balances were back up to $24,000, only this time they no longer had $50,000 in home equity to rely on. Within two more years, unable to keep up with the payments on their house, they sold it and rented an apartment (at least that ended the lawn service). Still, it wasn't enough, and they later filed for bankruptcy. It will be 10 years before they are able to buy another house — if ever.

I got a call one day from a viewer to my TV show. "I have $15,000 to invest and need your advice," he said. "By the way, I'd really like to talk with you about our debts." He explained that he and his wife owed about $40,000 to credit cards, so I told him to use the $15,000 to help pay down the debt. "No, I don't want to do that with this money. I want to invest it," he said. "I want to handle my debts separately."

I asked him about his income. "My wife and I both sell real estate," he answered.

"Oh," I replied. "I guess the recent softness in the real estate market has hurt your income."

"Not at all," he said. "We made about $225,000 last year and $165,000 so far this year. We just can't seem to get rid of these debts."

He asked for an appointment to come in and talk about it. "But we have to see you as soon as possible," he said. I wondered why. "Are you facing some deadline?" I asked.

"No," he said. "It's just that we're leaving for a two-week vacation to Cancun and I'd like to get started on this debt thing before we go."

Like I said, people get into debt because of attitudes, not incomes.

Focus on the Future

Although you must deal with your debts, don't beat yourself up over them — and don't let anyone else beat up on you, either. Not your spouse, not your parents, not your friends. No matter what your debt scenario, how you got into debt is relatively unimportant. The past cannot be changed, so focus your energy on what you can change: the future. Determine what you need to do from here forward, and then do it.

> Once, while I was presenting this information in a seminar, a woman asked, "Isn't there a shorter way to do all this?"
>
> I just stared at her.
>
> If there was a shorter, easier, faster, less painful way to accomplish your goal of becoming debt free, don't you think I'd have told you by now?

Simple Does Not Mean Easy

Everything I've described in this chapter is fairly simple to understand, but that doesn't mean it's easy to do, and I know this from personal experience.

Back in 1982, before Jean and I launched our financial planning practice, we were in another business, and it was several years before we admitted failure, ending up about $6,000 in debt.

To solve that problem, we decided to kill the business (before it killed us) and start over, rebuilding from scratch. With no income and no assets, we moved out of our three-level, 3,000 sq. ft. townhouse and into a one-bedroom, 900 sq. ft. ground-floor apartment.

We placed an ad in the paper which read, "Moving family must sell everything," — which we did, except for the kitchen table my best friend Andy built for me in high school, the bedroom suite that once belonged to my parents, and a sofa. We sold all our other furniture, the TV — everything.

If you've never had a bunch of strangers walk through your home, offering you ten bucks for a desk that got you through college, or $15 for your stereo, you can't imagine what this experience is like.

We accepted all offers and raised $2,000 that day, because I needed $600 for a security deposit on the new apartment, $200 to rent a truck to move our few remaining items, and to buy food and gas for the next few weeks while we got ourselves re-established. For three weeks, we spent $25 per week on food — mostly fruit and vegetables. If you think it can't be done, think again, for we proved it's possible. People who are eating peanut butter to save money are fooling themselves: We discovered that processed foods are so expensive we couldn't afford them. But you can eat well enough to survive on very little money.

The manager of a nearby retail store let us have some boxes he planned to throw away, and we used them to pack our clothes and dishes. I didn't want to pay $30 a month for a self-storage place, and since we had no furniture anyway, we stacked the boxes in our new apartment, creating a mountain in the living room. But I told Jean not to worry. "It'll only be for three or four months. We'll be out of here by then," I said.

We ended up living there for four years. During that time we did not own a television, nor did we buy a newspaper, because I refused to spend 25 cents each day when I knew I could get a copy at the office after someone else finished reading theirs.

Entertainment was the library and public parks. Years later, when we eventually bought a TV, we discovered how smart we were to sell our old one. By not having a TV, we were not constantly bombarded with messages to buy, buy, buy. By avoiding television's influence, we didn't feel the need to spend money. Perhaps you can control the TV shows you watch, but you can't control the commercials that air during them.

To rebuild income as fast as possible, Jean and I both had several jobs, working seven days a week, often leaving one job to arrive at another.

After living so frugally (made all the more difficult because life wasn't always like that for us) one day we splurged on dinner, spending $7 at a nearby Roy Rogers. We knew we shouldn't spend the money, that we'd regret it later, but we needed the release, and, boy, did those burgers taste good! That meal reminded us of the things we had given up and it increased our resolve to be able to return to a life that would allow us such luxuries. It was a year before we visited Roy's again.

Despite the challenge, we knew we weren't going to have to live that way forever, and for sure, we don't live that way any more. By denying ourselves the little pleasures, setting goals, and focusing all our energy on achieving them, we paid off those debts and in four years had saved enough to buy a townhouse. We've since sold that and built a single family home, which we later sold to move into an even bigger one. Indeed, Jean and I are able to enjoy our lifestyle now because we were willing to sacrifice it all for a time, something most people will not do. We give each other a "knowing glance" whenever people comment on the success we've achieved. "You're both so young," people tell us. "It's amazing how successful you've both become in such a short time." If they only knew. You might say it took us years to become an overnight success.

You, too, can become an "overnight success." You will be on this Earth for 40, 60, or 80 more years. You can choose to live month-to-month as you have been living, or you can choose to live better. Give up your materialism for a few years, reduce your needs for now, and one day, you'll be able to exceed your current lifestyle. All it takes is a little effort each day, and a lot of days.

There isn't any magic to this, no get-rich-quick scheme. And while you may be afraid of how much time it will take to succeed, that's nothing compared to how much time is really left in your life. So what if it takes you 10 years to get out of debt? You'll still have 30 or 50 or 70 years to enjoy after that.

Take advantage of this information. I know you can do it. The mere fact that you've read this far tells me that you've got the interest. I've given you the direction, so all you need is the initiative! Find it within yourself and as W. Clement Stone, the great motivational trainer, said, **Do It Now**.

> *"Nothing lasts forever —*
> *not even your troubles."*
> —Arnold H. Glasow

Chapter 52 - Should You Buy or Lease Your Next Car?

It'd be easy for me to tell you to take the bus or keep your junker for another 140,000 miles, but that's not realistic. Besides, you know all that stuff anyway. So, since you're going to get a new car no matter what I say, let's answer the question: Should you buy it or lease?

Let's take the example of a car whose sticker price is $34,000. To buy it, with a 7% four-year loan and a down payment of 20% ($6,800), your payment would be $650 a month.

However, if you were to lease instead, you would pay a one-month refundable security deposit and your payment would be $450 a month.

Thus, leasing would save you $200 a month, and you would need only $450 down, not $6,800 (plus, in both cases, sales tax). This is why leasing is so popular.

Why Lease Payments are So Cheap

Economically speaking, cars consist of three parts: equity (ownership), depreciation (loss in value over time), and interest expense (on the loan, if any). If you finance the purchase of a car, you pay for all three parts, and you will own the vehicle in, say, four years. But if you lease, you are paying only for use of the vehicle. Therefore, you pay for the car's depreciation and interest, not the equity, and you return the car at the end of the lease term. This is why monthly lease payments are lower than purchase payments. Leasing, quite simply, is the difference between owning a car and renting one.

Why would a car dealer want you to rent (i.e., lease)? It's simple: If you lease the car, you pay $450 a month for four years. Then you give the car back, giving the dealer the chance to resell it. In other words, the dealer gets to sell the same car twice!

This means the dealer doesn't have to charge you (the first buyer) the full $34,000; You pay only the difference between what the car is worth today ($34,000) and what it will be worth four years from now. The second buyer pays the rest at that time.

Say the dealer expects this $34,000 car to be worth $15,200 in four years. He would therefore want you to pay $18,800 and the second buyer to pay $15,200. Thus, your lease payments would be based on just $18,800, whereas your payments to buy would be based on the full $34,000. That's why your monthly lease payments are $450 instead of $650. When the dealer resells the car in four years, he'll get the other $15,200.

The Key Factor: Residual Value

Leasing, then, features lower monthly payments because dealers expect the car to retain a certain value. In reality, though, lease rates are not based on what the car's residual value will be, but on what the dealer *pretends* it will be.

That's why lease payments often are so attractive. If, according to industry standards, a $40,000 car will be worth only $12,000 in four years, the dealer would have to base your lease on $28,000 worth of depreciation. That would make the lease payment absurdly high, and no one would take the deal. So the dealer pretends that the residual value will be $30,000, leading to lower, more attractive, lease payments. This game is dangerous for the dealer, but a bargain for you.

The key to the cost of leasing, then, is the "residual value," or what the dealer says the car will be worth at the end of the lease. Expensive cars tend to offer better lease deals than cheaper cars, for they retain more of their value, and the higher the residual value, the lower your lease payments.

Three Money-Saving Tips When Leasing

As with most financial transactions, success or failure is found in the fine print. Here are three items to keep in mind:

> *"When you think no one cares if you're alive, try missing a couple car payments."*
>
> —Anonymous

Money-Saving Tip #1: Make Sure You Have Gap Insurance

This is perhaps the single most important — and most overlooked — element of leasing.

Say your contract says the car's residual value at the end of the lease will be $15,200, but the car's actual value will be only $10,000. If you wreck the car three months before your lease expires, guess how much your insurance company will pay in settlement?

The insurer will pay the dealer (who owns the car) the actual market value, which is $10,000. But your contract says the residual value is $15,200. That means you are responsible for the other $5,200.

This "gap" between the lease contract's stated residual value and the car's actual value has caused many lessees to incur huge losses due to accidents.

The solution: Make sure your lease contract includes "gap insurance" — even if you have to pay extra for it, for being without it is like driving without insurance.

Money-Saving Tip #2: Avoid the Cap Cost Reduction

When someone buys a car, the more money he puts down, the less his monthly payments. Similarly, to lower your lease payments, you can make a cap cost reduction, which is a large, one-time payment made at the start of the lease. And as with a down payment, the more you pay in cap (short for capitalized) cost reductions, the lower your monthly payments. However, this is where the similarity ends.

Remember that when leasing, you do not own the car. Thus, if you make a cap cost reduction, you are making a down payment on property that is not yours. Never do that — no matter how much the dealer wants you to, and no matter how much it reduces your monthly payments — for in the long run, you are throwing your money away. And the run might not be so long, either: Steve leased a $25,000 car and paid $3,000 in cap costs. Two months later, he totaled the car. Since he didn't own the car, his insurer repaid the dealer $22,000; Steve lost his $3,000.

Paying cap costs is a waste even if you don't wreck the car. Why? Because the only reason dealers want you to pay it is so they can offer you a monthly payment that sounds really low.

Would you visit a dealer who advertised a $20,000 car for just $199 a month? You bet! But would you get excited about having to pay $345 per month for the same car? Not likely. And that's why dealers want you to pay a cap cost reduction. You see, in one recent ad, a car dealer offered a $20,000 car for $199 per month for 24 months with a cap cost reduction of $1,525. But paying $199 per month with $1,525 down is the same as paying $345 per month with no cap cost reduction. If $345 doesn't sound so hot (and it's not), then the other deal isn't so hot, either.

Instead of paying a cap cost reduction to lower your payments, ask the dealer to let you make additional security deposits. This will have the same effect as a cap cost reduction, except you'll get the deposit back when you return the car.[23]

Money-Saving Tip #3: Never Buy Optional Equipment in a Car You're Not Buying

When leasing, you must keep in mind that you don't own the car. That means you must be careful when agreeing to options that the dealer offers you. Take Carmen for example. She worked out a fine deal on a car — $250 per month for 36 months, with no cap cost reduction. But then she decided to have the dealer install mats, fancier hubcaps, a 10-disc CD changer, and a telephone. The cost of all these items came to $1,800, so the dealer added $50 to the monthly payment. This not only made sense to Carmen, since $50 per month for 36 months is $1,800, she thought it was a heck of a deal — because although she would be paying for the options over three years, the dealer did not add in any interest.

It was a deal all right — but for the dealer, not Carmen. When the lease expired three years later, Carmen returned the car — and with it, the mats, hubcaps, CD changer, and telephone. Carmen paid the full cost of owning those items, but she only rented them. Dumb move, Carmen.

---

[23]Unless, of course, you wreck the car or return it with excessive wear and tear.

What she should have done is incorporated the cost of the options into the overall price of the car, and *then* negotiated the lease price. That way, she'd be renting the options along with the rest of the car.

Remember: When you lease, you are renting the car and everything in it. Don't pay the costs of ownership when you lease.

Leasing and Taxes

When leasing, you are liable for sales tax even though you do not own the car. If your state levies a personal property tax, you'll have to pay this, too. But to entice you to lease, many dealers offer to pay the property tax for you if you lease. Shop around for the best deal.

To Lease or Not to Lease: Here is the Answer

To determine whether you should buy or lease, answer these two simple questions:

1.   How many miles do you drive per year?

In most leases, you are allowed to drive only 15,000 miles per year, or 60,000 miles on a four-year lease. Anything more will cost you up to 25 cents per mile. Therefore, leasing works best for people who drive less than 15,000 miles per year, and if you know you'll drive significantly fewer miles than 15,000 per year, you can negotiate a lower lease payment.

2.   How long do you generally keep your car?

Leasing is best for people who keep their cars for four years or less. Remember that when leasing, you never enjoy a payment-free month. At the end of the lease, you must turn in the car and get a new one, with a new lease or purchase contract.

Thus, if you like to keep cars for seven or eight years, you'll find that, over the long run, is much more expensive than buying.

Don't Lease Beyond the Car's Warranty

If you choose to lease, don't lease for a term beyond the car's warranty. If the car comes with a two-year bumper-to-bumper warranty, for example, get a two-year lease. By opting for a three-year lease, you could be stuck with huge repair bills in year three — on a car you don't own!

Leasing for Business

Leasing makes great sense for business, regardless of how many miles you drive, because you are allowed to deduct the cost as a business expense. (If you buy a car for business, you must depreciate it instead.)

Since cars are one of the largest purchases you'll make, talk with your financial advisor before you decide whether to buy or lease, how much to put down, and whether or not you should finance. The right decision can save you thousands!

Chapter 53 - How to Pay for College (Really!)

The first seminars I ever presented were to PTA groups on "How to Pay for College." But rather than presenting them to parents of high school sophomores and juniors, I would speak to parents of elementary-age schoolchildren.

Why? Because if you wait until your child is 16, you won't have enough time to prepare for the costs of college. You've got to focus on this subject while your kids are still in grade school.

> Heck, you need to work on this *before* the kid is born. Most who think about college costs already *have* children. And planners routinely advise their clients to plan for college (as this chapter suggests) while their kids are still young.
>
> But if you think you've got at most 18 years to plan for college, think again: Nobody says you have to wait for the baby to be born before you start saving. If you know you'll have children one day, you might as well start saving for college now. That way, you give yourself 20 or 25 years to save instead of just 18, 15, 10 — or 3. And the more time you have to save, the easier it is to achieve your goal.

CURRENT COSTS OF THE IVY LEAGUE

School	1995-1996 Tuition and Fees	Change Since 1988
Yale	$27,630	+43.8%
Tufts	$27,336	+44.2%
Harvard	$27,575	+46.7%
Princeton	$23,861	+52.5%
Brown	$27,234	+47.2%

FIGURE 7-6

The cost of college for today's newborns will be more than $180,000. That's tuition, room, and board for a four-year education at a typical state college. The Ivy Leagues will be more than $300,000. That's *per child*. Get used to it: You're going to buy several houses in your lifetime; you'll buy them simultaneously and you'll only live in one of them.

Too often, parents either don't think about future college expenses until their kids register for the SAT test, or their "plan" is a simple one: My kid will win an athletic or academic scholarship. *Voilà! Zee Crisis, she eez solved!*

If it were only that easy. The truth is that nationally, less than one-third of students receive any form of financial aid, and of those who do, the average aid meets only one-third of the need. Thus, if you're assuming your third-grader will be a football star because he's the fastest kid in his class, or that your child will be valedictorian because she always gets straight A's, think again. Educators will tell you there is no way to predict whether your young child will be a star when he or she is 17 years old (funny things happen to kids when they hit puberty — remember?), and it's a foolish financial plan that relies on such a premise.

A better idea is to start saving now. And how will you come up with the hundreds of thousands of dollars it will take to get your kid through college? Well, let me ask you this: How do you eat an elephant?

One bite at a time.

To accumulate the savings needed to send a six-year-old to college, you'll need to start saving anywhere from $600 to $1,500 per month, depending on your rate of return and the cost of the school your child will attend.

Those are absurd numbers, and they lead parents to do absurd things, including the biggest of all absurdities, *doing nothing*. "I'll never be able to save that much, so I might as well not save anything." Like most attitudes, this one will become a self-fulfilling prophecy.

Another dangerous strategy is to rely on the equity in your home.

This is an extremely common tactic among parents of today's college students, because today's 50-somethings have been caught totally off-guard by the costs of college. During the 1960s and 1970s, a four-year college education

"The 'birds and bees' I know about, Dad. I need to know more about the 'bulls and bears'."

cost under ten grand, and often under five grand. It was no particular financial struggle — either for the students or their parents. So, based on that experience, they assumed it would be the same when their kids reached college age.

But **The Rules of Money Have Changed** and college costs have skyrocketed, far outpacing the rate of inflation.

COLLEGE COSTS

Increases 1980-1995

662% Public Colleges
245% Medical Care
165% Housing
162% New Cars
42% Food
10% Energy

FIGURE 7-7

The result is that Mom and Dad are shocked when they attend College Night at their 17-year-old's high school. Where will we get the money, they ask each other? They quickly scan their assets: They have some savings, but not nearly enough for even one year, let alone four. They have the money in their company retirement plans, but that can't be touched without severe tax penalties. And they have their house, which they bought a few years before their daughter was born and which now has substantial equity. Thus, the answer is clear: They will take out a home equity loan to pay for college.

Bad Idea #1: Using Home Equity to Pay for College

This strategy will work: The child can attend college. However, this tactic all but destroys Mom and Dad's retirement plans and creates a ticking time bomb.

Think about it: Mom and Dad bought their home in their early 30s for $25,000. With a 30-year mortgage, they knew the house would be paid off in their early 60s — around the same time as they plan to retire. (After all, this is how *their* parents did it.) The mortgage balance is now down to $13,000 — but the house also is now worth about $100,000 — allowing the parents to pull out not just the original

$13,000 they've repaid over the past 20 years, but $70,000 more. Indeed, Mom and Dad are able to send their kids to college, but they find themselves three or four times deeper in debt than when they bought their house, and 50% closer to retirement.

The result: Mom and Dad will not pay off their home until they are in their 80s — 20 years *after* they had planned to retire!

Thus, using equity in the home is a fine solution for your college plan, but it creates havoc with your retirement plan. Still, all too many of today's parents feel they have no choice if they're to give their kids a college education.

Bad Idea #2: Using Student Loans to Pay for College

The second solution, commonly used when parents don't have home equity to rely on, or not enough to cover the college costs of all their children, is to seek student loans.

But reality soon hits. Under current federal rules for Stafford loans, first-year students can receive a maximum of less than $3,000. Even college seniors are eligible for less than $7,500 — and these figures are a far cry from the actual costs of college.

The qualification rules are perverse: Federal rules say parents who have managed to save just a little money must spend all of it on college, while parents who have amassed large assets are not so obligated.

> *"A major problem these days is how to save money for your children's college education when you're still paying for yours."*
> —Doug Larson

For example, take two families, both earning $80,000 per year. The Smiths have saved $20,000 vs. $40,000 for the Browns. Under current rules, the Smiths are required to contribute $14,695 per year before becoming eligible for aid, while the Browns must contribute $14,790 — or just $95 more! On a percentage basis, the Smiths must contribute 73% of their assets per year, while the Browns must contribute only 37%!

It really doesn't matter, of course, because both will eventually run out of money. Assuming the cost of college is $15,000, the Smiths will run of out money in the second year, while the Browns will run out of money in the third year. Thus, the federal loan rules are telling parents to save a lot — so some of your savings can survive college — or save nothing. For if you save only small amounts, you'll have nothing left after college, anyway. Since many parents find it impossible to save a lot, the system encourages them to save nothing.

Those who follow this strategy live to regret it. Many college graduates are saddled with tens of thousands of dollars in student loan debt, which will haunt your kids for 10 years or more after they graduate. Try buying a house or even a car with so much debt load.

EXPECTED PARENTAL CONTRIBUTION TO YEARLY COLLEGE COSTS

Based on Assets and Income

Total Income	Net Assets				
	$20k	**$40k**	**$60k**	**$80k**	**$100k**
$20,000	0	83	611	439	1,667
$40,000	3,260	3,380	4,199	5,163	6,291
$60,000	8,815	7,007	10,135	11,263	12,391
$80,000	14,695	14,790	16,014	17,142	18,270
$100,000	20,574	20,670	21,894	23,002	24,150

Figures provided are for a family of four, with one child attending college. These figures also assume one working parent per family.

FIGURE 7-8

Bad Idea #3: Using College Prepayment Plans

Sponsored by both individual schools (the first was Duquesne) and states (Virginia is the latest to offer one), these programs all work basically the same way: You send in a certain amount of money now (normally the current cost), and they promise that college will be paid for when your child turns 18.

There's lots of fine print, though, to wit:

- These programs cover tuition only — not room and board, which constitutes 40% to 60% of the cost of college;

- There is no guarantee your child will be accepted to the school;

- Your child might not want to go to that particular school, to a school in that state, or to *any* school, and in some programs, refunds are limited only to the amount you paid, with no interest;

- There is no guarantee the program will succeed. Michigan, for example, suspended its program because it was unable to keep up with the cost increases of its own colleges; and

- There are tax liabilities. Say you invest $15,000 now to avoid having to pay $75,000 when your child goes to college. The IRS considers this to be a capital gain of $60,000, which means you'll owe roughly $20,000 in taxes.

If you're wondering why I haven't discussed the notion of kids getting a job, it's not because I don't believe in it. I do. The problem, though, is that kids working a few hours a week at some minimum wage job will not enable them to earn and save the $10,000 or $20,000 annual cost of college.

So, sure, putting the kids to work can help, but it's not a real solution to the problem.

A better idea is to put your money into a good investment where the odds are high that it will perform at least as well as any prepayment plan, yet allowing you to maintain full control over the assets in the meantime.

Three Reasons Not to Save Money in Your Child's Name

Parents trying to save for college often save money in the child's name. Don't do it, for three reasons:

Reason #1: There is Little Benefit Under Current Tax Law

In the old days, putting money in your kids' names made great sense, because the parents were in tax brackets as high as 70%, while children were in 0% brackets. That huge spread created a tremendous financial advantage.

But the Tax Reform Act of 1986 closed this loophole by creating the Kiddie Tax. Today, Mom and Dad are likely to be in the 28% tax rate, or maybe 31%. Few Americans are in the 36% bracket, and even the highest is just 39.6% — a far cry from the 70% top marginal bracket in the old tax code.

> **In case you haven't noticed, I've been talking about college as though your child will attend for four years and then enter the workforce.**
>
> **Think again. With increasing frequency, today's college graduates go on for graduate and postgraduate degrees. So while you're figuring out ways to pay for the B.A. degree, make sure you or your child have resources left for graduate school.**

And worse, kids today earn little money tax-free: Until age 14, the first $650 they earn is not taxed, income between $650 and $1,300 is taxed at 15%, and everything above that is taxed at their parent's rate. After 14, they pay taxes at their own rate, but by then — if Mom and Dad are saving regularly in the kid's name — the child could be in the 28% bracket, anyway.

Since Mom and Dad are paying 28% and their young kids are paying 15%, the spread is only 13% — and this is too narrow a margin to make saving in the child's name worthwhile, especially when you consider the next two points.

Reason #2: Kids Take Legal Control of Their Money at Age 18

When saving for a child, the account must be registered in the child's name under the Uniform Gift to Minors Act. In a UGMA, an adult (usually a parent or grandparent) serves as Custodian and is responsible for investing and managing the assets. But the child is the "beneficial owner," meaning the assets really belong to the child, not to the adult. At age 18, the assets must be turned over to the child.

> All states offer UGMAs and many have adopted the Uniform Transfers to Minors Act as well. The former allows children to own stocks, bonds, mutual funds, and other securities; the latter allows them to also own real estate. Also, under UTMA, you can delay giving the assets to the child until age 21.

Picture handing $50,000 to your 18-year-old. If he wants to spend the money on a trip to Europe or a car instead of college, you can't stop him (short of your parental influence). A better strategy, then, is to save the money in your name, perhaps in a separate account, and to know in the back of your mind that the account is intended for college. (Hey, if your child decides not to go, or wins a scholarship, you get to keep the money!)

Reason #3: Saving in the Child's Name Hurts Your Ability to Qualify for College Financial Aid

All other factors being equal, a family whose child has assets is less likely to qualify for aid than a family whose child doesn't have assets. Because virtually all of the child's expenses are college-related (while parents have additional financial obligations), colleges require that students spend a larger portion of their assets than parents. Therefore, putting money in the parent's name rather than the child's will increase the family's eligibility for financial support.

What To Do If You Have a UGMA

Unfortunately, many parents — perhaps including you — already may have established a UGMA for your child. Creating such an account constitutes an irrevocable gift, and legally you cannot cancel the account and return the money to your own name. (Doing so would annoy the IRS, so don't do that.)

What, then, can you do?

Here's the solution: Remember that under a UGMA, the assets belong to the child, and the law requires that the assets be used for the benefit and welfare of the child. Most parents think this means the money can be used only for college expenses, but that's not so. In truth, money in a UGMA can be used for almost anything — provided "anything" is for the benefit and welfare of the child.

> *"No man's credit is as good as his money."*
> —Edgar Watson Howe

After all, your child needs clothes, food, shelter, education, and medical care, and there's nothing in the UGMA rules that say you can't use the child's assets to pay these expenses. For example, say you take your child to the doctor for her annual check-up and the bill is $200. Instead of paying for that yourself, withdraw $200 from the UGMA account and use that money to pay the bill. Simultaneously, send $200 of your own money into an investment (in your name) that is similar to the one used by the UGMA.

In this manner, you'll slowly erode the value of the UGMA, while building assets in a new account in your name. If you pay for all of the child's expenses through the UGMA, such as private school, camp, music lessons, clothing, even their portion of food, shelter, utilities, and insurance costs, you ought to have no problem eliminating that account well before the child is 18.

Keep good records and maintain receipts to show the IRS (if they ask) that the money you withdrew from the UGMA was used for the direct benefit of the child.

And don't get carried away: Liquidating a UGMA to buy yourself a new car "to chauffeur the child to soccer practice" is unlikely to win IRS approval. If in doubt about the validity of any expense, ask your tax advisor.

One Case for Using a UGMA

All the above notwithstanding, there is one circumstance where I regularly recommend the use of UGMA accounts: When a grandparent wants to save for a grandchild's college costs. I am unconcerned that a UGMA will hinder the family's ability to qualify for aid when the source of the UGMA assets is someone other than the parents, because this money is a gift. What does it matter if college is paid for by gifts or financial aid?

If a relative or family friend wants to give the child money for a birthday, holiday, or other celebration, that money *must* go into a UGMA for the child. After all, the donor is making the gift to the child and they want to know the child will indeed be the ultimate recipient of the money. They don't want the money to be used for the parents' financial problems (if they did, they'd have given the money to the parents, not the child).

So don't fret, Mom and Dad, that gifts to UGMAs will hurt your college financial aid eligibility.

Beware of IRC Section 2036(c)

But grandparents and other donors need to be aware of Section 2036(c) of the Internal Revenue Code. This section of the code holds that transfers to minors are considered void if the donor acts as custodian of the account.

Thus, if Grandpa gives $1,000 to the child, he should not serve as the custodian to the child's UGMA account. A parent of the child or other adult should serve as custodian instead.

Congress created 2036(c) to close an estate tax loophole. Remember that the custodian decides how to invest and manage the assets, so if a grandparent gives money to the grandson but serves as custodian, the grandparent retains control over the asset — almost as though the gift was never made. Yet if the grandparent dies, the asset would be excluded from his estate, avoiding or reducing estate taxes.

Congress rightfully concluded that lots of folks were making "sham" gifts in this manner, so the law was amended to say if you make gifts to an account for which you serve as custodian, the value of your gifts will be included in your estate for purposes of calculating the estate tax.

You can avoid this problem simply by naming someone else as the custodian. For more on estate taxes, see Chapter 73.

Dealing with College Costs Realistically

Every book on college planning I've read focuses on the incredible cost of a college education, admonishing parents that they need to sacrifice for 20 years to be able to meet this huge expense.

I don't agree, and that's why you're not reading much on college saving strategies in this book. The truth is that almost everyone is dealing with college costs the wrong way. That's because they're dealing with college *the old way*. But remember, **The Rules of Money Have Changed**, and you cannot approach the costs of college in a traditional fashion.

There are two reasons for this: First, you probably don't have the two decades you need to save for college. Second, you've ignored what is perhaps the primary problem with this entire subject: your kid's attitude (and maybe yours, too).

Let's face it: Going to college today is far different than it was a generation ago. We graduated either debt-free or with a small debt that was both tax-deductible and easily manageable.

That's not the case today. The best example I can give you is Bertha, the daughter of Lois and Jim. Bertha wanted to attend a private college that cost $16,000 per year. Dad obliged, mortgaging his house to pay for it.

Bertha planned to be a physical therapist. Late in her junior year, Bertha discovered she needed a master's degree to practice in her field, and she selected a Florida university. Dad, who by now had sent three kids to college, had exhausted his savings, so his ability to assist Bertha was sharply reduced.

Determined, Bertha borrowed as much as possible from her family, qualified for financial aid, and obtained credit cards and other personal loans. It all paid off: Today, Bertha is a successful physical therapist working in a major sports medicine facility, earning $42,000 per year.

She is also $45,000 in debt.

Between her student and personal loans and credit cards, Bertha's minimum debt payment is $1,100 per month, and she'll be saddled with that debt until she's 36 years old. And because she chose a career with no upward salary potential, her income is unlikely to improve. (She has contemplated becoming an administrator to make more money, but that would require going back to school for an MBA in hospital administration.)

Bertha can't change careers because she can't afford to go back to school. She can't quit her job because of her debt load, and she can't ever imagine being able to buy a house. And Dad, meanwhile, nearly lost his house in the process.

It's similar with Jason and Andrea. Soon to graduate from law school, Jason will owe $90,000 in student loans and Andrea $72,000. They hope to work for big law firms — the only ones who will pay the $60,000 starting salaries Jason and Andrea are counting on to enable them to pay off their debts.

Still, as huge as Jason and Andrea's debts are, they actually are somewhat better off than Bertha. At least *their* incomes can grow as they build their careers. Bertha's can't, for when she becomes too expensive for her employer, they'll just dump her and hire some other kid fresh from grad school.

Too many careers are like Bertha's: There is no relationship between the cost of obtaining the degree and the economic reward for having done so.

It is my contention that because of today's costs of college, we must approach the concept of going to college the same way we approach all other investments. Because today more than ever, a college degree is an investment. If you don't believe me, just ask your kids.

According to the University of California-Los Angeles's survey of incoming freshmen (Class of 1998), 75% said a "very important reason" in deciding to go to college was "to make more money." Their "essential or very important" objective was "to be very well off financially." These numbers are in stark contrast to students of 20 years ago: In 1971, only 40% of UCLA's freshmen felt the same way.

> **And don't fret if the only thing your kids want from college is a wife or husband. According to Census Bureau data, the average married couple who both have degrees earns three times more than the average married couple who are both high school dropouts, and twice as much as couples who are high school graduates.**

Thus, in the majority of cases, today's kids regard college as a means to improve their financial future, whereas their parents — who went to college in 1950s and 1960s — more often than not wanted to make the world a better place.

So while today's high school seniors think of college in terms of economic reward, their parents don't. This is how the disaster begins: The kids are making what they consider to be a practical investment, but their parents (who fail to see college in that light) don't equate the cost with the result.

In yet another example of how **The Rules of Money Have Changed**, parents need to change how they look at college.

Can I Have a Car?

How would you reply if your 18-year-old son came to you and said, "I have been looking at this hot, red Porsche Turbo. I've got to have it! It's only $72,000! Can I have it?"

You would refuse, of course, and none too quietly.

Yet when your son approaches and says, "I have been looking at this great school. I've got to go there! It's only $18,000 a year! Will you pay for it?"

Too often, Mom and Dad not only say yes, they will do whatever it takes to pay for it: They'll spend all their savings, they'll cash out the equity in their home, they'll borrow from their life insurance policies, they'll pull money from their company retirement plans, they'll get second jobs, they'll even ask relatives for assistance — all because it never occurs to them that *they don't have to say yes.*

But Mom and Dad think they do have to say yes. "After all, we're talking about my child's future! If I don't say yes, I will be responsible for destroying the one chance my child has for success! Money is not a concern here! If my child needs to spend $72,000 to go to college, then I'll do whatever it takes to make it happen!"

Years later, the parents are financially destroyed and/or the children are horribly in debt, both beyond their worst nightmares.

All because Mom and Dad took the financial advice of an 18-year-old. The kid said, "Have I got an investment for you!" and the parents bought it.

Four Ways to Survive the Cost of College

It's time we started challenging our nation's system of higher education, forcing colleges and universities to associate the cost of a degree with the economic reward one will receive when earning it. Demanding that families and young adults mortgage their futures is madness, and it's got to stop.

But until the system changes, you've got to change how you work with the system. To survive the costs of college, follow these four rules:

Rule #1: Tie Benefits to the Cost

Recognize that most high school seniors — and your kids probably are included in this group — can avoid expensive schools without any adverse affect on their careers. There's nothing wrong with having your son or daughter become, say, a teacher. Teaching is a fine profession. But let's face it: Teachers don't get paid a huge sum of money. Therefore, instead of spending $75,000 on a teaching degree, consider a school that costs $25,000 instead. Chances are the less expensive school will not adversely affect the child's ability to succeed.

Think about it:

- Most employers don't care *where* you went to school. The fact that you have a degree is enough. They're more concerned that you've got experience and the ability to

It's one thing to be working in a field unrelated to your college major — but it's quite another to be working in a field that doesn't require a college degree at all. In Washington, D.C., one-third of the drivers for the local Dominos Pizza franchise have college degrees. While most took the job because they couldn't find work elsewhere, many stayed because of the money: They often earn more than $50,000 a year. Reports one driver, a lawyer by training who now hopes one day to manage a store, "Imagine how far ahead I'd be if I hadn't wasted all that time and money on college and law school."

do the job. If you don't believe me, ask the personnel office where you work about what they look for in a new hire.

- Many college graduates eventually settle in careers completely unrelated to their degree. Think about what your old college classmates are doing now. Ask around at work to see how many of your colleagues have a degree related to their current occupation.

- Many college graduates never get a job, or quit within a few years to raise a family. Many of these never return to the work force — or they do so only after 10 or 20 years (which forces them to return to school to update their knowledge and skills anyway).

Of course, many in today's workforce do owe their success to their alma mater, such as doctors, lawyers, engineers, scientists, and other professionals. But it's a small percentage of the total number of people who go to college.

Rule #2: Factor in the Cost of Going to Graduate School

If your child is planning to enter a field that requires an advanced degree, you'd better keep costs down at the undergraduate level.

Rule #3: Choose to Involve — or Exclude — Your Child

Either *completely include* your child in the process of deciding which school to attend, or *completely exclude* them. Too often, the child starts the conversation by announcing to the parents, "I am applying to Penn State, Brandeis, and Cornell!" leaving the parents to figure out how to pay for it. That's the wrong way approach it.

There are two right ways (take your pick):

1.   Determine on your own how much you can afford to spend on your child's college education, just as you would when planning to buy a car, and then present this figure to your child. Tell them they must select a school that costs no more than this figure.

      Prohibit — rather than allow — your son or daughter from selecting a more expensive school and being responsible for the difference. Although some parents do this to instill financial responsibility in their children, it's a lesson too expensive for them to learn: All you'll do is saddle your kids with huge student loan debts that will haunt them for 10 years after they earn their degree. Besides, why would you let them go into such debt if you're unwilling to let yourself do it? There are easier, better ways to teach them financial responsibility (including the next point).

2.   Or, require that your child present you not only with the names and costs of the school he wants to attend, but also a financial plan for paying for it. Provide him with all the information he needs to make these calculations, including your income, assets, and expenses. Join him in this effort, and teach him the economic realities of life. As you look for ways to reduce or manage the cost, let him be the first to suggest a less expensive school. If he doesn't, feel free to suggest it yourself. And always use your experience to guide him as he suggests impractical or unwise ideas, such as carrying huge debt loads or having you buy a house near the college to avoid the cost of a dorm.

> **If you're reluctant to ask your child to undergo this effort, or if you resist revealing the intimate details about your finances, remember that going to college is about becoming an adult. Besides, he'll learn all about your finances when you complete the financial aid form, anyway. So get over it.**

Rule #4: Consider Alternative Ways to Attend College

Nobody said you must attend college full-time over four years. Instead, consider:

- *Living at Home.* As much as 60% of the cost of college is room and board, not tuition. Living at home can cut the bill in half (but with a commensurate cut in the college experience, in my opinion).

- *Community Colleges.* Funny thing about a degree: It names only the school from which you graduated, not the school where you first enrolled. By attending a community college for the first two years and then transferring to a major university for the junior and senior years, you can save thousands. And there's no huge sacrifice to the quality of the education, either, since freshman classes are just introductory, anyway. The best part: Employers will never know, since your resume only need show where you graduated.

- *Home-State Colleges.* Attending a home-state school is far cheaper than an out-of-state or private college, and the quality of the education is often just as good — or better.

I actually had a client ask us to help him figure out how to pay the costs of sending his daughter to Penn State. Since she did not live in Pennsylvania, the cost would have been about $80,000, and my client, though ill-equipped to handle it, was determined to send her there. When I asked why, he replied, "Because she's in the top 3% of her high school class. She's so talented, she even got a full scholarship to [an excellent school in her home state]."

I found it amazing that he was willing to pay $80,000 (that he didn't have) so " daddy's baby" could go to the school of her choice, even though she could have gone elsewhere — and received a fine education — for free.

Such is the control that "a college education for my kids" has over parents.

- *Accelerated Programs.* Where is it written that it takes four years to get a degree? It often can be done in three. That would save 25% of the cost of room and board and enable your child to start earning a salary one year sooner than other students.

- *Employer Assistance.* Many employers provide tuition-reimbursement programs. So instead of shopping for colleges, maybe your child ought to shop for a job with a company that will pay for school.

- *Military Service.* The ultimate employer assistance program. Consider it.

- *Time Off.* Where is it written that it takes four consecutive years to get a degree? Your child can work for a year or two to save for school, and then go to college for a year. Repeat until done. Many employers prefer graduates who have solid work experience to complement their degree. Many schools have cooperative education (co-op) programs. Check them out.

Is College Right for Your Child?

Before you spend the tens of thousands of dollars it costs to get a degree, talk with your child to make sure college is the right choice. Today's economy is increasingly service-oriented, and with automotive diagnosticians (read: auto mechanics) earning up to $100,000, many fine careers are available that don't require a college degree. Others demand advanced degrees, even PhDs, so make sure your son or daughter is enthusiastic and committed (or as committed as an 18-year-old can be) before you agree to incur — or agree to let them incur — the massive financial expense that their decisions require.

Above all else, remember: Refusing to be held hostage by college costs does not mean you are a bad parent. To the contrary, in the long run, you'll be a hero.

Chapter 54 - Does It Pay for Both Parents to Work While Raising Young Children?

If you're married, it's likely that both you and your spouse work outside the home. DINKs — dual income, no kids — are the norm. But what happens when DINKs start having children? Does it really make sense for both parents to work while raising young children?

There are two conflicting answers. The first answer says the costs of raising and supporting a family are so high that, to survive financially, both parents must work. The other contends that the other costs of having both parents work — emotional and stress-related — are so high that it's better for one parent to stay home.

Why Both Should Not Work

Let's examine what it costs to raise children. As we saw in Chapter 1, the federal government pegs first-year costs at $5,490 to $11,320. Unreimbursed medical bills for the obstetrician and hospital alone will be $1,200; maternity clothes, nursery furniture, baby-related equipment, clothes, diapers, formula, food, pediatrician, and other expenses constitute the rest.

But that excludes day care. If both parents work, add $7,000 to the bill. Thus, you're looking at perhaps $17,000 in first-year baby costs. At that price, many couples are convinced both parents must produce an income, and if one parent wasn't working before, the pressure to start is very high.

But is this the right conclusion?

Let's assume our new parents each earn $30,000 a year, for a combined income of $60,000. To maintain their ability to support the family, especially considering the new expenses that came with their baby, they feel both must keep working. But is this second income really necessary for financial survival?

A $30,000 annual income is $2,500 a month. From that, most people spend about $250 a month in commuting costs; this covers either the cost of an automobile and parking fees, or public transportation — your choice.

Also, you'll spend an average of $125 per month on work clothes. (On-the-job wardrobes extend beyond those who wear uniforms. Office workers buy suits and ties or silk blouses and pantyhose. It all adds up to about the same expense.) You'll spend an additional $120 per month on lunch, office gifts, and obligatory donations. And don't forget day care, at about $600 per month. In total, you'll spend $1,100 per month in work-related expenses — about half of one spouse's total income. "That's no problem," you say. "I still net $1,400."

Oh, really?

Don't forget taxes. If you gross $2,500, you will lose about $1,000 in taxes. Therefore, your net after-tax, after-expense take-home pay is about $400 a month. That's less than $100 a week. If you work 40 hours a week and devote one hour daily dressing for work and commuting, you're going through all this for about $1.75 an hour. And that's on a $30,000 gross income!

And it gets worse. Not only are you netting way below minimum wage, think about all the time you're not spending with your child and the additional stress added to the family by the fact that both the husband and the wife are working. Who stays home when the baby is sick? Who leaves that important meeting to race to the day care center before it closes? Will it be you or your spouse who takes vacation or sick leave because the plumber is scheduled to stop by? Considering all the non-economic issues affecting the family, does it really make sense for both parents to work?

Five Reasons Why Both Should Work

From this analysis, I may have led you to conclude "no." But it's not that simple. Thus far I have presented only half the issue, so let me come to the defense of women who have young children and who work outside the home. There are five reasons why it can make a lot of sense for both Mom and Dad to work:

Reason #1: Protect Your Career

If the wife gives up her job,[24] she could do irreparable damage to her career, because her colleagues (competitors?) who don't take five years off continue to climb the corporate ladder.

Reason #2: The Lower-Earning Spouse Might Have The Health Insurance Benefits

That's a very good reason to keep working.

Reason #3: Don't Forget Retirement Benefits

Women in the U.S. typically retire with lower Social Security benefits than men, because women tend to work fewer years. Ditto for company pension plans; if you quit work for five years, you'll pay the price later in the form of a sharply lower retirement income. So forget about the small loss today — staying home with the kids can pose a huge economic loss later. For more on this subject, turn to chapters 62 and 64.

---

[24]Let's admit it: The wife is the one most commonly affected here. Please note, however, that deciding who stays home should not be based on gender but on economics and individual preferences. In most cases, the spouse with the lower income is the more likely candidate to stay home.

Reason #4: The Parent's Mental Health

Some people just are not well suited to stay home with their kids full-time. They need adult interaction. One of my clients, a working mom, had a job whose income was so low she actually spent $35 a week more, net of child-care expenses, than she earned. When I mentioned this to her, she replied, "Well, it's cheaper than therapy!"

Reason #5: Improve your Child's Development

A friend who has a little boy once told me, "If my wife were to quit her job and stay home with Billy, he would have a total social circle of one person — his mommy. But in day care, he's learning social skills by being around 20 other kids." Point well taken: The value of interpersonal communication skills for a child shouldn't be dismissed.

So, should you work or stay home? Clearly, it's not an easy choice. Yet, more and more employers are offering flexibility that might help make it easier than before for both parents to work. Job sharing, flexible work schedules, and working from home are some of the options available in today's workplace that you should explore as you try to resolve this issue.

My point is that *you have a choice.* Too many parents do not realize that options exist. Too often, parents assume they must work without considering the alternative. To be a success with your financial planning, you always must examine your options. And proper planning is perhaps nowhere more important than when it comes to raising your children.

Part VIII
The Best Strategies for Buying, Selling and Owning Homes

Part VIII — The Best Strategies for Buying, Selling and Owning Homes

Overview - The American Dream

In this part, you will learn:

- How to buy your first home

- How to sell your home and buy your *next* home

- How to lower your taxes when selling your home

- How to handle your mortgage

- How to work with real estate agents

- All about the settlement process

Chapter 55 - Incorporating Home Ownership into Your Financial Plan

Too often, people buy homes in a vacuum — without considering how that purchase is going to affect other aspects of their lives. This can be a big mistake, and therefore you must recognize that owning a home holds very important implications for the rest of your financial plan. Although a fine goal, owning a home is not the ultimate financial planning goal, and in fact how you handle the issue of home ownership may well determine whether you achieve financial success.

Therefore, let's consider home ownership within the context of your financial plan. First, is the real estate industry best serving your interests, and second, can only two-income families buy homes?

Ignore What the Real Estate Industry Says You Can Afford

There is a big difference between what the real estate industry says you can afford and what financial planners say you can afford. As you'll learn on the following pages, lenders permit you to spend up to 36% of your income on debt — meaning mortgage payments and other debts — yet 30 years ago, that limit was 30%. The mortgage industry has slowly increased this limit because housing prices have grown more rapidly than incomes, and if they didn't increase the limit, today too many Americans wouldn't qualify for a mortgage. That, in turn, would mean bankers wouldn't sell loans and builders wouldn't build houses. That's not in their best interests.

Unfortunately, their best interests can conflict with yours, and if you buy a home by pushing this lending limit to its extreme, or by using some of the no- or low-money down loan programs that are available today (because you have to, not because you choose to), you face the very real risk of becoming "house-poor."

If you want to reduce that risk, keep your total debt payments (including your mortgage) to 28% of income, not 36% as the real estate industry allows. This way, you'll have a much-needed cushion to help you deal with the other financial aspects of your life, such as saving for college and retirement. But there is a problem with this self-imposed limit: It forces you to (a) increase your down payment, or (b) buy a less expensive home. You may have difficulty accepting either limitation, but I urge you to do so, because if you don't, you'll find yourself back at the 36% level, with all of the impending problems that brings.

What Happens if You Exceed a 28% Debt Limit

It's important that you don't exceed this 28% figure, for several reasons. Take the example of Marvin and Beth. In their 30s, each earns $35,000, so they bought a house based on their combined $70,000 income. Sometime later they had their first child, and Beth decided she'd like to stay home with the baby for a few years.

Unfortunately, Beth can't quit her job, because without her income the family can't afford the mortgage payments. Thus, Marv and Beth discover that when they bought the house, they relied on incorrect assumptions — the key being that they would continue to have a household income of $70,000 or more. Now, in order to keep the house, Beth must keep working.

It's hard to have sympathy for Marv and Beth, because their crisis is of their own doing: Beth changed her attitude about having a job. But what if this dilemma was forced upon them? It easily could happen: One might get laid off, become injured or ill and unable to work, or die. Since their ability to keep the house is dependent on both incomes, Marv and Beth would be in serious financial jeopardy if one income was lost (and therefore, proper planning is needed to guard against such possibilities).

Marv and Beth can reduce the risk of such a crisis — or avoid it entirely — simply by obtaining a mortgage that does not require a $70,000 income. And that, in turn, means they should set their limits at 28% (or lower) instead of 36%.

Indeed, not only did Marv and Beth assume their income would remain intact, they made a similar miscalculation regarding their expenses. If you had asked if they ever planned to have children, they'd likely have answered, "Sure, someday" — yet they completely ignored the financial considerations of actually having children.

This is a real trap, because as we saw in Chapter 1, the federal government says you're going to spend $343,000 raising each child to age 17 — $21,000 in the first two years alone! And when the kid reaches 18, she'll be off to college, which will cost another $180,000 to $300,000.

So if you plan to buy a house with the attitude that all you have to do is get your income and expenses into the 36% ratio, you're setting yourself up for serious financial troubles later.

Friends of mine live in a $250,000 home. They had no children when they bought the house; today they have three. Visit their home, and you'll see aging cars and furniture from their college days. The youngest child will be wearing clothes discarded from the eldest, and a nice dinner out was years ago — let alone their last vacation. Yet this couple is supposed to be living the "American Dream."

To avoid this trap, you must put things in perspective: Never make a financial decision that you'll live with for 30 years based solely on today's financial circumstances. Instead, take into consideration what your future lifestyle, income and expenses are likely to be. For most young couples, one of those changes will be children, so if you haven't already read Chapter 54, do so now before continuing.

Chapter 56 - How to Buy Your First Home

Are You Ready for Home Ownership?

Answer these 10 questions to learn if you are ready to buy a home.

1. Are you sure you want to buy a home? Yes = 1 point.

2. Do you anticipate any large expenses in the next two years, such as buying a car or having kids? No = 1 point.

3. Do you expect to stay in your current job for the next two to three years? Yes = 1 point.

4. Do you expect your job to stay in the same location for the next three to five years? Yes = 1 point. (Is your employer thinking of relocating? How do you know until you ask?)

5. Do you know how much you can realistically afford to pay for housing? Yes = 1 point.

6. Do you have a favorable credit record? Yes = 1 point.

7. Do you have enough money for the down payment and closing costs? Yes = 1 point.

8. Have you been pre-qualified for a mortgage so you know how much you can borrow? Yes = 1 point.

9. Will your existing debt reduce your ability to qualify for a mortgage? No = 1 point.

10. Is the amount you can borrow sufficient to enable you to buy a home you can truly enjoy? Yes = 1 point. (Don't settle for something you don't love, for you could well live in your home a very long time.)

If you scored 8 points or more, you're ready to buy a home.

As I've said many times, **The Rules of Money Have Changed,** and this is perhaps more true in the area of home ownership than in any other aspect of personal finance. Therefore, be careful when seeking advice about buying a home, for asking the wrong people can cost you a ton of money.

For example, do not ask your parents for an opinion if the last time they bought a home was decades ago. The reason: The rules of yesterday do not apply today, meaning their advice could be 30 years out of date!

One thing, though, hasn't changed: Buying a home is difficult — perhaps even more so than ever before — and if you're not careful, your dream of owning a home can become a nightmare. Indeed, it is very easy to become house-rich and cash-poor.

The biggest difference between owning a home generations ago and owning one today is that homes no longer are the key to financial success. Owning a home was once the fulfillment of the American dream: If you had a home, a pension, and Social Security, you were set for life. But that's not true today. Still, owning a home does offer important benefits. To understand them, let's consider the alternative, which is to rent.

Compared to renting, owning a home has many advantages, including:

- the homeowner's monthly payment does not change, while renters face annual rent increases;

- a large portion of the homeowner's monthly payment is tax-deductible, but rent payments are not;

- the homeowner's monthly payments eventually stop (when the loan is paid off); Renters pay rent as long as they live;

- homeowners keep a piece of each monthly payment, while renters never get back any of their rent payments;

- any increase in the home's value belongs to the homeowner; Renters keep none of that profit; and

- homeowners can design and decorate their homes virtually any way they want, while renters suffer major restrictions.

For all these reasons, owning a home is an appropriate goal for most Americans. Let's show you how to do it right.

Do You Have Enough to Pay Cash for Your House?

Of course not.

With homes costing a national average of $130,000, it's clear that you don't have enough cash to buy a home. That means you'll have to borrow some money. This loan is called a mortgage, and it is the source of much confusion, frustration, and anguish for homebuyers.

Using a Mortgage to Help You Buy Your Home

Did you know that last year, Wal-Mart sold tens of thousands of drills to people who didn't want them? Scandalous!

Well, not really. These folks wanted a hole. To get it, they first had to buy a drill.

Indeed, sometimes we must work with a thing we *don't* want in order to get another thing we *do* want. So it is with real estate. In order to buy a home, you must have a mortgage. To get one, mortgage companies require you to work with septic and termite inspectors, appraisers, credit bureaus, settlement attorneys, title insurers, and others. Not that you want to deal with any of these folks, mind you, but you must deal with them if you want a mortgage. Not that you want a mortgage, of course, but you must get a mortgage if you want to buy a home. And you *do* want that. Thus begins what is for many a very frustrating, annoying, and time-consuming process — much of which seems completely unrelated to your goal of buying a home.

Part of the reason home buyers find the mortgage process so frustrating is that they don't understand it — nor do they want to. After all, they want a home, not a mortgage, so the mortgage is a mere detail — and an annoying one at that. But if you understand the process, you can make it work better for you, with less cost, inconvenience, and delay.

The Biggest Misconception in Real Estate

Many people believe a mortgage is a loan against the house. It's not. The truth is that a mortgage is *a loan against your income.*

I own a mortgage company which has processed more than $400 million in loans, and I can assure you that without sufficient income, you will not qualify for a loan. The reason lenders are willing to loan you money is because you have an income. (The reason they are willing to set the loan at such low rates of interest is because you post the house as *collateral.* Thus, if you fail to repay the loan, they can take your house and sell it to get back their money.)

Because your home's value is expected to remain intact (or even rise), bankers consider mortgages to be very low-risk investments. Therefore, they don't demand a high profit, and hence, the interest rate they charge you is very low compared to other interest rates in the marketplace.

> Car loans, too, are offered at low interest rates, because the car collateralizes the loan. Interest rates for car loans are higher than for mortgage loans because cars decline in value, which place bankers at a higher risk if they must repossess and sell your car in the future. (Cars are also portable, meaning bankers have to find the car before they can repossess it. No such worry with houses.)
>
> Credit cards have the highest interest rates because they are unsecured loans: If you default, the bank has no collateral to seize, and thus, they cannot recover their losses. This higher risk for bankers translates into higher interest rates for you — and higher returns for them, to compensate them for lending money to you at such a high risk.

Just because the bank accepts your home as collateral, don't think banks want you to default on your mortgage. Trust me: They don't want the house back. Banks are in the banking business, not the real estate business, and they want the interest you're supposed to pay, not your house. Witness the Savings and Loan crisis of the '80s: When people defaulted on their loans, S&Ls took back all the real estate. With no buyers at hand, the S&Ls went broke, too.

Believe me, bankers don't want your house. They want you to repay the loan. And they know the only way you can do that is if you have a good income. That's why mortgages are loans against your income, not your house.

> **This is why it is difficult for retirees to get a mortgage. Consider people who bought a house in 1957, paid it off in 1987, and retired in 1990. Now living on a small pension and Social Security, they want a loan, but the bank says, "How are you going to repay it?" With little income and no savings, they can't, so the bank refuses to give them a loan. This is why you should obtain home loans *before* you retire.**

The Four Steps to Determining How Large a Mortgage You Can Get

The formula for buying a home is:

$$\text{Available Cash} + \text{Maximum Amount You Can Borrow} = \text{Maximum Purchase Price}$$

As you can see, how expensive a home you can buy is directly related to how much money you can borrow, and how much you can borrow is determined by four factors: your assets, your income, your debts, and your mortgage's interest rate.

FRANK & ERNEST   BOB THAVES

©1996 United Features Syndicate, Inc. Reprinted by permission.

Step #1: Determine How Much Cash You Have — or Can Raise

Start by listing all your assets: checking and savings accounts, mutual funds, stocks, bonds, and any other assets. Include amounts you expect to receive as gifts from family and friends. This grand total represents how much cash you can apply to the purchase price. *Let's say you have $35,000 that you can apply to the purchase of a home.*

Step #2: Determine Your Income

Add up all your income (if you are married, or if a second person is going to buy the house with you, such as a parent or unmarried partner, add income from both people) and be sure to include:

- your gross pay, including overtime, part-time and seasonal pay, commissions, bonuses, and tips;
- dividends from investments;
- business income;
- pension or Social Security income;
- veterans benefits;
- alimony; and
- child support.

Let's say your total income is $60,000.

Step #3: Tally Your Debts

Include your partner's, if any, for such items as:

- car payments (whether you own or lease personally);
- alimony or child support payments;
- student loans;
- minimum monthly credit card payments (not the balance owed); and
- any other debts that will exist for 10 months or more (for example, you can ignore car payments if the car will be paid off in less than 10 months).

Let's say your total monthly debts are $800.

Step #4: Determine Current Interest Rates

Let's say you talk with a mortgage broker, who tells you that the following loans are available:

- **9% Fixed.** This loan lasts 30 years, and the rate will never change.

- **6% 1-year Adjustable Rate Mortgage.** This loan also lasts for 30 years. The interest rate is 6% for the first year, but will change every year, increasing or decreasing with current interest rates. The loan can rise no more than 2% in any one year and no more than 6% over the life of the loan. Thus, the highest rate this loan can charge is 12%, and it can't get that high before the fourth year.

The Two Mortgage Limits

> For more details about specific mortgage loan programs and how to work with a mortgage company, see Chapter 57.

Lending Limit #1

Now that you have all four pieces of information, let's determine how much you can borrow. **Lending Limit #1 states that your monthly mortgage payment (including taxes and insurance) must not exceed 28% of your income.** *Since your income is $60,000 (or $5,000 per month), the maximum you can spend on a mortgage payment is $16,800 per year ($1,400 per month).*

To translate a monthly loan payment into a loan balance, look at Figure 8-1. It shows how much money you can borrow based on different interest rates. As you can see, the higher the interest rate, the less money you can borrow. *If you choose the 9% fixed-rate loan, the maximum amount you can borrow is $173,995, while you can borrow up to $233,508 if you choose the 6% ARM.*

So, by adding your loan amount to the $35,000 cash you have, you can buy a home that costs up to $208,995 (if you choose the 9% fixed rate) or $268,508 (if you choose the 6% ARM).

HOW LENDING LIMIT #1 AFFECTS A PERSON EARNING $60,000

If the rate is...	...you can borrow up to:	If the rate is...	...you can borrow up to:
5.00%	$260,794	8.50%	$182,075
5.25%	$253,530	8.75%	$177,958
5.50%	$246,570	9.00%	$173,995
5.75%	$239,901	9.25%	$170,176
6.00%	$233,508	9.50%	$166,497
6.25%	$227,377	9.75%	$162,951
6.50%	$221,495	10.00%	$159,531
6.75%	$215,850	10.25%	$156,232
7.00%	$210,431	10.50%	$153,049
7.25%	$205,226	10.75%	$149,976
7.50%	$200,225	11.00%	$147,009
7.75%	$195,418	11.25%	$144,142
8.00%	$190,797	11.50%	$141,373
8.25%	$186,352	11.75%	$138,695

FIGURE 8-1

Lending Limit #2

But we're not done yet, because **Lending Limit #2 states that your mortgage payment plus other monthly debt payments must not exceed 36% of income.** *Since your income is $60,000, your limit for both a mortgage and other debts is $1,800 per month. This presents you with a problem, because your total monthly debt payments are $2,200 ($800 in current monthly debts plus your new $1,400 mortgage payment).*

Therefore, you must either reduce the size of your mortgage (meaning you borrow less money, which forces you to buy a lower-priced house), or you must pay off some of your debts.

Let's say you choose to lower the size of your mortgage. That means your monthly payment cannot exceed $1,000 (because $1,000 plus your current debt payments total $1,800 — which is the maximum that Lending Limit #2 allows). Based on a $1,000 monthly payment, then, the most you can borrow under the fixed-rate loan is $124,266, or $166,777 under the ARM loan. Combined with your $35,000 in cash, that means you can buy a house worth as much as either $159,266 or $201,777.

Now you begin to see why ARM loans are so popular: Their lower initial rates allow you to qualify for bigger loans, which in turn allows you to buy a more expensive home. The danger with ARM loans, of course, is that the first year's low rate could vanish in the second year. If interest rates rise in the economy, what could happen to your ARM over the next four years:

Year	Interest Rate	Monthly Payment
1	6%	$1,000
2	8%	$1,224
3	10%	$1,464
4	12%	$1,716

Thus, ARM buyers are gambling that interest rates won't rise, or that their incomes will rise fast enough to let them afford the higher payments. Those are mighty big bets, for if you're wrong, you could be unable to make the payments and you'll lose your home.

This is exactly why lenders have these two lending limits. Left unchecked, buyers would borrow beyond their ability to pay. And while it might seem that you're able to carry a larger payment than the $1,000 determined by our calculations above, lenders know better: They know that your mortgage does not represent the total cost of home ownership.

Indeed, you will incur many additional costs that renters avoid — including taxes, insurance, utilities, maintenance and repairs, improvements, and decorating.

You need to set money aside for these expenses, and that means you should not buy as expensive a home as you think you can afford.

Six Ways to Qualify for a Bigger Mortgage

All too often, home buyers discover they can't afford the house they want. Here are some ideas for increasing the amount you can borrow:

> Guess what buyers of new homes discover the day they move in? There are no curtains or drapes on the windows! Jean refused to walk into the bathroom of our new house until I tacked sheets over the windows, and curtains became the top item on our shopping list!

1. Reduce your long-term debt. Paying off credit cards, for example, can improve your ratios, allowing you to qualify for a bigger mortgage;

2. Wait until you get more income;

3. Have another person join you in obtaining the mortgage. By signing the loan application, their income is included (so are their debts) and they become legally obligated to fulfill the terms of the mortgage along with you. (So choose a co-signer carefully and make sure the co-signer understands the implication of this action);

4. Use financing options that require lower down payments;

5. Use financing options that allow you to make lower monthly payments; and

6. Wait for interest rates to drop, for the lower the rate, the more you can borrow. If you can't (or don't want to) wait, you can lower the rate yourself. How? Read on!

How to Get a Lower Interest Rate

If you can't afford the home you want because interest rates are too high, you can "buy" a lower interest rate. *Say you want to borrow $120,000, and your lender offers you a fixed-rate loan at 9%. Unfortunately, that requires a bigger monthly payment than you can afford. What you need is a rate of 8%.*

You can get the lower rate you want by paying something called "points." *By paying three points, your lender will give you an 8% rate.*

One point equals 1% of your loan. Note: One point does not equal one thousand dollars (a common misconception). *Since you seek to borrow $120,000, one point equals $1,200 (1% of $120,000). Three points, then, is $3,600. Thus, for a one-time payment of $3,600 in this example, you can "buy" your rate down to 8% from 9%.*

> This is why you should not seek advice from someone who last bought a house 30 years ago. Then, all loans were 30-year fixed-rate loans requiring 10% down, unless you were a veteran buying a house through the G.I. Bill.
>
> Today, you can choose from adjustable-rate loans, COFI loans, balloons, 5/25 and 7/23 programs, 10-year, 15-year and 30-year terms, 3% money down programs, no-documentation programs, and more. The advice of people whose last experience was 30 years ago is likely to be way out of date. Dozens of programs are available today that didn't exist until recently, and new ones are offered constantly. To learn about them, talk with a mortgage broker or lender.

Does it Make Sense to Pay Points?

The answer is: It depends[25] — in this case on:

- the spread between the no-point rate and the rate with points;

- how long you plan to keep the loan;

- whether you're dealing with a fixed-rate or adjustable-rate loan; and

- whether you have the cash to pay the points.

Which is better: the 9% loan with no points or the 8% loan with three points? A 9% loan would have cost you $965 per month vs. $880 for the 8% loan. Thus, paying three points lowers your mortgage payment by $85 per month. Since the points cost you $3,600, it will take you three and a half years to recover that cost — not to mention the fact that by spending $3,600 on those points, you gave up the ability to earn interest on that money. That aside, if you keep your home (and your loan) for at least three and a half years, you'll break even.

Clearly, the longer you plan to stay in your home, the more sense it makes to pay the points in exchange for a lower interest rate. If you're planning to sell your home in just a few years, it would be foolish to pay points. However, every situation is different, and because interest rate programs constantly change, there is no simple answer or "rule of thumb." A good financial advisor or loan officer can help you determine whether paying points is best for your situation.

---

[25]What a surprise.

Other Costs of Owning Homes

Points and other loan fees are not the only costs you'll incur when buying a house. You must obtain an appraisal, termite inspection, home inspection, credit report, and more. Together, these "settlement costs" will be roughly 1% to 3.5% of the purchase price of the home. This figure is in addition to any points you choose to pay.

> **Please ignore "rules of thumb." They are silly attempts to simplify complex issues and they rarely work. For proof, just look at your own hands: By that standard, rules of thumb can be expected to apply only 20% of the time.**

The Three Kinds of Insurance That Protect Real Estate

There are three different types of insurance that apply to homes, and many people get them confused, so let's cover them one at a time.

Protection #1: Mortgage Insurance

This type of insurance protects your lender, not you.

First-time home buyers, typically strapped for cash, want to buy their homes with as little cash as possible. But the lender knows through experience that the less you put down, the more likely you are to default. (Think about it: If you put down $100,000 to buy a $300,000 house, walking away means you lose your $100,000. But if you had put no money down, walking away costs you nothing. Thus, the more money you put down, the less likely you are to default.)

Therefore, if you put down less than 20% of the purchase price, your lender will require you to buy mortgage insurance. Known as PMI, Private Mortgage Insurance protects the lender in case you default. The cost, which is included in your monthly payment, is 0.65% of your original loan balance. Thus, if you borrow $100,000, you'll pay $54.17 per month ($650 annually). That's why it may make sense to make a down payment of 20%: Doing so will allow you to avoid this expense, which adds up to many thousands of dollars over the life of your loan.

How to Beat PMI — Without Putting 20% Down

Some lenders now let home buyers avoid PMI with as little as 5% down in exchange for a slight increase in the interest rate. Although this will translate into a somewhat higher mortgage payment, the payment will still be lower than if you were paying PMI. Also, remember that PMI payments are not tax deductible, but the extra interest you'd be paying is — further reducing the net cost of this alternative.

The recent introduction of these new loan programs serves as evidence of the continuing evolution of the mortgage industry, and why you need to seek counsel from those who monitor the latest developments.

Are you still paying for PMI on the home you bought years ago?

Most homeowners pay for mortgage insurance because they were not able to put down 20% when they bought their home.

But guess what? You could easily have 20% in your home now.

Say you bought a $150,000 house 10 years ago, with 10% down. You borrowed $135,000 and your monthly payment thus includes the cost of PMI (about $73 per month). Today, though, your current mortgage balance is only $123,000 (because you've made 10 years' worth of payments) and the value of your home has grown to $225,000. Thus, you now have $100,000 in equity in your home — which is well above the 20% needed to avoid mortgage insurance!

If you're still paying for mortgage insurance, you need to write a letter to your mortgage company to tell them to eliminate that charge. You'll save hundreds of dollars every year!

Protection #2: Homeowner's Insurance

Homeowner's insurance protects you, not your lender.

If the home is damaged or destroyed, this coverage provides you the money you need to rebuild the home and replace its contents. Only a fool would own a home without such insurance, and indeed, your lender will require proof that you have it. You buy it from a property/casualty insurance agent (as opposed to a life/health agent). Some financial planners offer it as well.

Protection #3: Title Insurance

Title insurance comes in two parts, one to protect the lender and one to protect you. You must buy the part that protects the lender; it's your choice to buy the part that protects you.

Your property may have changed hands dozens of times over the past 400 years, especially if it's on the East coast. Who's to say the person selling you the property really owns it? It is quite possible that the deed (or *title*) is defective. If that's true, you might not own the property you think you bought.

Title insurance protects you from the catastrophe of losing your home because someone challenges the validity of the title in court. This is why lenders require that you buy a policy to protect them, and why I strongly recommend that you buy a second policy to protect yourself.

You order a title policy for the lender during the mortgage application process, and if you order a second policy for yourself at the same time, the additional cost is quite low. Unlike other kinds of insurance, you pay for title insurance only once — at settlement — and it protects you for as long as you own the property.

The Settlement Process

Settlement is the formal process that transfers title (legal ownership) of the real estate from the seller to the buyer. The settlement also gives the buyer's lender (if any) a lien against the property. (A lien grants a financial interest in the property to the lender until the loan is repaid.)

The settlement process is governed by the Real Estate Settlement Procedures Act of 1974. RESPA requires that your lender give you a booklet which describes the settlement process in detail and advises you of your legal rights.

Pre-Settlement

Once your loan application is approved, somebody (chosen by either the buyer or the seller) will be designated to conduct the settlement. The settlement agent will order a survey of the property and a report on the status of the property's title. When these steps are completed, the settlement

> **When refinancing, the title is not transferred but many of the same events occur because the owner's old loan must be repaid and the new loan obtained. The new loan also must be secured by a new lien on the real estate.**

agent will prepare a Commitment for Title Insurance (sometimes called a Binder) and deliver it to your lender. The commitment informs your lender that, subject to certain approved exceptions, a title insurance policy will be issued for the lender at settlement to protect the lender's interests. All this preparation must be completed by the settlement date.

The Settlement

At settlement, the settlement agent will review the loan documents with you. The settlement agent's job is to:

- make sure all documents are properly signed and notarized;

- collect all funds required to pay settlement costs; and

- pay-off any pre-existing mortgages on the real estate.

When everything is done and all the papers are signed, the seller gives to the buyer the keys to the house.

Post-Settlement

Following settlement, the settlement agent will record with the court all required documents, pay off any pre-existing mortgages, and make all disbursements required to complete the transaction. When all recording has been completed, the settlement agent will issue a Title Insurance Policy to your lender and, if you ordered it, one to you.

About Settlement Costs

Costs will vary depending on many factors, including:

- **Location of the Property.** Recordation and transfer taxes are payable to the state and local governments where the property is located. Each jurisdiction sets its own tax rates.

- **Purchase Price and Amount of Financing.** The purchase price and amount of financing will affect the recordation and transfer taxes and the title insurance premium.

- **Loan Fees.** Fees vary according to the lender you select and general economic conditions at the time you obtain your loan.

Within three days of applying for your loan, your lender is required by RESPA to give you a Good Faith Estimate of the settlement costs you are likely to encounter.

Who Gets the Drapes?

Imagine you find your dream home. It's 10 years old and listed for $200,000. You offer to pay $185,000 and the owners accept your offer.

Who gets the drapes?

All too often, questions like this go unanswered until you reach the settlement table. If the contract is silent about the drapes and other items, arguments are sure to arise between the buyers and sellers. Disputes easily can be avoided if the buyers, sellers, and their real estate agents prepare a well-thought-out contract.

When buying or selling a home, remember that no transaction has occurred until you reach settlement, which is where the property transfer actually takes place.

For the settlement company, the contract is King: If the contract doesn't specifically state that an item is to *convey* (go to the buyers), then, it doesn't — period. So if the contract doesn't say the curtains stay, then the sellers can take them. Likewise for the washer/dryer, refrigerator, and even the landscaping. (Sellers have been known to dig up the rose bushes!) Generally, any item that is bolted to or made a part of the home will convey unless otherwise specified.

Also, if the contract doesn't say the seller pays the points, the buyers better not expect them to do so. You can imagine the fights at settlement when verbal commitments are not reflected in the contract.

To make the process go well, be sure the contract covers everything. You should do this when the contract is first written and signed, but amendments later are okay, too — provided both parties sign the amendment.

Use as much detail as possible in the contract. Standard contracts convey many items, but the choices are not always all inclusive and an item the buyers clearly want may be overlooked. To avoid this, buyers must make sure that everything they want conveyed is included in the contract and that the sellers acknowledge it in writing.

Remember: The settlement table is a poor place to try to renegotiate a contract. If all the terms are in writing, you'll avoid confusion. Be sure to write into the contract such stipulations as whether certain repairs are to be made before the final walk-through, or if the basement freezer comes with the house. Make no assumptions and don't let the other party's agent fool you into thinking that if it wasn't mentioned, it will be yours. Although the settlement company can help resolve differences, it can only enforce what is written in the contract.

Ask your real estate agent to tell you what conveys and what doesn't. Speak up if you suspect an item is not mentioned, for even the best real estate agents may miss what you see.

Above all, put it in writing. A properly written contract can help you avoid surprises on closing day.

Hire a Real Estate Agent to Help You Buy Your Home

Shopping for a new home is fun, and most first-time buyers enjoy their search for a new home. Regardless of whether you plan to buy a newly-built home or a resale, a real estate agent can prove very worthwhile.

Before you start looking, create your "wish list" of everything you want in your new home. Decide what you want in the way of:

- price range

- location: either for a particular part of town or proximity to work, schools, shopping, recreation, medical/rescue facilities, or family and friends;

- structure: condo, townhouse, single-family, or farm;

- style: ranch, Cape Cod, Tudor, Colonial, split-level, traditional, or contemporary;

- features: number of bedrooms, baths, first-floor master bedroom, washer/dryer, and other layout specifications; and

- amenities: circular driveways, side-load garage, deck, fireplace, security system, and other items.

> **Most agents can arrange for you to see 6-10 homes in a day (more than that and you'll forget what you saw).**

Once you develop your wish list, you have a choice: You can spend months visiting every home listed in the newspaper classifieds, or you can let a real estate agent do all the legwork for you. The vast majority of home sellers work with agents, and consequently, their homes are listed in the Multiple Listing Service, an electronic showplace of every home for sale in your area. Through the MLS, your agent can quickly identify homes that meet your criteria and arrange convenient times with the sellers for you to visit and inspect the properties.

In addition to identifying specific homes, real estate agents are a great source of information on the community and comparable prices. But the most important service they provide, once you find a home you want to buy, is presenting your offer to the seller.

> **Do not make an offer to the seller yourself, because you're not good at it. An offer is the first part of what often is the protracted, detailed negotiation of a legal contract, and you don't know how to play that game as well as real estate agents.**

As you'll soon discover, home buyers find themselves involved with a great many people, including lawyers, appraisers, mortgage companies, settlement companies, termite inspectors, home inspectors, and others, and your agent can refer you to qualified individuals and companies to help you through the entire process.

Who Does the Real Estate Agent Represent?

When working with a real estate agent to help you buy a home, be aware of one critical point: By law, the agent you hire works for the seller and anything you say to the real estate agent will be communicated to the seller. This is true even if you found the real estate agent, even if the agent shows you dozens of houses, gives you lots of advice, and spends lots of time with you — even if the agent has never met the seller before. **Real estate agents always legally represent the seller, and saying something to the real estate agent is the same as saying it to the seller.**

> Say the seller is asking $200,000, and you say to your real estate agent, "We love this house. Let's offer $180,000, but we're willing to spend the $200,000." Guess what? You just paid $200,000.

Most home buyers do not realize real estate agents legally represent sellers, and consequently, hundreds of thousands of home buyers pay more than they should for their homes because they lack representation in the negotiation process. In fact, not only do they lack representation, the person they think is on their side actually is a spy for the other team!

Think about it: You find and retain a real estate agent, as does the home's seller. Once negotiations begin, your real estate agent and the seller's real estate agent start negotiating. You think your real estate agent is negotiating with your best interests in mind, but the truth is your real estate agent doesn't work for you — he or she works for the seller! So, both real estate agents are teaming up against you, trying to figure out how much they can get you to pay for the benefit of *their* mutual client, the seller!

Too often, buyers fail to understand this legal relationship.

Working with a Buyer-Broker

You can avoid this problem by hiring a "buyer-broker." Under this arrangement, you and your real estate agent sign an agreement stating that your real estate agent legally represents you, the buyer. Many agents will agree to such an arrangement, and I strongly recommend it when you are on the buy-side of the transaction.

Some agents, depending on who their client is, sometimes will represent the buyer, and at other times, the seller. Working with such agents is fine provided you know what team each player is on at the time.

Who Pays the Real Estate Agent?

Whether you work with a traditional agent or a buyer-broker, real estate commissions — typically 6% of the sales price — are paid by the seller.

I mean, buyer.

Uh, let's try that again.

While it's true that the seller pays the agent's commission, let's face it: The seller would pay nothing to the agent if there's no buyer. Further, the amount of the commission is directly related to the sales price of the home: The higher the sales price, the higher the agent's commission. Since sellers know they are going to pay 6% to the selling agent (who will share it with the buying agent), sellers simply inflate their asking price by 6% to cover this cost. Thus, while agents get their commissions from sellers, it's really the buyers who pay for it.

In fact, "avoiding the commission" is the only reason people cite for wanting to avoid real estate agents. By skipping the agent, people think a given house will cost 6% less. Indeed, on a $200,000 house, that's $12,000 — a lot of money!

But it's unlikely you'll ever see the savings. Why? Because the seller already has an agent and their agreement entitles the agent to a 6% commission. If as a buyer you fail to retain your own agent, the selling agent's commission isn't cut to 3% — they just keep the entire 6% for

> When you're trying to buy a house, only work with one agent. Remember: Agents get paid only when a transaction occurs. If several real estate agents show you the same house, who is entitled to the commission?

themselves! So don't think you (the buyer) will save money by *not* hiring an agent. The commission is built into the price of the home whether you have an agent or not.

And I'll bet hiring a real estate agent — a good one — actually will *save* you money. They'll apply all their years of experience, salesmanship, and negotiating skills to convince the seller to lower the sales price, perhaps even more than the 6% you were trying to save on your own. A good real estate agent, for example, even may be able to convince the seller to pay some of the points and settlement costs for you.

If you are serious about buying a house, don't worry about wasting an agent's time. Most buyers inspect 20 to 30 homes before they buy, but can see only 6-10 in a day. That means you're going to spend at least two or three days with your real estate agent. Don't worry about all the time you're taking, for that's why agents get paid.

By the same token, if you're not serious about buying a house, please be considerate of the agent's time; if he's spending Saturday with you, he's not spending it with someone else — and time is money. Spend as much of the agent's time as you need to find the place you want, but only if you're serious.

Should You Buy a New Home Instead of a Resale?

Many first-time home buyers buy townhouses with the intention of moving up to single-family homes later. Given the choice of buying a newly-built townhouse vs. a resale, many prefer to buy new — where they get to choose floor plans, options, and even colors for carpeting, paint, and bathroom tile. But make sure you fully understand the economic implications of buying a new home vs. a resale.

First, the future value of your house will be determined by your builder. If you buy a brand-new townhouse in a new development, the builder likely will continue to build homes in your neighborhood for several years. That means your future selling price will be based on whatever he is then selling his homes for — and in fact, yours probably would sell for less than his. After all, why should prospective buyers choose your "old" townhouse when they can get a new one — giving themselves the same opportunity to buy state-of-the-art construction and appliances along with the same choice of designs and colors as you enjoyed?

Of course, if the builder raises his prices, your home's value will rise, too. But either way, you will compete against the builder for as long as he's building in your neighborhood.

Another concern is that since the homes are all being completed in roughly the same period of time, most buyers move in during the same period and many move out at the same time, too. The result is often a saturated market which keeps resale prices down.

Remember: When buying your home, think like a seller, for you will be one someday. To that end, don't wallpaper a newly-built house for at least one year. The house will settle and the wallpaper will tear. (It's okay to paint.) Design and decorate your home so it will be appealing to potential buyers. If you paint your dining room purple, as my wife and I did (don't ask), be prepared to repaint it before you sell (as we did), because just as you don't always like the decorating you find in other people's homes, buyers will not share your taste, either (as we learned).

Chapter 57 - All About Mortgages

Which Loan Program is Right for You?

As you explore financing options, be wary. Some programs offer low down payments, low interest rates, low closing costs — or a combination of all three — and they can be enticing. Remember, though, that mortgage bankers make money by selling you a loan, not by servicing the loan throughout its 30-year life. (Bankers actually sell their loans to loan servicing companies. If you later default on your loan, the bank which sold you the loan has no risk — nor does the real estate agent who sold you the house.)

Therefore, bankers create many programs simply because they know they can sell them, but that doesn't mean you should buy them.

Fixed-Rate Mortgages

A fixed-rate loan is the most common. With this loan, which normally is for a term of 15 or 30 years, your interest rate never changes, and your mortgage payments stay the same. Fixed-rate loans are considered "safe" because the rate never changes. Thus, you need not worry about your rate rising in the future. *If you choose an 8% 30-year fixed rate, you will pay 8% per year for the life of the loan. The rate will never change.*

Adjustable-Rate Mortgages

ARMs offer lower initial interest rates than fixed-rate loans, and many people who choose them do so because they are unable to qualify for loans at current fixed rates. Thus, many people must either choose the ARM or forget about buying a house. But if (when?) interest rates later rise, the buyers could find themselves unable to afford the new higher payments. The result: They lose the house anyway. So when choosing a loan program, make sure you can handle the loan under its *worst-case* scenario, not its *initial terms*.

As discussed in Chapter 56, ARM rates start low but can rise up to 2% per year, not to exceed 6% over the life of the loan. *Thus, if your ARM starts at 5%, your rate could rise to 7% in year two, 9% in year three, and 11% in year four. The rate could never exceed 11% over the life of the loan.*

A 1-year ARM changes its rate after the first year, and again every year after that. A 3-year ARM maintains a fixed rate for the first three years, then changes annually thereafter, although some 3-year ARMs change their rates only every three years.

The 5/25 Mortgages

In this 30-year loan program, the initial rate is lower than the fixed rate but higher than the ARM, and the rate will remain in place for the first five years. At the end of the 5th year, the rate will be reset to current fixed rates. Unlike ARMs, there is no upper limit to this loan. *Current fixed rates are 8%, but you obtain a 5/25 loan with an initial rate of 6.25%. After five years, current fixed rates are 14%, so your loan's rate changes to 14% and will remain at this high level for the next 25 years.*

Thus, while the 5/25 is a very good deal for the first five years, it becomes very uncertain thereafter. Therefore, the only home buyers who are suitable for this loan are those who are <u>sure</u> that they will sell the house within five years. If you know you're moving within five years, the 5/25 is a great program, because you essentially receive a fixed-rate loan for the five years you'll own your home, but at a rate lower than true fixed-loan rates. But woe to you if your plans change and rates jump: You could find yourself paying an astronomical rate, and you may even lose your house.

A similar program is the 7/23, which fixes the rate for the first seven years instead of five. Other variations exist as well.

The COFI ARM: Use With Care or It May Burn You

Which would you choose: a loan with a high rate of interest that cannot change or a loan with a low initial rate that might rise later?

This is the ongoing debate between fixed-rate loans and ARMs. Maybe an ARM will be cheaper in the long run, maybe not. Which would you choose?

The COFI ARM may be your answer. Its rate is based on an average that banks in the Western states pay their depositors (the rate that banks pay is their cost of attracting deposits), and this "cost of funds index" gives COFI its name. Most COFI ARMs are based on the Federal Reserve Bank's 11th District, whose rates move more slowly than interest rates in other indexes. For example, the COFI index in 1994 rose less than half a percent, while the T-bill rate rose by four percent — or eight times as much. Because ordinary ARMs rely on the T-bill and similar guides, homeowners who have an ordinary ARM are much more likely to see a big rise in their rate than those who have a COFI ARM.

While COFI rates are lower than ordinary ARMs, that's usually true only for the first three months. After that, the COFI rate changes every month and will for the next 30 years. ARMs, by contrast, lock in their rates for one-year or three-year periods.

COFIs Offer Three Payment Choices

You choose a COFI loan with an initial interest rate of 7%.

You will receive in the mail a monthly invoice instead of an annual coupon book, and this invoice will give you three payment choices.

Say the index later rises to 9%.

Payment Choice #1: The Fully Indexed Payment

This is the payment you need to make in order to pay off the mortgage in 30 years. This payment will change whenever the 11th District's rate changes. That's why the 11th District is so popular: Its changes are smaller and less frequent than other indexes, reducing the risk that next month's invoice will be a big jump over this month's invoice.

Under Choice #1, you'd make a full principal and interest payment based on the current 9% rate.

Payment Choice #2: Accrued Interest Only

This is a payment of interest only, no principal, and therefore the payment is less than that required by Choice #1. This is great if money is tight one month or if the index jumps suddenly, but the downside, of course, is that your loan's balance doesn't go down. Next month, you'll still owe as much as you owed this month.

To prevent you from having a "perpetual mortgage," homeowners who consistently choose this option will find their loans recast every five years. In other words, if you make interest-only payments every month, your loan is recalculated after the fifth year so it is paid off in the remaining 25 years. This way, the loan won't exceed 30 years.

Under Choice #2, you'd pay only the interest, but still based on the current rate of 9%.

Payment Choice #3: The Minimum Payment

This amount is the same as the payment that was in effect at the loan's inception, and therefore this payment will be lower than the other two choices. That's the good news. The bad news, of course, is that this option can create negative amortization.

Under Choice #3, your payment would be based on the old 7% rate — and since that's 2% less than the current rate, the shortfall would be added to your principal balance, meaning you now owe more than you did last month.

The effect is similar to that of paying the minimum payment on a credit card: Even though you are making a payment each month, you're not paying enough. Therefore, the debt not only doesn't go away, it continues to grow, making it even more expensive and difficult to pay off.

I don't like to recommend Choice #3 for obvious reasons, and there is concern that some consumers may not realize the impact of selecting Choice #3. If so, they could find themselves burned by this very hot COFI.

Figure 8-2 compares the monthly payment of a COFI loan vs. a 1-year ARM.

COFI vs. ARM

Principal and interest payment for $150,000 loan assuming no increases in base indexes

Year	Month	Rate	COFI			1-Year ARM	
			Option-1	Option-2	Option-3	Rate	Payment
1	1	5.70%	$870	n/a	n/a	8.25%	$1,126
	2	5.70%	$870	n/a	n/a	8.25%	$1,126
	3	5.70%	$870	n/a	n/a	8.25%	$1,126
	4	7.59%	$1,058	$965	$870	8.25%	$1,126
	5	7.59%	$1,058	$965	$870	8.25%	$1,126
	6	7.59%	$1,058	$965	$870	8.25%	$1,126
	7	7.59%	$1,058	$965	$870	8.25%	$1,126
	8	7.59%	$1,058	$965	$870	8.25%	$1,126
	9	7.59%	$1,058	$965	$870	8.25%	$1,126
	10	7.59%	$1,058	$965	$870	8.25%	$1,126
	11	7.59%	$1,058	$965	$870	8.25%	$1,126
	12	7.59%	$1,058	$965	$870	8.25%	$1,126
2	1-12	7.59%	$1,058	$965	$870	9.16%	$1,224
3	1-12	7.59%	$1,058	$965	$870	9.16%	$1,224

(Rates as of 9/95)

FIGURE 8-2

A COFI ARM can be attractive because it uses a more stable index, your payment options are flexible, and you get the ability to buy a home you otherwise might not be able to afford. You should consider a COFI ARM, though, only if you are comfortable with it; a person who will lie awake at night worrying about rate changes probably should avoid this loan — and all ARMs, for that matter.

Dozens of other programs are available, too, and more are added all the time. That's why you need to sit down with a financial professional who can suggest the program that is best for you.

How to Choose a Mortgage Company

Ask people what they look for in a mortgage, and they'll tell you, "The rate." But seeking a good rate is a poor way to choose a mortgage company — simply because all lenders get their money from the same place. Therefore, everybody has the same cost of doing business and the same loan programs with virtually the same interest rates.

Thus, it's rare that you'll find a "great deal" offered by one firm that another can't match. Our experience with my own mortgage company has convinced me of this. But there is one area where one firm can set itself apart from another: service.

As every home buyer has learned, the mortgage process is an ugly one. You are asked to submit a zillion documents (they ask for them one at a time), and then they want you to reverify what you already told them. Then all the third parties get involved: the appraiser, credit bureau, termite inspector, well and septic people, title company — and nobody ever seems to talk with each other, leaving you to do all the work, worrying about whether it will get done in time for settlement!

> *"A banker: The person who lends you his umbrella when the sun is shining and wants it back the minute it rains."*
> —Mark Twain

Therefore, after you verify that rates are competitive, you'll be much happier if you choose a mortgage broker or banker who has an excellent reputation for providing high quality service.

When to See the Mortgage Company

When preparing to buy a house, most people start with a real estate agent. That seems to be the correct first step — after all, it's a house you want to buy — but it's not. A house may be something you want, but you're not going to get it without a mortgage. Therefore, you should talk first with a mortgage broker, not a real estate broker!

Three Advantages of Getting Pre-Approved

Why bother looking for a house if you don't know whether you can get a mortgage, or how much of a loan you can get? After all, your mortgage will determine how expensive a house you can buy. Many real estate agents, in fact, will not work with a client until after they've been approved by a lender.

Advantage #1: You Avoid Disappointment

There's nothing worse than finding the home of your dreams, only to discover later that you can't afford it. By going to the lender first, you'll determine how much house you can buy before you start visiting homes beyond your price range.

Advantage #2: You Save Significant Amounts of Time

While you're searching for a home, the mortgage application process can be underway. Too often, people start this process only after they spend three months finding the home they want. This forces them to spend another three months waiting for their loan's approval. Starting the loan process now will save you a lot of time.

Advantage #3: Pre-Approval Can Be a Major Negotiating Weapon

With a pre-qualification letter in hand, you can complete the purchase of a home in as little as two weeks, instead of the usual three months. Many sellers are in a hurry to sell and will accept a lower offer in exchange for a quicker settlement. If two people bid on the same house, the person whose loan is pre-approved will win the contract.

So choose your mortgage company first, get pre-qualified, and *then* hire a real estate agent.

Mortgage Bankers vs. Mortgage Brokers

Most banks offer loans, and going to them is like shopping at a Ford dealer: You won't get a Chevy, no matter how good the Chevy might be. Therefore, you need to compare offers from several banks. Or you can work with a mortgage broker.

Brokers represents dozens of banks. Although the broker serves as middle-man, his or her services will not cost you anything extra. That's because brokers get loans at wholesale rates, and pass them along to their clients at retail prices, just like any business. The difference between wholesale and retail is how brokers make money. Therefore, you get the same rate from a broker as if you went directly to the lender yourself. In fact, because of their volume, many brokers are able to offer their clients better deals than you can get by talking to banks on your own.

The choice is yours.

Does Your Mortgage Company's Appraiser Even Know How to Count?

We've talked about how the mortgage process can be confusing. Often, that's a good description for the appraisal process, too. All lenders require an appraisal to confirm that the property is worth what they're planning to lend. Your mortgage company will hire an independent appraiser (the cost usually is $300 — at your expense, of course), and you have to accept whatever they say.

That's fine, except that they don't always say what you want them to say. Based on the description that follows, can you tell me...

How Many Bathrooms Are In This House?

John and Kathy want to buy a four-bedroom colonial. The main bedroom features a master bathroom, and the other bedrooms off the upper level share a full bathroom. A powder room is in the hallway on the main level. The finished basement has paneling and carpeting throughout, recessed lights, and a wet bar. It also has a fifth bedroom and full bath.

To obtain a mortgage, John and Kathy need to have the house appraised. According to the appraisal, *how many bathrooms are in this house?*

Before you read the answer below, please don't go nuts. Because you're wrong. You counted three and a half. Sorry, you're wrong.

The correct answer is two and a half.

When reviewing a property, appraisers include only those features which exist above-grade. The basement is below-grade, and thus neither the bedroom nor the bathroom built there are included in the normal count.

But don't worry. The appraisal form does provide for a separate section on basements, which is where you'll find information about those improvements.

The moral to this story is that the mortgage banking industry doesn't see the world as you might expect. What begins as a simple effort can become very complex, so as you move through the mortgage process, don't be surprised by the unexpected. If you see or hear something that doesn't look right, call your loan officer. Chances are, a simple explanation will alleviate your concerns. And should you discover a mistake, bringing it to your mortgage company's attention will enable them to fix it for you.

And above all, don't go nuts.

Chapter 58 - How to Buy Your *Next* Home

Just because you bought a house once doesn't make you an expert. The truth is that buying your *next* home offers many important differences — not the least of which is the fact that for the first time, you have a house to sell. So let's look closely at how to handle these two important financial transactions simultaneously.

Your real estate agent likely will suggest, among other things:

- **Clean and clean up! First impressions are vital;**

- **Repair major items such as windows, plumbing, and appliances;**

- **Repair little things, too, such as loose doorknobs or sticking doors;**

- **Repaint and recarpet as needed. Spending some money here will help you sell for a higher price;**

- **Get your lawn and driveway/walkway in good condition;**

- **Too much furniture makes a room look small. Remove some pieces to let the house show better;**

- **Too little furniture makes a house look barren. Add some pieces from another room;**

- **Make closets look bigger by keeping them organized; and**

- **Get the bathrooms and kitchen looking their best.**

Remember: Good real estate agents sell dozens of homes every year, and they know what motivates buyers. If your real estate agent makes a suggestion, act on it.

Disposing of your current home could take eight to 10 months (if all goes well). The first step is to hire a real estate agent to sell your home. Do this at least one month before you plan to put the house on the market. Your agent will tell you how to prepare the house for sale (this is the first of many ways the agent will prove his or her worth to you). The goal is to make the house as presentable as possible. Depending on how much work your home requires, it could take a month or more to get your house in selling condition. Depending on how active the real estate market is at the time you sell and the marketability of your home, it could take from several weeks to many months to find a buyer, so the sooner you get a real estate agent involved, the sooner you'll sell the house. Once you find a buyer and sign a contract, you must wait for settlement, which generally takes 60 to 90 days. The result: eight to 10 months to sell your home.

Should You Hire a Real Estate Agent to Help You Sell Your House?

I know a great real estate agent you should hire. He's very enthusiastic and well-intentioned. He's also completely honest and trustworthy, and he really wants to do a great job for you.

On the other hand, he has never sold a house before. He has never taken a real estate course, does not hold a real estate license, and knows nothing about real estate law. He has no background in sales or marketing and doesn't know anyone in the real estate business. He does not know how to find prospective buyers (although he's confident that won't be a problem) and he admits to being completely unfamiliar with the elements of negotiating a real estate contract — in fact,

> *"A good architect can improve the looks of an old house merely by discussing the cost of a new one."*
>
> **—Anonymous**

he's never even drafted a real estate contract. He does not have access to the Multiple Listing Service (he's not even sure what that is or what it offers) and he knows nobody in the mortgage, title settlement, or related fields, nor does he know anything about those businesses.

But like I said, this guy is honest, motivated, and wants to do a great job for you. Oh, and best of all, *he's free.*

Would you hire him?

No, of course not. It's obvious why such a person is willing to work for free: Nobody would ever think of paying him! Yet, if you're planning to sell your home on your own, without the benefits of a real estate agent, this is exactly who you are hiring: You're hiring yourself.

No other person would hire you to sell their home, so why are you hiring yourself to sell yours? Admit it: The only reason is because you want to save the 6% commission that real estate agents charge. Yet, as we discussed in Chapter 56, it's really the buyer who pays the commission, because sellers simply increase their sales price to cover this expense. So get over it. Hire the real estate agent and move on.

> Do you think you'll be able to inflate your price by 6%, skip the real estate agent, and pocket the difference? Nice try, but there isn't a buyer in the world — especially one who's using an agent, as most are — who will let you get away with that stunt.

Even if you were paying the commission (rather than the buyer), I can give you three reasons that make the cost worthwhile:

- A real estate agent is likely to get a higher price for your home than you will on your own because the sales price is determined by negotiation, and real estate agents are experts at contract negotiation;

- Buyers will say things to a real estate agent that they won't say to the seller, and the agent can use this information to your advantage; and

- The buyer is likely to be represented by a real estate agent. Do you want to negotiate alone?

Buyers are Liars, and Sellers are Tellers

Buyer was inspecting Seller's house.

Buyer casually mentions, "I was hoping the master suite was on the main level."

Seller, asked why he's moving, says, "I've got to be in Dallas next week for a new job."

When they start negotiating, Seller is at a disadvantage. He thinks Buyer is lukewarm about the house, because Buyer expressed disappointment about the location of the bedroom, yet Buyer knows that Seller is in a hurry to sell.

Buyers pretend that things are important to them which aren't, while sellers say things to buyers they should not say because it weakens their negotiating position. Either way, careless sellers hurt themselves by interacting with potential buyers.

The only way to make sure you don't hurt yourself *is to not have any conversation with a potential buyer.* That means someone else has to do the talking for you, and that someone should be your real estate agent.

Four Tips for Working Successfully with a Real Estate Agent When Selling a House

You need to hire a real estate agent and then follow these tips:

Tip #1: Leave the House When the Agent Shows it to a Potential Buyer

Sometimes, agents give you little notice. "I've got someone who'd like to see the house. Can we come over in 15 minutes?" You need to (a) say yes, (b) clean up, and (c) get out of the house.

Don't be in the house when it is being shown, for two reasons. First, you might say something stupid, like, "You can't see that water stain on the wall, can you?" Second, buyers feel uncomfortable walking around someone else's home if the owners are there. Your presence will intimidate buyers, and they will not spend a lot of time in your house. The less time they spend in the house, the less likely they will buy it. Get out of the house.

Tip #2: Take Your Pets With You

Some people hate animals. At best, a pet is a reminder that the house will be filled with stains, odors, or other problems. At worst, your pet could literally chase them out of the house. I know you love Muffy, but she will not help you close the sale.

Tip #3: Turn off the TV and Radios

Let them focus on the house, not Oprah.

Tip #4: Keep All Lights On, and Open the Curtains to Let the Sun Shine In

Make sure all the rooms of the house are inviting.

If you let agents do their job, you'll sell your home quicker, for more money, and with less hassle than if you try to do it yourself.

Should You Rent Your Current House?

Ask people where they plan to get the cash to buy a new home and most will answer, "From the equity in my old house." But by selling your old house, you give away any future growth in that property's value. Realizing this, many homeowners debate whether they should sell their old home or keep it as a rental. Here's how to decide which course of action is best for you.

Do you have any equity in your current home?

In other words, can you sell your house today for more than you owe on it? Remember to consider the costs you'll incur to sell the place, including the agent's commission.

If you *do not* have equity in your house, it's an ideal candidate for renting.

If you *do* have equity in the home, ask yourself the following question:

Do you need to use that equity as a down payment on the new home?

If you do, you must sell your home. If you don't, you can rent or sell it.

Renting can be enticing, for it offers these benefits:

- It lets you avoid selling your house now. This is especially valuable if selling now would produce a loss. By waiting, maybe you can get a higher price later;

- When you eventually sell the property, you might get a tax deduction if you sell it for a loss;

- Provided your annual adjusted gross income is less than $100,000, you may enjoy annual tax savings through "depreciation," which lets you slowly deduct from your taxable income the cost of the building (not the land under it); and

- You might be able to rent the property for more than what it costs you to maintain it.

But don't think renting is an easy road to riches. There are major drawbacks, including:

- If you don't sell now, your property's future value might be even lower later;

- You are likely to incur a "negative cash flow," meaning your rental income will not be enough to cover your monthly expenses;

- It is likely your property will be vacant at least occasionally, such as when a tenant leaves but a new one hasn't yet moved in. When predicting rental income, mortgage lenders assume rentals are vacant 25% of the time;

- Each time a tenant moves out, you'll incur cleaning and fix-up costs — from carpet cleaning and painting to major repairs.

- Depreciation, that oft-cited benefit of real estate investors, is not a gift from Congress — it's a loan! Every dollar depreciation saves you in taxes lowers your cost basis, which means that when you sell the house, you pay a larger capital gains tax. Thus, depreciation lowers your taxes today but increases your taxes later;

- It's difficult to refinance a rental property should interest rates drop; and most important,

- The Hassle Factor (see Chapter 18).

The Shared Equity Deal

What if you don't want to rent your house but can't sell it? Here's the answer, in the example of Tom and Karen. They bought their original house for $200,000, putting 10% down and financing the $180,000 balance; their monthly payment is $1,400. They now want to move to a bigger place, but due to a soft real estate market, their house would sell for only $180,000.

They don't want to sell their house because they don't want to lose the $20,000 they had put down, but they don't want to become landlords, either. Because they don't need the equity from the old house to get into the new house, they are ideal candidates for a shared equity deal.

Along come Ed and Trish. Newly married with a baby, they make good incomes and easily can afford a $1,500 mortgage payment, but they haven't been able to save the $20,000 or so it takes to buy a house. Like most young couples, they want to own, not rent, but buying a home seems out of reach. Like Tom and Karen, Ed and Trish also are ideal candidates for a shared equity deal.

Karen places an ad in the local paper saying, "Own your home with no money down," and Trish responds. Here's how the deal works: Tom and Karen, the two sellers of their home, agree to sell their home to four buyers: Tom, Karen, Ed, and Trish. Thus, Tom and Karen, who once owned 100% of the property, now own 50%; Ed and Trish own the other 50%. Thus, they are sharing the ownership, or equity, of the property.

In a separate legal agreement signed by all four parties, it is agreed that Tom and Karen contribute the down payment — the $20,000 they already have in the property. Ed and Trish agree to be responsible for all mortgage payments, repairs, maintenance, and decorating expenses. The four also agree to share any required repair expense of $1,000 or more.

They further agree to sell the property in five years. The proceeds of the sale will be disbursed in the following order:

1. The mortgage will be paid off;

2. All selling expenses will be paid, including the real estate agent's commission;

3. Tom and Karen will receive back their original down payment of $20,000; and then

4. Any remaining proceeds will be split equally among all four parties.

Let's assume the property grows 6% per year over the five years. If so, the house would be worth about $243,000. They owe the bank $180,000 and the real estate agents $14,500. Then Tom and Karen get their $20,000 back. The remaining cash — $28,500 — is evenly divided, giving $14,250 to each couple.

This is a great deal for everybody. From Tom and Karen's $20,000 downpayment, they get back $34,250. That's a total return of 71%, or an average annual return of 14% — very good by any measure!

And Ed and Trish, who got into the house with no cash outlay, now get $14,250 to use as a downpayment on their next house, which they'll own all by themselves. And because they made the mortgage payments during the five years, they enjoyed big tax deductions while the shared equity deal was in effect.

If Ed and Trish don't want to move at the end of the term, they simply use their share of the equity to buy out Tom and Karen. In fact, that's the most common way people end a shared equity deal.

This strategy is used most often within families, where the kids — young, newly married — have good incomes but no cash, while Mom and Dad have assets and lots of their own home equity. The kids don't want to ask Mom and Dad for a loan, and the parents don't really want to give them one...

...so they strike a business deal: They all buy the house together, with Mom and Dad owning half and the kids owning half. The parents make the down payment and the kids cover everything else. Three

A client called me one day rather discouraged. He'd been trying to sell his house for six months, without success. He originally listed the property at $410,000 (which he knew was too high), then dropped the price to $389,000 (in the range of other sales in his neighborhood.). Still, no offers.

"My Realtor wants me to cut the price to $379,000," he told me. "But I want to see if anyone will accept $389,000 first. "

"How long do you figure it will take to get an offer at $389,000?" I asked him.

"Four or five months," he replied.

"How quickly do you think the house will sell if you price it at $374,000?" I asked.

"Right away!" he gushed. "It's already on the low side compared to recent sales on my street, and I've got a finished basement. At $374,000, it's a heckuva deal."

I had one last question for him. "What are your

or five or seven years later (the parties decide), the parents get a great return on their investment and (assuming the house's price has increased) the kids get their own house.

If you're a would-be seller, you'll find that shared equity deals often offer you lower risk than if you treated your home as a rental, because your tenants regard themselves as owners and they treat the house accordingly. They don't trash it, they don't call at 3 AM to have something fixed, and most important, they won't miss any mortgage payments because doing so voids their share of the deal.

What's the downside? By offering a shared equity deal, you are giving away half the future growth of the property. And if home prices go down or stay level, your share will not grow. But considering the alternatives, this might be a price worth paying.

The Chicken or the Egg

So which should you do first — buy the new or sell the old? Most second-time buyers buy the new one first, so it ought to be no surprise that this is wrong. The reason: Since most buyers cannot afford to carry two homes, they offer the seller a "contingency contract," which says that their purchase of the new home is contingent on the sale of their old house.

For anyone who is buying a home while already owning one, contingency contracts make perfect sense, and if your circumstances require you to buy a new home before selling your old one, then I agree you should offer a contingency contract. But ideally, *do not buy a new home until you have already sold the old one.*

Why? Because everyone else is offering contingent contracts, too, and sellers hate them. Think a moment like the seller: You want to sell your house and along comes a buyer. "I want to buy your house, and I'll pay your asking price — but my house has not sold yet, and I will not buy yours unless and until it does." Do you have a deal? There's no way to tell. But accepting that offer forces you to take your home off the market anyway, for as much as 90 days. If the buyer fails to sell *his* home, *your* deal falls through. That's why sellers hate contingency contracts.

It's also easy to see why your real estate agent will be able to strike a better deal for you if you are able to buy a home without worrying about selling another. Again, think like the seller: Say you hold an open house and you receive two offers. The first agrees to pay your asking price of $200,000, on a contingency basis, while the other offers you only $192,000 and offers to go to settlement in two weeks with no contingency. Which will you take?

Most sellers will accept the lower offer, and with good reason: The contingency contract might not reach settlement for 90 or 120 days, and in the interim you must continue to make your mortgage payments. At $1,300 per month, that's an additional $4,000 or $5,000 — and then you've still got to hope the buyer sells

monthly carrying costs for the property?"

"Well," he answered, "between the mortgage payment, utilities, maintenance and such, I'd say about $4,000 a month."

I told him to price the house at $374,000 immediately, as his Realtor had suggested, and I hope you can see why. If it takes him four months to sell at $389,000, he'll spend $16,000 carrying the property until then — leaving him with $373,000. Thus, he'd actually make more money selling for $374,000 now than by selling for $389,000 in four months (assuming he's able to sell for that price at all! More likely, he'll end up cutting the price to $374,000 eventually, anyway, and he'll merely have wasted four months and $16,000).

Remember, as I showed you in Chapter 2, don't focus on how much you earn. It's how much you keep that counts.

their home. But by taking the lower offer, you *know* you've got a deal. And because of all the mortgage costs you'll save over the next few months, it's really just as good a deal as the higher offer. Your real estate agent knows how to make this a strong negotiating point — especially if you took my advice in Chapter 57 and got pre-qualified for your mortgage loan.

"Look, Mr. Seller, I know my client's offer is not as much as you wanted, but it's *not contingent*. If you take a contingent offer that's $10,000 more than what my client is offering, you've got to wait months for that guy to sell his house, and then another 90 days to close the deal. My clients are asking for no contingency, and they've been pre-approved for their mortgage: You could go to settlement and be outta here in just two weeks!"

That's a powerful pitch. So if you want to save money and increase the likelihood that the buyer will accept your offer, buy your next home *with no contingency*.

Of course, that means you need to sell your current home first. If you do, you could be homeless for a time — because you sold one before buying the other. If that worries you, here's the solution: Place a contingency on the home you're *selling* instead of the one you're *buying*. Tell the buyer of your old house that you need a 10-day or 30-day contingency to find a place to live. Most buyers won't object (since they're fumbling with their own mortgage application process anyway), and it'll give you the time you need to make an offer on a new home.

Remember: It is always easier to buy your next home than to sell your existing one.

What is Your Home Worth?

The client I described in the sidebar on the previous two pages had bought his house in 1988 for $425,000. He finished the basement, added a deck, landscaping, and other improvements. He figures he spent some $60,000 on all these extras, but he realizes that the market has gotten softer since he moved in. So, what is his home worth?

Whatever someone is willing to pay him for it.

What my client paid for his house irrelevant. How much he spent on improvements and upgrades is irrelveant. His current mortgage balance is irrelevant. And, most shocking to some, what he thinks the home is worth also is irrelevant.

The only number that matters is the one offered to him by a buyer.

If You're Building a New Home

Very often, home buyers and sellers (and you're both!) are working with tight timetables, often with deadlines imposed by others. If you are building a new home, have plans in place in case the builder does not finish on time.

And if you are working with a small builder, what would you do if your builder failed to complete construction? This happened to a client of ours: His builder was killed in a small plane crash, and the house was only two-thirds finished. I suggest that if you are working with a small builder, buy an insurance policy on the builder to protect your-self in case the builder dies or becomes disabled. The cost is low because you're buying the insurance only for a short time, yet you'll be protected in case the builder becomes unable to finish the house.

How to Handle the Mortgage on Your Second Home

As I've said, buying your next home is different from buying your first, and nowhere is that more true than when it comes to your mortgage.

The price you paid for your first home was determined by your mortgage company. They told you how much money you could borrow and how much cash you needed in order to complete the deal. You had no choice but to agree, so in the weeks and months before you bought the home, you scrimped and saved, you stopped eating out, you sold assets, you received gifts and loans from family and friends, and in the end, you became cash-rich. Then, on settlement day, you wrote the largest check you had ever written and in an instant you went from cash-rich to house-poor. You were never happier, more excited — or more scared.

The reason you wrote that large check is because the mortgage company said you had to, and as big as that check was, it was the least amount required in order for you to qualify for the loan. So you wrote a check for $20,000 or $30,000 or whatever — not because you wanted to but because they required you to. By brute strength, through sheer force of will, you came up with whatever cash was necessary to get yourself into that house.

Well, now you're in the house. Next, you sell it, and after commissions and other selling expenses, you have $50,000 in equity. You plan to buy a new home that costs $300,000.

Most buyers buy their second homes the same way they bought their first home: By writing a check for 100% of their assets. There are two reasons people do this: (1) because they did it before, and (2) because the price of their new home is frightening.

When you bought your first home, you did whatever it took to raise the money your lender required. Since you emptied your bank account last time, it seems natural to do it again. And you've got another reason to make a big down payment: The bigger the down payment, the lower your monthly payment.

But while it made sense for you to devote all your financial assets to a down payment when you bought your *first* house, it does not make sense to do it when buying your *next* house.

Last time, you bought your house on brute strength alone. This time you can do it with finesse. You see, you must recognize that there's a big difference between *what the lender requires* and *what you can afford*. The first time you bought a house, there was no difference. Then, what your lender required *was* what you could afford (barely!), so the two numbers were the same. Your lender required that you put down a certain amount, so you scraped the money together and wrote a check.

But this time, it's different.

This time you're buying a $300,000 house, and the lender is requiring just 10% down. That's $30,000. Yet you've got $50,000 from the sale of your first house. So this time, what they require is not the same as what you can afford. This time, you can afford to put down *even more* than what is required.

Don't do it.

Don't give lenders more than they require. Instead, give lenders only the minimum they want and take out as big a mortgage as they will give you.

Five Great Reasons to Carry a Big Long Mortgage

If you're concerned that reducing your down payment will increase your monthly payment, relax: That's a good thing. In fact, I want you to carry as big a mortgage as possible. Why? Here are five great reasons:

Reason #1: Mortgages Don't Affect Home Values

The value of your home will rise or fall regardless of the size of your mortgage. Its ability to grow has nothing to do with the amount of equity you hold in it. Therefore, having lots of money in home equity is like having money in a mattress: It's not earning any interest. You would never keep $100,000 under your bed, yet lots of people have a quarter million in their walls. In other words, *keep the money out of the house.*

Reason #2: Your Mortgage is the Cheapest Money You'll Ever Buy

Most people have debt, if only for an auto loan. Credit cards average 18%, auto loans 10%. But a mortgage (or home equity loan) costs much less.

And unlike other loan interest, you get a tax deduction for all the mortgage interest you pay. If you are in the 33% combined federal/state income tax bracket, the government subsidizes a third of your mortgage interest. That means an 8% home loan costs you only 5.4%. Compare that to an 18% credit card, where none of the interest is deductible. Result: Your home loan is less than a third of the cost of a credit card. So get a big mortgage, enabling you to use your cash to pay off other debts. In other words, *keep the money out of the house.*

Reason #3: Get the Cash Out While You Can

Ever see a retired person lose their home? Here's how it can happen: Many retired couples have little savings, but their house is paid for. Suddenly, there's a catastrophic illness, costing $4,000 a month in long-term care. Living on a fixed income, the other spouse can't pay these new bills. But the house is worth six figures, so the spouse seeks a bank loan, offering to post the home as collateral.

This sounds good, but banks do not like to lend money to a retiree, as discussed in Chapter 56. With no income, there's no way to repay the loan, and the bank doesn't want the house — it's in the banking business, not the real estate business. So the only way to get the cash out of the house is to sell it. Result: The couple loses their home of 40 years.

The solution is to take the cash out of the house before you and your spouse retire. Invest your equity and use the income to pay off the new mortgage. The loan will be a wash, and if your broker or financial planner is good, you may even be able to earn a bit more in interest than the loan costs you.

Now if a financial or medical crisis strikes, the cash would be readily available to you. And you could cancel the whole idea anytime by cashing in the investments to pay off the mortgage. The point is this: When you have the cash, you have choices. When the cash is tied up in a home, you have few options. In other words, *get the cash out of the house.*

Reason #4: If You Don't Borrow it When You Buy, You Can't Deduct it Later

Under tax law, mortgage interest is deductible only for acquisition debt, or in some cases, acquisition debt plus $100,000, subject to limitations. Say you sell your $300,000 home and buy a new one for the same price. If you pay cash for the new home (which you can afford to do with the proceeds from the sale of your old home), you will lose the tax break and liquidity discussed earlier. But worse, if you later decide to take out a home equity loan, only the first $100,000 will be tax deductible. On the other hand, if you took out a 90% mortgage ($270,000) when you bought the home, the entire amount would be deductible. In other words, *keep the cash out of the house.*

Reason #5: A 30-year Mortgage is Better than 15

On a $150,000 loan at 8%, a 30-year mortgage would cost $1,100 per month, but mortgage bankers will tell you that for only $333 more per month, you can get a 15-year mortgage instead. Thus, they say, you'll own your home in half the time and save $138,207 in interest charges. Sound great?

> **To avoid mortgage insurance, it's okay to put down as much as 20%, but not more.**

Well, try this: Choose the 30-year mortgage and invest the extra $333 you were willing to give the bank. Assuming you earn 10%, which is no great challenge, at the end of 15 years you'll have saved $113,022 after taxes — virtually the same as your mortgage's outstanding balance. So, you can pay off your mortgage if you want, giving you the equivalent of a 15-year note.

Why do this if the numbers are the same? For all these great reasons:

- Because your cash remains available to you if you need it for other purposes;

- Because cash tends to be tight after buying a new home, so the lower payment will prove very helpful;

- Because that extra $333 mortgage payment goes toward principal, not interest, so there's no tax break by making it;

- Because you lose your tax deduction quicker on the 15-year note than on the 30-year; and

- Because your mortgage payment stays fixed but your income grows with inflation, meaning you get to pay off today's fixed loan with cheaper, future dollars.

In other words, *keep the cash out of the house.*

> **There is one caveat to this strategy: You must religiously set aside the $333 each month. If you don't, you'll have nothing in 15 years but 15 years left on your mortgage. A good planner or advisor can show you how to set up a systematic investment program so you'll be sure to save that $333.**

At first thought, a big 30-year mortgage may seem risky. But if you really think about it, it's the only way to go.

Chapter 59 - How to Avoid Taxes When Selling Your Home

If you're like most people, eventually you will sell one house to buy another. This must be done carefully, or you could be hit with a potentially huge tax bill. In this chapter, I'll show you how to avoid this problem and how to minimize, defer, and avoid those taxes.

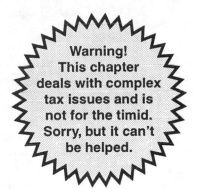

Warning! This chapter deals with complex tax issues and is not for the timid. Sorry, but it can't be helped.

If You are Selling Your Old Home for a Profit

When selling their house, most people make a profit, so let's start there. (Later in this chapter, we'll cover what to do if you will be selling for a loss).

If you are selling your house for a profit, you must pay taxes on that profit *unless* your new home costs at least as much as the selling price of the old house, in which case *you are prohibited* from paying taxes on the profit (like anyone would argue with that).

That sounds simple enough. (Okay, maybe it doesn't. Read it a few more times.) When it comes to taxes, nothing is simple, so let's take a closer look.

Determine Your "Adjusted Sales Price"

As stated above, you must pay taxes on your profit when you sell your house unless the purchase price of the new home is at least as much as the selling price of the old one. Thus, to determine how expensive a home we have to buy, we have to figure out the selling price of the old house.

You bought a house 10 years ago for $125,000, and you now sell it for $200,000.

Is $200,000 the selling price? Not according to the IRS. Instead, you must determine the *Adjusted Sales Price*. To get it, subtract from the actual sales price all the expenses you incurred in selling the home. You can include:

- commissions;

- advertising;

- legal fees;

- related taxes;

- title policy fees;

- escrow fees;

- points you pay to the buyer; and

- any fix-up expenses.

Although tedious, this effort is worthwhile, for it will produce for you a lower, or *adjusted*, sales price than the actual sales price. And the lower the Adjusted Sales Price, the less expensive your new home needs to be to enable you to defer the tax.

Fix-Up Expenses

Notice that the above list includes "fix-up expenses." Let's look closer at this item, for it is a source of significant confusion.

The 90-Day Rule

In order to include the cost of fix-up expenses, you must incur the expense within 90 days of signing the sales contract, and you must pay the bill within 30 days after settlement.

Which leads us to **IRS Annoying Rule #1:** Say you spend thousands re-painting, re-carpeting, replacing kitchen cabinets, and fixing the leaky faucets. Then the house doesn't sell within the required 90 days. The IRS says you cannot reduce your sales price by the amount of those expenses. *Boy, is that annoying.*

To avoid this risk, some sellers refuse to make the repairs. Instead, they plan to lower their asking price, telling potential buyers that repairs will be completed when the contract is signed. Although this might avoid the tax risk of doing repairs outside the 90-day window, it's a bad idea, for it will hurt your efforts to sell the house. The reason: Most buyers want to buy a house that's in good condition.

> **Furthermore, this idea is short-sighted. Often, spending $5,000 on needed repairs will enable you to raise your price by $10,000. So don't let your efforts to reduce taxes interfere with your efforts to sell the house. The better strategy is to make the repairs, price your home realistically, and hope for the best.**

Is It a Repair or an Improvement?

To be considered a fix-up expense, the expense must be for repairs, not improvements.

Fine, but is fixing the roof a repair or an improvement? There are no clear answers, but the IRS does provide some guidelines. Expenses are improvements if they:

- add to the value of your house;

- extend the useful life of the house; or

- adapt the house to new uses.

Repairs, on the other hand, simply maintain the property in good working order. Thus, fixing a few shingles on the roof would be a repair, while replacing the entire roof would be an improvement because it extends the useful life of the house.

Also, fix-up expenses must not be deductible elsewhere on your tax return. A common example is when somebody installs handrails in the bathroom, deducting the cost as a medical expense on Schedule A. By doing so, you cannot also include the expense as a selling expense in an effort to lower your Adjusted Sales Price.

Say you incur $25,000 in selling expenses.

Thus, your Adjusted Selling Price is $175,000, and that's what the price of your new home needs to be. Again, that sounds simple. And again, it's not.

The IRS says that in your efforts to spend $175,000 on your new home, the following expenses are **not** includable:

- real estate taxes;

- mortgage interest;

- points or loan origination fees;

- FHA mortgage insurance premiums; and

- fire insurance premiums.

However, the following expenses **are** includable:

- title insurance;

- commissions;

- legal expenses; and, most important

- improvements made within two years of the date of sale of the old house.

Pay particular attention to that last point. You do not have to buy a $175,000 home. Instead, you can buy a $150,000 home and later spend $25,000 in improvements — such as by adding a swimming pool, finishing the basement, or building an addition. You have *two years* to do these things to reach the total of $175,000.

Remember that only money you actually spend on the new home counts toward meeting the Adjusted Sales Price of the old house. If you're handy with tools and plan to work on your new home yourself, only your cost of materials will count. The IRS will not consider the economic value of your time, nor the equivalent retail cost of the improvements you make. If you're a skilled do-it-yourselfer, you might save so much money that you could fail to spend as much as the Adjusted Sales Price of the house you sold. You have my blessing (and my envy, too) to do things yourself if you're so inclined, but watch out for this trap.

Actually, *two* years is misleading, for there really are *two* 2-year rules. Let's look at them both.

The First 2-Year Rule

Get ready for more confusion: The first 2-year rule provides a 4-year window. This rule says you must buy *and occupy* your next home within two years of selling your old one. And this can occur either *before* or *after* you sell the old one.

You sell your house on February 9, 1997.

Thus, you have until February 9, 1999, to buy your new home. A home you bought as long ago as February 9, 1995, would qualify as well.

As we discussed in the last chapter, you should strongly consider selling your old house before buying your new one. And as you can see from this rule, that's okay as long as you buy the new one within two years.

> **IRS Annoying Rule #2:** Please note that construction and acquisition costs incurred outside this 4-year window do not count. I once had a client who sold his house and built a new home near the beach when he retired. He had bought a wooded lot for $50,000, and since the Adjusted Sales Price of his house was $250,000, he built a $200,000 home on the lot. But when he came to us, we gave him bad news: He had bought the lot ten years earlier, and because the purchase occurred outside the 2-year window, the cost of the lot — $50,000 — did not count toward meeting the Adjusted Sales Price. The result was that he owed $17,000 in taxes, a bill he could have avoided had he sought proper counsel in advance. *Boy, that's annoying.*

Before you get too excited, I should stress that meeting the terms of this 2-year rule does not mean you do not have to pay taxes on the profit you got from selling your house. It only means you don't have to pay the taxes *now*. You still owe the tax, but it is deferred. Until when? Stay tuned... we'll cover that a bit later in this chapter.

The Second 2-Year Rule

The second 2-year rule says that if you make a tax-deferred sale, you cannot sell the new home for two years. If you do, you must replace the new home within the First Rule's clock, and even if you do you'll still pay tax on the replacement home's gain.

I'm sure that's clear as mud, so let's try an example:

You sell A on March 10, 1996.

You have until March 10, 1998, to buy B.

You buy B in early 1997 [so far so good] and then, still in 1997 [okay, still within A's original 2-year clock], *you sell B for a profit and buy C.*

You must pay taxes on B's profit. The profit from selling A remains deferred until you later sell C. If you sell B before March 10, 1998, but fail to buy C by that date, you will be taxed immediately on all of A's profit. (There is an exception for sales triggered by job changes.)

If you find all this confusing, here's the simplest way to remember the rule: *If you sell a house and buy another, don't sell the new one for two years.*

> **The IRS created the second 2-year rule in part because of people who buy, fix up, and quickly sell — or "flip" — houses. This rule prevents these people — who are really real estate investors, not homeowners — from buying and selling house after house while deferring taxes each time.**

Can You Deduct Moving Expenses?

While we're on the subject of selling and buying, let's talk about moving. You can deduct moving expenses if:

- the distance between your former home and your *new* job location is at least 50 miles farther than the distance between your former home and your *old* job location;

- you work full-time for at least 39 weeks during the 12-month period immediately following your move (if you are an employee), or at least 39 weeks during the first 12-month period *and* at least 78 weeks during the first 24-month period immediately following your move (if you are self-employed);

- your moving expenses are incurred within one year from the time you first report to your new job or business;

- the move is connected with the start of work at the new location; and

- expenses are reasonable.

Moving expenses can include:

- traveling to a new location

- moving household goods and personal items, and

- lodging expenses en route to your new home.

To qualify for the moving expense deduction, you may not move to a home that has been owned or maintained by you or members of your family.

If You are Selling Your Home for a Loss

By now, you have long since given up the notion that taxation of real estate is a simple thing. Hey, we're just getting started. But before we move to the next major area, I thought you'd like to review a few more annoying IRS rules.

As we explained, if you buy a house and then sell it for a profit, that profit is subject to tax. **But IRS Annoying Rule #3** says that if you sell your house for less than you paid, you can't deduct the loss. Heads they win, tails you lose. *Boy, that's annoying.*

And it gets worse. Much worse. Let's look at **IRS Annoying Rule #4**.

People who lived in the southwest, New England, and other areas suffered horrendous real estate markets in the 1980s. In Texas, for example, the oil bust led to a severe recession, and thousands lost their jobs. Consequently, housing prices dropped as much as two-thirds: Homes that once sold for $150,000 fetched only $50,000.

Out of work and with no income, many no longer could afford the payments on their house. They couldn't sell it, either, because it would bring only $50,000 but they owed the bank $120,000. They couldn't rent it because they couldn't charge enough to cover their mortgage costs, and besides, there was no one to rent it to. So, many home owners simply mailed the front door keys back to the bank and just walked away.

But that wasn't the worst part. No, here's the true horror: If you walk away from a mortgage, the IRS holds that the unpaid balance becomes income and therefore is taxable. Thus, someone who walked away from a house owing the bank $120,000 is deemed to have "earned" $120,000 and therefore owes about $40,000 in taxes. Not only are you out of work, not only did you lose your home, but now you owe the IRS forty grand.

Why does the IRS take that position? As much as I hate to admit it, there is validity to the IRS' thinking. The IRS contends that you borrowed money to buy the house. You did not declare the loan as income, and you were not taxed on it. This was okay with the IRS because you promised to pay the money back. But when you decided not to pay it back, you converted the money from "loan" to "income," and income is taxable. The fact that you don't have the money anymore is your problem, says the IRS, not theirs.

Boy, is that annoying! In fact, annoying isn't quite the word for it.

> *"Collecting more taxes than is absolutely necessary is legalized robbery."*
> —Calvin Coolidge

When the New Home's Price is Less Than the Old House's Adjusted Sales Price

Let's return to our example, where your Adjusted Sales Price is $175,000.

You've moved to an area where real estate is less expensive, and your new home, including all expenses, cost only $150,000.

Since the new home costs less than the Adjusted Sales Price of the old house, you've got a tax liability. But how much?

> *"The language in which the act is couched is involved and [its] rhetoric, bewildering. It contains sentences hundreds of words in length in which clauses are added to clauses and provisos heaped upon provisos."*
>
> —Taxpayer A.C. Rearick, complaining in 1914 about the income tax law adopted the year before

To figure it out, we need to know how much profit you earned when you sold your house, and to calculate that, we need to subtract (a) the price you paid when you bought your house from (b) the price you received when you sold it. We know the price you received: $175,000. Now we just have to determine how much you paid.

As before, when we learned that the "sales price" was different from the "Adjusted Sales Price," we now find that the price you originally paid for your house is not necessarily the number we want. Indeed, the figure we want is called your "cost basis."

Determine the Cost Basis of Your Old House

The cost basis is the original price of your home plus the cost of any improvements.

You bought your house 10 years ago for $125,000.

At first glance, you might think to simply subtract this figure from $175,000, resulting in a profit of $50,000. But again, that's too simple.

You made improvements to the property. You paneled the basement and added a deck. And you incurred other costs associated with acquiring the house, such as title insurance, real estate commissions, and legal expenses. You spent $10,000 on all these extras.

That means your cost basis is not the $125,000 you originally paid, but $135,000 — and this becomes the elusive item "(a)" we sought six paragraphs above. So, since your Adjusted Sales Price is $175,000, your profit is $40,000 [(b)-(a)], and it is on this figure — $40,000 — that you will pay taxes.

Do you see what's happened? Money spent on improvements, which you could not use earlier to reduce your Adjusted Sales Price, can be used now to *increase* your cost basis. So while the selling expense didn't reduce the price of the replacement home you had to buy, it does reduce the taxable profit on the sale of the old house, which in turn reduces the tax you have to pay.

Read this again a few zillion times. It'll eventually become clear. Then again, maybe it won't.

You could have avoided taxes on that $40,000 if you had bought a house that cost at least $175,000. But since you didn't, this $40,000 becomes taxable. Or does it?

Notice that in all these calculations there is no mention of the mortgage. The IRS has no interest in the fact that you obtained a loan in order to buy your house. Aside from points being deductible for the seller, the IRS couldn't care less what you spent on closing costs, points, or interest payments.

So if you've been trying to figure out how your mortgage is involved, you can stop, because it isn't.

Not exactly. Let's go back to our example. You sold your house for $175,000 and bought a new one for $150,000. You're short by $25,000. And you've got a profit of $40,000. The result? You have to pay taxes only on the $25,000, not $40,000, and you continue to defer the tax on the remaining $15,000.

If your profit was less than the $25,000, your tax liability would have been limited to the amount of the profit.

For clarity, read until blind, then call an accountant.[26]

---

[26]While you're at it, throw your Congressman out of office.

The Six Rules Pertaining to the Capital Gains Exclusion

Before you rush off to send a check to the IRS, hang on a minute. Congress has provided a tax break that might help you. It's called the capital gains exclusion.

Congress is well aware that for many Americans, their home is their largest asset, and paying taxes on that asset would not endear members of Congress to their middle-class constituents. Therefore, Congress wrote into the tax code a provision that excludes from capital gains tax a certain amount of profits for certain people who sell their houses beyond a certain age. This is a very powerful benefit, but it is surrounded by a lot of misconception and fine print. So let's look more closely:

Rule #1: The Exclusion Lets up to $125,000 in Profits Skip the Capital Gains Tax

For most homeowners, that figure is high enough to effectively avoid taxes on *all* the profit you'll get when you sell your home.

Rule #2: The Exclusion is a One-Time-Only Option

Pay attention, for this is the first misconception many people have about the exclusion. To wit:

Mrs. Walker sold her house for $300,000 and had a $5,000 profit. To avoid taxes on that profit, she elected to take the exclusion. She then moved to Florida and bought a house for $75,000.

Ten years later, she moved again. Her current house is now worth $125,000, giving her a $50,000 profit. "No problem," she says. "I only used $5,000 of my $125,000 exclusion, so I've got $120,000 left."

Wrong.

The exclusion is available for use *one-time only*. You may claim a maximum of $125,000, but once you use it, you're done. By protecting $5,000 from taxes earlier, Mrs. Walker cannot protect $50,000 now.

So before you take the exclusion, think seriously about whether you should take it, for merely having a profit on your current house is not enough of a reason to take the exclusion. You might incur an even larger profit later, when you sell your next home.

Rule #3: You May Take the Exclusion Only if You are Over Age 55

And you must be over 55 by the settlement date, not just "this year." If you turn 55 in August, don't sell the house in July. The date you sign the contract is not relevant.

If you're married, only one of you has to be over 55 — provided both of you own the house. If only one of you owns the house, the owner must be over 55. Not sure you're "married"? The IRS says you are married if you are married on the date of settlement. Being separated or intending to divorce is not relevant.

Rule #4: The Seller Must Have Owned the House for Three of the Previous Five Years

Rule #5: The Seller Must Have Lived in the House for Three of the Previous Five Years

There are exceptions for incapacity, involuntary conversion, casualty, theft, and condemnation.

Rule #6: You or Your Spouse Must Not Have Taken Your Exclusion Since July 27, 1978

Note that the house does not have to be your principal residence. It could be a vacation home. It could be a vacation home — but the exclusion is available only once per person, not once per house. Also, if the house was not jointly held, whichever spouse does own it must meet all the above criteria. So: can you use this deduction?

Your Marital Status Determines Whether You Can Use the Exemption

Are you married or not? This is very important, especially if you are separated or planning to divorce, because you may not take the exclusion unless your spouse agrees with your decision.

This is true even if:

- you or your spouse own the home separately; or

- you and your spouse file separate tax returns; or

- the spouse not owning an interest in the home has not lived in it for the required period of time before the sale occurred.

I have a client who has been separated for 14 years. He bought his home 10 years ago, and he still owns it outright. If he wants to take the exclusion, he'll need his wife's permission (if he can find her), and if she doesn't give it, he will be prohibited from taking the exclusion.

THE EXCLUSION RULES

If you **have not** used the exclusion...	If you **have** used the exclusion...

...and you are **single**, then you can use the exclusion once.

...and you are **married**...

...then you may never use it again, and anyone you marry is prohibited from using it while they are married to you.

...and your spouse **has** used the exclusion, then you are prohibited from using the exclusion while you are married to that person.

...and your spouse **has not** used the exclusion, then you as a couple can both use the exclusion once.

FIGURE 8-3

Why You Might Never Be Allowed to Take the Exclusion

As stated, the exclusion is available as a one-time option. But we've also seen that married couples must agree to use the exclusion. That's easy enough for those who are happily married and will remain so. But the law plays havoc on those whose marital status has changed.

Many Americans never will be able to take the exclusion, whether or not they ever used it, because of their marital status. Examine Figure 8-3 to see how the rules work.

411

When Two Singles Marry

As you can tell from Figure 8-3, your marital status plays a key role in determining whether or not you are able to use the exclusion. Here's a common situation: Claudia, a widow, falls in love with Stan, a divorcee. Both in their late 50s, each owns a home with substantial appreciation. They plan to marry, sell the two houses, and relocate, buying a new home together. If they're not careful, they could incur a huge tax bill unnecessarily.

You've probably already guessed it. If they marry *before* selling the two houses, they'll be able to take the exclusion on only one. The proper strategy, then, is for them to marry *after* they sell the houses. That way, they each can take the full exclusion on each home even if they marry in that same year, provided they are single at the settlement of each home.

If they do it wrong, either Claudia or Stan will lose the chance to take the exemption.

They also can defer the gain on both houses by jointly buying a new home; half the cost of the new home must be at least as much as the Adjusted Selling Price of each of the two old houses.

For example, if Claudia sells her home for an Adjusted Sales Price of $200,000 and Stan sells his for $180,000, the new home they buy together must cost at least $400,000.

But even if they do it wrong, there are two solutions.

Say Stan sells his home and takes his exclusion. Then he and Claudia marry. This means Claudia cannot use her exclusion. No problem. All she has to do is divorce Stan, sell her home, take the exclusion, then remarry him.

Or she could kill him, because that, too, would make her unmarried and once again eligible for the exclusion.

Divorce? Murder? It's amazing what our nation's tax laws encourage people to do.

Revoking Your Choice to Take the Exclusion

If you take the exclusion and later regret it, you can revoke your decision at any time before the latest of:

- three years from the due date of the return filed for the year of the sale;

- three years from the date you filed the return; or

- two years from the date you paid the tax.

If You Used Your Home Partly for Business or Rental

If you took a tax deduction for use of your home as an office, consider the sale of your home to be the sale of two properties. Profits can be deferred on the home portion, but you must pay taxes on any gain on the business portion.

If You Converted Your Home into a Rental Property

As discussed previously, people often convert their houses to rentals because they cannot sell for the price they want. If you do this, be aware that when you eventually do sell the house, you cannot postpone taxes on the gain, even though you once used the house as your home.

This does not apply if you only temporarily rented either your old house before you were able to sell it or your new home before you moved in. Also, *intending to rent* does not create a problem. If you hire a real estate agent to rent your home and it is not rented, it is not considered to be business property or property held for the production of income.

Have You Considered an Installment Sale?

In an installment sale, the seller agrees to be paid slowly over time. For example, a seller of a $200,000 house might agree to be paid $20,000 per year plus interest for 10 years. If you do this, you pay taxes on any profits as you receive the money. The good news is that by deferring receipt of the money, you defer the tax — which is especially helpful if you are not eligible for the exclusion. Also, offering to sell the house on an installment basis might help you find a buyer in a weak market.

The bad news, of course, is that you do not receive the money for years — and many things can happen in the interim. Still, under the right conditions an installment sale might help you lower your taxes.

> **If the buyer defaults on an installment sale, is that good news or bad news?**
>
> **It's good news because you get the house back, and you get to sell it again, keeping whatever money the buyer had previously paid you. It's bad news because it's a legal hassle, and you have to go through the nuisance of selling the house all over again. Now that you're living hundreds of miles away and enjoying retirement, this is just what you wanted to do, eh?**

Keep in mind that installment sales to a spouse or to an 80%-controlled entity do not qualify, and if you sell to a related person who resells the house within two years, you must declare gains on the entire sale in the year of the resale. A related person is defined as a:

- spouse;
- child;
- grandchild;
- parent;
- partnership in which you are a partner;
- any estate or trust of which you are a beneficiary;
- any grantor trust of which you are treated as an owner; or
- a corporation in which you own at least 50% of the stock.

Must You Sell Your House at a Loss?

If you think you will lose money selling your house, you might want to consider converting it into a rental property. If you sell a rental at a loss, you might get a tax deduction for part of the loss. You can't do that when selling a residence, although legislation has been proposed to change that. Ask an accountant or other financial advisor to help you determine if it would be worthwhile.

Have You Lent Money to a Family Member?

Very often we find that clients have lent money to their kids or other relatives to help them buy a home. If you make such a loan, make sure you charge current interest rates. I've seen situations where Dad lends the kids $50,000 so they can buy a house, but does not charge interest.

And here's **IRS Annoying Rule #5:** Dad is liable for taxes on the interest he didn't earn. How would the IRS ever know? Through an audit of Dad — or the kids.

I can see Dad's face when the auditor says, "You should have charged your son 8% interest, and we're going to tax you as though you did." On a $50,000 loan, that's $4,000 in interest Dad should have earned per year, so he could get hit with big taxes on this "phantom income," plus interest and penalties for not reporting it. *Boy, that's annoying...*

...and then the IRS could say to the kids, "You should have paid your father $4,000 in mortgage interest. You didn't, but we're going to pretend you did and therefore you get a tax deduction." So Dad gets hit with penalties for not paying taxes on money he didn't earn, while the kids get a tax deduction for payments they didn't make. *Boy, does Dad find that annoying.*

> And, Dad, don't try to claim you made a gift to the kids, or they'll nail you with a 55% gift tax. Or charge it against your $600,000 lifetime exclusion for estate taxes (see Chapter 73).
>
> Boy, is all this annoying or what?

And don't charge a token interest rate, either, because if you do, the IRS could decide that the difference between what you charged and what the market bears constitutes a gift, and therefore a gift tax would be levied against Dad. The IRS, which publishes a table showing current rates, does permit loans to family members at below-market rates, but make sure you've got a bona fide agreement and make sure the kids make regular payments.

Gee, after all this, you might decide to just pitch a tent and forget that "Owning a Home is the American Dream."

Part IX
Retirement Planning

Part IX — Retirement Planning

Retirees have three primary sources of income: pensions, savings they've accumulated in their company retirement plans, and Social Security. (Yes, there is a difference between pension plans and retirement plans, and we'll cover both in this part.)

Chapter 60 - Pensions

Pensions are technically called *defined benefit plans*. Through them, your employer promises to give you a specific monthly income (or in some cases, a *lump-sum* check in lieu of a monthly income) starting at retirement. The amount you receive is calculated by a formula that considers your salary, the number of years you've worked for the company, and other factors. The formula is different at every company, so check with your employer to learn how much you can expect to receive at age 60, 62, or 65, based on your employer's calculations.

Most workers entitled to a pension at retirement are offered several options regarding how to collect the benefit. The two most common options are *single life annuity* (which gives you a monthly income for life, but which stops upon your death) and *joint and survivor annuity*

(which provides you with a smaller monthly income but which continues as long as either you or your spouse is alive).

Figure 9-1 shows the options faced by one of my clients who recently retired. The single life option would provide Tim with $3,500 every month for as long as he is alive, but following his death, his wife Marcia would receive nothing. The joint and

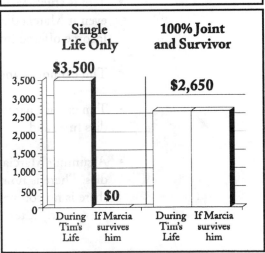

WHICH OPTION WOULD YOU CHOOSE?

FIGURE 9-1

survivor option gives him $2,650 a month ($850 less), but should he die prior to Marcia, she would continue to receive the same $2,650 he had been receiving for as long as she lives.

You can see Tim's dilemma: Should he choose a higher income which stops at his death or accept a smaller income which also protects his wife?

Which would you choose?

The overwhelming majority of workers choose the joint and survivor option. In fact, federal law requires that Marcia provide written consent if Tim chooses anything else, because after all, it's Marcia who is at risk here.

Single Life or Joint and Survivor Benefits?

When Tim chooses joint and survivor benefits, he's leaving Marcia a benefit payable upon his death. Quite simply, he's buying a life insurance policy! The cost of the policy in his case is $850 per month (the difference between the income provided by the single life option and the joint and survivor option), and the death benefit is $2,650 a month. But note these restrictions:

- Marcia is not entitled to a lump-sum check. She gets only a monthly check;

- Tim is stuck with the lower income for his entire lifetime, even if Marcia dies first. He can never return to the higher income offered by the single life option;

- Tim cannot change the beneficiary from Marcia to other heirs;

- Tim cannot name contingent beneficiaries in case Marcia dies first; and

- Assuming Marcia outlives Tim, all benefits stop when she dies. There is no residual value or inheritance for heirs, and there is no compensation to Tim's family in the event she dies shortly after him.

An Alternative to the Joint and Survivor Option

For all these reasons, Tim chooses the single life option, and uses the extra $850/month to buy his own life insurance policy. By cutting out the middleman (his employer), Tim got a better deal for these reasons:

If they both live:

- The policy can become fully paid-for, meaning they can stop paying premiums but the policy will continue to provide benefits; and

- This strategy can cost less, letting Tim and Marcia enjoy the money they save every month.

If Tim dies first, Marcia can:

- Take the entire lump-sum at any time if she needs it; and

- Pass any assets she didn't use during her lifetime to children or other heirs upon her death.

If Marcia dies first, Tim can:

- Cancel the policy and (depending on when she dies) get a refund of most or all of the premiums he had paid; and

- Name additional or replacement beneficiaries, such as children.

In Tim's case, we calculated how much Marcia would need as a lump sum if he died first. This money, when invested, would provide her with a monthly income of $2,650, equal to the joint and survivor benefit which she won't get because he chose the single life option.

This policy cost Tim $657 a month, meaning our strategy saved him $143 a month — every month for the rest of his life! On top of that, he and Marcia enjoyed all the benefits noted above.

COMPARING YOUR OPTIONS

	Pension Max	100% Joint and Survivor
Provide income for my survivor upon my death	yes	yes
Monthly premiums required	yes	yes
Premium payments are flexible	yes	no
Premiums cease if my survivor pre-deceases me	yes	no
Benefits payable if my survivor pre-deceases me	yes	no
Benefits payable if my beneficiary and I die at the same time	yes	no
I can cancel at any time	yes	no
If I decide to cancel, I can get some or all of my money back	yes	no
The benefit increases	yes	no
My survivor can elect a lump-sum payment	yes	no
My survivor has multiple options for income upon my death	yes	no
My survivor can designate a beneficiary to receive benefits after my survivor dies	yes	no
I can leave benefits to a favorite charity	yes	no
I have control of this plan from day one	yes	no

FIGURE 9-2

Eight Problems with Pension Max

This strategy is called *pension enhancement* or *pension maximization*. When it works, it's wonderful. Unfortunately, it doesn't always work. Watch out for these problems:

Problem #1: Health Risk

You must be healthy enough to qualify for the insurance. *Solution*: Obtain the coverage before you choose an option because your decision almost always is irrevocable. If you choose the single life option and then discover you can't buy insurance, your spouse will be in serious financial jeopardy if you die first.[27]

Problem #2: Age Risk

The cost of insurance increases as you get older. Thus, if you wait until retirement to implement this strategy, the cost of insurance might be too high to make the strategy effective. *Solution*: Buy the insurance 10 years *before* retirement. By obtaining coverage at age 50 or 55, the cost is significantly lower, and you can even arrange it so that your premium payments stop by the time you retire, if you choose.

Problem #3: Income Risk

If you lose income from other sources, you won't be able to pay the premium. No premium, no policy. No policy, no benefit. *Solution*: Use a vanishing premium policy and be fully committed to funding it.

Problem #4: Inflation Risk

Pension max doesn't normally provide for increases in income, but your pension might. *Solution*: Alter the strategy to match your pension's benefits.

---

[27]And you probably will die first because your spouse, so angry at what you've done, will kill you.

Problem #5: Interest Rate Risk

If interest rates drop, the cost of your life insurance policy could increase, altering the economics of your strategy. *Solution*: Use a whole life or universal life policy with very low interest rate assumptions (see Chapter 68).

Problem #6: Marital Risk

If the marriage goes bad, the retiree might cancel the policy or change the beneficiary to someone other than the spouse. *Solution*: Have the spouse own the policy. By owning it, the spouse controls it.

Problem #7: Management Risk

The spouse may not know how to manage the lump sum proceeds provided by the insurance policy, yet his or her lifetime income is dependent on doing so successfully. *Solution*: Establish a plan now for handling the assets, or have handy the name of a trusted advisor to whom the spouse can turn for guidance.

Problem #8: Health Insurance Risk

A spouse who doesn't receive survivor benefits from the company might lose the company's health benefits as well. *Solution*: Find out in advance and, if this is so, include in the pension max strategy the cost of replacement health coverage. (And of course, make sure you and your spouse can qualify for health insurance coverage, too!)

> **Pension Max generally doesn't work for federal or military employees. For these workers, the joint and survivor option is known as the Survivor Benefit Plan, which states that upon the spouse's death, the worker can cancel the SBP deduction, thereby returning the worker's pension benefit to the full amount of the single life option. Also, federal pension incomes rise with inflation and spousal medical benefits are tied to participation in the SBP. Most private employers don't offer these features.**

So before you choose the single life option, be sure you carefully consider all the risks.

Should You Choose Monthly Income or One Lump-Sum?

When you leave your company, you may be offered the choice of a monthly income or one single check, known as a *lump-sum distribution*. If you take a lump-sum, you must provide for your own monthly income — for the rest of your life. That frightens many people, for what if you lose the money?

It's so frightening, in fact, that many people refuse to take the lump-sum. Instead, they choose the monthly income. That's the wrong move, for these reasons:

- You are not in control of how your former employer handles your money;

- Your monthly income is almost certain to be less than if you were to invest the money yourself. Employer-provided annuities are rarely competitive in the marketplace;

- The cost of living will rise, but your monthly check will not. This will hurt as you get older; and

- In most cases, you won't ever have the chance to take that lump-sum again or leave it to your heirs.

For all these reasons, you're much better off investing your own money. So when your employer offers you that check, take the money and run.

When you do, you can put the distribution into an IRA to defer taxes, or you can keep the money and pay taxes. If you choose the latter, watch out for taxes and IRS penalties if the check exceeds $750,000 (see Chapter 61).

> *"Before you decide to retire, take a week off and watch daytime television."*
> —Dr. Laurence J. Peter

Using Income Averaging to Lower Your Taxes

You can reduce or avoid that penalty by taking advantage of "income averaging," a special IRS formula that lets you pay taxes at below-normal rates.

To be eligible, you must (a) retire, (b) receive a total distribution from the qualified plan in one taxable year, (c) be at least 59½ years old or age 50 by 1986, and (d) have been in the plan at least five years. Averaging is complicated, so let a tax advisor do the calculations for you.

Putting your distribution into an IRA is the simpler choice. This postpones payment of all the taxes until you actually use the money. Whenever we have compared the results, 5- or 10-year averaging has never worked better than a rollover.

Where to Invest Your Lump-Sum

Whether you income-average or use an IRA, your most important decision is where to invest the money, and it is here that competent investment advice is of the most value.

As we explored in Part I, don't make the mistake of focusing only on current income needs, or inflation will destroy your lifestyle. Instead, be sure to allocate at least part of your money for growth. Remember: If you and your spouse both live to age 65, odds are one of you will live to age 90. Make sure you don't outlive your money!

CLOSE TO HOME   JOHN MCPHERSON

5-5   © 1994 John McPherson/Dist. by Universal Press Syndicate

"Here's your allowance. You're free to do with it as you please, but I strongly recommend that you put 25 percent of it away for retirement."

Chapter 61 - IRA Accounts

An IRA is the most common type of retirement plan. These are maintained individually rather than in groups (we'll talk about company retirement plans in the next chapter). With any retirement plan, you know how much money is being placed into the plan, but you have no idea how much the plan will be worth when you retire. Thus, retirement plans are technically known as *defined contribution plans*, and they are the exact opposite of defined benefit plans (see prior chapter), where the result is known but the amount that needs to be contributed is not.

Like all retirement plans, including those established by companies for their employees, IRAs offer two major benefits:

- You do not pay taxes on any of the money that is contributed until you begin to make withdrawals; and

- Any interest, dividends, or capital gains that accumulate in the plan also are tax-deferred until withdrawal.

As we explained in Chapter 28, tax-deferred growth is a very important benefit because a dollar that is not taxed grows more quickly than a dollar that is.

Can You Deduct Contributions to an IRA Account?

Review Figure 9-3 to determine whether you're allowed to deduct a contribution to an IRA account.

"Retirement: The first day of the rest of your life savings."

—Anonymous

HOW MUCH OF YOUR IRA CONTRIBUTION CAN YOU DEDUCT?

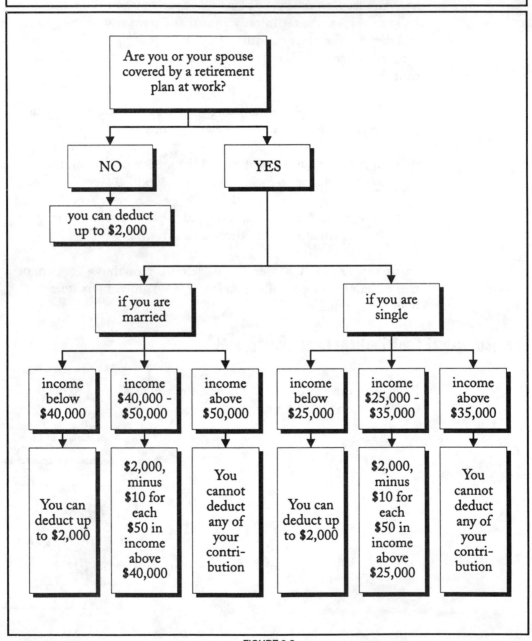

FIGURE 9-3

Prior to 1986, Figure 9-3 looked like this:

FIGURE 9-4

It was that simple. Then Congress passed the Tax Reform Act of 1986, which promised to simplify our tax code, and we got stuck with Figure 9-3. Next time Congress offers to make our lives "simpler," maybe we should Just Say No.

Ric's IRA Quiz

Let's see how much you know about IRAs by taking this quiz:

Question #1
True or false? IRA stands for Individual Retirement Account.

Question #2
True or false? An IRA is an investment.

Question #3
True or false? Banks sell IRAs.

The answer to all three questions is *false*.

IRA stands for Individual Retirement *Arrangement*, not Individual Retirement Account. An IRA is a provision of the tax code — Section 408 of the Internal Revenue Code, to be exact — under which you *arrange individually* (as opposed to through a group) *for your retirement.* An IRA, therefore, is not an investment, but simply money the tax code treats differently from other money.

Therefore, banks do not sell IRAs. What do banks sell? CDs. That means you can have a CD with or without an IRA. Is the CD in an IRA any different from one outside it? Not at all. Sure, the tax treatment is different, but the CD itself is the same.

If you open an IRA at a bank, you'll get a CD. In fact, banks have done such a good marketing job, everybody thinks IRAs are investment products and that banks are the only place to get them. It's so pervasive that my firm gets calls from people asking, "What are your IRAs paying these days?" This is a silly question: Since IRAs are not investments, they don't "pay" anything.

Rather, think of an IRA as a bucket. The IRS says if you put $2,000 into the bucket, you can deduct that amount from your income for tax purposes (based on the qualifying rules in Figure 9-3). Furthermore, the IRS says you can use that money to buy and sell investments as you wish, provided the money stays inside the bucket until you retire.

Thus, you can buy any investment you want with that $2,000: You can buy CDs, savings accounts, money markets, Treasury bills, and more. In fact, you can choose from virtually everything we have covered in this book, including stocks, bonds, U.S. Government Securities, mutual funds, variable annuities, fixed annuities, limited partnerships, gold, international securities, foreign currencies, real estate — almost anything, provided that any asset you buy stays in the bucket. You also may sell at any time any investment you previously bought, and replace it with something else, provided all the transactions occur — and the proceeds stay — in the bucket. You will pay no taxes until you withdraw money from the bucket. That's all there is to it.

Thus, if you get an IRA at the bank, you're going to get a CD; If you go to an insurance agent, you're going to get an annuity; And if you go to a stockbroker, well, who knows what you'll get!

Question #4

Tom, 35, has $4,000 to invest and has decided to place half the money into a high-risk growth stock and half into a U.S. Treasury Bond. Which of the two should Tom place into his IRA? *For this question, which is designed to show you the proper way to handle your IRA, assume you have an "either-or" choice between these two securities; ignore the notion of mutual funds.*

What do you think is the correct answer? If you answered, "The stock!" I'm willing to bet you thought, "Tom is not going to touch the money until he retires in 25 years, so he can tolerate a higher level of risk." That's what you said, isn't it? Well, you're wrong.

If you answered, "The bond!" I'm willing to bet you said, "Tom is depending on this money for his retirement, so he can't play games. He needs to be conservative with his IRA." If that's what you said, you're wrong, too.

There is a correct answer, which I'll give you in a moment, but first I want you to understand why both of the above answers are wrong. Both infer that the determining factor is *risk*. One answer favors high risk; the other low risk. Both are wrong. After all, Tom is going to buy both investments. If the stock goes broke, is he going to feel any better because that investment was or was not inside the IRA?

"Yes, Tom, you went broke — but don't worry: Your money was/wasn't inside your IRA!"

That sounds silly, doesn't it? And that's why both of the above answers are wrong. Since IRAs are not investments, the subject of risk is not relevant.

The correct answer is the *government bond*, and by now you should know why: because of tax law.

An IRA has a special tax advantage: The money grows tax-deferred. Chapter 15 showed you that the profit from high risk growth stocks comes from growth in value. Also remember from Chapter 15 that one of the advantages of owning stock is that you pay no taxes on the gain until you sell. In other words, your stock is *already* tax-deferred. But, as you'll recall from Chapter 5, bonds generate interest, and that interest is subject to tax every year.

431

So put it all together: By placing the bond in the IRA, its interest is sheltered from taxes until you withdraw the money at retirement. And if you keep the stock until retirement, it too grows tax-deferred, even though it is not in an IRA.

Remember: The whole idea of an IRA is to shelter from taxes money that ordinarily is not sheltered. That's why you need to place the bond inside the IRA. Putting the growth stock inside the IRA serves no useful purpose.

And I can give you two more reasons to choose the bond instead of the stock for Tom's IRA:

- By keeping the stock outside the IRA, its profits upon sale will be taxed at capital gains tax rates. If the stock was placed inside the IRA, its earnings would be taxed upon withdrawal at ordinary income tax rates, which can be higher than capital gains rates; and

- By keeping the stock out of the IRA, any losses in value are tax-deductible. This would not be the case if the losses occur inside an IRA.

Thus, both profits and losses enjoy tax-favored treatment outside IRAs. Clearly, tax law is telling us to place bonds inside IRAs and keep non-dividend-paying stocks outside.[28]

Question #5
True or false? You should contribute the maximum to an IRA even if you cannot deduct some or all of the contribution.

The answer is *false.*[29]

---

[28]Again, please note that this discussion is limited to individual stocks and bonds. Mutual funds, regardless of what kind, always are ideally suited for use both inside and outside IRAs. This is because all mutual funds pay annual capital gains distributions, meaning all mutual funds generate an annual tax liability, unlike individual stocks. (Mutual funds once enjoyed the same tax deferral as stocks, but the Tax Reform Act of 1986 eliminated that advantage.)

[29]Frustrated yet?

The true power of an IRA is the ability to deduct your contribution from your taxable income. For example, assuming you can take the deduction and a combined federal/state bracket of 33%, placing $2,000 into an IRA saves you $660 in taxes.

When you withdraw your original $2,000 in retirement, you'll pay taxes on that money since you have not done so yet.

But if you cannot deduct your contribution yet make one anyway, you must file IRS Form 8606, *Nondeductible IRAs (Contributions, Distributions, and Basis)*, every year you add to or make a withdrawal from an IRA. This form tells the IRS that you already paid taxes on a portion of the money that you had contributed to the IRA.

What happens if you don't file the form, or if you file but fail to keep a record of it for the rest of your life? There is a $50 penalty for failing to file, and if you don't keep your records in order, you'll have to pay taxes when you withdraw the money — even though you already paid taxes when you contributed to the IRA years earlier. Indeed, you'll pay taxes twice on the same money!

Occasionally, I come across someone who says Form 8606 is not a problem. "I do my own taxes, and I know how to do this," they say. But that's not the point! You've got to keep track of the form for the rest of your life, which could be 40 or 50 years from now, and I'm willing to bet that sooner or later (a) you're going to forget to file the form; (b) between now and retirement you're going to lose the forms you previously filed; or (c) you're going to become ill, and your spouse will take over the chore of filing the tax return — and your spouse won't know what you know.

Keep in mind that IRA rules are less than 20 years old, and the vast majority of people who have contributed to IRA accounts are still employed. Thus, all the attention has been focused on how to get money *into* IRAs, not *out*. Stockbrokers, for example, receive heavy training on how to establish IRAs, and they are well versed on the contribution rules, procedures, and limitations. But few brokers, and fewer investors, are familiar with the withdrawal provisions. It's a time bomb waiting to happen, and it's set to go off when today's generation enters retirement in the 21st century.

Have You Made Non-Deductible IRA Contributions?

When IRAs were created, anyone with earned income was eligible. But the Tax Reform Act of 1986 placed limits on eligibility. Consequently, many people who opened a deductible IRA in the early '80s continued adding to their accounts in the late '80s, but on a non-deductible basis.

> **Some people think Form 8606 is worth the hassle because they can withdraw their non-deductible contributions tax-free at retirement, but it's not true.**
>
> **Say you have $12,000 in IRA accounts, of which $2,000 was contributed on a non-deductible basis using Form 8606. If you think that at retirement you'll be able to withdraw the non-deductible money first, tax-free, you're wrong: IRS rules state that each withdrawal from an IRA must be a *pro-rata* distribution of deductible and non-deductible dollars. Thus, since ¹/₆th of your IRA (2,000/12,000) is non-deductible, only ¹/₆th of each withdrawal is tax-exempt. Clearly, non-deductible IRAs are not worth the hassle.**

Have you done this? Have you commingled deductible and non-deductible IRA contributions into one account? It's a common mistake, and if you've done this, you've got a big problem: You're going to be taxed on the entire account balance when you make withdrawals, even though only part of the money ought to be taxed.

The best solution is to establish two IRA accounts, one for the non-deductible contributions and one for the deductible ones. Label each account accordingly. For example, one account would read, "The IRA Account of Shirley Mason," while the other would read, "The Non-Deductible IRA Account of Shirley Mason." This way, it'll be easy to remember where the non-deductible monies are and how much you contributed on that basis. Simply place into the non-deductible account an amount equaling your total non-deductible contributions; leave all interest and profits in the regular IRA account. Contact your bank, broker, or financial planner handling your account for help correcting this problem.

A Great Alternative to the Non-Deductible IRA

Since you should not make a non-deductible IRA contribution, where does this leave you? Do you lose your only chance to let money grow tax-deferred?

Not at all! Just return to our discussion on variable annuities (Chapter 28). With annuities, there's no tax deduction, but the money grows tax-deferred until withdrawal — just like a non-deductible IRA!

And the annuity gives you three major advantages:

- There's no limit on the amount of money you can contribute each year, unlike the IRA, which limits you to $2,000;

- You can delay withdrawals until age 85, unlike the IRA, which requires that you begin withdrawals at age 70½; and

- You don't have to deal with IRS Form 8606.

So, instead of using a non-deductible IRA, you should be using a variable annuity, and you'll have all the benefits of the non-deductible IRA without the hassle.

Question #6:
True or false? It does not matter when you contribute to your IRA, provided you do so by April 15.

The answer is *false*.

As with all savings efforts, you should contribute to your IRA as soon as possible, but most taxpayers don't because they treat their IRA contributions as a debt, not an investment. "My goodness, taxes are due April 15th — I've got to get money into my IRA by then!" is the common attitude.

I actually have seen people borrow from their credit cards in order to make their $2,000 IRA contributions. They think buying an IRA is the same as buying a sweater!

With an IRA, of course, you're not *spending* money, you're *saving* it. That's why you need to contribute as soon as possible. Over 30 years, assuming you earn 10% per year, you will have $53,000 *more* by opening your account on January 1 instead of April 15 of the following year. Einstein taught us why in Chapter 3. Think about it: *15 months is worth $53,000.*

Two Methods You Can Use to Move Your IRAs

If you have an IRA in a bank, credit union, or S&L, I'll bet you're itching to move it by now — especially if you're like the many folks who have the bulk of their savings in IRAs.

You can move money from one IRA account to another in two ways: The first is fast but hard, the other is slow but easy.

Method #1: IRA Rollovers

The fast/hard method is a *rollover*. This occurs when you tell your IRA *custodian* (i.e., your bank, broker, or whoever is handling the account for you presently) to liquidate your account and give you a check for the proceeds. It is very important that you tell your custodian the following: "I intend to roll these funds over to another IRA account. Therefore, <u>DO NOT</u> withhold taxes." If you fail to state this (they might want you to sign a form containing this language), the custodian could withhold 20% of your account for taxes. Watch out for this trap.

When you liquidate an IRA at a bank, S&L, or credit union, be prepared for an argument, but they'll eventually comply — especially if you raise your voice in their lobby. My experience has shown that personnel at these institutions often claim that taxes must be withheld, to which you should loudly and defiantly yell, "Why won't you give me my money!?" The louder you say it, the quicker they'll cave in.[30]

When you get the money, simply deposit it into your regular checking account. You then have 60 days to "roll the money over" (hence, *rollover*) to your next IRA. If you do so within this time period, there is no tax implication of any kind.

Make sure you follow the rules perfectly. You are permitted to rollover each IRA only once every 12 calendar months (not once a year, mind you, but once every 12 months). Thus, if you have two IRA accounts, the 12-month clock on the first account does not affect the 12-month clock on the second account.

However, the 12-month clock does pertain to *all the money* inside that given IRA account. Say you have $10,000 in an IRA account and you rollover $2,000 from it to another IRA account. The remaining $8,000 cannot be rolled over for 12 months.

Don't blow this like Jeremy did. He had $150,000 in an IRA account, and via a rollover, he moved $25,000 of it to a new IRA account. Two months later, he moved the remaining $125,000 to the new account.

Bad move, said the IRS. Because only one rollover is permitted every 12 months within each IRA account, the second rollover is void. Therefore, the $125,000 was considered to be a premature distribution, and Jeremy had to pay taxes on the money.

---

[30]Make sure the bank is filled with customers when you do this.

And that's not all. Because Jeremy had rolled over the $125,000 into his new IRA — which he wasn't allowed to do — this contribution was subject to a 6% excess contributions penalty. That penalty is assessed for every year the money was in the IRA. Since it took Jeremy three years to learn all this, that penalty cost him an additional 18%. Thus, of the $125,000 he started with, Jeremy lost 49% — $61,250 — to taxes. *Yeouch!*

Thus, rollovers are *fast*, because you can do them in a day, but they're *hard*, because you've got to tolerate a shouting match with your bank, and you must follow the rules to avoid nasty surprises.

> It is not necessary to place all your IRA money into one IRA account. You can have an unlimited number of IRA accounts, with varying amounts of money in each.

Method #2: IRA Transfers

The other way to move your IRA — and the one that would have enabled Jeremy to avoid his problem — is called a *transfer*. Through a transfer, you instruct your *current* IRA custodian to send your money directly to the *new* IRA custodian. You do not personally receive the money as an interim step, as you do with a rollover. Thus, there is no 12-month rule regarding transfers; you are permitted to execute them without limitation. Transfers, therefore, are very easy. You simply sign a form (given to you by your new IRA custodian) and the new custodian will do the rest. But transfers are *slow*. They often take four to six weeks to complete.

> People often get confused between rollovers and transfers because the IRS uses the same words for different reasons.
>
> When you open an IRA, it is considered a *contributory* account. If you move that money to another IRA account, the new account is called a *rollover* account — and it's called a rollover account whether you move the money there via a rollover or a transfer.
>
> Thus, you can *roll over* money to a rollover account, and you can *transfer* money to a rollover account.

The delay should not surprise you. After all, what do you think your current IRA custodian does when it receives the transfer request? Loses it, of course! In my experience, the new custodian often has to send a second request to the old custodian before the transfer occurs. So be patient when doing transfers.

Combining Contributory IRAs and Rollover IRAs

Many custodians don't like to combine contributory IRA accounts with rollover IRA accounts because regulations require custodians to track the source of all the money in the account. But from a consumer's perspective, there's no difference between the two.

Well, okay, one difference: If you move money from an employer's retirement plan to an IRA, you are permitted to move that money back to another employer's plan later — but only if the money was held in a separate rollover IRA account in the interim. If you commingle the retirement plan money with other IRA money, you lose this option. (As you'll see later in this chapter, I am unimpressed with this feature; thus, my advice is to go ahead and combine your IRAs. It'll cut your paperwork.)

Beware the Tax Trap When Moving Money From an Employer's Plan to an IRA

It's the most Orwellian law I have ever seen, and it affects every company retirement plan in the nation. Under this law, which became effective January 1, 1993, the government can force your employer to give the IRS 20% of the money in your company retirement account and then, because you didn't receive the money, make you pay taxes on it plus a 10% penalty.

The law affects you if you leave your job and are eligible to receive distributions from your company's retirement plan, such as a 401(k), 403(b), or Profit Sharing Plan (all of which we'll discuss in the next chapter).

Before this law took effect, you were allowed to request that your employer send you a check for the full value of your company's retirement account, and you had 60 days to roll the money over to an IRA account. Provided you met the 60-day rule, you would not be required to pay taxes on the distribution and the money would continue to grow tax-deferred until you made a withdrawal at retirement.

But this new law changed all that. Employers now are required to withhold 20% of any rollover distribution paid directly to you, sending the 20% to the IRS.

Since 20% of your money will be withheld at the source, you have no opportunity to roll it over — and separate IRS rules say that any retirement funds you don't roll over are subject to both taxes and a 10% penalty. So, on the one hand, Congress says you can't have the money, and on the other hand, the IRS says you're going to pay taxes and penalties because you didn't roll over the money — even though the reason you didn't roll it over is because Congress wouldn't let you have it!

Here's how the law could hit you: Assume you have been with your employer for 15 years and are now separating from service (because of retirement, termination, layoff, office relocation, etc. — the reason doesn't matter), and further assume that you have accumulated $100,000 in your employer's 401(k) plan.

If your employer sends you a check, under the new rules you will receive only $80,000. The rest — $20,000 — will be withheld for taxes. Since you can't rollover what you don't have, you must pay taxes on that $20,000, which is about $6,600 (assuming a 33% combined federal/state income tax bracket). Then, the IRS will penalize you another 10% — $2,000 — if you are under age 59½, for a total of $8,600!

Two Ways to Avoid the New Tax

Here are two ways to solve the problem:

Solution #1: Use Other Savings

Take $20,000 from other savings, add it to the $80,000 your employer gave you, and roll over the full $100,000 into an IRA. Then, when you file your tax return in April, acknowledge the fact that your employer withheld $20,000 from your distribution, and you'll get it back as a tax refund.

There are three problems with this solution: First, most folks don't have $20,000 lying around to replace what the employer withheld. Second, you've got to wait until next April to get your money back (depending on what month you leave work, you could wait nearly a year). And three, most folks don't know they can do this.

Solution #2: Do a Transfer

Transfers, rather than *rollovers*, are not subject to the new withholding requirements. Thus, instead of having your employer send the money to you, withholding 20%, instruct your employer to send the money directly to your IRA account. The IRS also allows you to receive the check from your former employer provided the check is made payable to your IRA custodian. Either method will avoid the 20% withholding requirement.

If you are changing jobs, the new law also lets you demand that your old employer send your money directly to your new employer for deposit into the new employer's retirement plan. Unfortunately, the law does not require that your new employer accept the money.[31]

Although it might seem that the transfer rules effectively avoid the new withholding requirement, this law nonetheless is creating havoc on millions of Americans for these reasons:

- **The law has received little publicity.** Most workers are unfamiliar with the rules and therefore do not know they should do transfers instead of rollovers. And since the request usually must be made prior to leaving the company, and is irrevocable, many find out too late.

- **Leaving your job is traumatic, especially during a forced layoff.** For workers losing their jobs, how you handle your rollover seems like a trivial detail. After all, many displaced workers worry more about how they are going to *eat* than how they are going to *invest*.

For both these reasons, many workers lose significant amounts of money to this forced tax — meaning that this law is hurting most the group who can afford it least: the newly-unemployed. The biggest irony is that for all its mandated withholding, the law does not raise any new revenue. It merely accelerates the receipt of taxes that the IRS would have collected in the future anyway from workers who received but did not roll over their company retirement plan assets.

This situation demonstrates Congress' penchant for solving today's problems at the expense of tomorrow and is all too fine an example of how **The Rules of Money Have Changed.**

---

[31]Don't ask.

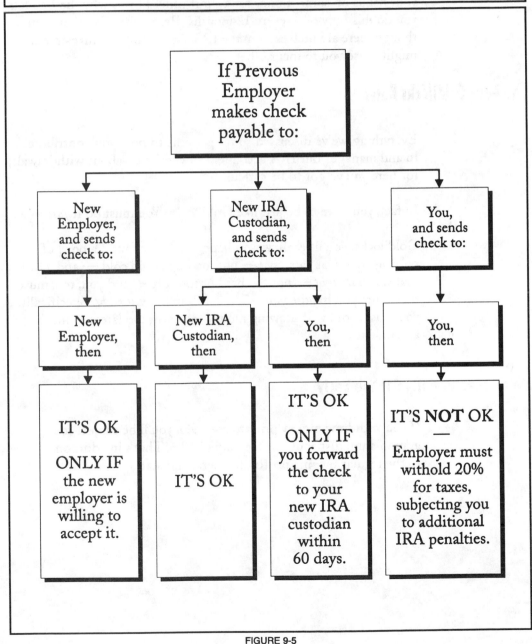

MOVING MONEY FROM AN EMPLOYER PLAN TO AN IRA

If Previous Employer makes check payable to:

New Employer, and sends check to:

New IRA Custodian, and sends check to:

You, and sends check to:

New Employer, then

New IRA Custodian, then

You, then

You, then

IT'S OK

ONLY IF the new employer is willing to accept it.

IT'S OK

IT'S OK

ONLY IF you forward the check to your new IRA custodian within 60 days.

IT'S NOT OK
—
Employer must withold 20% for taxes, subjecting you to additional IRA penalties.

FIGURE 9-5

441

Give Yourself a Short-Term Loan From Your IRA — Tax-Free

You can liquidate money from your IRA account and use it without tax consequences provided you put the money back into an IRA account within 60 days. I don't recommend this, but the strategy might come in handy if you have a temporary cash flow problem and you need to get your hands on some money for a short time. This is why the IRS lets you do this only once every 12 months. Remember also that even though there are no fees from the IRS, liquidating the investment might cause you to incur other costs.

The Four Goldilocks Rules

Everything we've discussed so far pertains to how you contribute to and manage your IRA accounts. Now let's talk about withdrawals, for here you've got to be careful.

In fact, you have to be just like Goldilocks: You must do it *just right*.

Goldilocks, you'll recall, was unhappy until she found a bowl of porridge that was *just right* — not too hot or too cold — and a bed that was *just right* — not too hard or too soft — and you, too, must make sure you handle your IRA distributions *just right*. Specifically, you must avoid withdrawing money too early, too late, too much, and too little.

Goldilocks Penalty #1: Too Early

If you withdraw money prior to age 59½, you'll be subject to a "premature distributions" penalty of 10%. That's in addition to the regular income tax (both federal and state).

Goldilocks Penalty #2: Too Late

You must begin to withdraw money from your IRA by April 1 of the year following the year in which you turn 70½.

For example, say you reach age 70 on July 10, 1997. That means you are 70½ on January 10, 1998, so you must make a withdrawal from your IRA by April 1, 1999, and by each December 31 thereafter.[32]

If you fail to make the withdrawal, you will pay a 50% penalty (yes, 50%!) on the amount you were supposed to withdraw but didn't. And that's in addition to the regular tax.

Goldilocks Penalty #3: Too Much

You are prohibited from withdrawing more than $155,000 from your IRA in any one year. Doing so will subject you to a 15% "excess distributions" penalty.

Goldilocks Penalty #4: Too little

The IRS publishes a table which shows the minimum amount you must withdraw at a given age, based on your life expectancy. If you fail to withdraw the minimum amount, you will pay a 15% penalty on the amount you were supposed to withdraw but didn't. And again, that's in addition to the regular tax.

It gets interesting for those who have large amounts in their IRAs and who have short life expectancies. To avoid the *"15% for taking too little"* penalty, the IRS's minimum distribution tables could require such people to withdraw more than $155,000, but doing so would subject them to the *"15% for taking too much"* penalty. Talk about rocks and hard places.

Just as you are prohibited from withdrawing "too much," you also are prohibited from accumulating "too much." If you die with a balance in your IRA greater than what the IRS tables allow, your estate will incur a 15% excess accumulations penalty — again, in addition to other taxes.

---

[32]If you wait until April 1, 1999 to make the distribution that was required for 1998, you'll have to make two distributions in 1999 — one for 1998 (due April 1, 1999) and one for 1999 (due December 31, 1999).

One Hapless Family

If you're trying to imagine the impact of all these rules and what might happen if you fall victim to them, consider the plight of Dr. Gabler's family.

Dr. Gabler practiced medicine for 47 years, and like many physicians he was able to accumulate substantial amounts of money in his retirement accounts. At his death at age 82, his IRAs and other retirement accounts[33] were worth $2 million. He also owned two homes and other assets of sizable wealth, which he left to his wife and children, but he chose to name as beneficiary his 12 grandchildren for their future college educations.

It was a few months after Dr. Gabler died that one of his daughters, Judith, came to see me. She had just seen the accountant handling the estate tax return, and she wasn't happy.

The IRS says a person who dies at age 82 is permitted to have an IRA balance of $1,034,000. Because Dr. Gabler's balance was $2 million — or $966,000 too much — this excess was subject to a 15% excess accumulations penalty. Cost: $145,000.

Further, Dr. Gabler's IRA is considered part of his estate, and although he gets a deduction for the $145,000 penalty he paid above, he's still subject to a 55% federal estate tax on the remainder (see Chapter 73). Cost: $1,020,000.

Dr. Gabler also made the unfortunate decision of leaving his IRA directly to his grandchildren. Therefore, his estate must pay a 33% Generation Skipping Tax. He does, however, get a deduction for the taxes already paid above. Cost: $275,000.

And, of course, money distributed from an IRA is taxable at both the federal and state levels as ordinary income. Although there are some adjustments for the above deductions, the tax nonetheless is at the 43% combined marginal federal/state bracket. Cost: $302,000.

---

[33]The Goldilocks rules pertain to the total value of all your retirement accounts, not just IRAs.

The result is shown below.

Gross Value of IRA:	**$2,000,000**
Less Excess Accumulations Penalty	(145,000)
Less Estate Tax	(1,020,000)
Less Generation Skipping Tax	(275,000)
Less Income Taxes	(302,000)
Net After-Tax Value to Heirs	**$258,000**
Split Among 12 Grandchildren	**$21,500**

I think you can see why Judith was so unhappy.

The Perils of Bad Tax Advice

And I didn't improve her mood. Because her father had already died, virtually nothing could be done to avoid the huge taxes his estate was incurring. As we'll learn in Part XI, proper estate planning could have avoided almost all of this cost, but planning must be done before death occurs. Once a person dies, it's almost always too late, as it was in this case.

The irony is that Dr. Gabler's tax preparer probably made the situation worse. People who hire accountants tend to give them one mission — lower my taxes! — and Dr. Gabler was probably no different. So, when he turned 71 and his accountant said he needed to start making withdrawals from his IRA, Dr. Gabler withdrew only the minimum. After all, he had plenty of money from other sources, and he didn't need income from the money in his IRA. And since any money he withdrew from it would be taxed, it made sense to him to keep those withdrawals to a minimum.

And since the accountant knew he needed to keep Dr. Gabler's taxes low or face his client's wrath — and maybe even lose the client's business — he didn't make a fuss when Dr. Gabler insisted on withdrawing only the minimum.

Unfortunately, by withdrawing only the minimum each year, the IRA continued to grow in value — so much so, that by the time Dr. Gabler died, the account was worth $2 million, resulting in the problem you saw above.

Thus, because he wanted to keep his income taxes low each year, Dr. Gabler's estate eventually had to pay an excess accumulations penalty, a federal estate tax, and a generation-skipping tax — on top of the higher income taxes he so desperately wanted to avoid. Remember: When it comes to taxes, you can defer and delay, rarely avoid.

Indeed, Dr. Gabler was penny-wise and pound-foolish. By keeping his current taxes low, he allowed his future taxes to soar. And because many tax preparers have tunnel vision — seeing only this year's tax return instead of their client's complete, long-term tax picture — they often fail to provide the guidance and counsel their clients need. Avoid this trap. Be careful when making financial decisions, for good short-term moves often can be very bad in the long-term.

How to Beat the 10% Penalty on Early Withdrawals

Ordinarily, if you withdraw money from your IRA (or from annuities, for that matter) before age 59½, you must pay taxes plus a 10% penalty. While you can't avoid the tax, you can avoid the penalty if you receive the proceeds in the form of *Substantially Equal Periodic Payments*.

Under SEPP rules, withdrawals must be made at regular intervals over a period of not less than five years or until you reach 59½, whichever is later. For example, someone starting SEPP withdrawals at age 40 must continue to do so until age 59½, while a 57-year-old must do so until age 62.

While SEPP won't help much if you need all the money right away, it could help if you simply need a steady income stream.

MARVIN   TOM ARMSTRONG

Reprinted with special permission of North America Syndicate.

Chapter 62 - Company Retirement Plans

As we discussed at the beginning of the last chapter, all retirement plans — whether individual or company-sponsored — offer two major benefits:

- You do not pay taxes on any of the money that is contributed to the plan until you begin withdrawals, and

- Any interest, dividends, or capital gains that accumulate in the plan are tax-deferred until withdrawal.

We've examined individual retirement arrangements. Now let's look at the different kinds of plans offered by companies for their employees.

SEP-IRAs: IRAs for the Self-Employed

Do you have any self-employment income? If not, skip this section. But if you are in business for yourself — even if only part-time — keep reading.

If you have any self-employment income, from baby-sitting to shooting wedding videos, you may qualify for a Simplified Employee Pension Plan, known as a *SEP-IRA*. SEPs are as easy to use as IRAs and almost identical as well. But they offer one major advantage over IRAs: Instead of being limited to a $2,000 annual deductible contribution, you can put away 15% of your self-employment income, up to $22,500. You are permitted to do this even if you or your spouse participate in another pension or retirement plan.

SEPs involve minimal disclosure and reporting requirements. You can contribute different amounts from year to year, and you can wait until April 15 to contribute for the previous year (or later if you file an extension). Other plans must be established by December 31.

When 15% Equals 13.04%

Although the law says you can place up to 15% of your net taxable income into a SEP-IRA, the correct figure is really 13.04%.

Here's why:

Say your net taxable income (that's your profit minus expenses) is $10,000. Fifteen percent would be $1,500, which you'd place into a SEP-IRA. But that would reduce your net taxable income to $8,500[34] — and $1,500 of $8,500 is 17.65% — meaning you've contributed too much to the SEP, leading to major headaches with the IRS.

Thus, the correct amount you would be permitted to place into your SEP would be $1,304, which is only 13.04% of $10,000.

Clear as mud, huh?

401(k) Plans — The Grandest of All Retirement Plans

The 401(k) plan — so-named by the tax code section that created it — is offered by more companies than any other type of retirement plan, so if your company offers a plan, it's likely to be this one. If so, you need to understand how it works.

The Four Contribution Methods of 401(k) Plans

Method #1: The Employer's Basic Contribution

This contribution usually is a percentage of payroll.

Ken, 45, makes $40,000 a year and his company contributes 1% of his pay to the 401(k) plan every year. Although the money is Ken's, he is not taxed on it, and the money grows tax-deferred inside the plan.

Method #2: The Employee's Voluntary Contribution

Depending on where you work, you may be permitted to contribute up to 15% of your pay.

Ken is allowed to invest up to 5% of his paycheck into the 401(k) plan. He gets a tax deduction for the amount he contributes, and like the employer's contribution above, this money grows tax-deferred.

---

[34]Contributions to a SEP reduce your net taxable income because SEP contributions are considered to be a normal business expense, and like all normal expenses, are deductible from your business's gross revenue.

Method #3: The Employer's Matching Contributions

Through this method, the company contributes a percentage of what the employee contributes.

Ken's company adds 25 cents to the plan for every dollar that Ken puts in himself. This increases Ken's stake by 25%, yet he is not taxed on this money, and it too grows tax-deferred until he retires.

Method #4: The Employer's Profit-Sharing Contribution

This is an additional contribution that the company voluntarily makes each year based on the firm's profits.

Ken's company typically gives Ken a bonus equal to 3% of his pay, which is deposited into the plan on Ken's behalf. Like the other contributions, this one too is not taxed and it grows tax-deferred.

Thus, of the four ways money goes into a 401(k), only one comes from the employee — making these plans a great deal for workers!

Some companies offer a retirement plan called a *Money Purchase Plan*. It works like the Employer's Basic Contribution to a 401(k): Deposits come from the employer, must be the same every year, and employees are not permitted to add money from their own paychecks.

Other companies offer a *Profit-Sharing Plan*, which is the same as the 401(k)'s Profit-Sharing contribution. The money comes from the employer, but the amount of the contribution can vary year to year. Again, employees are not permitted to contribute themselves.

Still other employers offer what's known as the paired-plan system, which is a combination of the two.

All told, Ken contributes $2,000 of his own pay to the 401(k), a contribution that costs him only $1,340 because the contribution entitles Ken to a tax deduction that saves him $660 in taxes. On top of that, Ken's employer adds another $2,100 — $400 in basic, $500 in matching and $1,200 in profit-sharing contributions — and all of it is in pre-tax dollars which grow tax-deferred. Thus, for every dollar Ken contributes to his 401(k), his employer contributes $1.05. Put another way, for a $1,340 investment, Ken's account is worth $4,100 — and that's before his account earns a penny from interest, dividends, or capital gains!

Without question, the 401(k) plan is indeed the grandest of all retirement plans!

Where to Invest Your 401(k) Money

In most 401(k) plans, each employee must decide where to invest his or her money, and employees usually can choose from four or five options. The most common choices are:

- a fixed account (equivalent to a CD or money market account)
- a bond mutual fund
- a balanced mutual fund
- a U.S. stock mutual fund
- shares of the employer's stock

Given these choices, which of the following is the best way to invest your 401(k)?

a) Invest 100% in the fixed account.

b) Invest 100% of *your* contribution in the fixed account and 100% of *your employer's* contributions in the stock fund.

c) Invest 100% in the stock fund.

d) Invest 100% in shares of the employer's stock.

e) Invest 20% in each of the five choices (or 100% in the balanced fund) so that you are highly diversified.

Which answer did you choose?

The worst choice is (a), yet 34% of all the money in 401(k) plans nationwide is invested there. People choose fixed accounts because, not understanding how money works, they have an excessive fear of losing money. But you know better (having read Part VI).

HOW EMPLOYEES INVEST THEIR 401(k)

Bonds 4%

Company Stock 40%

Fixed 34%

Balanced 14%

Stocks 8%

FIGURE 9-6

Likewise, (b) and (e) are the wrong choices, too, for they both involve fixed assets. If this seems to contradict my earlier discussion on diversification, you're right: It does. That's because *you must handle your company retirement plan different from the way you handle all your other money.*

To understand why, answer these questions:

1. How often are you paid? (*At regular intervals, right?*)

2. Does that ever change? (*Nah.*)

3. Is the amount of your paycheck the same each time? (*For most workers, yes.*)

4. Is the amount deducted from your paycheck for the 401(k) the same each time? (*Yes.*)

Have you figured it out yet? Your paycheck comes at regular intervals and, at each interval, you contribute the same amount of money. What does this sound like?

Dollar cost averaging, of course.

And as we learned in Chapter 46, dollar cost averaging works best with stock mutual funds. Therefore, the correct answer is (c): You should place 100% of your 401(k) contributions into the most volatile stock fund available in your plan.[35]

---

[35]Hah! I bet you thought the answer would be "it depends." Not this time. But for the one exception and two cautions that you'll soon discover, *everyone* should *always* place 100% of their retirement plan allocations into the stock fund *all the time.* This strategy is as smart as it is shocking.

Two More Reasons Why (c) is the Best Choice

If dollar cost averaging is not enough to convince you, here are two more reasons to choose (c):

Reason #1: Most of Your 401(k) is Free Money, So Treat it That Way

If your employer contributes to your 401(k) on your behalf, as Ken's does, you've got a profit even before your money is invested! In Ken's case, the stock market could drop by 56%, and the amount he contributed — $2,000 — still would be intact. So shed your fears about "losing money." It's not "yours" you lose.

Reason #2: Even a Total Loss Wouldn't be So Bad

Say Ken allocates 100% to the stock fund and, two days after payday, the stock market crashes. So what?

Think about it: Ken, age 45, is paid twice a month, or 24 times per year. Assuming he retires at 65, he'll get 480 paychecks over the rest of his career. If the market crashes this week, destroying the value of this week's contribution, so what? Ken's got 479 contributions to go. And all of them will be made *after* the market drop has occurred, giving Ken the chance to buy at new low prices. This is dollar cost averaging at its best!

One Exception and Two Cautions About Selecting (c)

They say exceptions prove every rule. So be it. Here are three pieces of fine print to consider before you implement this strategy:

The Exception: If You Plan to Withdraw the Money Within the Next Few Years

Dollar cost averaging needs time to be successful. If you're planning to withdraw the funds within two or three years, this strategy is not appropriate. Choice (e) would be a smarter idea.

Caution #1: Do Not Transfer into the Stock Fund all the Money Currently in Your Plan's Account

That's not dollar cost averaging — that's lump-sum investing. And the proper way to invest lump sums, as we discussed in Chapter 44, is to diversify. So, *existing assets* should be invested according to choice (e), and 100% of all *future contributions* should be invested according to choice (c).

Caution #2: Make Sure You Choose the Diversified Stock Fund

Do not choose (d): Do not invest in shares of your employer's stock, regardless of how successful your company is or how successful you expect it to be.

The reason is this: If you suddenly were in need of money, you might have to turn to the money in your retirement plan. But the reason you might need money is because you lost your job. And maybe you've lost your job because the company went broke. Yet if you had been placing all contributions into the company's stock, your retirement plan would be worthless — at the very time you need it most.

Therefore, I always advise employees to sell company stock. It's not because I don't like your company; it's simply a matter of diversification. Remember, in your efforts to achieve financial success, you have only two weapons: Your money and your time. Don't invest both in the same place.

> **If your employer lets you buy company stock at a 15% discount — many do — buy as much as they'll allow and sell it all the very next day. You'll have a 15% profit literally overnight. Not bad for a day on Wall Street. If you could do that every day, your annual rate of return would be 5,475%!**

Retirement Plans for Employees of Non-Profit Organizations

If you work for a hospital, school, or other non-profit organization, you may be eligible to participate in a 403(b) plan, also known as a *Tax-Sheltered Annuity* or *Tax-Deferred Annuity*.

403(b) plans are the non-profit version of 401(k) plans and, therefore, the strategy for a 403(b) is the same as for a 401(k). But there are a few differences between the plans themselves:

- 403(b) plan contributions may be placed only into mutual funds or annuities;

- Profit-sharing is not permitted, since you work for a non-profit organization;

- You can participate in a 403(b) plan even if other employees do not (unlike 401(k)s, which require participation by a majority of employees); and

- Contributions made into 403(b) plans prior to 1987 do not have to be withdrawn beginning at age 70½. Only contributions and earnings that occur after 1986 are subject to the age 70½ minimum withdrawal rules, and any money you withdraw in excess of the minimum requirements permanently reduce the pre-'87 account balance.

The Cost of Not Participating in Your Retirement Plan

If you are 30 years old, and

- You contribute $2,000 per year to your retirement plan for the next 35 years, and

- Your account earns 8% per year,

Then, at age 65, your account will be worth $344,633.

But if you delay your participation just one year, beginning instead at age 31, your account will be worth only $317,253 — a loss of $27,380!

If your employer matches as little as 25 cents on the dollar, your total loss would be $34,225!

And if you earn 10% and if your employer matches 50 cents on the dollar, your loss would be $41,069!

Yet despite the power of early and consistent savings, only 75% of eligible employees in the U.S. participate in their company retirement plans.

You need to participate in your retirement plan as soon as your employer permits and to the maximum extent you're allowed. It's the best place to save for the future.

And you might as well participate: Depending on your income and marital status, being *eligible* to participate in a company retirement plan (whether or not you do participate) makes you *unable* to deduct a contribution to your IRA. So you might as well join your employer plan. For many workers, it's that or nothing.

SALLY FORTH   HOWARD & MACINTOSH

Reprinted with special permission of King Features Syndicate.

Chapter 63 - Social Security

Will Social Security exist when you retire?

When I ask that question in my seminars, those over age 45 say yes and those under 45 say no. As a planner, I believe Social Security will continue in some form, if only due to political pressure, but I make no predictions about what the benefit levels will be or how old you'll have to be to receive them.

Under current law, the maximum Social Security benefit for a worker and spouse is $22,464 per year. Therefore, even if Social Security continues as is, it alone is not likely to provide you with a comfortable retirement.

The current age to be eligible for full Social Security benefits is 65. But that's only for workers nearing retirement. For younger workers, Congress already has cut back the benefits. As shown in Figure 9-7, those born after 1959 are not eligible for full Social Security benefits until age 67. (They can start receiving benefits at 62, but they will get 30% less than if they wait until 67, not 20% less like those retiring today.)

SOCIAL SECURITY

The Age You're Eligible for Full Social Security Benefits

Year of Birth	Years	Months
before 1938	65	0
1938	65	2
1939	65	4
1940	65	6
1941	65	8
1942	65	10
1943-1954	66	0
1955	66	2
1956	66	4
1957	66	6
1958	66	8
1959	66	10
1960 and after	67	0

FIGURE 9-7

Social Security at 62 or 65?

If you're a near-retiree, you can start receiving Social Security at age 62, although you will receive throughout your lifetime only 80% of what you would have received had you waited until 65. So, which is the right choice: Start at 62 with 80% of benefits, or wait until 65 in order to receive 100%?

The answer: It depends[36] — on whether you will stop working at 62. If you are planning to cease receiving *earned*

---

[36]Here we go again.

income (as opposed to investment income), go ahead and start collecting Social Security at 62 — for as Figure 9-8 shows, you'll be better off for the next 13 years. If you live beyond age 75, you'll wish you had waited until you were 65 to begin receiving benefits, but we don't know if you'll live that long! So, since you're here now, take the money and run.

But maybe you're 62 and you don't need the money. So you figure you might as well delay collecting Social Security benefits until you turn 65, to get the higher income at that time.

> *"The rich get richer and the poor get jobs."*
> —**Anonymous**

Wrong move.

If you start taking benefits at 62 and invest that monthly check, the interest you'll earn on that money over the next three years will more than offset the fact that you're receiving a smaller amount by not having waited until age 65. In fact, the interest can be so worthwhile that the person who does not start to collect Social Security until age 65 *may never catch up*. So, when you turn 62, take the money and run.

You get *earned income* from a job or business. *Investment income* comes from interest and dividends.

If, however, you plan to continue working, wait until you stop working, or until you reach age 70, before you begin receiving Social Security. The reason: Retirees under 65 lose one dollar in Social Security benefits for every two they earn over $8,280. (Retirees aged 65-69 lose one dollar for every three they earn over $12,500; retirees 70 and have no reduction.)

SALLY FORTH   HOWARD & MACINTOSH

Reprinted with special permission of King Features Syndicate.

TAKING SOCIAL SECURITY AT 62 IS BETTER THAN WAITING UNTIL 65

Starting at 62				Starting at 65			
Year	Age	Amount	Amount Received	Year	Age	Amount	Amount Received
1	62	$9,600	$9,600		62	$0	$0
2	63	$9,984	$19,584		63	$0	$0
3	64	$10,383	$29,967		64	$0	$0
4	65	$10,799	$40,766	1	65	$13,500	$12,000
5	66	$11,231	$51,997	2	66	$14,040	$26,040
6	67	$11,680	$63,677	3	67	$14,602	$40,642
7	68	$12,147	$75,824	4	68	$15,186	$55,827
8	69	$12,633	$88,457	5	69	$15,793	$71,620
9	70	$13,138	$101,595	6	70	$16,425	$88,045
10	71	$13,664	$115,259	7	71	$17,082	$105,127
11	72	$14,210	$129,469	8	72	$17,765	$122,892
12	73	$14,779	$144,248	9	73	$18,476	$141,368
13	74	$15,370	$159,618	10	74	$19,215	$160,582

It takes 13 years to catch up!
Will you live that long?

FIGURE 9-8

Chapter 64 - Why Retirement Plans are Not Enough

As outstanding as pensions and retirement plans are, they are not enough to satisfy your retirement income needs. Yet many workers who are covered by these programs often have terrible personal savings records. Many are in for a shock when they discover at retirement that their retirement income is a fraction of their pre-retirement pay.

For example, workers earning $50,000 a year who plan to retire with nothing but a pension and Social Security can expect their income to drop 36% the day they retire. That's right: They'll get pensions worth only 44% of pre-retirement pay and Social Security will provide only another 20%.

Could you afford a 36% pay cut right now? If you can't, what makes you think you'll be able to afford such a large cut at retirement? Remember "43,800" from Part I!

It's even worse for higher-paid workers. If your final pay is $150,000, pensions and Social Security together will replace only 36% of your income. You'll lose a whopping 61% of your income when you retire!

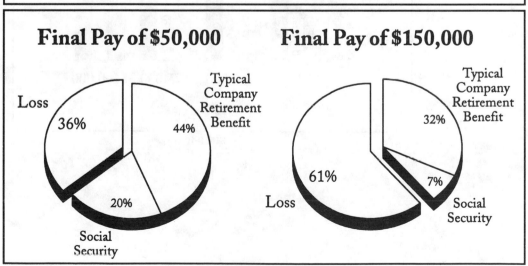

HOW MUCH INCOME WILL YOU LOSE AT RETIREMENT?

Final Pay of $50,000

Loss 36%

Typical Company Retirement Benefit 44%

Social Security 20%

Final Pay of $150,000

Typical Company Retirement Benefit 32%

Loss 61%

Social Security 7%

FIGURE 9-9

If you're thinking that's not a problem for you because you don't earn anywhere near $100,000, think again: If you and your spouse jointly earn $50,000 today, a mere 4% annual pay increase over the next 20 years will place your income above $100,000. So, as important as it is that you participate in your company retirement plan, you need to save even more.

YOU WILL CONTINUE TO EARN MORE AND MORE MONEY

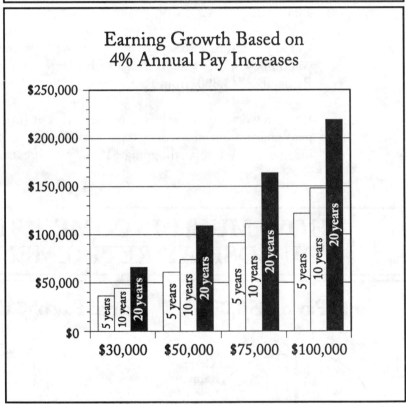

FIGURE 9-10

Chapter 65- Women and Retirement

Retirement planning is a critical issue for many women. Although the majority of adult women are married, 85% die alone — unmarried, widowed, or divorced. Also, older women generally have worked fewer years and earned less money than men.

The result, according to the Social Security Administration, is that only 37% of women over 62 receive Social Security benefits based solely on their own work records, and these women receive on average only 76% as much as men. In fact, 63% of all women over 62 qualify for higher Social Security benefits as the *wife* of a worker rather than as a worker themselves. Indeed, the Older Women's League reports that the total median annual income for women 65 and older is 43% less than the median income for men of similar ages.

While this trend may change over the next 40 years as women in today's younger generation achieve more economic parity with men, it is undeniable that many older female Americans face a difficult situation. In fact, in 1988, Social Security accounted for more than 90% of the total income for one third of older unmarried women.

The problem extends beyond Social Security, too: Since women tend to spend more years outside the workforce (raising families and maintaining the household), and since they tend to earn less when they do work, according to the U.S. Census Bureau, they qualify for pensions only half as often as men do.

Similar statistics are found in their rates of personal savings: Retirement-age women have half the amount of personal savings as men their age.

Perhaps the most telling statistic is cited by the American Association for Retired Persons: Although only 12% of all elderly people live in poverty, 74% of them are women.

Clearly, women who ignore retirement planning do so at their own peril, so if you're a woman and you didn't pay much attention to this page, read it again. And if you're a man, you need to share this page with your mother, your wife, and your daughters.

Part X
Insurance

Part X — Insurance

Overview - How to Manage Risk

Forget what you know, or what you think you know, about insurance. Ignore what you've heard from insurance agents and put aside your biases. In this part, I'm going to tell you the truth about insurance and its proper role in a financial plan.

No matter what you've been told, no matter what you think, there is one purpose — and only one purpose — for insurance: To protect against a financial loss. The key word is *financial*, for we are not protecting against *losses* themselves.

As a financial planner, I can't protect you from suffering a loss, but I can prevent you from suffering *financially* as a result of incurring a loss. For example, I can't prevent you from getting in a car accident, but I can prevent you from losing money as a result of it.

Thus, insurance protects us from the adverse economic impact caused by a loss. If there is no financial loss, there is no need to protect against it financially.

Have you insured your shoes?

I'll bet not, because if you lose them, you'll just buy another pair. You don't need to insure your shoes because losing them would not present a significant financial loss.

But your house is another matter. Losing *that* certainly would constitute a major financial loss. That means we've got to figure out a way to manage the risk that you might lose your house. Financial professionals often refer to insurance, therefore, as *risk management*.

> **Indeed, anybody who offers to conduct a "risk management analysis" for you is often nothing more than an insurance salesman.**

Four Ways to Manage Risk

Financial losses can occur if you die, are injured, become sick, if your property is damaged, destroyed, or stolen, or if you get sued. We must protect ourselves financially in case any of these events occurs. In other words, we must manage these risks, and there are four ways to do so.

To illustrate, say you need to get a package across town, but you fear the dangers of highway traffic. You could:

1) **Avoid risk.**   Refuse to drive. But then the package does not get delivered.

2) **Accept risk.**   Driving a car is dangerous, but you accept the risk in order to deliver your package.

3) **Reduce risk.**   Drive carefully and wear a seatbelt.

4) **Transfer risk.** Have someone else deliver the package for you.

To apply these four management techniques against, say, the financial consequences of having your house burn down, you can:

1) Refuse to buy a house in the first place (*risk avoidance*);

2) Buy the house and ignore the problem or hope it never happens (*risk acceptance*);

3) Install smoke detectors and fire extinguishers throughout the home to enable you to discover and extinguish the flames before major damage occurs (*risk reduction*);

4) Force someone else to pay for the loss if the fire occurs (*risk transference*).

The last strategy is what insurance is all about.

Chapter 66 - Protecting Your Largest Financial Asset

Your largest asset is not your house, your health, or your company pension.

For almost everyone who is still working, your largest asset is *your ability to produce an income*. Thus, the most important type of insurance is *disability income insurance* (DI). You need it more than any other kind of insurance — more than life, health, homeowners, or auto insurance. In fact, in my firm's planning practice, we typically are far more concerned that our clients own disability coverage than life coverage.

Although everybody who earns a living needs disability insurance, less than 15% of all workers in the U.S. have it. There are two reasons why:

Reason #1: "It won't happen to me"

I bet you think "bad stuff" only happens to the other guy. Well, to the other guy, you're the other guy. Consider this: 48% of all mortgage foreclosures in this country are caused by disability. When somebody gets injured or ill, they can't work. They then lose their job and thus their income. With no income, they can't make their mortgage payment and the bank forecloses. If you thought people lose their homes because they're deadbeats, alcohol or drug abusers, criminals, or compulsive gamblers, think again. They're good, honest people who merely suffer a disability.

Although only 15% of workers have DI coverage, virtually all homeowners have insurance on their homes. I'll bet you do, too. Yet has any house on your street ever burned down? Unlikely, because the odds of that happening are only one in 1,200.

Yet your odds of suffering a disability before age 65, one that lasts 90 days or more, is an incredible 1 in 8. So if you think it won't happen to you, maybe — just maybe — it might.

In fact, as Figure 10-1 shows, actuaries can predict with remarkable accuracy the probability that a disability will occur. For example, take any five people who are age 45. Statistically, it is 95% certain that at least one of those five people will suffer a long-term disability prior

ODDS OF DISABILITY

Probability of At Least One Long-Term Disability Occurring Prior to Age 65

Age of Group	Number of People in Group				
	1	2	3	4	5
30	52%	77%	89%	95%	98%
35	50%	75%	88%	94%	97%
40	48%	73%	86%	93%	96%
45	44%	69%	83%	90%	95%
50	39%	63%	78%	87%	92%

FIGURE 10-1

THE AIR BAG PHENOMENON

Chance of Occurrences Among Men and Women
Ages 45-65

Condition	Death	Disability
Hypertension	-73%	+70%
Heart Disease	-29%	+44%
Cerebrovascular	-48%	+36%
Diabetes	-27%	+36%
All Four	-32%	+55%

FIGURE 10-2

to age 65. Those are pretty awesome odds, and I certainly would not want to bet against them — yet that's exactly what you're doing if you do not have disability insurance.

The Air Bag Phenomenon

Interestingly, the reason you are so *likely* to suffer a disability is exactly because you are so *unlikely* to die. Since 1960, the frequency of death from the four leading causes have sharply *decreased*, while the frequency of disability has sharply *increased*. I call this the Air Bag Phenomenon.

If you live in a major metropolitan area, you'd agree that there are 10 rush hours every week, one each weekday morning and evening.[37] How often do you hear of a traffic accident in those rush hours?

Every time, of course.

But in how many do you hear that a driver was killed in a rush hour accident? That's much less common. Since fatalities are unusual, most of us don't give those accidents a second thought, other than to complain that someone made us late. But the truth is that someone is getting hurt in those accidents. After all, you're not likely to avoid injury after sustaining a collision at 55 mph.

---

[37]In many cities, people will argue that there's just one rush-hour per week: It starts Monday morning and ends Friday evening.

And that's my point: Due to the advent of airbags, many people now survive auto accidents who 10 years ago would have been killed. But this does not mean accident victims just walk away from the scene. Rather, it simply means they go to the emergency room instead of the morgue.

Indeed, a study by the University of Pittsburgh showed that people protected by an airbag who are involved in a high-speed, head-on collision often suffer a variety of injuries caused not by the collision, but by the airbag itself — including burns to the chest and face, loss of hearing and vision, and broken forearms. Airbags also fail to prevent legs from being broken. And research from the University of Florida revealed that many drivers whose lives were saved by airbags suffer injuries that are not readily apparent to rescue workers, such as lacerations to the liver. Thus, airbags do not assure that you will survive injury-free if you are in an accident.

So while airbags have been very good news for the life insurance industry (as the number of highway fatalities has dropped), it has been bad news for the health and auto insurance industries (which pay the medical expenses of accident survivors).

Indeed, medical advances can be felt far beyond the highway. A generation or two ago, a worker who suffered a heart attack on the factory floor would have died. Today, paramedics and emergency medical technicians arrive in minutes, ready to stabilize and transport the patient to the hospital — by helicopter, if necessary. Throughout much of the country, EMTs are able to install pacemakers *right at the scene.*

And there's more. Has your liver gone bad? No problem. We'll give you a new one. Clogged arteries? We'll predict the stroke before it occurs, give you a quadruple bypass, and you'll be back on the tennis court in six weeks. Failed kidneys? We'll hook you up to a machine that will take over the job.

Modern medicine can do many things. Above all else, it can *keep you alive.* But that doesn't mean you'll never miss a day of work.

Quite the contrary. In a study of more than 2,000 severely ill patients from five medical centers around the country, the *Journal of the American Medical Association* reported that nearly a third of the families lost most of their life savings as a result of the patient's illness. The study found that although 96% of patients had some form of medical insurance, 31% still lost their savings.

"Home care and disability costs may now be more devastating to patients and their families than the costs incurred in the hospital," said the study. These expenses include the unreimbursed costs of home care, health aides, special transportation, and related medical costs. In addition, 29% of the families studied lost a major source of income, either because the patient no longer could work, or because another family member had to quit a job in order to care for the patient.

So if you think a disability won't happen to you, or if you think it won't result in a financial burden, think again.

Reason #2: "It's Too Expensive"

Without question, DI coverage is expensive. Annual premiums can be 1% to 3% of your annual salary. And that's why many people ultimately reject DI insurance. "I can't afford it," they say.

Turn this argument around. The reason you need to buy disability insurance is exactly why you don't want to buy it.

Have you ever seen one of those insurance commercials on late-night TV? "For just two dollars a week... you cannot be turned down... veterans only..." and other nonsense. These policies are only two bucks a week because the insurance companies know they're not going to pay a claim!

If you look at the fine print, you'll see that the benefits for the first several years often are limited to a return of the premiums you've paid, minus administrative costs. Since most buyers of this awful coverage are a gizzillion years old, the carriers know the buyers will die before they qualify for a claim. Thus, the carriers collect $2 a month, for which they do nothing in return. That's why coverage is so cheap. For the carrier, that $2 premium is virtually pure profit!

This is the main thesis of the insurance world. A policy is cheap when the insurance company knows it is unlikely to pay a claim. But policies are expensive when there is higher probability that you will file a claim. Therefore, the more expensive the policy, the more you need the protection.

Think Like the Seller

It might help if you examine the situation from the insurance company's point of view. If only one house in 1,200 is likely to burn down and each house is valued at $250,000, then how much does an insurer need to charge each of the 1,200 homeowners to be able to pay the claim for the one house that burns down? The answer is:

$$\frac{1 \text{ Claim of } \$250,000}{1,200 \text{ Homes}} = \$208/\text{Per Home}$$

Toss in administrative expenses, profits, and payouts for other forms of damage, such as lightning, theft, and flood, and the typical homeowner's insurance bill is about $350. Thus, from the insurer's perspective, the cost of a policy is directly related to the likelihood and cost of a claim. This explains why homeowner's insurance is cheap, and why DI coverage is expensive.

The Cost of Disability vs. The Cost of Death

Look at Figure 10-3. Mike, a 35-year-old male nonsmoker in good health, buys a $250,000 life insurance policy. If Mike were to die, the insurance company would owe his survivors $250,000.

On the other hand, if Mike bought a $2,000 disability income policy and suffered a disability, the insurance company would owe him $2,000 per month — for as many as 30 years. That would be as much as $720,000 in claims!

That's why disability insurance is expensive — and why you need it.

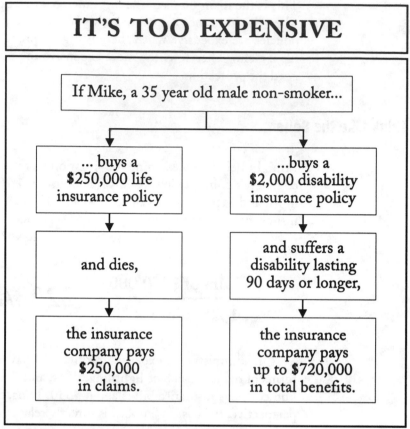

FIGURE 10-3

The Problems with Group DI Coverage

Of those who have DI coverage, most have it only because it is provided by their employer. But group coverage has several problems:

- The group policy's definition of disability is far too restrictive;

- Your employer can cancel the coverage at any time;

- The insurance company can cancel the benefit at any time;

- If you leave your employer, you lose the benefit; and

- The cost of the coverage can increase.

Two Groups of Workers Who Really Need Their Own DI Policy

In addition to these problems, red flags rise for two groups of workers: those who plan to leave their jobs, such as women to want who stop working for a few years while they raise children, and any worker who intends to become self-employed.

Group One: Moms-to-Be

One of my clients, about to have a child, planned to quit her law practice with the intention of returning to work after a few years. By leaving her firm, she would lose her employer-paid DI coverage, and she would not be able to obtain a policy on her own because homemakers have no income. (*Income* is the primary criterion used by carriers in deciding whether to give you a policy. No income, no policy.)

To solve this problem, we told her to buy a non-cancelable DI policy *before* she left the firm. Buying her own policy meant she could keep it even after she left the firm. If she later returns to the work force, regardless of her new occupation, the coverage moves with her.

If you're wondering why she needs DI coverage after she becomes a homemaker with no income, you're confusing *no income* with *no work*. As any mother can tell you, she'll be working plenty — and she'll be the only person in the world crazy enough to do her job for free. (Okay, maybe Dad or another relative also would be willing. Maybe.) If she gets hurt or falls ill, she'll have to pay someone else to take over, such as a nanny or housekeeper. Without DI coverage, from where would the money come?

Group Two: Budding Entrepreneurs

Similar problems occur for those preparing to become self-employed. Another client of ours, working for a defense contractor, planned to become a self-employed consultant in the same field.

Like the lawyer, he would be unable to obtain disability income insurance after he began his consulting practice because the insurance company would want to know the amount of his income over the past two years *from his current occupation*. Since his consulting business

473

would be brand new, his income would be zero, and he would not be eligible for coverage for two years. Therefore, you must buy your own non-cancelable DI policy *before* you become self-employed.

You Have Only Two-Thirds as Much Coverage as You Think You Have

If your DI coverage is provided to you as an employee benefit, you have only two-thirds the coverage you need. This is because your disability benefit probably equals 60% of your pay, a widely-followed industry guideline. It is based on the fact that insurance payments are tax-free under federal law. Thus, earning 60% of your pay tax-free is the same as earning 100% of your pay and then paying taxes on it.

But — and this is a big *BUT* — if your employer pays the premium for you, the disability income becomes taxable, yet the amount you receive *is still only 60% of your pay*. Since you'll lose about a third (20%) to taxes, you'll have only 40% left. That's a problem.

Therefore, if your employer pays for your coverage, you need to consider buying a supplemental policy on your own. The good news is that you probably need to buy only enough to replace the 20% you lose to taxes, and since that's not much insurance, it's not very expensive (often only a few hundred dollars a year).

Eight Reasons Never to Buy a Policy Based on Price

When shopping for a disability policy, don't buy based on cost, for the cheaper the policy, the less likely your claim will be covered — or if it is, the less money you will receive. In fact, there are several factors affecting the cost of a policy. Let's take a look at them.

Cost Factor #1: Who Says You're Disabled?

Disability insurance is not as simple as life insurance. With life insurance, there is no debate regarding the legitimacy of the claim: If you die, they pay. But what about a disability? What exactly does *disabled* mean? And who decides you've met the definition — your doctor or the insurance company's doctor?

This is perhaps the most important factor affecting the value —
and cost — of a disability contract, and why you cannot buy a policy
merely based on price. Cheap polices have a definition so strict that
it is unlikely you will ever qualify to receive payments, while more
expensive policies have more favorable definitions.

For example, is a surgeon who loses a finger disabled? Don't be too
quick to say yes. After all, a surgeon certainly can teach or consult,
and her income might not suffer in the least — despite the fact that
she no longer can perform surgery.

Thus, standard disability income policies would not consider her to
be disabled. Standard contracts say you must be unable to perform
the duties of *any occupation* for which you are prepared by training
or experience. In other words, if you can sell magazine subscriptions
over the phone, you might not be considered disabled. This is why
the Social Security Administration, which uses a "totally disabled"
definition, denies more than 90% of the claims filed.

If you are a white-collar worker, therefore, or one who works in
a specialized field, you need a policy that will pay benefits if you
are unable to perform the duties of *your own occupation*. With an
"own-occ" policy, our surgeon would be considered disabled and
entitled to benefits even if she continued to earn a living as a
professor of medicine.

Cost Factor #2: Your Occupation

The more dangerous your job,
the more likely you'll be hurt,
and thus the more expensive
the policy. Workers in high
risk occupations find that DI
coverage is either unusually
expensive with benefits payable
only for five years or less, or
not available at all. By contrast,
general office workers can get
coverage at a lower cost with
full benefits payable to age 65.

> A freelance writer, working out
> of his home, cannot qualify for
> disability insurance. Why?
>
> It's not because many acci-
> dents occur in the home. Ask
> yourself this: If you became
> disabled, where would you go?
> Home, of course! Well, if you
> *work* at home, how will they
> know when you're better?
> Thus, insurers often don't like
> to provide benefits for people
> who work in their home.
>
> This example shows that the
> insurance industry looks at DI
> in strange and unusual ways.

475

Occupational classes are very specific, with several classifications for many occupations. For example, nurses who work in an emergency room might be classified differently from nurses who work in an administrative capacity. Each classification would be charged a different premium — all based on the risk of injury. In addition to your job's specific duties, insurers consider your age, sex, even leisure activities (insurers frown on scuba-diving, hang gliding, motorcycle riding, car racing, and piloting airplanes, for such activities often lead to serious injury), and then they price your policy accordingly.

Cost Factor #3: The Waiting Period

You can set your waiting period (i.e., the amount of time that must elapse before you will receive benefits) at 0, 30, 60, 90, 180 or 365 days. The shorter your waiting period, the more expensive the policy. A 90-day waiting period generally is the most cost-effective because most disabilities do not last 90 days. Insurance companies know this and, therefore, you'll save a lot of money by choosing a 90-day wait over a 60-day wait, but you'll save less by choosing a 180-day wait over a 90-day wait. Keep in mind, though, that "self-insuring" for the first 90 days could cost you $10,000 or more in out-of-pocket expenses. So make sure you maintain sufficient cash reserves (see Chapter 6).

Cost Factor #4: Inflation Protection

Buying a policy based on today's income is fine for now, but inflation will cut the value of your policy. Therefore, better policies either guarantee to automatically increase your benefits each year or give you a guaranteed option to increase your coverage along with increases in the Consumer Price Index.

Cost Factor #5: Does Protection Increase as Your Income Grows?

Since your income will grow over time, you need a policy that will let you increase your coverage to keep pace with it. Because your health may change, it's important that the benefit be guaranteed without you having to repeat the application process — which could prohibit you from obtaining additional coverage in the future.

Cost Factor #6: How Long are Benefits Payable?

Lots of policies pay benefits for only five years. That doesn't do you a lot of good unless you're close to retirement. Therefore, get a policy that pays benefits to age 65. But be forewarned: This is not always possible. Workers in high-risk occupations or those with pre-existing conditions often cannot get full-career coverage.

Cost Factor #7: Will the Policy Pay a Partial Benefit if You're Partially Disabled?

Say you suffer a back injury and your doctor wants you to work only four hours a day. Some policies would pay nothing because you're not totally disabled, but better (and more expensive) policies pay partial benefits to make up for the hours you can't work, or the money you can't earn (provided you show a loss of hours or income of at least 20%).

Cost Factor #8: Is Your Policy Both Guaranteed and Non-Cancelable?

Guaranteed means the policy's cost can't rise. Non-cancelable means you are covered as long as you pay your premiums — even if you change jobs or quit working.

"Everything is funny as long as it is happening to someone else."

—Will Rogers

One Dumb Feature You Need to Avoid

To overcome the objection that DI coverage costs too much — and to help agents make the sale — many insurers offer an option called the *Return of Premium Rider*. This rider (so-called because it's an addendum to the insurance contract) says if you do not suffer a disability, you are entitled to a partial refund (usually 50%) of the premiums you paid.

This is a popular option, but it's really quite dumb. After all, buying the policy is in direct conflict with the rider. You buy the policy in case you become disabled, but you buy the rider in case you don't. It doesn't make sense!

It makes even less sense when you realize the cost. Buying the rider increases the cost of the policy by 20% to 40% for the privilege of getting half your money back. It's a wonderful example of the smoke and mirrors that are so pervasive in the insurance industry. Avoid this trap.

Why You Should Not Deduct Premiums as a Business Expense

If you own a business, you can deduct the cost of your DI policy as a normal business expense. If you do, you'll give yourself a tax deduction, which in turn lowers your cost of buying the policy.

Don't do it.

If you do, the disability income, should you ever receive it, would become taxable. Therefore, you should pay your premiums personally, with no tax write-off, so that any disability income payments you receive will be tax-free.

Chapter 67 - Long-Term Care

Long-Term Care insurance is, in a sense, disability income insurance for retirees and an excellent example of how **The Rules of Money Have Changed**. Many people have not dealt with this subject for the simple reason that until now nobody ever had the need.

In ancient Greece, for example, life expectancy at birth was 20. When the Declaration of Independence was signed, life expectancy was still just 23; the median age was 16. Even as recently as 1900, most Americans died by age 47.

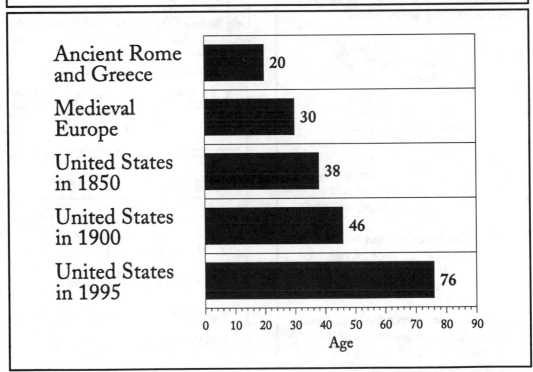

LIFE EXPECTANCY AT BIRTH

Ancient Rome and Greece	20
Medieval Europe	30
United States in 1850	38
United States in 1900	46
United States in 1995	76

Age

FIGURE 10-4

If you're under the age of 40, you probably think the subject of long-term care doesn't apply to you. But it does — not only because you will one day be old enough to worry about it — but because you will be faced with the problem as your *parents* get older.

Indeed, the Marriott Corporation found that although the median age of its employees is 35, some 15% say they have elder-care responsibilities. And in a study of workers are several major corporations, the consulting firm Cobley & Hunt found that, of caregiving employees:

- 1% were forced to quit their jobs in order to provide care for an elder;

- 11% take off an average of six days per year to provide routine elder care;

- 100% incur workday interruptions to provide routine elder support; and

- 20% incur excessive use of physical, mental health and Employee Assistance Plan services.

Face it: long-term care is an issue you will face at some point in your life — and probably much sooner than you think.

These figures are confirmed by the percentage of Americans who reach age 65. In 1870, only 2.5% of all Americans made it. By 1990, that percentage had increased five-fold to 12.7%. Today, 31 million people are over 65 — and the figures continue to grow, bolstered by advances in medicine and public health.

To understand why, just look at the leading causes of death in the United States. In 1900, communicable diseases were the scourge of the nation. Today, most deaths are caused by heredity, lifestyle and the environment. That's why people in the 1940s and 1950s rarely died of heart disease: They were more far more likely to die from a contagious disease long before they reached what we would now consider "old age."

LEADING CAUSES OF DEATH

1900	1990
1. Pneumonia	1. Heart Disease
2. Tuberculosis	2. Cancer
3. Diarrhea	3. Stroke
4. Nephritis	4. Lung Disease
5. Diphtheria	5. Accidents

FIGURE 10-5

To understand just how different our world is today, consider:

- Life expectancy at birth is 76;

- People in the fastest-growing age group in this country are those over 85;

- If you and your spouse both reach age 65, the odds are that one of you will reach age 90;

- 90% of all the people in world history who ever reached age 90 are alive today; and

- Willard Scott won't wish you a happy birthday unless you are least 100.

Old cars break down more often than new ones, and the same is true for people. As our bodies begin to wear out, we require assistance with the Activities of Daily Living, usually defined by insurance companies as eating, dressing, toileting, tranferring (walking, or getting from bed to chair), and maintaining continence. As a result:

- More than half the women and about one-third of the men who reach age 65 will spend some time in a nursing home;

- Seven out of 10 couples can expect at least one partner to use a nursing home after age 65;

- The average cost of a nursing home is around $50,000 per year;

- Half of all older Americans who live alone will spend them-selves into poverty after only 13 weeks in a nursing home;

- 56% of couples spend their income down to the poverty level after one spouse has spent six months in a nursing home; and

- Two out of five people 65 and over will need long-term care. Half will stay in a facility six months or less, while the other half will stay an average of two and a half years.

These statistics come as a shock to most of us. Indeed, as a nursing home admissions officer once told me, the most common remark she hears when admitting a new patient is, "I never thought I'd live this long."

The Three Levels of Long-Term Care

We'll talk more about the cost of care and how to pay for it. But first, it is important that you become familiar with the three types of care.

Level #1: Skilled Care

Defined as *continuously medically necessary*, these cases represent the horror stories about growing old: of people tied to their beds, connected to tubes, suffering from some chronic ailment. But in reality, only one-half of one percent of Americans require this level of care, so unless you have a medical or family history that predisposes you to it, it's statistically unlikely that this will happen to you.

Level #2: Intermediate Care

This is care provided under a doctor's supervision. Only 4.5% of the nursing home population falls in this category.

Level #3: Custodial Care

All other long-term care patients — 95% — receive custodial care, which is little more than room and board. It is not related to medical or health care, but is based on the mere premise that you're finding it difficult to maintain one or more of the Activities of Daily Living. Often, Mom is in a retirement facility because she cannot live alone at home anymore, and the kids are unable to care for her.

The result: Mom enters a retirement home. She will find her meals prepared, her room cleaned, and someone to remind her to take her medication.

> **And, almost always, it is Mom. Wives survive their husbands 80% of the time, And 72% of nursing home residents are women. More than 85% of all women in this country die single —unmarried, widowed, or divorced. (See Chapter 64.)**

How to Pay for Long-Term Care

This is why neither private medical insurance nor Medicare pays for long-term care. It's simply not a medical need. So who pays? *You do*, until you can no longer afford it. Thus, we can group all Americans into three broad groups: the wealthy, the middle class, and the poor.

If you are wealthy and can afford the $50,000 annual cost, long-term care may not be a financial concern for you.

If you are middle class, you must pay for the cost of long-term care from your income and assets until you run out of money.

If you are poor (which is where many in the middle class eventually find themselves) and cannot afford to pay for the care you need, you will be covered by Medicaid.

> **Do not confuse Medicaid with Medicare.**
>
> **Medicaid is the federal welfare program for the poor. Medicare is the federal medical insurance program for those over 65. Although virtually all American retirees qualify for Medicare benefits, Medicare does not pay for long-term care expenses. Medicaid does, but only the poor qualify to receive its benefits.**

Supposedly, therefore, everybody in the U.S. who needs care will receive it, even if they can't afford it. But if you're going to rely on Medicaid, you are assuming:

- a Medicaid-approved facility is available;

- you are accepted by that facility; and

- Medicaid still exists. As this book went to press, Congress was considering massive changes to Medicaid.

Even assuming that the patient requiring institutionalized care is able to find it, a problem remains for his or her spouse. If all of the family's income and assets are devoted to paying for the care of the institutional spouse, where does that leave the community spouse?

A Crisis for the Middle Class

This is why long-term care is a crisis for the middle class. The wealthy, after all, can afford the cost without sacrificing the lifestyle of their spouse or family members. And the poor enjoy a similar advantage, not because they can afford it, but because they are not required to.

Thus, it's the middle class which suffers the most, economically-speaking.[38] Unfortunately, those in the middle class also have the most misconceptions about who pays for long-term care. As already mentioned, health insurance does not cover this cost. And according to the U.S. Health Care Financing Administration, Medicare pays for only 6% of the nation's long-term care costs. Here's why:

- Medicare pays only if the patient has been hospitalized for three consecutive days within the 30 days prior to entering a nursing home (60% of patients fail this test);

- The facility must be Medicare-approved (only 20% of the nation's 20,000 nursing homes qualify); and

- Even if the above two criteria are met, Medicare pays only for the first 20 days in full. Medicare requires a patient co-payment of $89.50 per day for the next 80 days, and Medicare pays nothing after the 100th day.

"No problem," you say to yourself. "I'll just become poor and get Medicaid to pay." Before you try that, make sure you know the truth about Medicaid. If you decide to spend down your assets — or if you're forced to — you need to know how Medicaid operates (again, assuming it still exists).

The Medicaid Asset Test

As the rules stand at this writing, Medicaid places your assets into three categories: non-countable, countable, and inaccessible.

- **Non-countable assets** include your house (but only if you have a spouse who lives there), car, jewelry, household goods, personal effects, prepaid funeral, and $2,000 in cash.

- **Countable assets** include second homes and any additional cars, plus all savings and investments, including CDs, stocks, bonds, mutual funds, annuities, IRAs, and retirement plans — even the cash value of your life insurance policies.

---

[38]What else is new?

- **Inaccessible assets** include gifts and anything placed into irrevocable trusts. These assets will be deemed by Medicaid to be *exempt transfers* (meaning gifts or transfers into trusts will be allowed) or *non-exempt* transfers (meaning the gifts or transfers are disallowed). If the transfers are deemed non-exempt, Medicaid will deny benefits for a period of time based on when the non-exempt transfers occurred.

Under Medicaid rules, the community spouse may keep non-countable assets, but is forced to liquidate countable assets. Furthermore, in most states, the community spouse is allowed a monthly income of less than $2,000; the institutional spouse is allowed just $30. Medicaid takes all income above those amounts, including Social Security income, pensions, interest income, annuity income, and alimony payments.

Although Medicaid will not take your house if a spouse lives there, you will lose your home when your spouse dies or goes to a nursing home. When your house eventually is sold, Medicaid will recover the sale proceeds — even if it has to wait until after you've died to do so. So you can forget about leaving your house to the kids.

The solution? Actually, there are three of them. Let's look closely at each:

Solution #1: Qualify for Medicaid By Transferring Assets

Clearly, Medicaid will pay only if you have few assets. Logically, then, make sure you don't have assets. Therefore, *transfer your assets to your children now*. This will make you poor, and by being poor, you'll qualify for Medicaid.

If you don't transfer your assets to your children, you'll just spend everything you own on long-term care costs until you have nothing left anyway. Either way, you'll be broke. So wouldn't you rather give your assets to your kids instead of to a nursing home?

Four Problems with Transferring Assets

If you think this sounds reasonable, watch out for these four big problems:

Problem #1: Yeah, Right

You'll find it very hard to give everything you own to your (spoiled rotten!) kids just as you've reached that time in your life when you can start enjoying yourself. In other words, this recommendation, um, usually doesn't go over very well.

> **Try convincing your parents to give you all their money.**
>
> **"No, really, Dad, you need to give me everything you own right now. It's for your own good!"**
>
> **Yeah, right.**

Problem #2: Medicaid is Aware of This Trick

If you made gifts during the 36 months prior to filing your claim for benefits, Medicaid will deny the claim. This rule is specifically intended to prevent people from asset-shifting. And please note an important change in Medicaid rules: If you file a claim at any time during the 36-month waiting period, *Medicaid will restart the clock.* Therefore if you plan to use this strategy, assets must be transferred well in advance of the need for long-term care, and be sure you don't file a claim until *you're sure* the 36-month waiting period has expired. Also, be aware that transferring assets to a spouse does not shield the assets from Medicaid.

> **Have you brought assets into your marriage?**
>
> **Many people who marry later in life bring assets into the marriage, like Ruth. Her husband died when she was 47, leaving her his 401(k), their home, plus life insurance proceeds. Five years later, Ruth remarried. She kept all her assets in her name and filed a separate tax return. When her second husband needed long-term care, he quickly spent down all *his* assets.**

But Medicaid required Ruth to spend all *her* money on his care before it would pay benefits. Over the next several years, Ruth was forced to spend down to the poverty level, too.

Regardless of whose money it was or where it came from — inheritances, savings, retirement plans, or insurance proceeds — Medicaid will deny claims until *both* spouses spend virtually all their money on long-term care. The fact that the money originally belonged to the community spouse does not matter.

Problem #3: Attempts to Asset-Shift are Stymied by the IRS

Under gift tax rules, you may give to any one person only $10,000 per year (you may give unlimited amounts to your spouse, but as shown above, doing so has no effect). Any gifts greater than $10,000 will be subject to taxes, and the rate starts at 37%. (By the way, the IRS taxes the person who gives the gift, not the person who receives it. See Chapter 15.) So, even if you try to give your money away, the IRS will restrict the speed with which you may proceed.

The $10,000 per-person per-year rule might not be as restrictive as you might think. Take a married couple with three children (themselves married) and five grandchildren. Grandma can give $10,000 to each of her three children ($30,000), to each of her children's spouses (another $30,000) and to each grandchild ($50,000). That's $110,000. And Granddad can do the same thing, for total annual gifts of $220,000 — all without incurring any gift taxes. On January 1, they can do it again. Thus, this family can transfer $440,000 to the kids in a remarkably short period of time.

Of course, making gifts to all these people might not be a good idea. If a divorce occurs, for example, the grandparents could discover that they've given perhaps $120,000 to an ex-daughter-in-law and her children, who they may never see again. Think hard before using this strategy.

Problem #4: This Strategy is Unethical

Please remember that Medicaid is funded by taxpayers to help the truly needy of our society — not as a middle-class tax-dodge to protect your assets.

Solution #2: Divorce Yourself From Medicaid

For all four reasons noted above, transferring assets is not as simple or as easy as it first appears. This is why some elder care attorneys suggest strategy number two: *Divorce*. The institutional spouse leaves all assets under a divorce decree to the community spouse; Medicaid cannot claim assets transferred in such a manner.

Three Problems with Divorce

This isn't necessarily a great idea, either, because:

- The same ethical problem exists as noted above;

- If you thought it was tough for Mom and Dad to handle the thought of giving everything to their kids, just try to get them to file for divorce after 45 years of marriage simply because one of them is declining in health. Not only is it unlikely they'll do it — it's one heck of a commentary that our laws even encourage such an action; and

- Medicaid is aware that many couples are divorcing for economic rather than marital reasons, and the agency is starting to challenge this strategy. Where claimants have recently divorced and decreed all their assets to their ex-spouses, Medicaid has gone to court, arguing that under the divorce decree, the institutionalized spouse did not get his or her fair share of the marital assets. Why argue that position? Because if Medicaid wins, as much as half the marital assets return to the institutional spouse, which Medicaid then can seize.

Solution #3: Long-Term Care Insurance

This is the least-evil solution.

Although buying insurance is never fun, given the alternatives of transferring assets or getting a divorce, it is the least evil choice. For that reason, clients who are not independently wealthy should consider buying a policy — and as early as age 50.

Here's why: The cost of coverage is related directly to your age (rates are unisex; there is no cost difference between men and women) and

Many wealthy Americans buy long-term care insurance even though they don't need to. Why? Because they'd rather spend several hundred dollars on a policy instead of many thousands on the care itself, preserving their assets for their children.

Indeed, for many people, long-term care insurance is not just a smart way to protect you, it's a smart way to protect your assets, too.

once you buy the policy, the cost remains the same for life.[39] Since a person age 50 is not likely to file a claim for 20 years or more, the carrier has many years to collect premiums. Thus, the cost for that 50-year-old is quite low — about $50 a month in many cases. That's extremely affordable, especially considering that the cost of policies skyrockets with age. If you don't buy a policy until age 65, the cost could exceed $1,500 a year, or $2,300 by age 75.

Many feel that buying a policy in their fifties is unnecessary, since it is likely to be years — even decades — before they'll need the coverage.

Two Reasons to Buy Long Term Care Insurance at Young Ages

Although it's true that a 50-year-old is unlikely to need the coverage for many years, it nonetheless makes sense to buy it young. Why? Consider Figure 10-6, which compares the cost of a typical long-term care policy for different ages:

LONG-TERM CARE INSURANCE

Age	Years of Coverage	Basic Policy		"Cadillac" Coverage	
		Annual Cost	Total Cost to Age 85	Annual Cost	Total Cost to Age 85
50	35	$530	$18,550	$1,293	$45,255
55	30	$712	$21,360	$1,626	$48,780
60	25	$989	$24,725	$2,097	$52,425
65	20	$1,454	$29,080	$2,875	$57,500
70	15	$2,242	$33,630	$4,112	$61,680
75	10	$3,624	$36,240	$6,240	$62,400

FIGURE 10-6

---

[39]While the cost of most policies will remain unchanged once they are purchased, your policy's cost could increase if you select an inflation protection option. Also, while insurers can't increase the cost of a single policy, they are permitted to seek state approval to change the cost of their contracts for all policyholders.

Here's a list of some "uninsurable conditions" that would cause an insurance carrier to deny long-term care coverage:

- Reliance on another person or assistance devices to perform two or more of the Activities of Daily Living
- AIDS, AIDS-related Complex
- Alzheimer's Disease, Dementia, Memory loss
- Amputation or Blindness due to disease
- Cirrhosis
- Cystic Fibrosis
- Kidney Failure — Dialysis
- Lou Gehrig's Disease
- Multiple Sclerosis
- Osteoporosis
- Pancreatitis
- Paralysis
- Parkinson's Disease
- Schizophrenia
- Sickle Cell Anemia
- Spinal Cord Injury/Myelitis
- Stroke

There are a lot more exclusions, but you get the point. People in their 50s and 60s often do not display any of these conditions, but many in their 70s and 80s do. If you wait too long to obtain your policy, you might be no longer insurable. Make sure you obtain your policy *before* you need it.

Reason #1: It's Cheaper When You're Younger

Thus, the 50-year-old pays 45% less in total payments over his lifetime than the 75-year-old and is protected for 35 years instead of just 10. The insurance industry is sending you a clear message: Buy this policy when you're young, because you'll save a lot of money in the long run.

Reason #2: You're More Able to Qualify

And you're more likely to qualify for it, too — and that's the second reason you need to protect yourself at younger ages. On the application form, you'll be presented with a list of medical conditions. If you have any of them, you will be declined. But at age 50, when you're unlikely to have symptoms, you are better able to get the coverage.

Thus, you need to buy a policy when you're young enough to afford it and healthy enough to qualify.

Eight Features to Look for in a Long-Term Care Policy

Feature #1: $130 Per Day in Coverage

This figure approximates the current cost of nursing homes. You can obtain more or less coverage, with corresponding changes in cost. Remember: Many people do not need a policy covering 100% of the cost of care because of other income sources. Depending on your situation, you might be fine choosing reduced benefits in exchange for a more affordable premium.

Feature #2: At Least Three Years of Coverage

Five or six years of coverage is better. Shorter benefit periods are available, but if you plan to use the strategy of giving away your assets, you need at least 36 months and, since you probably won't start asset-shifting right away, an extra 12 to 36 months of coverage will be needed.

Most people don't need lifetime benefits. Not only is the cost exorbitant, but less than 2% of residents stay in a nursing home more than five years. Thus, the odds are small that you'll use benefits beyond five years.

Feature #3: A 100-Day Waiting Period

Delaying the start of benefits is an excellent way to reduce the premium, but this means you "self-insure" for the first 100 days, which could cost you about $10,000. Make sure you have enough in cash reserves to afford this outlay (see Chapter 6).

Feature #4: Inflation Protection

Because the cost of care will increase over time, you need to make sure that the benefit amount you buy today maintains its purchasing power in the future. Inflation protection is a must for those under 65, strongly suggested for those between 65 and 70, and optional for those over 70.

Feature #5: No Prior Hospitalization Required

Many illnesses afflicting the elderly, such as Alzheimer's, never place you in a hospital, so it makes sense that your LTC policy doesn't require such a stay. Avoid policies that require prior hospitalization.

Feature #6: Coverage Not Limited to Skilled Nursing Homes

Since less than 1% of all nursing home residents require skilled care, your policy should pay regardless of the type of facility you enter.

Feature #7: Waiver of Premium Included

This feature allows you to stop paying premiums once you've received benefits for 90 days.

Feature #8: Home Health Care

When it comes to nursing homes, people wait as long as possible to go, and they return home as quickly as they can. This crucial feature pays for adult day care or for home visits by a nurse or home health aide to assist you with medication, dressing, bathing, and preparing meals. Make sure the benefit you receive for home health care is the same as you'd get for care in a facility. Many policies either do not pay at all for home care, or they pay only 50% of the regular benefit.

As with disability insurance, never buy LTC coverage based on cost, because the cheaper the policy, the less likely it will meet your needs.

> **We find that many adult children buy these policies for their parents, because the kids would rather spend $4,000 on a policy now than $50,000 on mom's care later. That's smart planning.**

Chapter 68 - Life Insurance

When it comes to the subject of life insurance, I'm willing to bet that

> ...you don't *understand it...*

> ...you don't *like it...*

> ...but you *bought it anyway.*

That doesn't make sense, does it? Can you imagine any other product that millions of people buy but which so few understand?

It is also noteworthy that the only source of information for most consumers is the agent who sells you the policy. That's hardly the proper environment for a proper education. Therefore, this chapter is devoted to ending your confusion about life insurance. Hold your applause, because it's not that complex a subject — it's just that the insurance industry wants you to think it is.

Consider, for example, the following list:

- Mortgage Insurance
- Credit Life Insurance
- Accidental Death Insurance
- Stock Redemption Policies
- Key Man Coverage
- Second-to-Die Coverage
- First-to-Die Insurance
- Cross-Purchase Policies
- Split-Dollar Policies
- Reverse Split-Dollar Policies

These policies do not represent different types of insurance, but rather different uses of plain ol' life insurance. But in many cases, you could be hard pressed to realize it.

The Basic Elements of a Life Insurance Policy

Actually, life insurance is quite simple. Like all insurance policies, life insurance is a contract between you and the insurance company. You promise to pay a certain amount of money over a certain period of time and, provided you do so, the insurance company promises to pay a death claim.

Steve, a non-smoking male age 35 in good health, buys a $250,000 policy to make sure his young son will be able to afford college even if Steve dies before he has a chance to save enough money.

In this example:

- The *owner* of the policy is Steve, and as owner he is responsible for paying for it. The money Steve pays is called the *premium*.

- Steve is the *insured*, too, meaning that when he dies, the insurance company has to pay...

- ...the *death benefit* (also called the *face amount*) which in this case is $250,000, and the insurer must pay this money to...

- ...the *beneficiary* of the policy, whom Steve (as the policy owner) chooses.

Despite all the marketing glitz, there are only two kinds of life insurance contracts: temporary and permanent. Let's examine them one at a time.

"Whoever created the term 'life insurance' had to be the sales genius of all time."
—**Robert Half**

Term Insurance

Temporary insurance, more commonly known as *term*, has two main features: the amount of the death benefit and the price of the policy. The contract is quite simple: When you die, the insurance company pays.

Term insurance gets its name from the fact that it covers you for a specific term, or *period of time.*

Auto insurance is another type of term insurance: When you buy auto insurance, you're betting you're going to have a car accident within one year. Term life insurance works the same way: You're betting you're going to die, and the insurer is betting you won't. If you don't die, you must buy the insurance again — and you must do this every year until... well, until you win the bet!

The Three Kinds of Term Insurance

You can choose from three kinds of term insurance:

- **Annual renewable term (ART).** The cost goes up each year because, as you get older, you become more likely to die. This type of policy costs little when you're young and is very expensive when you're old.

- **Level term** locks in the cost for a period of 5, 10, 15, or 20 years. At the end of each period, the cost increases dramatically. It stays at this new level until the end of the next period, when it increases again. Over the long run, level term is less expensive than ART.

- **Decreasing term** is the opposite of ART: Instead of increasing the cost each year to adjust for the increased likelihood that you'll die, decreasing term keeps the cost the same but does so by lowering the death benefit.

BABY BLUES KIRKMAN & SCOTT

Reprinted with special permission of King Features Syndicate.

One of the Biggest Rip-offs in the Insurance Industry

The most common form of decreasing term sold today is so-called "mortgage life" and it's one of the biggest rip-offs in the industry.

Mortgage life is sold primarily to new homeowners. The pitch goes like this: Kevin and Harriet are thrilled with their new home, and they really stretched to buy it. Since Harriet stays home with the kids, the family depends on Kevin's income. If Kevin dies, Harriet and the kids could lose the house.

Mortgage insurance to the rescue! (Or so claims a pesky insurance salesman.) For one low annual premium that will never increase, Kevin can buy a policy *with a death benefit equal to the outstanding mortgage balance on his house*. Thus, if Kevin dies, Harriet will own the home outright.

That's a nice idea, but it's completely smoke and mirrors, because there's no such thing as "mortgage" insurance. After all, Kevin's not insuring his *mortgage*; he's insuring his *life*. But by calling it "mortgage" insurance, companies fool you into thinking the policy is something other than what it is, and they slap a huge price on it — as much as 300% or 400% more than what they would have charged if they just called it what it really is: life insurance.

If that weren't bad enough, mortgage policies have two other problems:

- As Kevin pays off the mortgage, the mortgage balance goes down, and with it the amount of insurance, even though the cost of living goes up.

- If Kevin dies, the insurance company writes a check directly to the mortgage lender. Harriet will never see the money, even though she might need it for other, more pressing reasons (such as paying for college — or just buying food). Who says she'll want to pay off the mortgage, anyway, just because Kevin dies? (See Chapter 59.)

If you're worried that your spouse might lose the house if you die, a better idea is to buy life insurance *sold* as life insurance. The policy will be much less expensive and, since the death benefit will be paid directly to Harriet, she'll be able to choose for herself how the money should be used.

Permanent Insurance

The other type of insurance is permanent, and there are three varia-tions, just as there are three variations of term life. The original type of permanent insurance is known as *whole life* because it covers you for your "whole life."[40] There are also *universal life* and *variable life* policies, and we'll discuss them all in detail for you.

First, let's return to Steve to see how permanent life insurance works.

Steve thinks about buying a term policy for a cost of about $300 a year.

Term life is cheap, because Steve's age and health suggest that he's unlikely to die within the next year. As he gets older, of course, his chances of dying increase, and the policy's cost increases as well. By the time Steve is 70 years old, the policy could cost $5,000 or more per year.

> That's the problem with term insurance: 25% of all life policies sold in the U.S. are term policies, yet less than 5% ever pay a claim. Why? Because young people buy them — and relatively few people die when they're young. Thus, young people pay until they can't afford it anymore. Then they cancel the policy just as they reach an age when they are most likely to need it.
>
> This is why the insurance industry loves to sell term life insur-ance. They know the premiums they collect are almost entirely free money, since policyholders will cancel the policies before they die — meaning the insurer will never have to pay a claim.

This problem was solved by the introduction of whole life insurance.

"Instead of insuring you for one year," the industry tells Steve, "How about if we insure you for your whole life — for the fixed price of $3,000 per year, guaranteed never to rise."

The insurance company is willing to give Steve a policy for his whole life (instead of just one year) but they want him to pay $3,000 per year for the policy. Why are they charging Steve $3,000 for the policy when the term cost is only $300? Because they know that in future

---

[40]Real creative, these insurance people, huh? Like I said, this stuff isn't very complicated.

THE COST OF COVERAGE

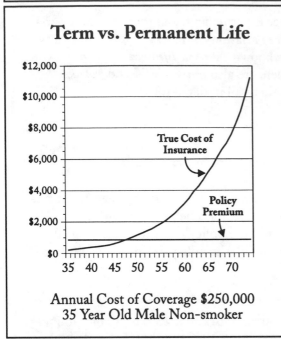

Term vs. Permanent Life

True Cost of Insurance

Policy Premium

Annual Cost of Coverage $250,000
35 Year Old Male Non-smoker

FIGURE 10-7

years, $3,000 won't be enough. Thus, like the squirrel storing acorns for the coming winter, they place the excess ($2,700 in the first year alone), into a side fund (called the *accumulation account*) where it will earn interest.

As Figure 10-7 shows, Steve's premium payments are higher than the actual cost for about 12 years, after which they become too little. At that time, the insurance company takes money out of the accumulation account to make up the shortfall between Steve's payment and the policy's actual cost.

Therefore, a whole life policy has three features: the same two as term (the death benefit and the cost of coverage) plus the *cash value build-up* of the accumulation account.

This third feature is critical, for the more your accumulation account grows, the less you must pay in premiums. Indeed, the cash value is responsible for all the smoke and mirrors found in life insurance policies. Here's the story of how it all began.

Whole Life

In permanent life's original form, called "whole life," *everything* is guaranteed: the cost of the policy, the death benefit, the future cash value, *and* the interest rate that the policy earns in order to achieve that cash value.

If you were the insurance company, would you make these guarantees conservative or aggressive? Conservative, of course, because you must deliver what you promise. And so it is with whole life: You can be confident that a whole life policy will do what the agent tells you it will do.

The problem, though, is that this conservative structure produces an expensive product. Since the carrier must guarantee the rate of return on the policy, it must set a low rate (and whole life policies do just that: The guaranteed rate is usually 4% to 5%). Meanwhile, other players in the financial world, such as mutual funds, can generate much higher returns because they're not making their customers any promises.

Buy Term and Invest the Rest?

This led to the "buy term and invest the rest" school of financial planning. This strategy holds that Steve is nuts to pay $3,000 for a policy that costs $300, because the carrier credits the $2,700 excess with such a low rate of interest. Therefore, it is argued, Steve should buy term insurance for $300 and invest the other $2,700 into mutual funds. In future years, he'd be able to use profits from the mutual fund to pay for the increased premiums of the term policy.

This is all very logical (assuming you have the discipline to fully execute the strategy), and it has caused thousands of people to cancel their whole life polices — to the joy of the mutual fund industry and the consternation of the insurance industry.

To counter the competition, insurers responded in 1977 with the second form of permanent insurance: *universal life*.

Universal Life

Universal life offers Steve a guaranteed interest rate similar to that of a whole life policy, but if the carrier earns more interest, it will credit Steve with the higher rate. Thus, if the carrier earns 9%, Steve will get 9%, but if the carrier earns 2% or even loses money, Steve is still guaranteed to get 4% (the policy minimum).

What's the point of all this? Well, by assuming that they'll earn a higher return than the 4% guarantee — say, 7.5% — the carrier can assume its future cash value will be much higher, too. Since the carrier would be amassing more money in the accumulation account, it would need to collect less from Steve. Therefore, the carrier charges Steve much less than $3,000 — $1,700 in fact — and this makes the policy much more competitive in the marketplace.

One Problem with Universal Life

Universal life has proved to be a very popular product. However, you need to be aware of one significant potential problem: The interest rate assumption used by the carrier might be wrong and, if so, the policy will not perform as planned. If the carrier fails to earn that return, Steve will find that his premiums will increase. Worse, he could be unable to pay the higher cost. If that were to happen, the policy would be canceled.

This is exactly what happened to thousands of people who bought universal life policies in the late 1970s and early 1980s. Back then, interest rates were 15%. Thus, carriers assumed they would earn 15% for the next 40 years. Of course, rates since then have been much lower, and carriers are no longer earning anywhere near those high levels.

As a result, insurance companies have cut their rates like everyone else. Thus, the assumptions they once used have become invalid — meaning that since the carriers are not earning 15%, their policies are not accumulating as much cash as projected. That means policyholders must make up the difference — in the form of higher premiums. Thus, many policyholders are being told that their premiums are increasing — even though they bought "permanent" insurance to avoid that problem. And they have little choice, for if they don't pay the higher premiums, they'll lose their coverage.

This can be a big problem, but you can avoid it. How? Simply by knowing what you're buying. If you understand universal life and recognize the possibility that future premiums might increase, there's no problem. After all, your alternative is to by whole life and pay those higher premiums today. So, many people conclude that it's better to choose universal life (and acknowledge the possibility that premiums might rise) instead of paying those higher costs now as whole life would demand. Others argue that whole life is better because you enjoy the confidence of knowing that your premiums never will increase.

So which is best? It depends.[41]

---

[41]This is getting tiresome.

If you want to be certain that your premium will never rise, choose whole life.

If you want to pay less now, choose universal life, and be aware that you may have to pay a higher amount later if current assumptions about future interest rates prove to be wrong.

Variable Life

The third type of permanent policy is *variable life*. This type of policy allows you to invest your excess premiums into mutual funds. The good news is that your accumulation account may grow more quickly than in either whole life or universal life. The bad news is that it might not grow at all, for in a variable life policy, *there are no guarantees.* If the mutual fund goes down in value, so does your accumulation account. In fact, if you choose a stock fund and the stock market crashes, your policy might be canceled for lack of funds.

For this reason, I am not a fan of variable life policies, but I must emphasize this is a personal bias. Put me in a room with other qualified advisors and we'll argue all day. In my opinion, the increased profit potential is not enough of a reason to buy it. After all, the policy's primary purpose is to protect against a financial loss, not to generate profits. If you seek profits, why not buy a mutual fund or variable annuity and skip the insurance altogether? It's a question no variable life proponent has ever answered to my satisfaction.

How to Comparison Shop for Permanent Life Insurance

As mentioned, each of the permanent life policies have three variables: the death benefit, the premium, and the assumed interest rate. Thus, when comparing one permanent life proposal to another, make sure two of the three variables are the same. This allows you to solve for the third: Whichever has the best answer (i.e., the highest death benefit, the lowest premium, or the most cash value as projected in the 20th, 30th, or 40th year) is the best buy.

> There is a fourth variable, but neither you nor your agent can manipulate it. It's the policy's efficiency, which determines how much of your premium will earn interest. (All premiums first pay the mortality charges, underwriting expenses, and other costs of the policy; what's left then earns interest in the cash value account.)
>
> For example, say carrier ABC credits the cash value with 5% interest and carrier DEF credits 6%. You'd think DEF would produce a higher cash value in 20 years, but that's not necessarily true. If DEF's expenses are higher than ABC's, DEF's cash value in the 20th year could be lower than ABC's — even though DEF offered the higher rate.
>
> This often happens, and is an another example of the smoke and mirrors used by the insurance industry.

For Which Variable Should You Search?

It depends[42] — on whichever one is most important to you. Some people want the most death benefit they can afford. Others want to keep their premiums within a certain budget, while still others want to build up a certain amount of cash value by a certain date in the future.

Regardless of which variable you shop for, it is vital that the assumed interest rates in each proposal be identical — and realistic. If one carrier currently is paying 5% and another 5.5%, have both produce proposals showing identical interest rates. And make sure the rate they use is reasonable. The rate should be similar to current CD rates.

> An agent can use any figure he or she chooses in order to make the policy look as good as they want.
>
> By jacking up the assumed interest rate, a clever (deceptive) agent can knock hundreds of dollars off the annual cost shown on a policy proposal. An unethical agent once gave a client of mine a proposal featuring a 14% interest rate assumption — even though the carrier was then paying 6%. Not only would the carrier be unable to sustain a 14% annual rate over 20 years, it wasn't even doing it at the time!
>
> Remember: To help them close the sale, agents can change the variables to make an insurance proposal look *any way* they want. In fact, this is one of the causes of the insurance industry's bad reputation.

[42]Aaaarrrrrrrgh.

SAMPLE PERMANENT LIFE PROPOSAL

End of Year	Age	Annual Premium	Total Paid	Cash-In Value	Death Benefit
1	36	$1,698	$1,698	$0	$250,000
2	37	$1,698	$3,396	$0	$250,000
3	38	$1,698	$5,094	$45	$250,000
4	39	$1,698	$6,792	$1,680	$250,000
5	40	$1,698	$8,490	$3,404	$250,000
6	41	$1,698	$10,188	$5,236	$250,000
7	42	$1,698	$11,886	$7,164	$250,000
8	43	$1,698	$13,584	$9,191	$250,000
9	44	$1,698	$15,282	$12,681	$250,000
10	45	$1,698	$16,980	$18,638	$250,000
11	46	$1,698	$18,678	$21,014	$250,000
12	47	$1,698	$20,376	$23,506	$250,000
13	48	$1,698	$22,074	$26,124	$250,000
14	49	$1,698	$23,772	$28,871	$250,000
15	50	$1,698	$25,470	$35,116	$250,000
16	51	$1,698	$27,168	$38,427	$250,000
17	52	$1,698	$28,866	$41,900	$250,000
18	53	$1,698	$30,564	$45,537	$250,000
19	54	$1,698	$32,262	$49,355	$250,000
20	55	$1,698	$33,960	$58,812	$250,000
21	56	$1,698	$35,658	$63,453	$250,000
22	57	$1,698	$37,356	$67,394	$250,000
23	58	$1,698	$39,054	$73,651	$250,000
24	59	$1,698	$40,752	$79,306	$250,000
25	60	$1,698	$42,450	$92,438	$250,000

FIGURE 10-8

When 7.5% is not 7.5%

Figure 10-8 shows a $250,000 universal life insurance proposal for Steve. The cost is $1,698 per year.

In 25 years, according to this proposal, Steve will have paid a total of $42,450 in premiums, yet the cash value will be $92,438! Thus, an insurance agent would say that if Steve is alive in 25 years, he could cancel the policy and get back twice as much as he paid. Steve can double his money — and have free insurance for 25 years!

Wow! This is great! (Or, at least, that's how the agent wants you to feel.) There's only one problem: The agent has lied. To produce this proposal, the agent told Steve the policy's assumed rate of return on the cash value is 7.5%. That's not a problem *per se*. After all, that was comparable to long-term U.S. Treasury rates in effect at the time the proposal was produced, so it would be fair to assume the carrier could earn such a return.

No, the problem is much more insidious than that.

If you invested $1,698 per year (the annual cost of the policy) for 25 years at an average annual return of 7.5%, you would have $124,131. But the proposal says the cash value would be worth only $92,438. What happened to the other $31,693?

Obviously, the policy is not really paying 7.5% (compounded monthly) on your premium payment of $1,698. You see, the insurance company first subtracts commissions, then mortality charges, administrative expenses, policy fees, underwriting costs, and so on, and what's left *then* earns 7.5%. The effective return, in fact, is really just 5.95%.

Don't be too hard on Steve's agent. I am an approved continuing education instructor for insurance, and I can tell you that many agents are unaware that the assumed rate shown on their company's proposals do not reflect the true effective rate paid by the policy.

> *"What if everything is an illusion and nothing exists? In that case, I definitely overpaid for my carpet."*
>
> —**Woody Allen**

Insurance is for Insurance's Sake (Duh!)

This is why you must never buy insurance for *investment* purposes. Buy insurance for *insurance* purposes.

Never buy insurance with the goal of creating a gain. Buy it only to protect against a loss. In fact, it is illegal to make a profit from insurance, and those who try to do so are guilty of insurance fraud.

> **If that's true, you might be wondering how Steve can buy a $250,000 life policy. Won't his family "profit" from his death?**
>
> **Not at all. That $250,000 death benefit merely compensates the family for lost wages if Steve dies. If Steve wanted his family to truly profit, he'd buy a $10 million policy. Yet, no carrier would let him because there is no "insurable need," meaning Steve's death would not produce a loss to anyone of $10 million.**
>
> **So why doesn't Steve just buy ten $1 million policies from ten different carriers? He can't do that, either, because each carrier would ask how much coverage he has in force or *applied for* with other carriers. If he lies in order to get the coverage, well, that's insurance fraud.**

This is not necessarily intended to imply that you should buy term and invest the rest, nor that you should buy whole life instead of variable life.

I am simply saying that when buying a permanent policy (of whatever flavor), pay only enough in premiums to allow the cash value to grow to an amount *sufficient to keep the policy in force*. Do not try to accumulate huge sums of cash value for the simple reason that *you're never going to see the money*.

The reason? Either you die, or you don't.

- **Say Steve were to die in the 25th year.** If so, the death benefit to his heirs would be $250,000 — not $250,000 + $92,438 = $342,438. The fact that the policy shows $92,438 in cash value is meaningless to Steve's beneficiaries.

- **Say Steve doesn't die.** Instead, if he borrows from the $92,438 as his agent said he could, the annual cost of the loan (at 8% interest) would be more than $7,000 — and that's in addition to the cost of the policy premium. And guess how much the death benefit will be when Steve does die? It will be $157,562 — $250,000 minus the $92,438 Steve took. At that point, Steve will be required to pay interest on the money he "borrowed" from his policy.

In other words, Steve won't "earn" $92,438 — he'd just be stealing it from his heirs! Taking the money negates the very reason he bought the policy in the first place: to protect his family.

Heads, the insurance company wins. Tails, Steve loses. Do not play with a two-headed coin, and do not allow your insurance policy to build up a large cash value.

Which Type of Insurance is Best?

Like so many other areas of personal finance, the type of insurance you should buy depends[43] on your circumstances. Each offers strengths and weaknesses, as Figure 10-9 shows.

Generally, the longer you plan to keep your policy, the better off you will be with a permanent policy. The cross-over point is between 8 and 12 years, depending[44] on your age and health. If you plan to keep the policy for eight years or less, term has the lowest overall cost, but if you keep the policy longer than 12 years, permanent will be cheaper in the long run. This is because you can cancel the policy and get a refund of the cash value that has accumulated, which ought to compensate you for the extra premiums you paid. Between eight and 12 years, which policy is best must be determined on a case-by-case basis.

---

[43]I'm gonna quit highlighting this.
[44]Seriously.

COMPARING TYPES OF INSURANCE

	Term Insurance	Whole Life	Universal Life	Variable Universal Life
Low Initial Cost	✓			
Permanent Protection		✓	✓	✓
Guaranteed Premiums		✓		
Current Returns			✓	✓
Premium Flexibility			✓	✓
Choice of Investments				✓

FIGURE 10-9

For most of us, though, it's not a question of one or the other, for most people have more than one need for insurance. Steve, for example, needs to be sure his son can afford college, but he also must be sure his wife doesn't lose their home. One need will disappear soon, the other may not. Thus, some of Steve's insurance needs are temporary while others are more permanent. For this reason, many clients need two policies, one temporary and one permanent.

The One Group of People Who Never Need Insurance

Nineteen percent of all life insurance policies sold in this country insure children under the age of 12. What an incredible waste of money.

About half the time our firm advises clients to cancel the life insurance they already have because they don't need it anymore. If the kids are out of college, if the house is paid for, and if you're retired, your death may no longer present the financial loss to others as it once did. If so, you can cancel your policies, save yourself some money, and skip the rest of this chapter.

507

We all love our children dearly and no loss could match the tragedy of the loss of a child. But, such a loss would not be *financial*, which of course is the reason for buying insurance. If you are concerned about funeral costs, add a $10,000 child rider to your own policy. The cost will be less than $25.

What bugs me are the mail and phone calls from agents that new parents start receiving within weeks of their baby's birth. Often, these pitches warn mommy and daddy that they need to start saving for the baby's future. Another pitch says parents need to buy insurance "while your child is healthy enough to qualify for the coverage."

One example has the parents buy a $75,000 policy for just $26 a month. The pitch says that when the child reaches age 21, the child can cash in the policy. Thus, you get $5,410 at age 21 — plus free insurance for 21 years!

Sounds great — until you realize that if you instead had invested that $26 per month over 21 years into a mutual fund earning 10% per year for 21 years, you would have $22,138 — far more than what the policy would have produced!

If an agent tells you to buy a child policy, ask yourself whether the agent is thinking about the benefits to your child — *or his!*

Six Problems With the Life Insurance You Already Own

First, your coverage has been eroded by inflation. If you bought a policy 20 years ago, your death benefit is a fraction of what you need today. Maybe you need more.

Second, you have too much insurance. Although the policy you bought 20 years ago is not worth very much, it nonetheless could be too much because the reason you bought the policy may no longer exist.

Third, you have the wrong kind of coverage. If you have only group insurance, your coverage is dependent on your job. This lack of portability poses the same problems we discussed earlier regarding disability insurance (Chapter 66).

Fourth, you're paying too much for the coverage you do have.
If you bought your policy before 1980, the insurer priced it as
though you were going to die in your 60s, since that's what the
actuarial tables back then said would happen. Today's mortality
charts, of course, say you'll live well into your 80s and insurers have
lowered the cost of coverage accordingly. So, swapping your current
policies for new ones could save you lots of money, even though
you're older now.

Fifth, your policy's assumptions are invalid. If you bought your
policy in the '70s or early '80s, the interest rate assumptions may
be wrong and, if so, your policy is not accumulating as much cash
value as you think. At best, your premiums may rise. At worst, the
policy may be canceled. Either would be unpleasant.

And sixth, you have too many policies. Buying one $200,000
policy costs less than two $100,000 policies. Why? Because every
policy contains flat expenses, such as policy fees, that are unrelated
to the amount of coverage. If you buy two policies instead of one,
you pay these costs twice instead of once. Therefore, explore
swapping your many policies for newer, fewer ones. You could
save hundreds every year.

One Dumb Feature You Need to Avoid

In an effort to increase your premium — and therefore the commission
— your agent might suggest you add a rider to your policy called an
accidental death benefit, sometimes called "double indemnity."

Under this rider, your heirs receive additional money if your death is
caused by an accident. This is absurd, because death is death: Dying
from a bus accident instead of cancer is not going to change your
family's need. Therefore, get the coverage you need and skip this
rider. Ditto for "cancer life" and similar policies which pay only if
you die from certain causes, such as cancer or an airplane crash.
Remember: Life insurance should cover death itself, not merely
certain causes of death.

A woman once told me that her husband's company provided five
times his salary if he died in an air crash while on business travel. "If
he dies of a heart attack," she joked, "I'm driving him to the airport!"

Chapter 69 - How to Protect Yourself From ~~Lawyers~~ Lawsuits

In a world where you can sue and win for being served coffee that is too hot, you need to protect your money.

You can, too, with an umbrella liability insurance policy. These policies provide a minimum of $1 million in coverage for nearly anything that might happen. Merely having a homeowner's or auto policy isn't enough, for too many things can happen that are unrelated to your home or car. Besides, most homeowner's policies cover you for only $100,000 to $300,000, and auto liability insurance often provides just $50,000. Those figures are peanuts in a liability suit.

What if you bump into an elderly woman with your grocery cart, causing her to fall and break her hip, or if your foot slips off the brake causing you to hit the car in front of you, which causes that car to hit a pedestrian?

Remember: If a claim against you exceeds your insurance limit, you're on your own for the rest. Don't risk it. Get an umbrella liability insurance policy instead. They are very affordable, typically costing under $250 per year. But because insurers are providing a lot of coverage at little cost, getting a policy is not always easy. Your premium — and whether or not you qualify — is based on where you live, the cars you own, whether your household has drivers under age 26, your driving record, prior claims, and other factors.

Many carriers will sell you an umbrella policy only if you buy your homeowner's and auto coverage from them as well. A few carriers will provide a stand-alone umbrella policy, but only if you maintain "minimum" coverage on your primary policies. The best course is to talk with the agent who sold you a homeowner's policy.

Chapter 70 - Should You Buy from an Insurance Agent or Insurance Broker?

When buying any form of insurance, should you work with an insurance agent or broker? To understand the answer, first understand the difference.

Captive agents are employees of an insurance company. As such, they represent the carrier exclusively, just as a Ford dealer sells Fords exclusively: No matter how good a Chevy is, no Ford salesman will sell you a one. Some of the biggest insurance companies are captive agencies.

I have seen agents claim to be brokers in an effort to dissuade their clients from talking to the competition. If you are unsure, ask your broker to name the carriers he or she works with, and if you doubt his or her veracity, ask to see their licenses. In most states, agents must have one license for each carrier they represent. Another good test is to ask for a business card. If it contains the name or logo of a specific insurance company, that's who they represent. Period.

Independent agents, or *brokers*, represent many carriers — often dozens. Thus, independent agents are free to shop with many carriers to find the one that offers the best policy at the best price for the client. Brokers, therefore, do the shopping for their clients, alleviating the need for their clients to shop on their own.

Therefore, you should either work with one broker, or with *several* agents, since agents will give you policies from only one carrier each.

Chapter 71 - How Safe is Your Carrier?

Although consumers have always had questions about their policies, few ever questioned the stability of their insurance company.

Until recently, that is.

With the collapse of Baldwin United, Executive Life of California, Mutual Benefit of New Jersey and Confederation Life, among others, consumers rightfully are concerned that their insurer might go broke — taking much-needed insurance protection with them. An unfortunate example of how **The Rules of Money Have Changed,** consumers must be certain that their carrier is financially healthy, for it must be in business when you file a claim decades from now.

Five major ratings companies evaluate carriers, and their rating systems are shown in Figure 10-10.

The easiest way to learn the rating and strength of a carrier is to ask your agent (if she won't show you documentation, find another who will).

Keep in mind that high ratings do not guarantee that a company is in good health: Executive Life was top-rated only weeks before it went broke.

Also, don't be worried if an agent recommends a carrier you've never heard of. There are 4,000 life insurance companies in the United States, and the vast majority don't sponsor golf tournaments or half-time shows on television.

RATING SERVICES

Description	A.M. Best	S&P/ D&P	Moody's	Weiss
Superior Negligible Risk	A++ A+	AAA	Aaa	A+
Excellent Small, Slightly Variable Risk	A A-	AA+ AA AA-	Aa1 Aa2 Aa3	A A- B+
Very Good	B++ B+			
Good High Claims-Paying Ability For Now	B B-	A+ A A-	A1 A2 A3	B B- C+
Adequate Less Protection Against Risk	C++ C+	BBB+ BBB BBB-	Baa1 Baa2 Baa3	C C- D+
Below Average Higher Risk Factor	C C-	BB+ BB BB-	Ba1 Ba2 Ba3	D D- E+
Financially Weak High Risk Factor	D	B+ B B-	B1 B2 B3	E E-
Not-Viable (or about to be)		CCC CC D	Caa Ca C	F
State Supervision	E			
Liquidation	F			

FIGURE 10-10

Part XI
Estate Planning

Part XI — Estate Planning

Overview - Managing and Distributing Wealth

Thus far, you've learned how to protect, accumulate, and manage wealth. Now you're going to learn the final phase of money management: how to distribute wealth.

To preserve your wealth for your heirs, we're going to try to make you broke — because the more money you have when you die, the more the IRS will collect. If you're like most people, you're probably intimidated by the subject of estate planning. No doubt you've heard it's complex. But, like insurance, the basic concepts are quite simple.

To begin, please understand that everyone — including you — has to deal with estate planning for the simple reason that everybody has an estate, not just rich people. That often comes as a surprise: When I once asked a new client about the size of his estate, he replied, "I don't have an estate. I just have a house and some savings." He thought estates were the exclusive domain of the Kennedys and Rockefellers, but the truth is that everyone has an estate.

Your estate is simply the total value of everything you own minus debts. And the goal of estate planning simply is to transfer your assets to your heirs after your death, or for you to receive assets from a deceased relative. This part will show you how to do it.

Chapter 72 - Your Will

When a person dies, their assets are given to their heirs. This raises a question: Who gets what?

That's why you need a will. Through it, you leave instructions for the disposition of your assets. Typically, wills tell us:

- Whether to pay off mortgages and auto loans;

- What debts are to be eliminated;

- What debts are not to be paid off;

- What assets are to be sold, such as real estate or businesses;

- To whom remaining assets are to be given, including family heirlooms and items of sentimental value as well as financial assets;

- When assets are to be distributed (immediately, at some specified time in the future, or upon satisfaction of certain conditions);

- Who is to be "legal guardian" and assume responsibility for raising minor children;

- Who is to ensure that all these instructions are implemented correctly (called the "executor" or "personal representative"); and

- Any other instructions you wish to leave.

Your Will or Theirs?

Do you have a will? If you answered, "No," think again, because the truth is that *everybody has a will.*

If you die without having written your own, your estate will use a standard one written by your state government. It's called *dying intestate* and, if you rely on it, you give up the opportunity to disburse your assets as you wish. Odds are, in fact, you won't like what the state will do with your assets. For example, in some states, if you have children from a prior marriage, dying intestate means your spouse gets only one-third of your assets, the kids get two-thirds. In other states, intestacy means assets might pass to parents, in-laws, brothers, sisters, even aunts, uncles, and cousins instead of the people you wish.

Furthermore, failing to write a will means you give up the right to name a guardian for your minor children. Do you really want a judge to make that decision for you?

> *"Money doesn't solve problems — it just creates new ones!"*
> — Ric Edelman

Nine Questions to Help You Choose a Guardian for Your Kids

The most common excuse offered by parents of young children for putting off writing a will isn't the thought of dying. No, what brings the process to an immediate halt is trying to decide who will raise the children.

Because of this question, many parents do the worst thing: nothing. And that means the decision, if it becomes necessary, will be made by a judge in probate court. Don't let that happen to you. Don't let a stranger decide who will raise your kids.

If you're stuck on how to choose a guardian, the following will help you:

With pen and paper, answer the following questions, providing as much detail as possible. If you are deciding as a couple, answer these questions separately and then compare your answers. Many of these questions will take some thought, so you might not be able to answer right away. That's okay. Answer what you can in the first sitting and set a deadline to finish the rest.

Question #1:   Who Are All the Candidates?

Listen to your gut instinct and answer the remaining questions with these people in mind.

Question #2: **Is it likely that the candidate(s) will live for many years?**

Remember, you are planning for the event that your kids have just lost their parents... losing your replacements can be twice as devastating. A lot of people want to name grandparents, but are your parents too old?

Question #3: **How is each candidate's health?**

Are they physically and mentally able to accept the responsibility? Do they have the energy? This is another caveat for grandparents. They may be great as weekend baby-sitters, but having your kids permanently is a very different notion. Are they up to it?

Question #4: **Do the candidates have kids of their own? If not, do they know how to raise children? If so, would adding yours to their household be too much for them to handle?**

Raising a family is expensive and hectic, particularly for two-income families. Your proposed guardians already may have a full plate. Conversely, if they don't have kids, are you confident they know how to raise children?

Question #5: **Do the candidates have time to raise your kids?**

Are they a two-career family or does one parent stay home? Is one or the other particularly important to you?

Question #6: **What are the candidate's views on education and religion?**

Do you insist upon home-schooling or private education? Do they share your religious beliefs? Will the candidates raise your children with the same values and cultural traditions as you would have provided?

Question #7:   Where do the candidates live?

Moving your kids to some far-away place after losing their parents can make a difficult transition even more difficult, for they will have lost not only their parents, but literally *everything* they are familiar with — school, friends, nearby relatives, favorite places and pastimes. You'll want to try to avoid this problem, but sometimes the best candidate doesn't live nearby. In such cases, perhaps the transition can be eased. For example, let them finish the school year where they are, if possible, or provide the money for them to visit friends for extended periods.

Question #8:   Are the candidates a young married couple?

If so, you might want to consider adding a statement about who gets your kids if they divorce. And if one of them dies, would you feel comfortable letting the survivor raise your kids?

Question #9:   Are the candidates financially secure?

While you shouldn't let wealth (or lack thereof) be the sole basis for choosing one candidate over another, you do want to know your kids will be in a financially stable and safe environment. While you probably want to leave all your money to your kids,[45] be realistic about the financial impact raising them will have on their guardians. Indeed, the guardians are sure to incur expenses associated with raising your kids, such as adding a room onto their house or buying a bigger car, let alone providing food each day, so you should make your assets available to help them. Otherwise, the guardian (or the guardian's spouse or children) could become frustrated. Thus, you must carefully balance several issues: You want your money used for the benefit and welfare of your kids and to have the assets available to help the guardian as needed, but at the same time you want to protect against the squandering of the assets by the guardians or others (maybe even your own kids!). A good estate planning attorney can help you achieve these goals.

---

[45]See the following section for important information about leaving money to minors.

As you consider these questions, feel free to change your mind. You also may find that you preferred certain people for some questions but not others. That's okay, too. This process is all about identifying the strengths and weaknesses of potential guardians. Often, the most appropriate person is the one who scored generally well, as opposed to one who scored great in some areas but terrible in others.

If you are deciding as a couple, only after you each reach a decision should the two of you compare notes. By having written down the *reasons* for your preferences beside each question (and not just the names), each of you can better understand the other, and perhaps his or her reasoning is more sound than yours.

Then: *Choose someone!* Pick a guardian you both can agree on, even if that means you each accept someone who is not necessarily your favorite — and please, after choosing, be sure to ask your choice to accept the nomination. Force him or her to sleep on it, and require that his or her partner (if any) consent.

Above all, remember: Failure to make a choice is itself a choice. Until you name someone, you are agreeing to let the probate court decide, where all the people you considered above (and possibly others) will fight it out with the judge acting as referee. It's a very difficult task for a judge, since he or she has never met you and will have no idea what you would want. That's why judges often select the first family member to show up at the courthouse!

If the thought of making a choice sends you into a panic, remember that you can always change your mind. Several of our clients change their minds every other year, as circumstances in their families change. If your parents seem the best option today, pick them. In a few years, when they've gotten older or become ill, you can change your selection. Or maybe today's choice marries someone you don't like, or suffers a setback of some kind. No problem. Just base your decision on the facts as they are today, and rest assured that as times change and people change, your mind can change as well.

Why Not to Leave Big Bucks to Little Kids

The most common estate planning mistake parents make is to name children under 18 as direct beneficiaries of IRAs or life insurance policies (usually as the secondary beneficiaries).

It seems to make sense to do so. After all, you bought the policy (or, your employer gave it to you) to protect your spouse and pay for your kids' future college costs, so it seems logical to name your spouse as the primary beneficiary and your kids as the secondary beneficiaries in the unlikely (and unthinkable) event that both of you die. Indeed, your life insurance agent (or benefits officer at work) didn't object, so what's the problem?

The problem is that your kids (if they're under 18) will not get the money, even though they are named in the policy as the secondary beneficiaries.

Instead, the money will go into the registry of the court, which will name a guardian of the money for the kids. Even if your will names a guardian for the kids, the *money* must get its own guardian.

> *"Money isn't everything, but it sure keeps the kids in touch."*
>
> —Anonymous

Why isn't the money covered by your will? Because IRAs and life insurance proceeds go directly to beneficiaries named in the policy, bypassing any instructions contained in a will. Although your will names a guardian for the kids (it better, or the court will decide that, too! — see the prior section), the IRA account or insurance policy control those assets.

Thus, by naming your minor children as beneficiaries, the IRA or insurance proceeds will be turned over to the court, which will appoint a financial guardian to manage the assets, and most distributions must be approved by the court. There is no assurance that the court will appoint as financial guardian the same person you named as the children's guardian in your will.

Chances are, after a year and thousands of dollars in legal fees, the life insurance money will be placed into a custodial bank account for the kids (until they turn 18, which typically is the latest age that a court may place money beyond the reach of a child). But once they're 18, the kids get the money — and they just might choose a sports car over college, despite your intentions.

What's the solution?

In your will, establish a children's trust and name it as the secondary beneficiary. You can even set up the children's trust in your own living trust (more on that later). That will avoid probate as well as court guardianship proceedings — and you get to determine at what age your kids are entitled to receive the money. (You may decide to withhold the funds from them until well beyond age 18.)

A second, simpler option is to designate as the insurance beneficiary a custodian under a Uniform Gifts to Minors Act account. The insurance money will go directly into the UGMA account, which will be managed for the benefit of your kids by the custodian you've named. This custodian can be the same person who's serving as the kids' guardian, and distributions can be made at any time for the kids' support and education.

If you name as your secondary beneficiary "my estate," that means the asset will be distributed in accordance with your will. That means, in turn, that you need to specifically address in your will how the IRA or insurance proceeds are to be handled. For example, you might state that the assets are to be held in trust until the children graduate from college.

Protecting your family through IRAs, company retirement accounts, and life insurance is a smart thing to do, but you need to make sure you handle them properly or your plans could be thwarted. So, don't name your kids as direct beneficiaries. That may be the easy thing to do, but it could prove very costly.

For more on IRAs and company retirement plans, see Chapters 61 and 62. For insurance, see Part X. For trusts continue with this part and for UGMAs, turn to Chapter 53.

Even Single People Must Write a Will

With no spouse or children, many single people think they don't need a will, but this is wrong. Why? Because even single people have debts, assets, and family members, and instructions still are needed.

Do you want your parents to receive your assets or would you rather split your assets among your siblings? What if you want to leave money for nieces or nephews for their college education? Without a will, your family won't know your intentions and, hence, your wishes will not be enacted.

Do You Have a Non-Married Partner?

Take the example of Joe and Susan, who have been living together for five years. They've accumulated some joint assets (furniture, cash, and a car) and some joint debt (a line of credit and a car loan), and they're living in a townhouse Joe bought the year before he met Susan. Then Joe has a car accident.

What Happens if Your Partner Dies

Say Joe died in the crash, and like many young people, he had no will. Consequently, his assets — including his savings, the townhouse, and his half of the property he owned with Susan — all pass to his parents. Susan receives nothing. Not only that, Susan is now homeless and dependent upon Joe's parents to help her pay off the loans and other bills she and Joe accumulated together.

Clearly, the law does not protect unmarried partners. Oral agreements and understandings are not recognized under state law: If you have an unmarried partner (whether you live together or not), the only way to protect each other is for you both to write wills naming the other as your heir so that when either one dies, the assets will pass to the surviving partner.

If you have no will, or if you do not specifically name your partner in your will, he or she likely will receive nothing upon your death. Assuming you have no children, whatever you own will go to your parents (if they are alive) or to your brothers and sisters (if your parents have pre-deceased you).

What Happens if Your Partner Lives

Let's assume Joe survives the accident, but is injured and hospitalized. What can Susan do to help manage his affairs, such as paying bills and authorizing medical treatment? Without two additional legal documents (a durable power of attorney and a health care power of attorney), not much. Susan does not have the rights of a spouse; she cannot access Joe's checking account or sign a release for surgery — even if she knows Joe's wishes. Joe's doctors won't discuss his condition with her, and Joe's family can even bar her from seeing him in the hospital! Her only alternative is to go to court to seek permission to act on his behalf, a time-consuming and costly proposition — and one likely to meet with opposition from Joe's family.

These problems can be avoided with durable powers. With a durable power of attorney, you name a person to act on your behalf should you become unable to manage your own financial affairs. The person you name as your "attorney-in-fact" can access your bank account to pay bills, sell securities to obtain cash for medical expenses, file your income tax return, and renew leases. A second durable power — the health care power of attorney — appoints someone (typically the person named in your durable power of attorney) to make health care decisions on your behalf, assuming you're unable to make them for yourself. The health care power of attorney also allows physicians to discuss your medical treatment with that person, even though they are not related or married to you.

If your partner is the person you most trust and to whom you would like your assets to go when you die, each of you needs to get wills and durable powers now to save each other problems in the future.

Being Married is Much Simpler, Right?

Most married people write a "simple will," leaving everything to their spouse, or to their children if their spouse dies first. Yet this strategy, simple in concept, could lead to unexpected problems for the simple reason that life isn't so simple.

A Simple Will Might Not Protect Your Children

Richard and Ashley have two children. Richard dies, leaving everything to Ashley. Ashley then marries Tom, a widower with three children of his own. Then Ashley dies, leaving everything to Tom. When Tom dies, he leaves everything to his three kids. The result: Richard's money goes to Tom's kids; Richard's kids get nothing. Got that?

This is an excellent example of the problems created by a simple will. A better solution is for Richard to leave his assets to a trust, not to Ashley. Under the law, a trust is the same as a person. It can own

> *"A man becomes a conservative at that moment in his life when he suddenly realizes he has something to conserve."*
>
> —Eric Jubler

assets, have debts and financial obligations, and so on. But a trust is a pretty dumb person, so it needs someone to tell it what it is supposed to do, and it needs someone to help it do these things.

For example, Richard can create a trust and give it all his assets upon his death. He can instruct the trust to give to Ashley all the money she needs, whenever she needs it. Or, he can place limits on how much or how often she is allowed to receive money. It's his trust, so he can set the rules any way he wants.[46] (Ain't America great?)

Since the trust doesn't get Richard's assets until he dies, someone other than Richard must be appointed to operate the trust (in conformance with Richard's rules). Who should Richard appoint as trustee?

In this case, his wife Ashley. After all, the money is for her benefit, so why force her to turn to a third person every time she needs money? The trust in this example is intended to protect Richard's kids in case Ashley dies, not to protect Ashley from herself, so naming Ashley as trustee is a fine idea.

> **If we were concerned about Ashley's ability to handle the money, we'd name someone else to serve as trustee or co-trustee. Richard could name another family member, a friend, even a lawyer, banker, or financial advisor.**

Thus, Ashley has access to the trust's assets during her lifetime — the same access, in fact, as though Richard had left it all to her directly. But Ashley doesn't "own" the assets, so in the event of her death, the money stays in the trust for the benefit of their kids; Ashley can't give the money to anyone else when she dies, and Tom can't make a claim on it. Thus, Richard has succeeded in protecting his kids without hurting Ashley. Since we don't know who will die first, Ashley would write a will with the same provisions in case she dies first and Richard remarries.

---

[46]Well, within certain limits, actually. This trust is called a QTIP Trust, for Qualified Terminal Income Property, and certain IRS rules must be followed. Talk with an estate attorney to learn the details.

A Simple Will Might Not Protect Heirs Who Cannot Handle Money

Do you *really* want to leave all your money to your 18-year-old? Images of sports cars and weeks at the beach flash through my mind, and I don't see a textbook anywhere.

Do you *really* want to leave your money to your relative who has a drug or alcohol problem, who gambles, who can't hold a job, or who is abusive? Or to that relative who never seems to have any money, is always bouncing checks, living paycheck to paycheck, and is constantly borrowing money from family and friends?

Do you *really* want to leave your money to these people?

> **This is why I don't like those will-making software programs. Although they can produce simple wills, you now have lots of reasons why a simple will might not be best for you.**
>
> **And these programs might not reflect laws in your state. The bottom line: You don't know if the program is producing a document that gives you everything you need. You can't ask it questions, and you can't hold it liable for its errors.**
>
> **Forget the software. See a lawyer. A small amount of money spent here may save your family thousands or hundreds of thousands of dollars and a lot of grief.**

Of course you do, because you love them. But you also realize that giving money to someone who can't handle it is like giving a drink to a drunk — you're certainly not doing anybody any favors.

This is perhaps the most fatal flaw of a simple will: Named heirs will receive your assets without restriction. And often, restrictions are exactly what are needed.

In such situations, a better idea may be to leave your money to a trust. You can set rules stating:

- **How soon.** You can delay availability of money for a certain period of time or until heirs reach certain ages; even spread out distributions over time.

- **How much.** You can grant heirs access to interest only, to a certain percentage of the trust's principal, to both, or to any combination.

- **How often.** You can state whether money is to be distributed whenever the person requests it, or you can release assets on a schedule, like an allowance.

- **How so.** You can require that your money be made available only for certain purposes, such as paying for college, or only under certain conditions, such as a medical need.

As you can see, "simple" wills are not always best, because life is not always so simple. Talk with an attorney who specializes in wills and trusts before you write your will.

A Terrible Place to Keep Secrets

Do you know what your parents plan to leave you? Have you told your kids what you plan to leave them?

Many parents never plan ahead. Even those who do rarely discuss the subject with their kids. Take the quiz below and see how you score.

If you're the son or daughter:

- Do you know where your parents keep their wills?

- Do you know who their executor is?

- Do you know how they plan to divide their assets?

- Do you know who they want to receive certain items of sentimental value?

- Have you told them how you feel and what you think about the above questions?

If you answered "no" to any question above, you need to have a serious conversation with your parents.

If you're the mother or father:

- Have you told *all* your kids where you keep your will?

- Have you told *all* your kids who your executor is?

- Have you told *all* your kids how you plan to divide your assets?

- Have you told *all* your kids who you want to receive certain items of sentimental value?

- Have you asked *all* your kids how they feel and what they think about the above questions?

If you answered "no" to any question above, you need to have a serious conversation with *all* your children.

A will is a terrible place to keep secrets, yet that's exactly what most Americans have done. The reasons don't matter. What does matter are the consequences of keeping secrets. Maybe you have not experienced any problems yet, but chances are you will.

I say this because my colleagues and I have seen problems arise in dozens of our clients' families. If you haven't talked with your family, you are setting the stage for them to suffer the same problems. Here are some we've seen:

Family Problem #1: The Child's Plan Thwarts the Parent's Plan

Mom, a widow, has $400,000 in assets. She's concerned about her health and anticipates that she'll eventually live in a nursing home. She fears that spending all her money on long-term care[47] will mean leaving nothing for her only daughter and grandson.

To avoid this problem, Mom hires an estate attorney and executes an elaborate estate plan designed to protect her assets from the costs of long-term care. Mom's plan effectively supports her desire to leave her assets to her daughter and, in turn, to her grandson.

Some years later, Mom, now 84, indeed enters a nursing home. Her assets have been protected: Her daughter now owns and controls all $400,000. Since Mom has no assets, her expenses are covered by Medicaid.

Next, the daughter, herself now 63, suffers a heart attack and dies. *She had not written a will of her own.*

Because the daughter dies intestate, the state orders that her son receive only one-quarter of her money. The rest is awarded to her surviving mother. Mom gets back $300,000 of the $400,000 she was trying to pass on. And because Mom now has the money, Medicaid claims it as reimbursement for the expenses it had paid on her behalf.

Thus, while Mom had created an estate plan to shelter her assets, her efforts were thwarted because her daughter did not create an estate plan of her own. If her daughter had written even a simple will — naming her son as sole heir — he would have gotten the entire $400,000. Instead, he got only a fraction.

---

[47]For a complete discussion of planning for Long Term Care, see Chapter 66.

When you write your will, make sure the people to whom you're giving your money understand what you're doing — and why. Make sure they understand what they have to do and make sure they do it. Otherwise, all your efforts might be for naught.

Family Problem #2: You Love Your Children Equally

Many parents are terrified of showing favoritism among their children.[48] To avoid that problem, many parents avoid writing a will at all. By saying nothing, you eliminate the risk of hurting your children. But as we've seen, this is a terrible solution.

The next most common tactic is to leave all your assets equally to all your children. You love them all equally (or, at least, you want them to think so), so let's just let them divide up everything equally. This is often the worst thing you can do.

When one of my clients died, she left everything to her son and daughter equally. Among her assets was a condo at the nearby shore, worth about $140,000. The son, who lived far away, wanted to sell it and split the money with his sister. The daughter, who lived an hour's drive from the condo, wanted to keep it, as her own family enjoyed using the condo on weekends each summer.

He wanted to sell. She didn't. He offered to buy her out. She refused. He is now suing her, and they haven't spoken to each other in three years. *Thanks, Mom.*

The correct strategy would have been for Mom to either (a) leave the condo to one child, and other (equivalent) assets to the other child, or (b) sell the condo and give equal amounts of the cash proceeds to each child for them to do with as they please.

Remember: The only asset that can be split evenly and easily is cash.

Family Problem #3: You Think Your Kids Love Each Other

My kids get along great, you say. They'd never fight with each other over something like an *inheritance*.

---

[48]Not that parents *don't* favor one child over another, just that they don't want their children to *find out about it.*

Oh, yeah?

I'll concede that your three children love each other and are great friends. But funny things happen over time. Such as marriage. Your three children will bring into the family three spouses. And just wait until in-law #1 finds out that, upon hearing news of the death, in-law #2 raced over to the house, rifled through the drawers, and is now in possession of Grandma's diamond ring or Granddad's coin collection.

"She always intended it for me!" someone all-too-often claims. If you don't expressly tell everyone your intent, you're setting the family up for a huge fight.

> **And I mean tell everyone — not just the person to whom you plan to give the item. If you make a private promise, no one else will believe them. Tell everyone, write it down in something called a "letter of intent," and attach it to your will.**

Rather than leaving property to everyone equally, have your will instruct that all your assets be liquidated, with the resulting proceeds divided equally. It's easy to split dollars, not so easy to split houses, televisions, cars, jewelry, and furniture.

This idea might be hard to accept because many people associate their sense of self with their possessions. Therefore, you might resist the idea of instructing that all your worldly goods be sold at auction. But if this attitude prevents you from establishing clear rules for the handling of your assets at death, you're setting the stage for a major fight among your heirs.

You're also being unrealistic. If you leave all your worldly possessions to your kids, guess what they're going to do with all your stuff? Sell it at auction, of course. Haven't you ever seen those signs along the highway? *"Estate Sale This Saturday."* That sign means someone died and their kids are having a big yard sale.

If you think your kids are going to keep all the stuff in your house, think again: Your kids already have a house of their own, and it's already full of their own stuff. So get over it and instruct that your assets be liquidated. That way, your kids won't have to fight about it.

Family Problem #4: You're Mistreating the Problem Child

If you're like most parents, you consider your children to be your pride and joy. Unless one of your kids is a lazy, no-good, rotten bum — the kind of person who would spend in a month whatever money you left, no matter how much you leave.

You might be tempted to cut this person out of your will, leaving your money to the rest of the family. Be careful if you plan to do that, for the strategy might not be as effective as you think.

> **Also, if you totally omit a family member from your will, they can challenge the will in court. Talk with a lawyer before you disinherit someone.**

You see, as a loving parent, you're always there for this child. Others of your family, in fact, have had to go without as you've devoted additional effort and attention to the problem child. Now, in your will, you want to set things straight. You'd like to give money to the other family members. They could use it, they deserve it, it's their reward for their years of helping the problem child, too. Besides, if you give the money to the problem child, he'll just squander it in a short time.

So, you might think, you'll just cut the problem child out of the will.

I've come across several cases where this was done, and in each case, the result was the same: The other children feel remorse at the fact that the problem child was disinherited and, knowing this, the problem child takes advantage of their guilt and generosity. The result: Each of your pride and joy becomes a surrogate parent to the problem child.

By giving your money only to your pride and joy, you condemn those children to a lifetime of supporting the problem child. A better solution, although it might not seem so at first, is to give the problem child an equal share and let it be known throughout the family that *that's it*.[49] "Don't rely on your brothers and sisters like you relied on us. We took care of you because we're your parents, but they are not. They have their own kids to care for. *Leave them alone.*"

If you do not give this instruction to the problem child — with the full knowledge of the pride and joy — your hopes will not be realized.

---

[49]Better still, put the problem child's money into a trust, having the trust pay an allowance over the child's expected lifetime. This is called a Spendthrift Trust. To learn more, talk with an estate attorney.

Family Problem #5: You're Mistreating Your Pride and Joy

One of my clients had four children. One became a surgeon, another a teacher, the third "wants to be an actor," and the fourth has three children and is happily married to a civil servant.

In their wills, my clients intended to leave their assets to three of their children, with only a token amount to the one who became a doctor. When I inquired as to why, they explained, "He's doing much better than his brother and sisters, so he doesn't need the money." They wanted to leave their money to the kids who needed it most.

Without realizing it, my clients had chosen to punish their son for achieving success. They had not told him of their plans, because it never occurred to them that he might not understand.

And he might not. "I should have become an actor, instead of working my butt off for eight years in medical school!" he may say. Animosity between him and his siblings could ensue.

Or maybe he would understand — but his wife and kids may not.

If the son does not learn of his disinheritance until after his parents have died, his brother and sisters will be the recipients of his anger and frustration. And that's assuming he knows his parents' reasoning. An even worse case is that he doesn't know why they cut him out of the will — only that they did. He could become very hurt and confused. In the end, he could challenge the will in court, demanding his share.

His parents had not envisioned any of this. They could prevent all these problems merely by talking with him, explaining their thoughts and concerns and asking his opinion. He's going to offer his opinion sooner or later, and sooner is much better, while there is time to change it.

The One Asset You Must Pass On

If there's one thing you must leave your family, it's this: Peace. Don't set the stage for a family war, or Thanksgiving dinner will never be the same. Talk with your family about your plans and about theirs. Above all else, remember: A will is a terrible place to keep secrets.

Chapter 73 - Estate Taxes

The reason people get so confused about this subject is that estate taxes operate exactly opposite from how all other taxes operate. Here's what I mean:

- If you **do not** earn income, you **do not** pay income taxes.

- If you **do not** purchase goods, you **do not** pay sales taxes.

- If you **do not** smoke cigarettes, you **do not** pay cigarette taxes.

- If you **do not** drive a car, you **do not** pay gasoline taxes.

- If you **do not** earn a profit on your investments, you **do not** pay capital gains taxes.

But...

- If you **do not** plan your estate, you <u>do</u> pay estate taxes.

Thus, in all other areas of your life, you avoid taxes simply by *doing nothing*. But doing nothing when it comes to estate planning is exactly how you will pay taxes. Indeed, estate taxes are optional: You pay them only if you fail to take the proper steps to avoid the tax. This chapter is designed to show you how to do just that.

The Magic Number

When a person dies (the *decedent*), his estate is distributed to his heirs.[50]

Before heirs receive anything, the IRS has first dibs. The *estate tax* is assessed against the estate's *net worth*, which is simply what the decedent *owned* (the assets) minus what the decedent *owes* (the *liabilities*).

---

[50]For the purposes of this discussion, we're using "he" as the one who dies and "she" as the survivor, because that's what happens to married couples 80% of the time. And while we're at it, let's offer one *"G-d forbid"* to cover the rest of the book.

ARE YOU KEEPING SCORE?

Net Worth	% of U.S. Population
$0 or negative	11%
$1,000-4,999	15%
$5,000-9,999	6%
$10,000-24,999	12%
$25,000-49,999	13%
$50,000-99,999	17%
$100,000-249,999	17%
$250,000-499,999	6%
$500,000 & over	3%

FIGURE 11-1

And in case you're keeping score, only 3% of the U.S. population has a net worth in excess of a half million dollars.

If your net worth is less than $600,000, your estate is not subject to estate taxes. But every dollar above that figure will be subject to tax — and the tax rate starts at 37%!

Two Mistakes in Your Arithmetic

If you think you're not worth $600,000, don't make the mistake of thinking you have nothing to worry about, for two reasons.

Math Mistake #1: You Did Not List All Your Assets

In addition to your ordinary assets, such as your home, cars, bank accounts, investments, IRAs and personal possessions, you also need to include:

- **the face amount of your life insurance policies.** Remember Steve from Chapter 68, who bought $250,000 worth of life insurance? For tax purposes, that $250,000 — the death benefit — is included in his estate. (That's right: the death benefit, not the cash surrender value.)

- **the present value of future pension benefits.** If you were to die, will your surviving children be entitled to your pension? If so, you must include in your estate the current value of the pension income that your kids are to receive during their life times. In other words, your estate will pay taxes on money it doesn't yet have![51]

---

[51]This is not a concern if your pension income will be paid to a surviving spouse.

Math Mistake #2: You Think You are Worth Less Than $600,000

Keep one point in mind: *You're not dead!* (I know because if you were, you wouldn't be reading this book.) By the time you are dead, you almost certainly will be worth $600,000 — *and more!*

Let's look at Beth, age 45, whose net worth is $200,000. Assuming her assets double every 10 years (which would happen with a mere 7% annual growth rate), Beth will be worth $400,000 at age 55 and $800,000 by 65 — thus presenting her with a tax problem. And she's still not dead! By 75, she'll be worth $1.6 million and $3.2 million by age 85. Her tax liability by then would be well over $1 million. Now that's a problem!

WHAT WILL YOUR ESTATE BE WORTH?

If your net-worth doubles every decade
(7.2% annual growth rate)

Age	Assets	Tax Rate
45	$200,000	0%
55	$400,000	0%
65	$800,000	32%
75	$1.6 million	41%
85	$3.2 million	55%

FIGURE 11-1

How to Reduce Your Estate Tax

To solve this problem, you need solid planning. Let's see the difference we can make. Each of the following examples are based on Mike and Sue, who have a net worth of $2 million. For simplicity, we'll assume their assets are split equally between them, although in real life it's rarely that simple. We'll also assume Mike dies first and that Sue dies shortly afterward, before the estate increases in value.

Simple Wills

Our first example, shown in Figure 11-3, assumes that Mike and Sue leave everything to each other, then to their kids after the surviving spouse dies. As we discussed in Chapter 72, this is called a *simple will*.

Mike dies, leaving everything to his wife Sue. When she dies, she leaves everything to their children.

We showed earlier the administrative problems posed by simple wills. Now we see that simple wills create huge tax liabilities as well. But interestingly, the tax problems occur not at Mike's death, but at Sue's. This is because you are permitted to leave an unlimited amount of money to your spouse without incurring any estate tax. Thus, Mike can leave his entire $1 million to Sue (making her worth $2 million) and no tax is due. This often lulls people into falsely believing that they need not worry about estate taxes.

The kids expect to inherit Sue's assets tax-free when she dies. After all, there was no tax when Dad died, so it follows that there will be no tax when Mom dies, too. Right?

As mentioned earlier, 85% of all women in the U.S. die unmarried, divorced, or widowed. Thus, women cannot assume that a man always will be around to handle the finances. If you find this comment degrading, mention this to your mother or grandmother. She will react with fear or denial, not indignation.

Wrong. When Sue dies leaving $2 million to the kids, only the first $600,000 passes tax-free. The rest — $1.4 million — is subject to taxes at a rate of 43%. Sue's estate thus will pay $588,000 in taxes, and her children will inherit only $1.4 million, instead of the $2 million Sue expected.

It doesn't have to be this way. Through proper planning, we can dramatically cut that tax bill, safely and securely, simply by following the rules provided by Congress.

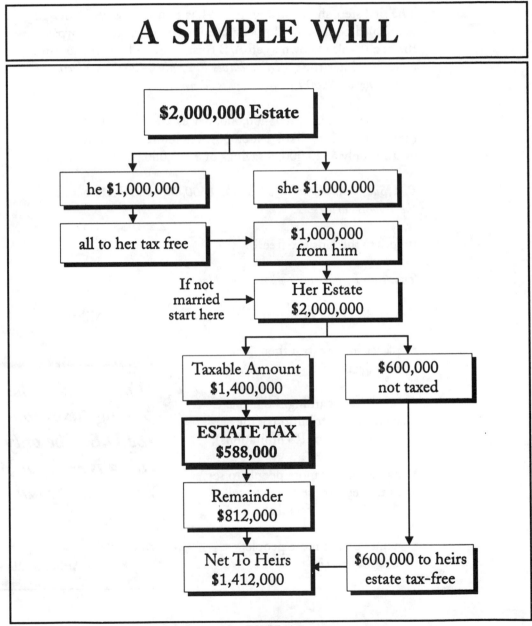

A SIMPLE WILL

FIGURE 11-3

Estate Taxes Are Optional

Congress made estate taxes *optional*: You pay only if you fail to take the steps needed to avoid the tax.

The first step, shown in Figure 11-4, is to use a *Bypass Trust* (so named because it allows a portion of your estate to "bypass" the tax; It's also known as an A/B trust, a unified credit trust and a credit shelter trust). *Mike leaves Sue only $400,000, placing the remaining $600,000 in the Bypass Trust.*

Since Sue receives only $400,000, her estate is worth $1.4 million (her million plus Mike's $400,000). Therefore, the estate tax at her death is only $320,000, a savings of $268,000.

But, Sue wonders, what about the $600,000 that Mike placed into the Bypass Trust?

It goes to the kids tax-free.

That's great, but what about me? Have I lost $600,000?

Not at all. Think of a trust as a bucket. As the *donor*, Mike:

- places money (or other assets) into the bucket;

- sets rules regarding the management and distribution of the money (within IRS limitations);

- names one or more people to serve as trustee, whose job is to follow the rules Mike established; and

- names one or more people as *beneficiaries*.

> *"I'm proud to be paying taxes to the U.S. The only thing is — I could be just as proud for half the money."*
> —Arthur Godfrey

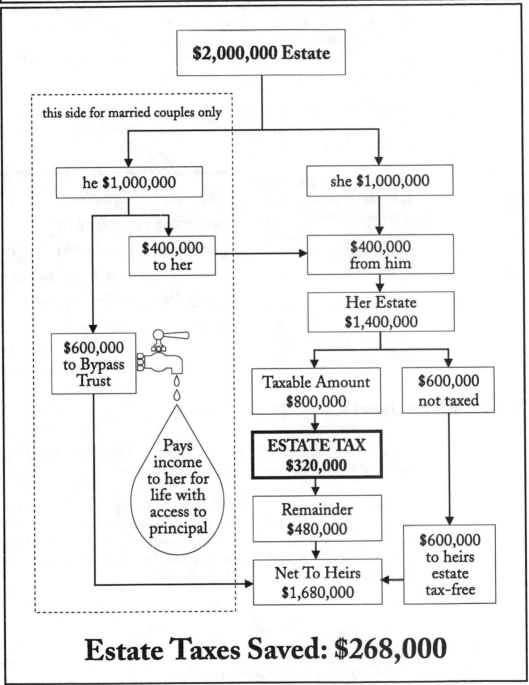

WILL WITH A BYPASS TRUST

$2,000,000 Estate

this side for married couples only

he $1,000,000

she $1,000,000

$400,000 to her

$400,000 from him

Her Estate $1,400,000

$600,000 to Bypass Trust

Pays income to her for life with access to principal

Taxable Amount $800,000

$600,000 not taxed

ESTATE TAX $320,000

Remainder $480,000

$600,000 to heirs estate tax-free

Net To Heirs $1,680,000

Estate Taxes Saved: $268,000

FIGURE 11-4

When Mike creates his Bypass Trust, he names his wife Sue as both trustee *and* primary beneficiary; the kids are secondary beneficiaries.[52] Mike further states that Sue, as beneficiary, is entitled to receive both income and principal from the trust throughout her lifetime, provided that the trustee agrees that the distribution is needed for her *maintenance, education, support, and health* (known in estate planning circles by the acronym MESH). Any assets remaining in the trust at Sue's death then pass to the children, who are the secondary beneficiaries.[53]

Thus, has Sue lost the $600,000 that Mike gave to the trust? Not at all. To get the money, she simply needs permission from the trustee — who is herself!

But since Mike placed the $600,000 into the trust, it is excluded from the estate tax calculation, which in turn saves $268,000 in estate taxes.

The kids, therefore, inherit $1,680,000 — $1,080,000 from Sue and $600,000 from Mike's Bypass Trust.

> *"The art of taxation consists in so plucking the goose as to obtain the largest possible amount of feathers with the smallest possible amount of hissing."*
>
> —John Baptiste Colbert

Bypass Trusts Are Limited to $600,000

If the Bypass Trust is such a great deal, why is Mike placing only $600,000 there? Why not his entire million?

Because it won't do him any good. Remember that Congress allows you to leave an unlimited amount to your spouse, but only $600,000 to a non-spouse. Therefore, if Mike had left more than $600,000 to the trust, everything above that amount would have been taxed, defeating the purpose.

---

[52]Unless they are minors. If so, see Chapter 72.
[53]Since this subject involves lawyers, fine print abounds. Talk with a legal advisor for more details.

Figure 11-4 actually shows only half of the actual estate plan. The second half, a mirror image of the first, is for Sue, and her will also contains a Bypass Trust. We need both halves because we don't know who will die first.

This reveals the secret to the Bypass Trust: It preserves Mike's ability to pass $600,000 to his kids tax-free, an ability he would have lost if he had first left everything to his wife. Since Sue also is able to pass $600,000 tax-free to the kids at her death, Bypass Trusts allow married couples to shelter up to $1.2 million from taxes.

Bypass Trusts are not needed when the estate is less than $600,000, since there is no tax on that amount. But for married couples whose estates are between $600,000 and $1.2 million, the Bypass Trust will completely avoid all estate taxes.

The Bypass Trust Works Only for Married Couples...

It's an example of how the tax code discriminates against those who are not married — and why, if you are married, you *must* establish these trusts while you both are alive. When one spouse dies, it's too late.

...and Only for U.S. Citizens

Bypass Trusts work only when both spouses are U.S. citizens. If you are worth more than $600,000 and married to a non-citizen, you need to see an estate attorney to learn about a Qualified Domestic Trust. This trust was designed to reduce the estate taxes for Americans who marry non-citizens.

"The difference between a taxidermist and a tax collector? The taxidermist takes only your skin."
—Mark Twain

Insurance Trusts

Although the Bypass Trust protect $1.2 million of Mike and Sue's money, we still have work to do, for they still would lose $320,000 to taxes. The solution can be found in Figure 11-5, which uses an *Irrevocable Life Insurance Trust* in addition to a Bypass Trust.

While both are alive, Mike and Sue establish and give money to an Irrevocable Life Insurance Trust. They name the children as both trustees and beneficiaries. The trustees (read: children) use the money in the trust to buy a special type of life insurance policy, called a "survivorship life" policy.

This type of policy, also called *second-to-die*, (a) insures the lives of both Mike and Sue, (b) is owned by the trust, and (c) names the trust as beneficiary.

Although Mike and Sue are *both* insured, this policy does not pay a claim at the first death. There's no need because there's no tax liability at that time. Rather, the death benefit is paid at the second death (hence, the policy's name), and it insures both Mike and Sue because we don't know who will die first. (We could buy two policies instead — one on Mike and one on Sue — but that's more expensive. Besides, we don't need coverage on both of them — just on the one who dies second. This is why the insurance industry created this type of policy.)

At the second death, the insurance policy pays the death benefit to the trust, which in turn distributes the money to the children.

> *"It isn't what you earn as much as what you save that counts in the long run."*
>
> **—Anonymous**

How much money? If you set it up correctly, the amount of insurance paid to the trust will equal the amount owed in estate taxes. Thus, instead of estate taxes being paid out of the estate, the taxes are paid by the proceeds of the insurance policy. Sure, Mike and Sue pay the policy's premium, but that's a tiny amount compared to the actual estate tax itself. In fact, you can save 90% of your estate taxes or more this way.

Second-to-die life insurance also makes it possible to obtain insurance even if one spouse is uninsurable. Since the carrier doesn't pay until the second death, it is largely unconcerned about a spouse who might be in poor health, provided the other spouse's health is better.

WILL WITH A BYPASS TRUST AND AN INSURANCE TRUST

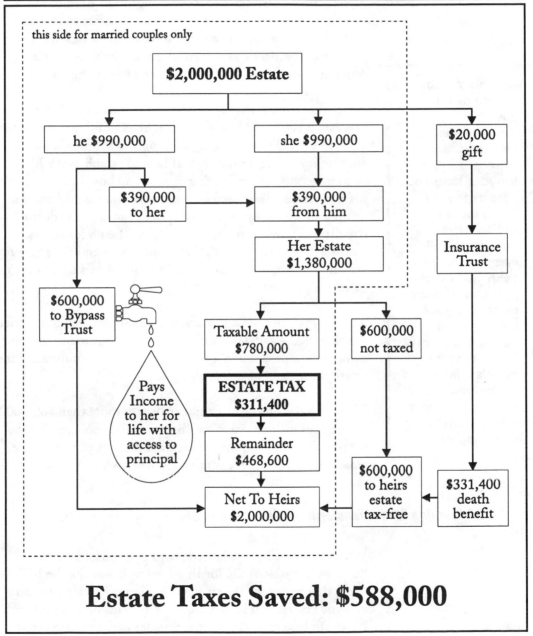

this side for married couples only

$2,000,000 Estate

he $990,000

she $990,000

$20,000 gift

$390,000 to her

$390,000 from him

Her Estate $1,380,000

Insurance Trust

$600,000 to Bypass Trust

Pays Income to her for life with access to principal

Taxable Amount $780,000

$600,000 not taxed

ESTATE TAX $311,400

Remainder $468,600

$600,000 to heirs estate tax-free

$331,400 death benefit

Net To Heirs $2,000,000

Estate Taxes Saved: $588,000

FIGURE 11-5

Not Just a Clever Way to Sell Insurance

This strategy is not simply a back-handed way to get you to buy life insurance. The alternative is to pay the taxes out of your assets, which would be far more expensive.

Besides, if you already own insurance, you might not need to buy a new policy. You may be able to transfer existing policies to the insurance trust. This provides two benefits: It removes the insurance from your estate (which lowers your estate tax liability) while providing the money that the kids need to pay the tax.

Another reason for not owning your own life insurance is Medicaid. Before Medicaid will pay for your long-term care expenses, it can force you to cancel your insurance policies, using the cash value that has accumulated to pay for your long-term care costs. But if your trust owns the policies, Medicaid cannot make this demand. For more on long-term care, see Chapter 67.

I once met with a new client whose net worth was $10 million. His estate tax would have been roughly $5 million, or half his estate. To avoid that problem, he bought a $5 million insurance policy. When I asked him if he had established a life insurance trust, he replied that, no, he had bought the policy in his own name. His insurance agent never mentioned anything about a trust. But by owning the policy himself, the death benefit was now part of his estate. Thus, he no longer was worth $10 million, but rather $15 million — and the estate tax was now $7.5 million instead of $5 million! His agent didn't solve the problem — he made it worse!

This is why you need an insurance trust: If Mike and Sue tried to solve their estate tax problem by buying insurance on their own, instead of through a trust, they would have *increased* the estate tax instead of reduced it!

Thus, if you are 65 or older and are worth more than $600,000, you should not own your own life insurance policies, for the death benefits would merely increase the size of your estate, which increases the tax your estate will owe.

A Warning When Transferring Policies to an ILIT

When you transfer a policy you own to an insurance trust, make sure you don't die for three years. If you do, the IRS will deem that you made the transfer "in contemplation of death," and your estate will be required to pay taxes on the value of the death benefit as though the transfer had never occurred.

Chapter 74 - Estate Administration

Estate administration deals with transferring assets from your parents to you after they've died, or from you to your heirs following your death. As we begin this chapter, it is important that you remember this point: *Estate administration has nothing to do with estate taxes*. That's because *estate administration* is based on laws set by individual states, while *estate taxes* are assessed by the federal government.

Since we're going to leave estate taxes behind and focus on estate administration, set aside for the moment everything we covered in the previous chapter.

How Assets Pass to Heirs

When a person dies, everything he or she owned is transferred to heirs in one of two ways: through operation of law or through probate court. *Operation of Law*, as the name implies, pertains to assets covered by specific laws. This includes:

- **Accounts which feature a named beneficiary,** such as a life insurance policy, an IRA or other retirement account. When the account owner dies, the beneficiary receives immediate ownership and control of the asset; and

NON SEQUITUR WILEY

...SO, BY UTILIZING THE ACTUARIAL TABLE IN CONJUNCTION WITH AN I.R.A. IN MUTUAL FUNDS AS RECOMMENDED IN CHAPTER 11...

TAP TAP TAP TAP TAP

OK, DOC... HE'S OUT COLD.

THE HOLISTIC ANESTHESIOLOGIST

©1994 Washington Post Writers Group. Reprinted with permission.

- **Joint accounts,** legally called either "Joint Tenancy With Rights of Survivorship" or "Tenants by the Entirety." When one joint owner dies, the asset immediately is owned by the other. A common example is when a husband and wife have a joint checking account.

All other assets — and I mean *all* — pass to heirs according to instructions in the will. (As Chapter 72 revealed, those who have not written a will use one provided by your state government.)

Just because Steve's will says his wife Sue is to receive everything doesn't mean she does: All wills first must be proved valid, even those provided by the state. And this is the job of the Probate Court.

The Three Dreads of Probate Court

Probate has several disadvantages, as anyone who has gone through the process can tell you, including:

Dread #1: Extensive Time Delays

In most states, probate lasts a minimum of one year and, due to backlogs, it can last several years. During this time, the assets are frozen and generally unavailable to heirs. This delay is intended to give creditors time to get paid and relatives time to challenge the will. The more challenges, the greater the delays — perhaps for decades.

Dread #2: High Legal Fees

Depending where you live, lawyers can charge as much as 5% of the value of the estate. Therefore, you should try to avoid naming a lawyer or bank to serve as your will's executor (now called the personal representative). Instead, appoint a family member and give them the authority to hire a lawyer for assistance as needed. This will save your estate tens of thousands of dollars in legal fees.

Dread #3: No Privacy

Probate is a public process, meaning anyone curious enough to inquire can read your will and learn the value of your estate, and who you named as your heirs.

Probate is not without its advantages, of course. It provides court oversight of the executor's actions and limits the time for someone to dispute the will.

The Longest Probated Will in History

This dubious honor belongs to Marilyn Monroe. When she died on August 5, 1962, she left equal shares of her estate to her psychoanalyst and her manager. The psychoanalyst, in turn, left his half to a mental health center, while the manager's portion went to his children.

The estate is still being probated. The manager's children feel they are entitled to the psychoanalyst's share, because he left the money to an institution instead of to a person, and the manager's children contend this was not Marilyn's intent.

Why are they fighting 30+ years after her death? Because Marilyn's estate generates an income of more than $1 million a year. That's worth fighting over.

Two Ways to Avoid Probate

Avoiding probate is an appropriate goal. Unfortunately, as with everything else we've learned, there's a right way and a wrong way to do it. The wrong way could cost you thousands.

The Wrong Way

Avoiding probate is simple: Just title all your assets jointly with your spouse. This works fine, provided (a) you have a spouse, *and* (b) your combined estate is below $600,000. But if *either* (a) or (b) is not true, holding assets jointly with another person is a terrible solution, for while it avoids probate, it creates another — very expensive — problem. Let's see how this often happens:

Mom, a widow, owns one major asset, a house worth $180,000. She wants her only daughter Ann to inherit it.[54]

Ann and her mom know about probate all too well, having gone through it when Ann's father died a few years ago. Mom is getting up in years, and she wants Ann to avoid probate on Mom's estate.

Mom thinks Ann can avoid probate by having Ann become a joint owner of the home, along with Mom. Therefore, Mom retitles the house from her name only to joint ownership with Ann.

This indeed enables them to avoid probate. But as I've stressed, probate is an administrative matter, not a tax matter. So this is where it gets interesting.

Since Mom's estate is below $600,000, she knows no estate taxes will be due at her death.

She's right. But in one of the nastiest tricks of the tax code, Mom and Ann are fooled into thinking they do not have to worry about taxes at all, when in fact they merely do not have to worry about *estate taxes*. Since Mom's estate is below $600,000, they are right that Mom's estate will not incur an estate tax, but they have forgotten about the *capital gains tax* (see Chapter 15).

Mom bought the house 40 years ago for $30,000. It is now worth $180,000.

Tax law says that if you sell an asset for more than you paid for it, you must pay taxes on the profit (the *capital gain*), which in this case is $150,000. If Mom had remained sole owner, leaving the house to Ann via her will, Ann would have received the house as an heir via the (dreaded) probate court.

But that's not what they did. To avoid probate, they put Ann's name on the deed of the house along with her mother. Ann, no longer an *heir*, is now an *owner*. And tax law treats owners very differently than heirs.

---

[54]Although the case described here refers to real estate, you should be aware that it applies equally to *any* type of financial asset, including bank accounts, mutual funds, stocks and other property.

If Mom remained sole owner, Ann would have inherited the house at its current value of $180,000 (the *stepped-up basis*), meaning she'd be able to sell it without incurring any capital gain and thus with no capital gains tax. But as an owner, she inherited the house with Mom's original cost basis of $30,000 intact. As a result, when Ann sells the house, the $150,000 profit will be subject to capital gains taxes. In other words, while Ann has avoided probate and does not incur any estate tax, she could have to pay capital gains taxes of as much as $50,000. That's a pretty stiff cost to avoid probate.[55]

Four More Reasons Not to Title Assets Between Generations

If Mom and Ann's story isn't enough to stop you from titling assets between generations — or, frankly, with anyone other than your spouse — following are more horror stories for you to consider. Remember: These pitfalls apply to all kinds of assets — mutual funds, stocks, bonds, and bank accounts — not just real estate.

Reason #1: The Child Might Die First

Dad has a bank account containing $40,000. He adds his son's name to the account. Then, his son dies. The IRS, holding that the son was a 50% owner in the property, requires the son's estate to pay estate taxes on $20,000. Thus, Dad loses as much as $11,000. Dad can avoid this only if he can prove that the property was originally his, and not his son's — something that can be difficult to prove.

Reason #2: The Child Might Steal Your Property

Sometime after Dad adds his son's name to his bank account, the son makes a substantial withdrawal. The bank permits the son to do this without notifying the father, because the son — being a joint owner —now has legal access to the assets.

---

[55]It's possible that the capital gains tax might be somewhat lower than this example suggests, because Mom herself enjoyed a stepped-up basis on Dad's half of the house, which she inherited when he died. You should rely on a good tax or financial advisor who can calculate the tax for your situation.

Reason #3: You Render Your Will Moot by Leaving it
All to Just One Child

Not realizing that operation of law takes priority over a will, Mom adds the name of her eldest daughter to all her bank and investments accounts for convenience. When Mom dies, her will — which instructs that all her assets be distributed equally among her four children — is moot, because all her money and investments passed directly to the one daughter listed as joint owner on Mom's accounts! If the daughter chooses, she can keep all the money, and there's little her brothers and sisters will be able to do about it. If she tries to fulfill Mom's wishes by redistributing the assets to her siblings, she'll discover that doing so constitutes making a gift from her to them, rather than an inheritance from Mom to her children. That means the IRS will subject the redistributed assets to a gift tax — at the same tax rates as those used to assess estate taxes.

Reason #4: The Parent Causes the Child to Lose Big Tax Breaks

In each of the above cases, it's the parent who suffers. But sometimes the child can be the one at risk. In a recent case, Dad helped his son buy a house, and to protect his father's financial interests, the son added his dad's name to the deed. The son then accepted a job transfer in another state and sold the house. He returned to his dad the money his father had put up. The son then deducted his moving expenses on his tax return. The IRS denied 50% of the deduction, arguing that the son owned only 50% of the property. It didn't matter that the father was on the deed merely to satisfy the lender's requirements. Nor did it matter that the father was a family member — the IRS held that the father didn't qualify as a "family member" because he was not a dependent. And the IRS even ignored the fact that the father's name was removed from the deed prior to settlement. The key issue, the IRS said, was that the father was an owner at the time the son agreed to take the new job.

Such are the games that tax laws play. By solving one problem, you create another. How then, can you avoid both?

The Right Way

Enter the Revocable Living Trust.

In our example, Mom should establish a revocable living trust, naming herself as both trustee (to retain control over the assets she places in the trust) and beneficiary (during her lifetime), and naming Ann as the beneficiary upon her death. *Revocable* means Mom can put assets into the trust and take them out at any time. *Living* means this trust is in effect only during Mom's lifetime, and *Trust* means the assets are owned by the trust, not by Mom.

> **Too many lawyers who prepare living trusts never make sure that their clients actually retitle assets into the trust. Yet without retitling your assets, all that legal work is for naught. As soon as your lawyer completes your trust document, take it to your bank, broker, and other financial advisors. And make sure your attorney handles any real estate you own.**

Because the house is owned by the trust, not by Mom, it does not go through probate when Mom dies, but passes directly to Ann (the beneficiary). Because the house is worth less than $600,000, there is no estate tax, and because Ann inherits the house at the stepped-up basis of $180,000, there will be no capital gains tax when she sells it for that amount, either.

Thus, the revocable living trust allows Ann to inherit the house without probate and without taxes.

This illustrates how the easy solution (in this case, joint ownership) often is the wrong solution, and why proper estate planning is critical.

Pros and Cons of Revocable Living Trusts

A revocable trust has many advantages. Through it:

- **Your estate avoids probate;**

- **You distribute your assets as you wish** (your instructions simply are in the trust agreement as well as in your will);

- **Your decisions are not public.** Nobody knows about John Wayne's estate because he used a living trust;

- **You make it harder for disgruntled heirs to complain.** In most states, a disinherited heir cannot challenge a trust as easily as they can a will; and

- **You can direct how you want your assets to be managed during your lifetime should you become incompetent.** You can set the rules in the trust and appoint someone to manage your affairs for you.

> Notice that the first four bullets are irrelevant to the person setting up the trust, because they address things that occur after you die. But the final point addresses an area that should be of critical importance to you, for it could well determine your quality of life in your final years. That is reason enough to establish a living trust.

Like all legal matters, living trusts do have disadvantages:

- **The trust is of no value unless you move assets into it.** Remember, a trust is a bucket: Unless you place assets into the bucket, the bucket itself is of no value. Thus, after you establish the trust, you need to change the name of all your assets from "John Smith" to "The Revocable Living Trust of John Smith." Doing so does not change John's access or legal control of the account; it simply allows the asset to skip probate upon John's death.

- **Living trusts do not avoid taxes.** These trusts are revocable, meaning you can put assets into them and take assets out at any time. Since you have this control, the assets continue to be considered yours for tax purposes (for annual income taxes, capital gains taxes, and estate taxes). That's why a comprehensive estate plan consists of several trusts, some (such as Bypass Trusts) to avoid estate taxes and others (such as living trusts) for estate administration.

- **It's more expensive to set up a trust than simply to retitle an asset into joint names.** You've got to decide if you have sufficient probatable assets to make the effort worthwhile. If you are married and all you own is a house and some IRAs, a living trust could be of little benefit.

> *"Put not your trust in money, but put your money in trust."*
> —Oliver Wendell Holmes

Chapter 75 - How to Make Money by Giving It Away

That might sound a little crazy. But you really can do it, through the little-known *Charitable Remainder Trust*.

In fact, with the CRT, you can lower your current income taxes, avoid capital gains taxes, maintain or even increase your income for life, donate large sums to charity, and still leave everything to your kids and grandkids.

Sound good? Read on.

You establish a trust with some of your assets, such as stocks, bonds, or real estate. You then name a favorite charity as beneficiary. You get an immediate income tax deduction because the gift is irrevocable, although the charity must wait for the death of you and your spouse before receiving your gift.

Next, the trust converts these assets into income-producing ones (if they aren't already). If you donated land, for example, you might have the trust sell the property and buy bonds.

Don't worry about capital gains taxes, either, because a charitable trust doesn't pay any taxes. (If the asset had appreciated, you would have lost a third of the value to taxes if you had sold them yourself. But the trust can sell the assets for you — tax free.)

> *"Many people who are not charitably inclined sure are patriotic."*
> —Anonymous

This trust annually must pay out at least five percent of its initial market value.[56] You decide who gets the income, how much they get, and for how long — *and you can name yourself if you want.*

Assuming you take the income for as long as you or your spouse live, the charity will receive whatever's left at the second death. But what about your kids? After all, their inheritance is going to charity.

---

[56]Based on the date the asset was transferred to the trust.

To replace that inheritance, the trust buys an insurance policy on you and your spouse equal to the size of your gift, naming your children (or whomever) as beneficiaries.

Premiums are paid from the income produced by the trust's assets and, upon the last death, they'll receive the policy's death benefit — which is as much as they would have gotten had you left the original assets to them in the first place.

And here's another advantage: Because your heirs receive their inheritance from insurance, not your estate, the cash passes to the kids free of income taxes, estate taxes, and probate.

These trusts once made sense only when giving away millions of dollars. But today, you can set up a CRT at little cost or effort for gifts as small as $20,000.

So take a close look at these trusts. You could help yourself, your family, and charity.

Some fine print: You can name more than one person or organization to receive income, but at least one must be a non-charity. You must specify whether the payouts are to be in dollars, or percentages. Your tax deduction is based on a complex formula involving the value of the trust's assets, the annual income you're to receive, and how long you're to receive it. The IRS publishes tables determining these figures. Also, there are limits on tax deductions for charitable gifts and the Alternative Minimum Tax could apply if your gift involves appreciated property.

Use Your IRA for Bequests to the CRT

Another good idea if you want to make bequests to a CRT is to donate your IRA (or a portion of it) instead of your cash or other assets. Why? Because when you make a donation from your IRA, you avoid both the estate tax *and* the income tax on that money. That reduces your taxes and increases the amount you leave for your family — or the charity itself.

Chapter 76 - Other Estate Planning Tools

The law provides for many solutions to estate planning needs. Some of the basic ones that most people need include:

- **Living wills,** which you use to declare your preferences for medical treatment in the event you become terminally ill;

- **Durable powers of attorney for health care,** which allow another person to make medical decisions for you if you are unable to make them for yourself; and

> **In many states, these two documents have been replaced by a Medical Directive.**

- **Durable general powers of attorney,** which allow another person (usually a spouse) to sign legal documents for you. The key word here is *durable*, for ordinary powers become void if you become incapacitated. Be aware that you are granting the person you name in this document unlimited access and control of all your assets.

By executing these documents now, you avoid the risk that someone else might go to court to be named your guardian in the event you become incapacitated.

FRANK & ERNEST   BOB THAVES

©1996 United Features Syndicate, Inc. Reprinted by permission.

Chapter 77 - When to Revise Your Will

Like financial plans, estate plans require periodic review to make sure they remain current and viable. You should review your estate plan if:

- your marital status has changed;

- your state of residence has changed;

- your income or net worth has changed;

- your health has changed;

- family members have died or been born; or

- five years have passed.

Part XII
How to Choose a Financial Advisor

Part XII — How to Choose a Financial Advisor

Overview - The Most Important Financial Decision You Will Make

The world of personal finance was once simple.

In the old days, if you wanted a savings account or if you needed to borrow money, you went to a bank. If you wanted to invest, you went to a stockbroker. And if you needed insurance, you saw an insurance agent.

It's not so simple anymore. Today, there is an incredible array of new products, as we've discussed throughout this book. You want to buy a bond? That sounds easy enough. But which kind? There are municipal bonds, government bonds, and corporate bonds. You can buy convertible bonds, bonds with equity warrants, Dutch auction notes and dual currency bonds. Then, of course, there are indexed bonds, junk bonds, option-related bonds, and pay-in-kind debentures. And don't forget zero-coupon bonds and flip-flop notes, not to mention zebras, bunny bonds, and LYONs and TIGRs and STRIPs (oh, my!).

And that's just bonds. I haven't even mentioned stocks and options. Or mutual funds. How about annuities, limited partnerships, real estate investment trusts, and guaranteed insurance contracts. Then there are oil & gas deals, foreign currency options, and collateralized mortgage obligations. But then again, I think maybe I don't want to mention them after all.

As if all these new products weren't enough, today there is a seemingly endless variety of people who will sell them to you. Today, everybody is moving in on everyone else's turf. Bankers are selling stocks and bonds, while stockbrokers will lend you money. Some insurance agents will sell you anything *but* an insurance policy. IBM offers its own mutual funds. AT&T has its own credit card. General Electric and General Motors each have bigger consumer loan programs than Citibank. And Sears actually makes more money charging interest on its credit card than selling merchandise in its stores.

So, today, you are faced not only with the dilemma of what products to buy but who to buy them from. How do you go about it, to where can you turn for help with all this?

Enter the financial planner.

Created in the past 25 years, the financial planning profession is a response to the increasing complexity of today's economic market-place. Financial planners can be found in many different companies — banks, brokerage firms, accounting firms, insurance companies, and of course, in financial planning firms. They use different titles, and carry lots of different credentials. But once you boil it all down, you reach a common denominator. All planners work with one goal in mind: to help you make financial decisions.

No matter what they call themselves, whether it's account executive, investment advisor, financial consultant, or financial planner, their job is to help you analyze your finances and give you advice regarding investments, insurance, taxes, wills & trusts, and mortgages — in a way that helps you achieve your financial goals.

Working with a financial planner should be a fun, close, warm relationship. It should not be adversarial. You should like your planner as a person, and they should be someone with whom you want to spend time.

If you choose your planner well, your planner should become an important part of your life, and you should be together for a lifetime. After all, financial planning is a lifetime activity, and a good planner can help make the process both fun and profitable for you.

FRANK & ERNEST   BOB THAVES

©1996 United Features Syndicate, Inc. Reprinted by permission.

Chapter 78 - The Four Ways Planners Get Paid

To evaluate financial planners, start by examining how they are compensated. No matter who your planner is or what type of organization they work for, all planners are compensated in one of four ways: commission-only, fee only, fee plus commission, and fee-offset. We'll look at each of these fee schedules one by one.

Compensation Method #1: Commission-Only

Planners who are commission-only are different from traditional stockbrokers and insurance salesmen (who also are commission-only). Traditional stockbrokers make money by selling investments, such as stocks, bonds and mutual funds, while insurance agents sell life insurance, annuities, and sometimes mutual funds, too.

Like traditional brokers, commission-only planners almost always work for a bank, brokerage firm, or insurance company, and as far as their employers are concerned, they are salesmen — nothing more, nothing less. But what sets commission-only planners apart from traditional stockbrokers and insurance agents is their methodology.

If you were to ask a traditional stockbroker, "How should I invest $10,000?" he'll tell you, because brokers traditionally have been trained to focus on investments, not on non-investment-related matters such as taxes, mortgages or wills. This is not a criticism of traditional brokers: They know whether you should buy Ford stock vs. General Motors, but they are not trained to review broader financial issues, such as the tax implications of selling a stock.

That's the difference between a traditional stockbroker and a financial planner who happens to hold a broker's license and work in a brokerage firm. If you ask a planner what to do with ten grand, he or she will not tell you. Instead, he or she will ask you lots of questions about your income and expenses, need for liquidity,

"With an evening coat and a white tie, anybody, even a stockbroker, can gain a reputation for being civilized."

—Oscar Wilde

how you feel about risk, and about your goals and objectives. They'll also want to discuss seemingly unrelated issues, such as family, job status, debt and budget issues, taxes and estate matters. Only after analysis of all this information would a planner feel comfortable giving you investment recommendations.

So, go ahead and take investment and insurance advice from traditional stockbrokers and insurance agents, but don't let them pretend to be financial planners.

> **It kills me when a person approaches me after a seminar and asks, "I have some money to invest. What looks good?"**
>
> **That's like phoning a physician and asking, "Hey, doc, what drugs are hot this week? I thought I'd try some."**
>
> **Stockbrokers believe that some investments are good and others are bad. Planners don't. Planners believe there's no such thing as a "good" or "bad" investment. Rather, planners seek "appropriate" investments and strategies designed to help each client achieve his or her goals.**
>
> **So while a planner might recommend the same investment as a broker, the planner's thought process and methodology that is used to arrive at that conclusion are very different from the broker's.**

How do you tell them apart? The quickest way is this: Brokers and insurance agents tend to talk about their *products*, while planners tend to talk about *you*.

Financial planners who are compensated by commission-only argue that anybody who pays a fee for financial planning is out of their mind. After all, they argue, the number-crunching and analysis that goes into your situation is all well and good, but if you never act on the recommendations, then the planning itself is of no value. Until you implement the plan, they argue — until you buy the investments or insurance that the planner says you need — the plan itself does you no good at all.

BROOM HILDA RUSSELL MYERS

Reprinted by permission: Tribune Media Services.

And since *all* investments and insurance products feature some form of transaction fees, expenses, sales charges, or commissions, you'll end up paying twice: once to be told what to do and again when you do it. So the commission-only planner argues that they are working in the consumer's best interests: If you don't like their recommendations, you are free to walk away, having spent no money on advice you're not using.

Thus, commission-only planners say their form of compensation demands that they emphasize the *implementation* phase of a financial plan. The result, they say, is that they produce better recommendations than other types of planners. They have to, they say, or you won't buy, and if you don't buy, they won't make any money.

The Problem with Commission-Only

Critics say commission-only planners can suffer from a serious conflict-of-interest. Since the planner makes money only when you buy, like stockbrokers and insurance agents, they only recommend products that have fat commissions. In other words, are they telling you to buy something because it's good for you or good for them?

Compensation Method #2: Fee-Only

To avoid this conflict, some people turn to *fee-only* planners, who do not earn commissions. Instead, they charge fees. This fee can be an hourly rate (usually ranging from $100 to $250 per hour) or a flat fee (usually $1,500 to $5,000).

Whatever their rates, fee-only planners will conduct their analysis and give you recommendations, but you'll have to go elsewhere to buy the investment, insurance, or mortgage products they say you need. Because fee-only planners do not earns commissions, they argue that they do not have any conflict of interest.

Three Problems with Fee-Only Planners

Commission-only planners, in their own defense, offer three criticisms of fee-only planners.

Problem #1: Why They Do Not Earn Commissions

In order to sell investments and insurance products, you must hold a federal securities license and a state insurance license. Stock-brokers and insurance agents go through extensive training and testing, with subsequent auditing and review by federal and state regulators, including the SEC, the NASD, and state insurance commissions. There also are periodic continuing education requirements that must be fulfilled. With the exception of medicine, law, and accounting, the securities licensing exam is considered the most difficult. (The six-hour test has only a 30% pass rate.) It's similar with state insurance examinations. Maintaining a license requires passing state-mandated classes and tests, as well as ongoing continuing education requirements.

These licenses are the only government-recognized demonstrations of expertise and knowledge in the field of investments and insurance, and they constitute legal authorization for a person to make specific recommendations to you. So, commission-only planners argue that fee-only planners don't earn commissions simply because they aren't allowed to. And they're not allowed to because they do not have the required licensing, training, or experience.

For more on licensing, see the following chapter.

Problem #2: No Conflict, But No Interest, Either

While commission-only planners agree that their fee-only colleagues have no conflicts of interest, they say this lack of conflict creates a new problem.

> Not too much of a turf war going on here, huh?

They say that because fee-only planners are compensated to analyze, not to implement, they are objective to the point of disinterest. It makes no difference to a fee-only planner whether your investments succeed or fail, since their fees are not based on performance. Say a fee-only planner tells you to put 30% of your money in stocks, so you go down the street to a stockbroker and buy them. When the stocks go down, you return to your planner who says, "I didn't mean those stocks!"

So commission-based planners say they are more accountable for their recommendations because they are implementation-oriented, not design-oriented like fee-only planners.

Problem #3: What They Earn vs. What You Pay

The final point commission-only planners make is this: Even though fee-only planners *earn* only fees, that doesn't mean you *pay* only fees. You've still got to implement, and that means you've still got to pay commissions or sales charges or transaction fees — *to somebody*. The fact that you're paying these expenses to someone else, rather than to your planner, might be small consolation.

Compensation Method #3: Fees Plus Commissions

The objections of the commission-only planners make sense. Still, it's nice to know that your planner is objective. So, which is the better choice? Before you choose, let's examine the third type of planner, the most common of all.

According to industry surveys, more than 70% of all financial planners charge their clients fees plus commissions. In other words, most planners do hold insurance and securities licenses. Therefore, they charge you fees for the analysis, then they sell you the investments you need and charge you commissions for doing so.

Many fee-plus-commission planners also charge asset management fees. These fees, anywhere from 1% to 3% of the value of the assets they are monitoring for you, are in addition to the fees and commissions you pay.

When Fees are Really Commissions

Asset management fees, such as those charged by wrap accounts (see Chapter 26) are all the rage today. Although not yet used by a majority of planners, it is emerging as the compensation method of choice for both planners and consumers.

Consumers like asset management fees because they can avoid paying up-front commissions. Further, since the fee grows with the size of the assets, the planner's compensation is directly related to how well those assets perform. This puts the planner on the same team as the client: If the client's investments fall in value, so will the fee that the planner earns, while an increase in the client's account gives the planner increased compensation, too. This gives the planner a strong motivation to offer good recommendations.

And planners like asset management fees, too. Why? Because fees provide steady streams of income, enabling the planners to devote their energy to serving their existing clients. Commission-only and fee-only planners, on the other hand, must continually find new clients because their compensation comes from the commissions and fees that new clients pay. Asset-based planners do not have this concern — for the benefit of their clients.

Three Problems with Asset Management Fees

But while the benefits are strong, there can be some problems.

Problem #1: Asset-Based Fees Should be a _Substitute_, Not an _Addition_

The whole point to asset management fees is that they provide an alternative form of compensation for the advisor. Therefore, paying asset-based fees in addition to commissions defeats the purpose.

Problem #2: Asset-Based Fees are Often Too Expensive

Many planners charge such exorbitantly high asset management fees that their clients would have been better off paying commissions or flat rates. Asset management fees never should be more than 2%, and the percentage should decrease as the size of the assets increase.

Problem #3: It's Not Really a Fee Anyway

Many financial planners who charge asset management fees claim — with the blessing of the regulators and the media — that they are "fee-only." It is argued that such planners are not earning commissions because the products they are recommending, such as no-load mutual funds, do not pay commissions, and that their only form of compensation is paid by the client.

This argument is nonsense. A *fee* is a fixed rate based on time or work. A *commission* is based on the size of the transaction. And since asset management fees are expressed as a percentage of the assets that a client gives the advisor for management, it is clear that asset management fees are commissions. They are simply another form of commissions.

Think about it. If you invest $10,000 in a mutual fund that has a 4% load, you are paying $400, of which your advisor will receive all or part as compensation. Thus, the more you invest, the more they are paid. If you don't invest at all, the advisor is not paid anything. *Sounds like a commission to me.*

But if your advisor charges you a 3% asset management fee, he or she will receive $300 on that $10,000 — but, again, only if you agree to invest the money. If you invest, the advisor is paid. And, again, the more you invest, the more they are paid. If you do not invest, they are not paid. *Sounds like a commission to me.*

Don't misunderstand me: There's nothing wrong with asset management fees *per se*. What is wrong, though, is (a) charging a fee that's too high, and (b) pretending that it's not a commission — even though it is a benign, even consumer-friendly commission.

> It's easy to understand why advisors don't like to refer to asset management fees as "commissions." First, there is a negative connotation to the word — it reminds people of the conflict-of-interest issue. Second, unlike traditional commissions that are based on the size and frequency of *transactions*, this compensation method is not based on trading. Instead, it's based on *results*, which is how many feel it should be. Therefore, it is argued, asset management fees are fees, not commissions.
>
> It's more important that you understand what it is than what you call it.

Compensation Method #4: Fee-Offset

Whereas fee-plus-commission planners are the most common, *fee-offset* planners are the most rare.

Planners who use this method charge fees to do the plan, just as fee-only planners do. The client is then free to go elsewhere to buy whatever investments or insurance products the planner recommends.

But here's where the fee-offset planner differs: If the client buys those products from the planner, or if the client agrees to pay asset management fees to the planner (either way providing the planner with additional compensation), the planner reduces his or her fee by whatever commissions or asset management fees the client incurred. Thus, a fee-offset planner will be paid one way or the other, but not both. Thus, it is the client's prerogative to choose the method they prefer.

Fee-offset planners say they have the most consumer-oriented method of all. Because they charge fees only, they have the same objectivity of fee-only planners. But because they are fully licensed, they are highly skilled in implementing their recommendations. All they are doing, they say, is reducing their compensation to be competitive in the marketplace.

Fee-offset planners wonder why consumers are willing to pay twice: once to be told what to do and once again to actually do it. Nobody would tolerate such practices in other industries, fee-offset planners contend, but consumers let financial planners get away with it all the time. Fee-offset planners avoid this redundancy for the benefit of their clients.

The Problems with Fee-Offset

Fee-only planners don't go for those arguments, however. They accuse fee-offset planners of being commission-based in disguise, while fee-and-commission planners claim the fee-offset group cannot afford to maintain that aggressive fee schedule indefinitely. In other words, they say, fee-offset planners either must change to fee-plus-commission or they'll one day be out of business.

Chapter 79 - Industry Designations vs. Federal and State Licensing

There is a big difference between federal licensing requirements and industry designations.

You may come across planners with a variety of credentials, virtually all of them obtained through correspondence schools. They include:

- **CFP — Certified Financial Planner**

  Now in its third decade, this is the most well-known of all planning designations. The CFP coursework covers the broadest range of topics, takes two years to complete, and ends with a rigorous two-day examination. Continuing education requirements also must be met by its licensees.

- **CFA — Chartered Financial Analyst**

  Although this is the only other accredited designation (aside from the CFP), it is less relevant to financial planners and their clients. Those holding the CFA designation typically are analysts or money managers working in mutual fund companies, institutional asset management organizations or pension funds.

- **ChFC — Chartered Financial Consultant**[57]
- **CLU — Chartered Life Underwriter**

  Both are offered by the American College in Bryn Mawr, Pa. which was founded by the life insurance industry. Virtually all graduates are (or were) insurance agents. The overwhelming majority of agents who hold one of these designations also hold the other. It is the position of the American College that insurance serves the crucial role in a financial plan, so in most cases, you can expect that a planner who holds these designations is both an expert in insurance and likely to emphasize insurance when offering recommendations. It generally takes two years to complete the coursework, followed by a 10-part series of exams and continuing education requirements.

---

[57]That's *not* a typo!

- **CFS — Certified Fund Specialist**

This designation was created by the Institute of Certified Fund Specialists in response to the increasing popularity, variety, and complexity of the mutual fund industry. The program emphasizes portfolio theory and the selection and monitoring of mutual funds. The self-study course generally takes six months, followed by rigorous examination and continuing education requirements.

- **CMFC — Chartered Mutual Fund Counselor**

Developed jointly by the National Endowment for Financial Education (the same group that sponsors the CFP designation) and the Investment Company Institute, this designation — like CFS — reflects an advisor's specialty in the ever-growing mutual fund industry. The self-study course is followed by a three-hour exam and continuing education credits are required.

- **CRP — Certified Retirement Planner**
- **CRIA — Certified Rollover Investment Advisor**
- **CFKA — Certified 401(k) Advisor**

Each of these designations are sponsored by the American Institute of Retirement Planners. The CRP designation reflects the advisor's work with clients concerned with retirement planning issues. The CRIA is held by planners who specialize in lump-sum distributions. (Most advisors who hold the CRP or CRIA designation also hold the other.) The CFKA designation tends to be held by advisors who work primarily with corporate and institutional clients in the development and management of 401(k) plans (see Chapter 62). Each of the designations requires extensive coursework, followed by rigorous examination and continuing education requirements. Candidates must satisfy licensing, academic or professional prerequisites in order to enroll.

- **RFC — Registered Financial Consultant**

The International Association of RFCs takes a philosophically different approach. Rather than offering its own exam, members must possess a federal securities license and state insurance license (see below), have at least four years of demonstrated experience as an advisor, a college degree in a related field or an industry designation (such as those described here), and a clean disciplinary record. The IARFC believes it is critical that advisors to be on top of current trends, and therefore, members are required to complete 40 hours of continuing professional education courses per year. By contrast, other organizations require only eight or 16 hours of continuing education per year.

- **PFS — Personal Financial Specialist**

  Offered by the American Institute of Certified Public Accountants to CPAs who (1) pass an additional exam, or (2) hold the CFP or ChFC[58] designation.

All these designations are awarded by private organizations. While they can suggest that a planner has a certain amount of experience or training, none is recognized by any federal or state government or regulatory agency. The planners of my firm and I hold many of these designations, but in the eyes of the government, all of them are meaningless.

Federal Securities Licenses

In order to sell securities, planners must hold a federal securities license. These licenses are offered by the National Association of Securities Dealers, a quasi-governmental agency empowered to license and regulate the industry. Although there are many NASD licenses, planners tend to hold one of two:

- **NASD Series 7 - General Securities**

  This is the license held by virtually all stockbrokers and the majority of financial planners. It permits advisors to offer and execute transactions pertaining to stocks, bonds, government securities, municipal bonds, mutual funds, unit investment trusts, closed-end funds, limited partnerships and options. The only security not covered by the Series 7 is commodities trading (which requires the Series 3). If the advisor also holds a state life/health insurance, the advisor also is permitted to offer variable annuities. The Series 7 examination is considered

---

[58]Really! It's *not* a typo!

Although being a Registered Investment Advisor does not constitute financial planning expertise, you should never work with a planner who is not registered. Why? Because it's a federal crime not to register (do you want to work with an advisor who is not obeying the law?)

Besides, the only advisors who are not registered are (a) crooks, or (b) people who are so uninformed that if they don't even know about SEC registration rules, you have to wonder what else they don't know.

Actually, there is another group of advisors who are not registered. They are (c) those who don't have to register. This includes stockbrokers, insurance agents, attorneys, and accountants, because the SEC holds that such persons provide advisory services that are merely incidental to their other activities. Therefore, such professionals are exempt from SEC registration. So, don't be surprised if your broker, insurance agent, lawyer, or tax preparer is not registered — provided that the advisory service they provide is merely incidental to the other services they give you.

"What did you expect a financial wizard to look like?"

to be among the most difficult of any field, with a national pass rate of only 30%. Continuing education requirements also must be met.

- **NASD Series 6 - Mutual Funds**

  This allows an advisor to recommend only mutual funds, unit investment trusts and closed-end funds. Many insurance agents who seek securities licensing choose the Series 6 because, being much more limited, it is much easier to obtain than the Series 7. Continuing education requirements also must be met.

- **NASD Series 63 - Blue Sky Laws**

  Each of the states require that advisors demonstrate expertise with state securities laws as well, known as the "blue sky" laws. After passing the Series 6 or Series 7, an advisor must satisfy state regulators by passing this examination. Until both the Series 6 or Series 7 and the Series 63 are passed, advisors are prohibited from offering recommendations to clients.

State Insurance Licenses

Advisors wishing to offer life insurance and annuities must pass state-administered insurance examinations. Most states require that applicants attend a 40-hour class, followed by rigorous examination. There are substantial continuing education requirements as well.

Registered Investment Advisors

Any person who provides financial planning services also must be registered with the Securities and Exchange Commission, and, increasingly, with state regulatory authorities as well. Registration consists of:

- submission of Form ADV

- payment of a one-time filing fee of $150

- passage of the NASD Series 65 - Investment Advisor Examination

While all financial planners must be Registered Investment Advisors, please do not assign a greater importance to this than it deserves. The Series 65 examination merely tests knowledge of SEC rules, not expertise or competence, and there are no continuing education requirements.

Notice that I continually use the phrase "Registered Investment Advisor" instead of the acronym "RIA." That's because the SEC frowns on use of the initials. Why? Because the SEC recognizes that the mere filing of Form ADV (see Chapter 82) does not bestow any expertise upon the planner, and the agency does not want consumers to be mislead into thinking a person is an expert just because they happen to be an "RIA." Thus, legitimate planners who are registered with the SEC refer themselves as being Registered Investment Advisors, not RIAs.

Chapter 80 - Ten Taboos Between You and Your Planner

Here are some things you should never do when working with a financial advisor:

1. **Never write a check made payable to your planner, other than for his fee.**

   Your checks should be made payable only to mutual funds, brokerage firms, or insurance companies. No legitimate planner would ever allow a client to write a check for investments or insurance payable to him personally or to his firm.

2. **Never allow your planner to list himself as a joint owner or beneficiary on your accounts.**

   Your money is yours, not your planner's. Keep it that way. The only place your advisor's name should appear on documents is as the advisor of record.

3. **Never lend money to your planner.**

   Period.

4. **Never give your planner discretionary authority.**

   This allows your advisor to execute transactions without your prior knowledge or consent. If your advisor earns commissions, this is a license to steal.

5. **Never let your planner sign your name to any document.**

   Forgery — however well-intentioned — is a felony.

"The aim of all legitimate business is service, for profit, at a risk."
—Benjamin C. Leeming

---

6. Never let your planner allow you to sign a blank form or contract.

It's a violation of NASD rules and a pretty dumb thing to do. Cross out sections that do not apply.

7. Never let your planner use his address on account statements instead of yours.

You should receive routine, periodic statements directly from the mutual fund, brokerage firm, or insurance company. Never allow your planner to have such documents go to his office instead of to you.

8. Never let your planner sell you something that isn't available from others.

There can be only one reason why an advisor would want you to buy in-house, or *proprietary*, products: Because he makes additional compensation for doing so. If a product is not generally available, you could find it extremely difficult to sell in the future. Like a box of cereal, all investments and insurance policies your planner recommends should be available from any number of sources.

9. Never let your planner share in your profits.

Unless you invest a minimum of $500,000, or your net worth is at least $1 million (exclusive of homes, home furnishings and cars), it is an NASD violation for an advisor to share in the profits of a client's account. Besides, from a practical perspective, I'd never let an advisor share in my profits unless he was willing to reimburse me for my losses, too — and while you might find a planner offering the former, none would ever agree to the latter.

10. Never let your planner assign any agreement with you to another advisor.

One day, your planner may retire or sell his practice. If so, you immediately are relieved of any and all contractual obligations you may have had with your planner. Never let a planner — or his successor — let you think you are obligated to work with the successor. Assignment is an SEC violation.

"He that won't be counseled can't be helped."
—Benjamin Franklin

Chapter 81 - Financial Planners vs. Money Managers

A financial planner creates custom-designed plans and investment programs for each client. A money manager, in contrast, invests each client's money identically.

If a manager decides to sell Ford stock, he or she will sell Ford out of every client's portfolio, and if he or she wants to buy Intel, every client will own it. Thus, every client's portfolio is identical and their results will be identical.

Mutual funds, for example, are run by money managers, and every investor in a given mutual fund has the same results as every other investor of the fund. The only differences are caused by the dates a given client might open or close an account. In many cases, financial planners refer their clients to money managers — often via mutual funds, annuities, or wrap accounts

Private money managers — those not running mutual funds or annuities — are expensive. They typically charge annual asset management fees of up to 3% per year — in addition not only to your planner's fee, but to the trading expenses the manager incurs on your behalf as well.

Planners who work with private money managers say their clients receive personal attention. Others argue that private money managers really do nothing you can't get from ordinary mutual funds at far less cost. For more on the comparison between private money managers and those who operate mutual funds, see Chapter 26.

Chapter 82 - How to Find a Planner

Now that you know the different ways financial planners are paid, you know one of the first questions to ask when interviewing them: How are they compensated? Make sure you understand how they earn a living and what your costs will be.

Interview two or three planners. Shop around as you would for a car or washing machine. To get the names of potential candidates, talk to your neighbors, friends, or co-workers. One note of caution, though: Before you ask someone for the name of their advisor, make sure the person you're asking is similar to you in age, income, net worth, and objectives.

Your neighbor might be very happy with his financial advisor, but if your neighbor is a real risk-taker and you're not, his planner might not be well suited to you. Likewise, if you make $20,000 a year, asking your rich uncle for the name of his advisor also might lead to a bad match.

Another good way to find an advisor is by watching some in action. Maybe you saw one on TV, at a seminar, or read a news article they wrote. If you were impressed, add them to your interview list.

10 Points to Ponder About Prospective Planners

Once you identify a few planners to talk to, here are ten questions you should ask:

1. **How many years have they been in business, and how did they get started?**

   If the planners you interview are former stockbrokers, their emphasis will be on investment management, whereas if they were insurance agents, they probably will emphasize insurance products. Planners with neither of those backgrounds are not licensed and therefore most likely are fee-only planners.

2. **What kind of people do they work with most often?**

   Do not tell the planner about yourself right away. Instead, ask them to describe their typical client. If they describe you, it could be a good match. If they describe someone totally different, you could be out of place.

   As part of this question, ask how much money their typical clients invest. If you have $50,000 to invest, you don't want a planner who works primarily with millionaires, or you'll be ignored. Likewise, if you have $1 million and the planner works mostly with assets of fifty grand, the planner may not have the expertise you require. Ideally, you want a planner who works extensively with people like you.

3. **What is the ratio of support staff to professional staff?**

   Too few and the advisor will never get any work done. Too many means his office is not operating well, and you're paying for the firm's big expenses.

   Here's a good test: The planner should not be answering his own phone, but he or his associates should return phone calls within one business day.

4. **What is the planner's reputation in the field and in the local community?**

   Planners who have roots and who are well-known have reputations to protect and therefore tend to be more careful than the planner who just blew into town.

5. **When setting your appointment, go to the planner's office instead of inviting him to your home.**

   It takes more effort on your part, but it will allow you to inspect his office. How often does the phone ring before it's answered? Is the office neat and organized? Is there a bustle of activity? Don't be taken in by offices that are too opulent, though. Remember: Clients pay the rent, not the owners! If there's a huge pile of papers, files, and documents all over the place, remember too that one day, *your* file will be somewhere in that mess!

6. **Do you understand what they tell you?**

Here's the easy way to know: If you understand what they're telling you, you should be able to repeat to others what they've said. If you can't, you might be getting bamboozled.

7. **Does the planner have a clean record?**

Don't be afraid to ask this question and, if you like, follow it up with a phone call to the regulatory authorities. If your planner has a securities license, see if there have been any complaints by calling the NASD.

If the planner has an insurance license, call your state insurance commission, too. Check with the SEC to see if your planner is a Registered Investment Advisor. All planners are required to provide clients with a copy of the planner's Form ADV Part II, which is the registration statement they filed with the SEC. It will disclose everything you need to know about their background, methodology, compensation, and other important data.

8. **Ask about the planner's investment methods.**

What types of investments does he normally work with? Are they high risk or low risk? Is your money accessible after it is invested or are there restrictions? Who makes decisions to buy or sell investments — you or the planner? Can the planner execute transactions without your prior approval?

Make sure you're comfortable with all the answers.

9. **Get referrals.**

This isn't a bad idea, but it's not that great, either. After all, no planner will give you a negative source. Still, you can use referrals to verify basic facts.

Do not ask the referrals how their investments are performing. (It's a bad basis from which to make a decision and it's rude, too.) Instead, ask what it's like to work with the planner.

Do they return phone calls timely? Are mistakes often made or difficult to get corrected? How quickly and effectively are questions answered? How often do you hear from the planner? Why do they contact you — just to sell you something or with bona fide news? Questions about style can tell you a lot about substance.

10. **Must you sign a contract?**

What does it obligate you to do? Many financial planners do use contracts, but never sign one that doesn't let you cancel in 30 days or less. For planning work, never pay more than 50% in advance, with the balance payable upon completion of the work. When paying asset management fees, never pay for more than one year in advance.

And always pay only for what you are getting, and make sure you get what you pay for.

Sources

1980 CSO Mortality Table
1984 Commissioner's Disability Table
American Association of Individual Investors Journal
American Association of Retired Persons
American Demographics Magazine
American Medical Association
Associated Press
Brides Magazine
Business Week
Center for Nutrition Policy and Promotion, USDA
Coberly & Hunt
College Board
Employee Benefit Research Group
Family Economics Research Group
Financial Analysts Journal
Financial Planning Magazine
Fitch
Forbes
Fortune
Gallup
Health & Society
Hulbert Financial Digest
Ibbotson Associates
Institute of Management and Administration
Investment Company Institute
The Journal of the American Medical Association
Kiplinger Tax Letter

Metropolitan Life Insurance Company
Money Magazine
Morgan Stanley Capital International
National Center for Health Statistics
Older Women's League
Panic Profits
Pension Benefits
Personal Business
Philadelphia Inquirer
Profitable Investing Bulletin
Provident DIMAC
Standard & Poor's
Tax Foundation
U.S. Administration on Aging
U.S. Bureau of the Census
U.S. Department of Agriculture
U.S. Department of Commerce
U.S. Department of Health and Human Services
U.S. Health Care Financing Administration
U.S. Internal Revenue Service
U.S. Senate Special Commission on Aging
U.S. Social Security Administration
University of Miami
University of Pittsburgh
The Wall Street Journal
The Washington Post
Washingtonian Magazine
Woman's Day
WRAP Fee Advisor

About the Author

Ric Edelman, CFS, RFC, CMFC is one of the nation's best-known and most successful financial advisors. He is on the faculty of Georgetown University, a state- and AICPA-approved instructor for continuing professional education and a member of the NASD Board of Arbitrators. He was named Financial Planner of the Year three times by World Invest Corporation, and in 1994 *Washingtonian* magazine named him one of the top financial experts in the Washington, D.C., area.

Ric has been the subject of feature stories in *The Washington Post, Dow Jones Investment Advisor, Registered Representative, The Washington Times, Washington Business Journal* and *Wall Street Computer Review,* and he has been quoted by *The Wall Street Journal, The Washington Post, Fortune* magazine, *Financial Planning on Wall Street, Bottom Line Personal* and *Family Circle.*

In addition to Mr. Edelman's substantial financial expertise, he is a highly-regarded financial educator and communicator. Ric is one of the most sought-after speaker for seminars, conventions and conferences across the country, and he is widely acknowledged as one of the most entertaining and informative speakers in the personal finance field.

Ric is the popular host of radio's *Your Money Matters* (for which he won the Washington, D.C., A.I.R. Award for Best Talk Show Host), which airs on WMAL Radio AM630 in Washington (Saturdays 10am-noon EST) and WLS AM890 in Chicago (Saturdays 6pm-8 Central). He also hosts two call-in television shows, one on the national NET cable network (Thursdays 10pm EST) and another on the DC-area's Newschannel 8 (Mondays 7:30pm), writes a syndicated news column, and publishes a monthly newsletter. Ric created one of the most popular personal financial programs on America Online (keyword: EDELMAN). Ric also has produced a popular series of video tapes and audio cassettes on a variety of personal finance topics.

Whatever the medium — print, broadcast, electronic or live presentation — Ric is able to explain difficult financial concepts in plain English, and he is consistently rated as one of the best communicators in his field.

In addition to his achievements as a financial planner and educator, Ric has created one of the most impressive business organizations in the nation. Winners of 30 professional, business and community service awards — including "1994 Service Business of the Year" Award by the Fairfax Va. Chamber of Commerce — The Edelman Financial Center Inc., today manages $600 million in client assets and was twice named by *Inc.* magazine as the fastest-growing privately-held financial planning firm in the country.

Through its six subsidiaries, The Edelman Financial Center Inc. offers clients around the country and the world comprehensive financial planning and investment management services through Edelman Financial Services Inc.; valuation, litigation support, tax preparation and business accounting through Edelman Tax and Valuation Services Inc.; home mortgages and refinancings through Edelman Mortgage Services Inc.; back-office, human resource and operational support for businesses through Edelman Business Services Inc.; and complete video production, marketing, public relations, advertising, media training and event planning activities through Edelman Communications Inc. In recognition of these activities, Ric was three times named as a finalist for the Washington, D.C., Entrepreneur of the Year Award (he still hasn't won).

THE
EDELMAN
FINANCIAL CENTER

12450 Fair Lakes Circle
Suite 200, Fairfax, VA 22033
703/818-0800
Fax: 703/818-1910
Internet: RicEdelman@AOL.com

FRANK & ERNEST BOB THAVES

©1996 United Features Syndicate, Inc. Reprinted by permission.

Index